Canadian Minor
League Baseball

Canadian Minor League Baseball

A History Since World War II

Jon C. Stott

McFarland & Company, Inc., Publishers
Jefferson, North Carolina

LIBRARY OF CONGRESS CATALOGUING-IN-PUBLICATION DATA

Names: Stott, Jon C., author.
Title: Canadian minor league baseball : a history since World War II / Jon C. Stott.
Description: Jefferson, North Carolina : McFarland & Company, Inc., Publishers, 2022. |
Includes bibliographical references and index.
Identifiers: LCCN 2021058952 | ISBN 9780786469925 (paperback : acid free paper) ∞
ISBN 9781476645001 (ebook)
Subjects: LCSH: Minor league baseball—Canada—History. | Baseball
teams—Canada—History. | BISAC: SPORTS & RECREATION / Baseball / History
Classification: LCC GV863.15.A1 S76 2022 | DDC 796.357/640971—dc23/eng/20211223
LC record available at https://lccn.loc.gov/2021058952

BRITISH LIBRARY CATALOGUING DATA ARE AVAILABLE

ISBN (print) 978-0-7864-6992-5
ISBN (ebook) 978-1-4766-4500-1

Front cover: (left to right) Roy Partlow, Jackie Robinson and John Wright
of the Montreal Royals in 1946 (National Library and Archives of Quebec)

Printed in the United States of America

McFarland & Company, Inc., Publishers
Box 611, Jefferson, North Carolina 28640
www.mcfarlandpub.com

Table of Contents

Acknowledgments   vii

Preface   1

Introduction   5

Part I. 1946–1951: The Minors Expand and Contract in Canada   9

1. From Jackie Robinson to Jack Kent Cooke: The International League   10

2. Canada's Border Leagues Teams: PONY League, Border League, Western International League, Canadian-American League   22

3. Mexican Jumping Beans, Hockey Players, and Negro Leaguers: Quebec's Provincial League   43

Part II. 1952–1977: The Lean Years   51

4. International League Departures   53

5. Vancouver's Pacific Coast League Mounties Come and Go … and Come and Go   69

6. Canada's Border League Teams Go South: Western International League, Provincial League, PONY League, Northern League   78

7. Struggling to Survive in the '70s: Northern League, International League, Eastern League, Northwest League, Pioneer League   96

Part III. 1978–2020: Boom and Bust II— Independence and Survival   107

8. Another Minor League Boom in Canada, 1978–1990: Pacific Coast League, Northwest League, Pioneer League, New York–Pennsylvania League, Eastern League   110

9. Canada's Minor League Teams Go South Again, 1991–2007: New York–Pennsylvania League, Eastern League, International League, Pioneer League, Pacific Coast League   127

10. On Their Own: Canadian Teams in the Independent Leagues   153

11. Thriving in the Twenty-First Century: Vancouver Canadians,
les Capitales de Quebec, Winnipeg Goldeyes   176

Conclusion   207

*Appendix. Directory of Canadian Minor League and Independent
League Teams by Year: 1946-2020*   211

Bibliographical Essay   223

Index   229

Acknowledgments

"Although this book bears my name as author, it would not have been possible without the assistance and support of many individuals and organizations." That statement is found in so many acknowledgments that it seems almost to be a cliché. It is not. Without the help of many people, a book such as this could never have come to fruition. I would first like to acknowledge the encouragement and support of two people from McFarland: Layla Milholen, who, many years ago, invited me to take up this project, and David Alff, who has been patient and encouraging throughout the process, always willing to grant an extension and offer valuable advice. The staffs at the City of Victoria Archives, City of Edmonton Archives, City of Toronto Archives, City of Ottawa Archives, and Bibliotheque et Archives Nationales du Quebec have provided invaluable assistance in tracking down photographs, as has Jason Beck of the B.C. Sports Hall of Fame. I am also grateful to Chad Scarsbrook of Way Back Winnipeg, Jeffrey Reed of London Ontario Sports (londonontariosports.com), and Daniel Papillon of Quebec City, who have generously provided photographs. John Horne of the National Baseball Hall of Fame located photographs of Hall of Fame managers and players who had played in Canada earlier in their careers. Stephani Ellis of the Vancouver Canadians, Dan Chase of the Winnipeg Goldeyes, and Jean Grignon-Francke of les Capitales de Quebec provided photographs of the stadiums of three of the most successful twenty-first-century Canadian teams. A special thank you to Gary Tater and Denyse Conroy who, when I rediscovered my love of minor league baseball in the 1990s, adopted me into the Edmonton Trappers' family. And, as usual, to my daughter Clare, who has provided a warm home, great meals, and continued support during my many writing ventures, thank you.

Preface

During the 75 seasons of professional baseball played between 1946 and 2020, 71 teams represented 35 Canadian cities and played in 21 minor leagues operating either under the aegis of the National Association of Professional Baseball Leagues (called Minor League Baseball since 1999) or independently without any relationship to the National Association. During this period 16 teams operated for less than a year (most notably the eight teams of the Canadian Baseball League of 2003), while another 14 lasted three seasons or less. Only seven have operated continuously for 20 or more years, the longest-tenured being the Winnipeg Goldeyes of the independent Northern League and American Association who, since 1994, have played 27 consecutive seasons.

The teams were manned by future major leaguers (including 14 who would be elected to the Hall of Fame—four as managers), veterans of the Negro Leagues who had been prohibited from playing for National Association teams until late in their careers (three were named to the Hall of Fame), aging players seeking to extend their careers, younger players hoping to advance their way up the minor league ladder, and rookies, some of them only weeks out of high school. Although most of the players were from the United States, there were many Canadians (including future Hockey Hall of Fame defenseman Doug Harvey), as well as players from Mexico and the Caribbean and around the world, most notably from Japan. Beginning in 2014 Cuba allowed players to become members of les Capitales de Quebec of the independent Canadian-American League.

The Montreal Royals and the Toronto Maple Leafs played in classic ball parks, stadia that had been built for the purpose of housing professional teams and could seat well over 10,000 spectators. Many teams shared fields with local amateur or semi-pro teams and the outfield dimensions were often much shorter than those of professional parks. In Winnipeg and Ottawa, teams performed on diamonds that had been laid out on the playing fields of Canadian Football League teams. And in Saint-Hyacinthe, Quebec, a team played on the infield of a horse racetrack. It wasn't until the early 1990s, when the Professional Baseball Agreement, which governed the relationship between the minor leagues and the major leagues and established rigid playing field and facility standards, that many stadiums were extensively renovated or new ones constructed.

Canadian Minor League Baseball: A History Since World War II is a chronicle history of the minor and independent league teams that have played in Canada since 1946, when leagues that had suspended operations during World War II were reactivated and new ones formed through 2020, when, because of restrictions resulting from the Covid-19 pandemic, only one Canadian team, the independent Winnipeg Goldeyes, took the field (but played their home games in Fargo, North Dakota). The history is organized in three main parts. Part I, "The Minors Expand and Contract in Canada," examines the six seasons following the war, a time when hundreds of ball players were returning from duty in the armed services anxiously hoping to resume their interrupted careers and when war-weary citizens searched for types of entertainment that had been restricted during the war years. However, by the middle of the twentieth century, attendance began to drop off as other outdoor summer activities, along with the indoor watching of television, engaged fans' time and entertainment budgets. In Canada, the number of minor and independent league teams reached a high of 17 in 1947 and dropped only by one at the start of the 1951 season. However, in July 1951, the Border League, which included teams in Kingston and Cornwall, Ontario, ceased operations.

Part II, "The Lean Years," traces the continuing decline of the minor leagues between 1952 and 1977. The relocation of nine major league teams and the granting of 10 major league expansion franchises displaced many minor league teams and caused a domino effect among many of the minor leagues. In addition, major league teams, faced with declining attendance, began cutting back on their farm systems and many cities found themselves without minor league teams. The increasing number of major league games on television, along with easily available alternate forms of outdoor recreation and entertainment, caused a sharp decline in minor league attendance. The number of teams and leagues not returning at the beginning of each new season increased steadily. By the early 1970s, those minor leagues that survived did so mainly because of extensive financial aid from the major leagues. During the lean years, the number of Canadian teams dropped to a low of one in 1968. Five Triple A teams, including the Montreal Royals and the Toronto Maple Leafs, once the jewels of the International League, relocated to the United States. Five leagues in the lower minors that spanned the Canada-United States border ceased operations in the 1950s; three teams went out of business in mid-season. Attendance dropped steadily for those Canadian teams that remained active. During the 1970s, four Canadian teams were accepted into the short season low minor leagues, the Pioneer and Northwest, mainly because otherwise the leagues might not have had enough clubs to operate.

Part III, "Boom and Bust II—Independence and Survival," chronicles the increase in the number of minor league Canadian teams in the late 1970s and 1980s, an increase which reversed itself beginning in the early 1990s. During the 1980s, minor league baseball grew in popularity, as new stadiums were built and minor league operators cleverly marketed their teams and created game-day experiences that included between-inning fan events, mascot antics, and a range of imaginative food offerings. Because the number of minor league franchises increased only slightly (as a response to the need of four major league expansion franchises to establish farm teams), the value of franchises increased. In 1992, a total of nine minor league teams operated in Canada, the most since 1955. Beginning in 1993, Canadian minor league franchises were purchased by Americans with very deep pockets and moved to American cities with newer and more state-of-the art stadiums. When the Triple A Ottawa Lynx of the International League relocated in Allentown, Pennsylvania, after the 2007 season, only one Canadian minor league team remained: the Vancouver Canadians of the short season Class A Northwest League. During the 1990s, as the exodus of Canadian minor league teams was beginning, the first of the modern independent leagues, which were not members of the National Association and whose teams were not farm teams of major league clubs, were formed. Many of these leagues were underfinanced, poorly organized, badly run and lasted only a few seasons. Canadian teams were members of seven of the leagues and disappeared when these leagues failed.

Their stories are included in Chapter 10. Only the Winnipeg Goldeyes of the American Association and les Capitales de Quebec, formed in 1994 and 1999, respectively, survived to the end of the second decade of the twenty-first century. Their stories, along with the story of the Vancouver Canadians, are recounted in Chapter 11.

In the Conclusion, the characteristics of Canada's minor and independent leagues are considered, how they reflect trends and tendencies of minor and independent leagues in general and, more important, how they differ, what makes them Canadian. An appendix provides a year-by-year list of minor and independent leagues and teams that have operated in Canada since 1946.

In the narratives of the individual seasons of Canadian teams and the leagues they played in, several aspects have been considered: the course of the specific season for each team along with managers and players who have contributed to it: all-stars, league leaders in individual categories, and future major leaguers of note who were part of the team's roster. Each team's annual attendance has, where available, been noted, for it is the rise or fall of attendance that frequently determines the continued existence of a team. Front office matters, including relationships with officials of city-owned stadia and with the farm-team organizations of major league parent teams, also influence that continued existence. Each team's season is also considered in relation to the state of the league as a whole, to minor league baseball in general, and to the major leagues' shifting, and frequently self-interested, views about the role of minor league baseball. In the case of the independent leagues, the fates of the teams and leagues are generally dependent on the financial stability, business sense, and the front-office baseball experience of owners and league officials.

The terms "minor leagues" and "minor league teams" refer to leagues or teams that are members of the National Association of Professional Baseball Leagues, the governing body of minor league baseball and negotiators of the Professional Baseball Agreement that specifies the relationship between major league baseball and the minor leagues. Since 1999, the National Association has been legally known as "Minor League Baseball." "Organized baseball" and "affiliated baseball" are informal synonyms for the above terms. "Independent leagues" is a generic term referring to leagues that are not members of the National Association and have no formal relationship with major league baseball. The teams in these leagues are not members of major league farm systems. The term "unaffiliated leagues" and "unaffiliated teams" are synonyms for independent leagues and teams.

A note on terminology: The abbreviations RBI and ERA, standing for Runs Batted In and Earned Run Average, respectively, are frequently used.

Introduction

On a cool early May Saturday afternoon in 1952, I attended my first professional baseball game. That morning, my twin sister and I had trekked to the sporting goods department of Eaton's Department Store in Victoria, British Columbia, to sign up for a membership in the Knot-Hole Gang, a club whose members could attend Saturday matinees of the Victoria Tyees of the Class A Western International League for free. (The regular kids' admission was ten cents.) That afternoon there were hundreds of us yelling and stamping our feet in the far-distant left field bleachers of Royal Athletic Park.

I don't remember who won the game or who the opponents were. (Decades later, while scanning newspaper microfilm for a research project, I discovered that the home nine had defeated the Yakama Bears 6–4.) I do remember that, to the delight of all of us, left fielder Bob Moniz did a headstand after one of the innings and that, after numerous raucous requests from the left field bleachers for an encore, he obliged. More important, on that long ago afternoon, I saw African Americans for the first time. The Tyees had three: infielder Lou Branham, outfielder Granny Gladstone, and pitcher Jehosie Heard. Branham and Heard, I would learn many years later, had played in the Negro Leagues; only Heard, of all the 1952 Tyees, would go on to play in the majors—he appeared in 3.1 innings for the 1954 Baltimore Orioles. Years later, I learned that the trio's appearance on the Victoria roster was no accident. Beginning in 1946, when Jackie Robinson broke the color line in baseball playing for the Montreal Royals, Canada had the most hospitable professional baseball diamonds for African American athletes.

That long-ago Saturday marked the beginning of an intermittent but long-lasting love of minor league baseball. My sister and I attended Tyee games for another two and a half seasons before the team went out of business, a victim, like so many clubs, of falling attendance and shifting recreational priorities. But every Wednesday, I would ride my bicycle two miles to the nearest store that carried the *Sporting News*, learning each week about the various leagues, teams, and players in, it turned out, the decreasing number of leagues. Although with the folding of the Tyees, my attendance at minor league games was sporadic, limited to going to games in cities where I was passing through or visiting friends, I continued to read the *Sporting News*, which was often referred to as the "Bible of Baseball," religiously.

In the mid–1990s, my dormant love for minor league baseball resurfaced. A recently widowed empty-nester, I began visiting John Ducey Park, the home of the Edmonton Trappers of the Pacific Coast League. Around this time, I discovered *Baseball America*, the bi-weekly newspaper that had replaced the *Sporting News* as the sport's "Bible"; read David Lamb's *A Stolen Season*, the account of his travels though minor league America;

and started making sure my own travels included overnights in cities that had minor league baseball teams.

As a kid, I had a glove with a hole in it, a weak arm, an inaccurate throw, and a pathetic swing at the plate. In pickup games in the school yard, I was always assigned to distant left field. But I had a father who had been a sportswriter in his younger days, and at one time my ambition was to follow in his footsteps. I'd always thought it would be fun to write articles for team programs. In 1995, I hesitantly approached Dennis Henke, assistant general manager of the Edmonton Trappers, offering to write program articles in exchange for free tickets. He accepted my offer and, when I saw the next year's program with three of my pieces in it, I was as happy as I had been when my first academic article had appeared in a "learned" journal. A few years later, Gary Tater, media director for the team, invited me to write a weekly column for the team's website, which I did for several seasons.

I kept thinking about Lamb's baseball travel book and how much I'd enjoyed it. I'd been a fan of travel literature since I first read John Steinbeck's *Travels with Charlie* in the 1960s, and when William Least Heat Moon's *Blue Highways* appeared in the early '80s, I read it two or three times. It would be fun, I thought, to do one on baseball, focusing on teams in the independent leagues that had started popping up in the 1990s. Happily, McFarland liked my idea and, retired from the University of Alberta and freed from the responsibilities of churning out professional articles, I travelled one summer from Bridgeport, Connecticut, to Tri-City, Washington, reporting on my visits with players and team officials. Writing *Leagues of Their Own* (published in 2001) whetted my appetite, and I then visited affiliated teams, writing about them in *Minor Leagues, Major Boom* (2004).

At the time I was doing this travelling and writing, Canadian minor leagues teams had become members of an endangered species; at the end of the 2003 season, only the Ottawa Lynx, the Vancouver Canadians, and the Edmonton Trappers remained as Canada's minor league teams. In the fall of that year, just as I was finishing reading the page proofs for *Minor Leagues, Major Boom*, I learned that the axe had fallen on the Edmonton Trappers. The Edmonton Eskimos of the Canadian Football League, who had purchased the baseball team in 2000 for a price reported to be $8 million Canadian ($4.3 million American at the time), had sold the Trappers to a Texas group headed by Hall of Fame pitcher Nolan Ryan for an estimated $10.5 million American. (The Eskimos original purchase price was later reported to be $6.5 million.) The 2004 season, the Trappers' last in Edmonton, was a sad one for fans and team officials alike. But there was some optimism: a new team, to be called the Cracker-Cats, would join the independent Northern League in 2005. The 2005 season proved to be even sadder: the new owners, real estate developers from Florida who had no experience in running a professional sports team, overrode the decisions of the experienced front-office staff (many of whom had served the Trappers for many years), demoralized the front-office personnel, firing many of them, and alienated the fans. I had been writing program articles and a weekly column for the new team, but discouraged and disappointed, I did not return for the second Cracker-Cats season and attended only a handful of games over the next few years.

My interest in the minors was revived at the end of the first decade of this century. I had just finished a project and was looking around for a new one when Layla Milholen of McFarland contacted me to see if I would be interested in another baseball book. We decided that a history of the minors in Canada since World War II would be an interesting and worthwhile topic to explore. For nearly a decade I have been reading and writing. The project has gone into many, many extra innings. It has been a trip down memory lane—I found myself reading the *Sporting News* papers I'd peddled my bike over three or four hills every Wednesday to buy, and I even talked to one of my childhood heroes. And it has been a journey of discovery—I learned about Canada's key role in the integration of baseball in the minor leagues and of the, to me, increasing incursion of American interests into the Canadian teams. To slightly shift the metaphor, as I head toward home plate, I realize how enjoyable it has been. I am happy to share this record of the trip/journey with other fans of minor league baseball.

PART I

1946–1951
The Minors Expand and Contract in Canada

The United States' entry into World War II in December 1941 had a major impact on minor league baseball. In 1941, 292 teams had played in 41 leagues. The number declined to 210 teams in 31 leagues in 1942, 80 in 12 leagues in 1943, and 68 in 10 leagues in 1944, before rebounding slightly in 88 teams in 12 leagues in 1945. In Canada, only the Toronto Maple Leafs and the Montreal Royals of the International League played throughout the war years. After the 1942 season, the Canadian-American League, which included Quebec City and Trois-Rivières, and the Western International and the Northern leagues, which had teams in Vancouver and Winnipeg, respectively, suspended operations. In the same year, Hamilton withdrew from the PONY league.

Even if there had not been travel restrictions or gas rationing during the war, the number of minor league teams would still have dropped drastically. There were simply not enough trained ball players around to stock teams. Large numbers of them had enlisted in the American armed services, as had many recent high school and college graduates who might have taken over for enlisted or aging and retiring players.

In the summer of 1945, as it became apparent that World War II would soon be over, the National Association, the governing body of the minor leagues, encouraged the return of leagues that had suspended operations and the formation of new ones. The 1946 season opened with 43 leagues: 12 that had operated in 1945, 28 that returned after the World War II hiatus, and three new ones. Three hundred eighteen teams took the field, nine of them Canadian: Toronto and Montreal in the International League, Trois-Rivières and Quebec City in the revived Canadian-American League, Vancouver and newcomer Victoria in the reorganized Western International League, and Hamilton in the PONY League. Kingston, Ontario, and Granby and Sherbrooke in Quebec became members of the newly formed Border League. Between 1946 and 1951, 18 Canadian cities would host teams from six minor leagues. Two teams operated in British Columbia, five in Ontario, and 11 in Quebec.

In each of the next three seasons, the number of leagues in Canada and the United States increased: to 52 in 1947, 58 in 1948, and 59 in 1949. Attendance also increased annually, reaching a high of nearly 42 million in 1949. In 1950 the number of leagues dropped to 58 and attendance to just over 34.5 million. In 1951, 27.5 million people watched teams in 50 leagues.

1

From Jackie Robinson to Jack Kent Cooke

The International League

The International League, which had had been formed in 1885 as the New York State League, begin the 1946 season in a new classification. Along with the American Association and the Pacific Coast League, it was now labeled "Triple A" instead of "Double A." The Southern Association and the Texas League, which had been designated "A1" now became "Double A."

The International League operated in Maryland, New Jersey, New York, Ontario and Quebec. Jersey City and Newark played in New Jersey, just across from New York City, while the Syracuse, Rochester, and Buffalo teams were in upstate New York. Baltimore, Maryland, hosted the league's southern-most team. The Toronto Maple Leafs, who played in Canada's largest English-speaking city, had jointed the International League in 1886 and had been a continuous member since 1895. The Montreal Royals, who represented Canada's largest French city, had become a member of the league in 1890 and had played in every season since 1928.

The two Canadian teams, which played in the league's largest cities, each with a metropolitan population of around one million, are an interesting study in contrasts. Since the 1939 season, the Brooklyn Dodgers had owned and operated the Montreal Royals. Beginning in 1942, these operations had been closely supervised by the Dodgers' new president, Branch Rickey, the baseball executive who, when he ran the St. Louis Cardinals, had created a far- reaching farm system. He had spent his first three years in Brooklyn laying the groundwork for a similar system. He searched for suitable locations for farm teams and scouted players who had not enlisted and been sent overseas He paid careful attention to African Americans, who had been excluded from playing major and minor league baseball since the late 1880s. By the opening of the 1946 season, Rickey had signed five African American (Colored/Negro players as they were then called) and assigned three of them to Montreal.

Over the period 1946–1951, the Montreal Royals, stocked with returning service men, African Americans, and other prospects who had worked their way up through the classifications of the minor league system, dominated the International League. They won three regular season championships, appeared in the post-season playoffs every year, winning four, and were the victors of two "Junior World Series," played between the champions of the International League and American Association. Just how strong the Royals teams were during that period is indicated by the fact that when the Brooklyn

Dodgers won their first World Series in 1955, 12 members of the squad along with manager Walter Alston had played in Montreal. Five were African American. Four, including Alston, would become members of the Hall of Fame.

Until the summer of 1951, when they were purchased by Jack Kent Cooke, the Toronto Maple Leafs were owned by a group of local businessmen, one of whom, Peter Campbell, had served as general manager and president since 1941 He knew little about baseball when he assumed the position and constantly turned to major league owners Connie Mack (of the Philadelphia A's), Sam Beardon (of the Boston Braves), and Branch Rickey (of Brooklyn) for advice. He was a hands-on administrator, roaming the stands to retrieve foul balls, interfering with his field managers, and taking issue with the game stories filed by reporters. The team did not lose money during his tenure in spite of the fact that, until 1950, the City of Toronto did not allow the club to play on Sunday, the day on which teams generally drew their largest crowds.Unlike the Montreal Royals, who were assured every year of building a team that featured a large number of the Brooklyn Dodgers' best prospects, the Toronto Maple Leafs in the six seasons after World War II had only a series of limited working agreements with major league clubs. While they received some players from these teams, Campbell would have to work very hard both during and between seasons to purchase enough experienced players from other minor league teams to field competitive ball clubs. In 1945, the Maple Leafs began a two-year agreement with the Philadelphia Athletics, who hadn't finished in the first division of the American League since 1932. In 1947, Campbell signed a working agreement with the Boston Red Sox, who sent their better farmhands to their other Triple A affiliate, the Louisville Colonels of the American Association. The Philadelphia Phillies supplied some players between 1948 and 1950. In 1951, the St. Louis Browns, who had finished in the first division only twice in their history, provided limited assistance. It is small wonder that Toronto assembled a dismal on-field record during the six-year period, never escaping the second division and finishing seventh and eighth one time each.

1946. The Montreal Royals' 1946 season—indeed the entire post–World War II professional baseball era—may be said to have begun on October 23, 1945, when the Royals announced that Jackie Robinson, a "negro" ball player who had served as a lieutenant in the American Army, had been a four-sport star at the University of California, Los Angeles, and, in the summer of 1945, had played several games for the Monarchs, a Negro League team based in Kansas City, would play the 1946 season in Montreal. Branch Rickey explained that he had been searching for three years for the right Negro player to break the color barrier. He stressed the importance of both character and playing ability but understated the racial aspect.

Although some people wondered whether, with only 63 professional at-bats, Robinson would be ready for Triple A baseball, Rickey decided Montreal would be the best testing ground for the new recruit. He was clearly too good to play in the lower minors and sending him to Memphis of the Double A Southern Association would have exposed him to some of the most racially intolerant segments of the American population. The city of Montreal was relatively free of the racial intolerance that Robinson would have faced if he played for an American team.

The Royals opened the 1946 season on April 18 in Jersey City, playing against the Giants, the top farm team of Brooklyn`s cross-town National League rival, the New York Giants. Montreal won 14 to 1 in front of over 25,000 spectators jammed into Roosevelt

Stadium. Robinson had a spectacular debut in Organized Baseball, with four hits in five plate appearances. He proved his power in his second at bat with a three-run home run, and his speed with bunt singles in the fifth and eighth and two stolen bases.

By the time the Royals returned to Montreal to open their home season at Delorimier Downs, the team occupied fourth place. Robinson was batting close to .400 and George Shuba had blasted seven home runs. Before a record opening day crowd of 16,133, the Royals defeated Jersey City 12–9. During the 22-game home stand, the team won 17 and lost five and, after it was over, occupied first place 2.5 games ahead of Syracuse. Over 115,000 fans attended the 22 games.

On May 27, the Royals left on an extended road trip that would see them meet each of the six American teams in the league. They returned home, with a 4.5 game lead over Newark and steadily increased their lead during the summer. They finished the season with a record of 100 wins and 54 losses, 18.5 games ahead of second-place Syracuse. Robinson won the batting title with a .349 average. Six Royals made the league all-star team: Robinson at second, Lew Riggs at third, Marv Rackley and Tom Tatum in the outfield, Herman Franks behind the plate, and Steve Nagy, who led the league with 17 wins, on the mound.

The Royals defeated the Newark Bears four games to two in the first round, and Syracuse defeated the Baltimore Orioles four games to two in the other semi-final. Syracuse took the first game of the Governor's Cup final 5–0 before the Royals came back to win four straight and capture the International League pennant. They travelled Louisville, Kentucky, to meet the Colonels, winners of both the regular season and playoff championships of the American Association, in the Junior World Series.

The trip to Louisville was the Royals' first foray into the South since Robinson had integrated Organized Baseball, and there were questions about whether Montreal would be allowed to play their all-star second baseman. They were, but when he trotted out to the field to start each inning and when he came to bat, Robinson faced a verbal viciousness so intense that the local newspaper printed an article deploring the conduct of white spectators. It is little wonder that, in the games he played in Louisville, he managed only one hit in 11 at bats. The Royals won the opening game 7–5 but were shut out 3–0 in the second game, only managing two hits. Louisville also won the next game, 15–6. The team was glad to get on the train back to Montreal.

The weather in Louisville had been cold, but it was colder still in Montreal. On October 1 it had snowed. But the 14,685 fans warmed themselves up by hurling insults at the Colonels' players. After the first half of the eighth inning, the Royals trailed 5–2. The Royals came back to tie the game in the bottom of the ninth. In the bottom of the 10th, Jackie Robinson's two-out single scored the winning run to tie the series. Robinson was the star of the fifth game, going three for five, including a double and a triple, and participating in three double plays as Montreal defeated the Colonels 5–3. The next night, the Royals scored only two runs. But that was all they needed, as veteran pitcher Curt Davis shut out the Colonels.

A great season had ended. The Montreal Royals had won the first Junior World Series title in their history. Jackie Robinson had more than earned his stripes: his quality of play on the field, as well as the strength of character he displayed, proved that Black players truly belonged in Organized Baseball. During the regular season 412,744 people attended games at Delorimier Downs, the second highest total in the International League. Another 127,154 attended eight home post-season games.

For the Toronto Maple Leafs, the 1946 season was as undistinguished as the Royals'

When Jackie Robinson (center) played for the Montreal Royals in 1946, his teammates included former Negro Leaguers Roy Partlow (left) and John Wright (right), who split the season between Montreal and Trois-Rivières, home of the Brooklyn Dodgers Class C team in the Canadian-American League (courtesy Bibliothèque et Archives Nationales Quebec, P833 S1 D1434 no. 5).

season was distinguished. Managed for a second season by Harry Davis, who had played three major league seasons in the 1930s, the club was in its second year of a working agreement with the Philadelphia Athletics, who offered pathetic support to its International League affiliate: a few aging returned servicemen, war-time major league replacement players, and several roster fillers. The most notable name on the roster was Jim Konstanty, a 29-year-old who would play with Toronto for three seasons before being purchased by the Philadelphia Phillies where he became a star for the National League team's 1950 championship club.

The Leafs won their opening game 7–2 at Syracuse, finished their first road trip with three wins and five losses. By the end of May they had evened their record at 16 wins and 16 losses. That wasn't good enough for Peter Campbell. Davis was fired and replaced by coach/outfielder Bill Norman. The Leafs promptly began an eight-game losing streak and by the end of June were in sixth place, 13.5 games behind Montreal, and would remain there for the remainder of the season. They finished the season with a 71–82 record, 28.5 games behind Montreal, and 8.5 games out of fourth place and a playoff berth. The Maple Leafs drew 182,193 fans to their home games, the fifth-lowest total among 24 Triple A teams.

1947. On April 17, two days after Jackie Robinson had broken the major leagues' color barrier, the Montreal Royals opened their 1947 season with only two of the previous year's regulars, Al Campanis and Earl Naylor, in their lineup. The Royals had strong pitching: twenty-two-year-old Jack Banta would, during the season strike out 199 batters, an average of one per inning, while winning 15 and losing five. Ed Heusser, a 38-year-old veteran of eight major league seasons, would post the league's best win-loss record: 19 and 3.

The most important member of the 1947 squad was Roy Campanella, a 25-year-old catcher who had spent 1946 playing in Nashua of the Class B New England league. By the time he arrived in Montreal, he already had 10 professional years under his belt including nine seasons in the Negro Leagues. Campanella was much different in temperament from Robinson. Whereas Jackie had been reserved and intense, Campy was more relaxed and outgoing. The only African American in the International League in 1947, he posted a .273 average and was named to the league's All-Star team, along with first baseman Ed Stevens and pitcher Ed Heusser. In 1948, he would become a regular with Brooklyn. He later spent 10 seasons with the Dodgers and was elected to the Hall of Fame.

During the first month of the 1947 season, the Royals seemed to prove the press experts correct. They won their opening games at Syracuse 11 to 10, but by the time they returned to Montreal for their home opener—which was delayed three days by snow, sleet, rain, and wet grounds—they had won four and lost five and were 1.5 games behind Jersey City. On June 3, the team moved into first place and, by July 7, led second-place Syracuse by 11 games. But, by September 1, Montreal's lead over Jersey City had shrunk to one game. When the eighth-place Toronto Maple Leafs defeated the Royals in the second to last game of the season, the Royals ended up in second place, half a game behind Rochester. The third-place Syracuse Chiefs won the semi-final series against Montreal in four straight games. The Royals' regular season attendance increased by 30,000 to 442,485.

For the Toronto Maple Leafs, their 6–3 victory over the Montreal Royals on the last day of the season did nothing for their standings in the league, but it did prevent their greatest rivals from winning the pennant. The Ontario team had started the season hoping to improve on the previous year's sixth-place finish. Peter Campbell, dissatisfied with the slim pickings provided by the talent-thin A's in 1946, had signed a working agreement with the Boston Red Sox, defending American League champions, but received none of their promising minor leaguers.

Toronto won its opening game, 14–2 in Baltimore, but managed only 11 wins during May and at one point lost nine in a row. By the end of June, the Leafs were 20 games out of first place and by mid–August 24.5 games out. Their final record of 64 wins and 90 losses put them in eighth place, 30 games behind Jersey City. The team had the lowest team batting average, .249, and the fewest runs per game, 3.55, in the International League. No regular batted above .300. Luke Hamlin with 15 wins and Jim Konstanty with 13 accounted for 44 per cent of the team's victories. Hamlin's ERA of 2.22 was tops in the International League. Third baseman Oscar Grimes earned a berth on the All-Star team. Attendance dropped 11,000 from the previous year. The figure of 171,730 was the lowest in the league and the third lowest among 24 Triple A teams.

1948. Although for Montreal and Toronto fans, the 1947 season had been disappointing, the reports from the 1948 training camps were positive, especially for the Royals. The Brooklyn farm system had several prospects who were ready advance to Triple A ball. One of these, Chuck Connors, would later become the star of the television show

The Rifle Man. Don Newcombe had won 19 and lost six at Class B Nashua, and Bobby Morgan, a slick-fielding infielder, had hit .293 in Class B Spokane. Training camp gossip had it that, should he not make the Dodgers' starting lineup, 19-year-old Duke Snider might wind up with the Royals.

During the winter the Maple Leafs entered into a working agreement with the Philadelphia Phillies. The Phillies had not finished in the first division since 1932 and since then had amassed a total of nine eighth-place, five seventh-place, and one fifth-place finishes. However, several players from the Phillies Eastern League's Utica Blue Sox, including future major leaguer Stan Lopata, along with manager Eddie Collins, were ready for Triple A experience. Willie "Puddin' Head" Jones would make the jump from Terre Haute, Indiana, of the Class B Illinois-Indiana-Iowa League. In addition to bright young prospects, the Leafs brought back some of their old standbys: 33-year-old Oscar Grimes, 43-year-old Luke Hamlin, 31-year-old Jim Konstanty, and 31-year-old Jocko Thompson.

The Montreal Royals opened the 1948 season in Newark, losing to the Bears 3–2 in 11 innings. By the time they arrived in Montreal for their home opener, their record was eight wins and three losses, which placed the club in a first-place tie with Syracuse. During the month of May, Montreal won 15 and lost 12 and by June 1 was in third place, 1.5 games behind Newark. The team moved into first place on June 15 and at the end of the month held a six-game lead over Newark. They would clinch the pennant with nearly two weeks to play and ended the season 13.5 games ahead of Newark.

Two of the most notable players contributing to the Royals' resurgence were future Dodger stars Don Newcombe and Duke Snider. Newcombe was both temperamental and erratic. He began the season with two complete game wins, then put in a number of performances that didn't see him make it past the second inning, was relegated to relief and then, in June turned in three more complete game wins. As the season progressed, Newcombe became more consistent. Between early June and the end of the regular season in September he won 14 games, including a seven inning, 8–0 no-hitter against Toronto, and lost 3. The 21-year-old Snider had begun the season with the Dodgers but had been bothered by leg injuries. He was optioned to Montreal on in mid–May and, after six weeks, when he was called up, he was leading the club with a .349 batting average. In 140 plate appearances he had slugged 11 home runs, driven in 44 runs and compiled a slugging average of over .600.

Many others contributed to the Royals' dominance. Sam Jethroe a 31-year-old star from Cleveland in the Negro Leagues, hit .322, and stole 18 bases, tops on the team. Chuck Connors, with a .307 average and 17 home runs; Jimmy Bloodworth, whose .294 average and 24 home runs and strong performance at second base earned him the league's MVP award; and Al Gionfriddo, who also posted a .294 average and hit 25 home runs all boosted Montreal's reputation as the most feared of the IL's offensive teams. On the mound, Jack Banta's 193 strikeouts led the league and his 19 wins tied him with Rochester's Bill Reeder as tops in that category. Bloodworth, Banta, shortstop Bobby Morgan, and manager Clay Hopper made the all-star team. Attendance increased by 35,000 to 477,638, the best in the league.

Like the Royals, the Maple Leafs lost their season opener, falling to Jersey City 6–4. They returned home with a 3–6 record, took their home opener against Jersey City 9–8, but, by the middle of May, had dropped into eighth place, seven games behind first-place Syracuse. In June the club won 16 and lost 12 and by late July, when manager Eddie Sawyer was promoted to the Philadelphia Phillies, it was in a three-way tie with Rochester and Jersey City for third place. For the rest of the season, the Maple Leafs, now managed by Dick Porter, played just over .500 ball and bounced between second and sixth in the standings. They were in the hunt for a playoff berth until the final day of the season, but finished in fifth place, half a game behind Rochester

Disappointing though the final outcome was, the season had been a relative success for the Maple Leafs. Four of Toronto's old men enjoyed strong seasons. Johnny Welaj, age 34, batted .315, and 32-year-old Barney Lutz .307. Oscar Judd, at 41 years, compiled a 14 and eight record, which included a seven-inning no-hitter, and 31-year-old Jocko Thompson won 12 while losing eight. Thirty-year-old Jim Konstanty, whose contract had been purchased by the Phillies before the start of the season, won 10 and lost the same number. Konstanty, along with Puddin' Head Jones, who was named all-star third baseman, Stan Lopata, and Ed Sanicki, would be promoted to Phillies for the 1949 season. A total of 291,977 fans, 120,000 more than in 1947, showed up at Maple Leaf Stadium.

Montreal was heavily favored going into the semi-finals against fourth-place Rochester. The Royals won the first two games, both at home. Games three, four, and five were played in Rochester, with the home team winning all three. Back at Delorimier Downs, the Royals took game six to even the series. The final game was scoreless going into the bottom of the ninth. With two men on Tommy Bloodworth hit a three-run walk-off home run to send the Royals into the finals against the Newark Bears.

The Royals had a come from behind extra inning victory against Syracuse in the first game of the finals. Syracuse had a come-from-behind win in the second game. When the series moved to Syracuse for three games, Montreal dominated, taking all three to reach the Junior World Series for the second time in three years. Their opponents were the St. Paul Saints, Brooklyn's American Association farm team.

The series opened in St. Paul, with the Royals winning two and the Saints one. Back in Montreal for the rest of the series, the Royals cruised to two easy wins, 8 to 3 in the fourth game and 7 to 2 in the fifth. In these two games, over 30,000 fans cheered the home team to its second Junior World Series championship in three years.

1949. Given the Royals' success and the Maple Leafs' vast improvement during the 1948 season, Montreal and Toronto sports writers, club officials, and fans greeted the 1949 season optimistically. Bobby Morgan, Lou Welag, Al Gionfriddo, Sam Jethroe and Don Newcombe, who was called up to the Dodgers in midseason, were back. Manager Clay Hopper began his fourth season at the helm. Newcomers included Dan Bankhead and Bob Addis, who were "promoted" from the Dodgers' other Triple A team, the St. Paul Saints. On May 15, John Van Cuyk, Chuck Conners, Bud Podbielan, and Pat McGlothan joined the team.

The Philadelphia Phillies didn't send the Toronto Maple Leafs any future "Whiz Kids." But they did provide the Leafs with a new manager, their sixth in since the beginning of the 1946 season: Del Bissonnette, who had been managing since 1937. The Phillies promoted to the Leafs promising young players Alex Garbowsky and Bill Glynn. The team was not without its gray beards: Oscar Judd, 41, Johnny Welaj, 35, and Jocko Thompson 32.

Neither team justified the preseason confidence people had in them. The Royals, along with the Leafs, spent most of the season struggling to stay in the first division. By September 1, the question was which of Montreal, Toronto, and Jersey City would earn third and fourth places and berths in the post-season playoffs. For a few days, the three leap-frogged each other or fell back. Going into the final day of the season, the Leafs needed to win their two remaining games to make the playoffs. They lost to the Bisons. The Royals and the Giants met in a one game playoff to decide third place. The Royals won 5–1.

The Royals received stellar individual performances from Bobby Morgan, who won the batting championship with a .337 average and was named all-star shortstop and league MVP, and Sam Jethroe, who placed second highest among league batters, with a .326 average and who broke a 30-year-old record for most stolen bases with 89. Jethroe was named one of the three all-star outfielders. Although he did not win an all-star berth, Dan Bankhead won 20 games, second best in the league, and struck out a league-high 176 batters.

Toronto's Jocko Thompson, who won 14 and lost five, while posting a 2.73 ERA, was named to the all-star team while Bubba Church, who had a league leading 2.35 ERA was not. Montreal again led the league in attendance: 473,798 fans (down four thousand from the previous year) attended the Royals home games. Toronto's attendance increased by 27,000 to 364,962.

The Royals won the semi-finals against Rochester in four straight and then, after losing the opening game of the finals, defeated first-place Buffalo four games in a row. Montreal faced the Indianapolis Indians in the Junior World Series. Montreal's bats were cool during the first three games of the series, all played at Delorimier Downs. The club managed only five runs on twelve hits. Indianapolis won games one and two, while Montreal took the third. In Indianapolis, the Royals seemed to come to life, evening the series with a 7 to 2 victory. Indianapolis won a come-from-behind 5–4 third victory and then belted five Montreal pitchers for 17 hits on their way to a 12 to 2 victory and the Indiana city's first Junior World Series championship since 1928.

1950. During the winter of 1949–1950, the International League's first franchise shift since 1938 took place. The New York Yankees sold the Newark Bears, whose 1949 attendance had been under 1500 a game, to the Chicago Cubs, who relocated the team to Springfield, Massachusetts. The Bears, along with their neighbors the Jersey City Giants, had suffered drastically at the gate because New York City's three major league teams had begun telecasting many of their games.

On March 7, the Dodgers announced that they would be moving manager Clay Hopper to St. Paul and appointing the Saints' manager, Walter Alston, as his replacement. Alston, a first baseman who had played only one major league game, had been recruited by Rickey to manage in the Cardinals system and, after World War II, had been brought over to the Dodgers. It was rumored that Alston had been sent to Brooklyn's top minor league club in preparation for his eventual taking over of the big club. The speculation was correct. In 1954, Alston began a 27-year career as manager of the Dodgers.

The Royals' opening-day roster was dominated by returnees. Toby Atwell, Chuck Conners, Al Gionfriddo, Clyde King and Turk Lown were back for a third season; Rocky Bridges, Geno Cimoli, and George Schmees for a second. In retrospect, the most noteworthy addition to the lineup was Tom Lasorda, a 22-year-old left-handed pitcher whom the newspaper reporters referred to as cocky. He would play nine seasons in Montreal. Like Royals manager Walter Alston, he would have a brief major league career, appearing in 26 games over three years. But also like Alston, he would enjoy a long and distinguished career as a major league manager. In 1977, he succeeded Alston at the helm of the Los Angeles Dodgers and managed the team for 21 years. During the season, the Dodgers sent three players down to Montreal: Jack Banta, George Shuba, and pitcher Carl Erskine, who would become one of the most important members of the great Brooklyn teams of the 1950s. The 23-year-old right hander would win 10 and lose six for the Royals.

Montreal started the season beating Jersey City 13 to 6 and returned home on May 3, in first place, with a 6–1 record. However, between mid–May and mid–June, the Royals hit the skids, winning only 13 of 34 games, falling into fifth place. They spent the next two months bouncing around between second, third and fourth before settling into second place, where they finished the season, seven games behind Rochester.

The Royals faced the Baltimore Orioles in the semi-final, travelling to Baltimore to play the first three games. Montreal lost the opener, took the second, but they lost the third. Back at Delorimier Downs, Tommy Lasorda pitched a one hitter and Turk Lown a three hitter, to lead them to 5–0 and 8–1 wins. But Baltimore came back to take the series with 6–3 and 4–3 wins.

The Royals did not dominate the individual statistics as they had in previous years. Two players made the all-star team: Don Thompson, who led Montreal with a .311 average and 11 home runs, was named one of three outfielders, while Rocky Bridges, who played superb defense, was named shortstop. Ronnie Lee was the top Royals pitcher with a 14–4 record. Over 80,000 fewer people than in 1949 attended regular season home games. The final regular season total was 391,001.

Before the Toronto Maple Leafs began the 1950 season, general manager Joe Zeigler made two predictions: the Leafs would finish in the first division and attendance records would be set at Maple Leaf Stadium. The first prediction was based on the fact that nine members of the 1949 team that had just missed the playoffs would be returning and the Phillies had assigned their top pitching prospect, 21-year-old Steve Ridzik, to Toronto. He made the second prediction come true because, at last, the law that prohibited the Leafs from playing home games on Sunday had been rescinded. Playing Sunday games would not only increase attendance, but it would mean that the team would not have to travel Saturday night to play a Sunday game in another league city.

Five games into the season, Zeigler's first prediction seemed to be a real possibility. The Leafs won their opening game, 7–6, at Syracuse and took three of the next four, to occupy first place. But by the time they had returned home, their record stood at four wins, four losses and, when the first home stand was over, they had lost eight straight and had dropped to seventh place, where they would remain for the rest of the season. Their final record of 60 wins and 90 losses placed them 31.5 games out of first place. The Maple Leafs did not set a season's attendance record. In fact, attendance dropped by 138,000 to 226,951.

1951. The 1951 season was one of both déjà vu (almost)—1949 all over again. The Montreal Royals dominated regular season play and moved quickly through the International League playoffs on their way to the Junior World Series, and the Toronto Maple Leafs started the season with a new manager and were in the hunt for a playoff berth until the last weekend of the season. There were changes as well. For the second year in a row, a team located on the outskirts of New York City relocated; the Jersey City club became the Ottawa Giants. For the first time since 1942, the Royals were not under the control of the venerable Branch Rickey who had taken over operation of the Pittsburgh Pirates. Midway through the season, the Maple Leafs acquired a new owner.

Montreal's power was evident during its road and home openers, both against Baltimore. On the road, they trounced the Orioles 15 to 7, and a week later, at Delorimier Downs, won 9–4. At the beginning of June, the team held a seven-game lead over Syracuse, and, by early July, that lead had increased to 10 (now over Buffalo). The Royals clinched the pennant on September 2 and finished the season with 95 wins and 59 losses, 11 games ahead of Rochester. Hector Rodriguez, with a .302 average, the only Royals batter above .300, led the league in stolen bases with 26. The team had no one dominant pitcher, but got steady performances from Bob Alexander, with 15 wins and eight losses, Tom Lasorda, who won 12 and lost eight, and Chris Van Cuyk, who joined the club in early June, with 11 wins, four loses. Four Royals were voted to the all-star team: Junior Gilliam at second, Rodriguez at third, Bobby Morgan at short, and Van Cuyk on the mound. Rodriguez was also named rookie of the year. In spite of the Royals' excellent season, attendance increased by a total of only 106, up to 391,107.

The Royals moved quickly through the International League playoffs, defeating Buffalo in four straight games and then taking the Syracuse Chiefs four games to one. Their opponents in the Junior World Series were the Milwaukee Brewers, who had dominated the American Association during the regular season, finishing nine games in front of St. Paul. The first three games were played in Montreal and, when the Royals won the first and third, fans and sports writers spoke enthusiastically about a third Junior World Series championship in six seasons. When the series shifted to Milwaukee, the Royals managed only 10 hits and two runs in games four and five, as the Brewers won 4–2 and 6–0. After the top of third inning of game six, it seemed as if the Royals would even the series. They led 10 to 2, but the Brewers scored 11 unanswered runs to take the Junior World Series.

The Toronto Maple Leafs began their season with a new affiliation and a new manager. The Leafs established a working agreement with the lowly St. Louis Browns. The new manager was Joe Becker, who had managed Jersey City in 1949 and 1950, winning International League manager of the year honors both seasons. The Browns gave the Maple Leafs limited assistance. Most of the players they provided were career minor leaguers well past the mid-points of their careers.

By July 1, Dominion Day, the celebration of Canada's birth as a nation, Toronto baseball fans had settled in for what would be a typical Leaf's season. The club was in fifth place and unlikely to improve. The Leafs had drawn just over 100,000 fans, many of them baseball die-hards, and if the weather stayed good the figure might be doubled. Then, on July 5, things changed radically—off the field. The group of businessmen that owned the Maple Leafs sold 80 percent of the club for a reported $200,000. The new majority owner was 36-year-old Jack Kent Cooke, the owner of several Ontario and Quebec radio stations and newspapers. The price included the lease to Maple Leaf Stadium and the fifth-place team—over a dozen players, a manager and a coach, along with assorted bats, balls, and uniforms. The greatest asset of ownership of the city's International League franchise was that it gave Kent a foot in the door should the major leagues decide to place a team there.

Over the next several weeks, he gave away free soda pop and hot dogs, comic books, orchids, fur coats, cars, and a few ponies. Entertainers such as Victor Borgia and the Mills Brothers (who were appearing at Toronto nightclubs) preformed before games or between games of doubleheaders. After many games, fireworks lit up the sky behind the right field fence. People started coming to Maple Leaf Stadium in large numbers, lured not so much by the games on the field, as by the promotions and entertainment. Over 40,000 people attended the six games of the first home stand under Cooke's ownership. Cooke was even able to convert the Leafs' seeming inability to rise above in fifth place into a promotion. At the end of July, he hired Don Buchanan, a currently unemployed young man, as a flagpole sitter. Until the Leafs moved into the first division, he was to live in a tiny cabin erected on a platform atop a flagpole. His sojourn didn't end until the second to last day of the season, when the Leafs were eliminated from playoff contention. Their final record of 77 wins and 76 losses placed them 1.5 games behind fourth-place Buffalo. The final attendance of 296,847 was nearly 70,000 more than 1950.

During August, the Leafs played their first three African Americans, all sent from the St. Louis Browns. Frank Barnes was a 24-year-old pitcher began the 1951 season with Muskegon of the Class A Central League and had posted a 15–6 record before his contract was acquired by the Browns and then assigned to Toronto. He appeared in only two games during the season. Leon Day, a 34-year-old veteran of the Negro Leagues who would become a member of the Hall of Fame, had begun the 1951 season as a pitcher for the Winnipeg Buffalos of the Mandak League, a high-level semi-pro circuit, had also been signed by the Browns and sent to Toronto. He appeared in 14 games, winning one and losing one. Catcher Charlie White, who also played for Winnipeg, appeared in 60 games and had a .283 average.

Canada acquired its third International League team in December 1950, when it was announced that the Jersey City Giants would move to Ottawa. Baseball operations would be run by the Giants, administration by Tom Gorman. The 64-year-old Gorman was a legendary sports figure in Canada. He'd been a member of Canada's gold-medal lacrosse team in the 1908 London Olympics, a sportswriter, and a general manager of four National hockey League teams. In 1946, he'd resigned his position as General Manager of the Montreal Canadians, who had just won the Stanley Cup, to return to Ottawa, where he took over control of the Ottawa Senators hockey team, purchased a professional baseball franchise for a Border League team, and promoted professional wrestling and a cross-Canada tour for Barbara Ann Scott, Canada's world champion figure skater.

Gorman confidently announced that, given the fact the Class C Ottawa Senators of the Border League had drawn 125,000 fans for a slightly shorter season, the Triple A club would certainly attract double that number. Gorman was wrong about both figures. The Senators had attracted only 97,000 fans; the Giants would draw only 117,000. One of the problems was that, as had been the case in Toronto, Ottawa by-laws did not permit the Giants to play Sunday home games. In addition to having to give up lucrative Sunday dates, they would also have to give up lucrative Saturday nights, playing in the afternoon so that they could make a long trip to other International League city and have enough time to rest before the usual Sunday doubleheader. People also wondered about the quality of players the parent New York Giants would provide. In spring training, it became apparent that the best players would be going to the New York's American Association team in Minneapolis, among them Willie Mays (for the first few weeks of the season), Hank Thompson, Davey Williams, and Hoyt Wilhelm All would be members of New York's 1954 World Series champions.

The "Little Giants," as sports writers oxymoronically named them, won their opening game, a 5 to 4 victory in Springfield. But by the time they arrived at Lansdowne Stadium, which was also the home of the Rough Riders of the Canadian Football League, for their own home opener, their record was one win, four losses. They again defeated Springfield, before a crowd of 7,469. By mid–May, they'd climbed to second place 3.5 games behind Montreal. But over the next month, the team won 13 while losing 18 and had sunk to seventh place, a position they would occupy for the remainder of the season. Their final record: 62 wins 88 losses, 31 games out of first place. Ottawa's sports fans were very displeased with the team; crowds of well under two thousand were frequent. And the New York Giants were unhappy with the Central Canada Exhibition Board and with Gorman's front-office operations. At the end of July, they announced that they would be cutting back on the number of farm clubs at the season's end and that Minneapolis would be their only Triple A affiliate.

2

Canada's Border Leagues Teams

*PONY League, Border League, Western
International League, Canadian-American League*

With the exception of teams in Quebec's Provincial League, all of Canada's minor league teams operating between 1946 and 1951 participated in cross-border leagues containing both Canadian and American teams: the PONY League (the acronym for Pennsylvania, Ontario, New York), the Western International League in the Pacific Northwest, and the Border League and the Canadian-American League in the Northeast. For the American teams, having Canadian clubs in their leagues was financially beneficial; most of the American clubs were located in smaller cities, while the Canadian cities were much larger and usually drew considerably more fans to their games. Since visiting teams received a portion of gate receipts, between 10 and 19 percent a ticket, playing in Canada was generally more lucrative than playing games with their state-side league rivals. Hamilton was the largest city in the PONY League; Kingston, and later, Ottawa in the Border League; Quebec City in the Canadian-American League; and Vancouver in the Western International League.

In 1946, twenty-seven of the twenty-nine new or returning minor leagues were in the lower classifications: B, C, and D. Life on these teams was not easy either for young players starting a career that would lead to the fulfillment of their dreams or for older players newly returned from the Armed Forces clinging to fading dreams. The pay was very low. From the period from 1946 to 1951, the monthly maximum for all 15 players on a Class D roster rose from $1,800 to $2,600; for 15 in Class C, from $2,200 to $3,000; and for 16 players in Class B, from $3,000 to $4,000. Playing conditions were primitive. Lighting was often poor; fields were lumpy and uneven; club houses were cramped with nails pounded into the walls often serving as coat hooks; and, if there were showers, a decent supply of hot or even warm water could be considered a bonus. Travel on old busses along narrow, twisting, badly paved roads was time consuming, tiring, and dangerous. In 1946, nine members of the Spokane Indians were killed when their bus was forced off the road while travelling on a mountain highway in Washington state.

PONY LEAGUE (Class D): Hamilton Cardinals (1946–1951)

The PONY League, formed in 1939 with Hamilton as a charter member, was one of only two Class D leagues to play throughout World War II. However, the Hamilton Red Wings franchise was suspended after the 1943 season. In 1946, the St Louis Cardinals enthusiastically returned a PONY League to Hamilton. They hired local people to run the administrative side of the club, but owned the entire operation including all the players. Like the other clubs in the Class D league, nearly all the Hamilton players were in their late teens and early twenties, usually rookies and sophomores at the beginning of what they hoped would be a baseball journey ending in the major leagues. Only 10 members of the Hamilton Cardinals between 1946 and 1951 would reach that destination. Often the oldest member of a PONY League team would be the player-manager, who was usually in his late 20s or early 30s.

1946. In mid–April, Johnny Newman, a 32-year-old career minor leaguer who had been honorably discharged from the services three weeks earlier, was named the Hamilton Cardinals manager. The average age of his team was 21.9 years; however, 12 men had served in World War II. The St. Louis Cardinals assigned several local players to Hamilton, one of whom, 18-year-old Tom Burgess of London Ontario, would later play 104 games for the St. Louis Cardinals and Los Angeles Angels. The only other Hamilton player to make the majors, Jim Clark, who was also 18, would appear in nine games with the Washington Senators.

The Hamilton Cardinals opened the season at Jamestown on May 1, losing 12–4, and, a day later, lost their home opener, 11–1, also to Jamestown, before 3,521 fans. A 14-game losing streak in late May and early June plunged the Cardinals into the PONY league cellar, where they would stay in until early August, when they moved into seventh place and then fifth place, six games short of a playoff berth. In spite of Hamilton's disappointing season, there were some bright spots. Frank Gravino hit .334 and Robert Schnurr, .325 in 101 games. Final home attendance was 65,206.

1947. If the 1946 performance of the Cardinals had been disappointing, that of the 1947 season was more so. Hamilton won the season's opener, 1–0, in Jamestown. Then the rainouts came—five of them during the first 10 days of the season. During June, the Cardinals played .500 baseball and shifted back and forth between fourth and fifth place. But during July, they lost six more than they won, dropping into sixth place. Shortly after, they moved into seventh, where they spent the remainder of the season. Their 49 and 76 record left them 37.5 behind first place Jamestown. Manager Johnny Newman was the only .300 hitter on the team; he posted a .332 average. Pitcher Vince Stine, in his only season in professional ball, won 13 while losing nine and led the league in strikeouts with 194. Surprisingly, in spite of the early season bad weather and the poor performance on the field, attendance increased by nearly six thousand to 70,608.

1948. There was a new manager, 27-year-old George Kissell. The Cardinals lost four of their first five games but moved above .500 during May and into the first division in early June. They would stay there for the rest of the season, finishing third with a record of 73 wins and 52 losses, 2.5 games behind first place Batavia. Hamilton won the first game of their semi-final against Jamestown before losing the next four and being eliminated.

The Cardinals' regular season was a success both off and on the field. A record 122,725 fans attended games at Civic Field, the second highest total for all Class D teams. James Hersinger's .349 batting average was third highest in the league; manager George Kissell's .347 was fourth. Chick McCombie won 15, including a 6–0 no-hitter. His 2.42 earned run average topped the league.

1949. After opening with a 6–4 record, the team lost four straight and soon after won eight in a row. By June 6, the Cardinals and the Jamestown Falcons were tied for first. However, in June, the Bradford Blue Wings moved to the top of the standings and, from then on, it was what might be called a bird-fight for the pennant. Four losses in their last five games left the Cardinals in third with a record of 75 wins and 50 losses. Attendance, up 13,000 to 137,340, was tops of all teams in Class D leagues.

The Cardinals faced the Jamestown Falcons in the first round, splitting the first two games before winning the next three. Hamilton was well rested when it entered the finals (for the first time since 1941) against Bradford, who had taken seven games to overcome Batavia. The regular-season champions took the first three games from the Cardinals. Hamilton staved off elimination winning the fourth game, before Bradford won the fifth and the playoff championship.

During the season four Hamilton regulars hit over .300, with player-manager Kissell leading the team with a .332 average, sixth highest in the league. Second baseman Bruno Casanova, a Canadian from Windsor, Ontario, who hit .313 and led the team with 10 home runs, was named to the all-star team, as was outfielder George Schachle, who hit .301. Rookie Willard Schmidt, who would go on to a seven-year major league career, led the league in victories with 22.

1950. George Kissell, who had been promoted to Class B Winston-Salem, was replaced as manager by Vedie Himsl. Even though four members of the 1950 Hamilton team, including future major league all-star Ken Boyer, would go on to the majors, the Cardinals turned in a relatively lackluster overall performance. Although for most of May they were close behind early-season leader Oleon, the team slipped into fifth place in June. Playing .500 ball in July the team moved into third place, where they remained until the end of the season: their final record 68 wins and 57 losses. Two Cardinals were voted to the all-star team. Pitcher Thomas Keating's, won-loss percentage (.929 on 13 wins and only one defeat) was the best in the league. He also set a league record, striking out 19 men in one game. Joseph Ossola shared all-star catching honors with Hornell's James Tuite. The first round of the playoffs was a high scoring affair, with the Oleon Oilers, who had finished second, scoring 38 runs to Hamilton's 32. Oleon took a two to one game lead, then split the next two games before winning game six and a berth in the finals.

Although Hamilton made the playoffs, home attendance for the season fell by 45,000. Five other PONY League teams experienced declines, which totaled 136,000. Perhaps the facts that there were no close races during the regular season along with the fact that television stations had recently started broadcasting in Buffalo and Rochester, New York, as well as Erie, Pennsylvania, help to explain the drop.

In retrospect, the most interesting season by a 1950 Cardinal player was that of Ken Boyer. The year earlier he'd been signed out of high school as a pitcher and assigned to Lebanon of the North Atlantic League where he won five and lost one and had a .455 batting average. Boyer lost his first two starts with Hamilton. For several weeks, he was used as both a starter and reliever, performing unevenly in both roles. But he was also used as a third and first baseman and an outfielder. On the July 4 doubleheader, he hit 5 for 10. In late July, he was replaced on the mound after 7.3 innings, having given up nine runs on eleven hits and walking seven men. But he finished the game in left field. At the plate he was three for four, with one home run and a double. In August, while pitching a complete game 6–1 victory, he went three for three, with an RBI triple. At season's end, he had a losing pitching record: six wins, eight loses, with a 4.39 ERA record. But his batting average was .342 and his slugging percentage was .575. In 1955 he began a 15-year major league career, establishing himself as one of the greatest of all St. Louis Cardinals third basemen.

1951. The Cardinals lost their opening game 7–1 in front of 2,508 home fans and then went on to lose their next nine home games. Luckily, they were victorious in half of their road games, so that by the end of May, they were only in sixth place. Hamilton began July in a three-way tie for fifth place but sparked by a 25-game hitting streak by Lee Leftridge, won 17 of 23 games in late July and early August to move into fourth place. They clinched fourth place and the final playoff berth by winning the first game of a season-ending double header. In the first round of the playoffs, Hamilton faced the Olean Oilers. The teams traded victories until the seventh game, which was won 7–0 by the Oilers.

Leftridge was Hamilton's top hitter with a .337 average; Wally Shannon was second with.323. Milt Bayne, who was named to the all-star team, won 16 games and lost 10. Attendance dropped by 30,000 to 62,000 causing some people to wonder how long the St. Louis Cardinals would continue to keep a team in Hamilton.

Border League (Class C): Kingston Ponies (1946–1951), Granby Red Sox (1946), Sherbrooke Canadians (1946), Ottawa Nationals/Senators (1947–1950), Cornwall Canadians (1951)

One of the new leagues that began play in 1946, the Class C Border League included teams in eastern New York state; Kingston, Ontario; and Granby and Sherbrooke, Quebec. The Kingston Ponies were owned and operated by Nelles Megaffin, the proprietor of a local hotel and active supporter of amateur sports in the area. The Sherbrooke Canadians were controlled by a group of Rochester businessmen who also owned the Niagara Falls Frontiers of the Class C Middle Atlantic League. Omar Cabana, a Quebec businessman, owned the Granby Red Sox.

The average age of the players in the Border League was higher than that in the PONY League. Border League regulations specified that, after June 1, each team must carry four veteran players (those with three or more years of service) and six rookies. Of the total of fifteen players on each roster, at least five had to be returning servicemen. During the season, the three Canadian clubs signed a total of 53 rookies, many of them recruits from semi-pro leagues in Ontario and Quebec. Several of the players on the Canadian teams were hockey players, including current and future National Hockey Leaguers Norm Dussault and Gilles Dube (Montreal Canadiens) and George Gee (Chicago).

1946. Sherbrooke and Granby opened the Canadian teams' Border League season on May 12 and 13. Granby won its opener 8–7, before 2,500 hometown fans, while the next night Sherbrooke won 2–0 before only 500 attendees. On May 15, the Kingston Ponies won 11–10 at the home of their cross-border rivals, the Ogdensburg Maples. After two days of rain, the Ponies opened their new home park, Megaffin Stadium, which had been built in just over four months, losing to the Maples 6–3 in front of a crowd of 1,920. By the end of the season, 60,957 fans, tops in the league, attended games at Megaffin Stadium.

The figures might have been greater had the Ponies been permitted to play home games on Sundays.

At the end of May, Granby and Kingston occupied third and fifth, respectively. Sherbrooke was well-settled in sixth and last place and would remain there, except for a few days in July when they were tied with Kingston for fifth place. For most of June, July, and August, Granby and Kingston battled each other for third and fourth place, with the Ponies finishing third and the Red Sox fourth. Granby clinched a playoff berth by winning their last five games—all without taking the field. On the Saturday morning of Labor Day weekend, the owners of the Sherbrooke Canadians announced that the team was bankrupt and would be forced to forfeit its final five games, all against Granby.

One of the season's highlights involved Arnie Jarrell, 23-year-old rookie right hander of the Kingston Ponies. He pitched two complete games in a doubleheader against Ogdensburg and won both. Jarrell, a Kingston native, would end the season with the most wins, 21, in the Border League and its best earned-run average: 2.30. He would be named to the league's all-star team, as would teammates catcher Charles Alltop, outfielder James Heximer, and pitcher Peter Karpuk, who led the league in strikeouts with 175.

In the first round of the playoffs, Kingston lost its first game in Auburn and then returned home to take the next three and the right to advance to the final against the Watertown Athletics, who had defeated Granby by three games to one. The Athletics won the first two games, lost the third, and won the fourth, to take a commanding lead into game five, which would be part of a doubleheader. The Ponies took the opener but lost the nightcap and the inaugural Border League championship.

The two Quebec teams drew poorly during the first month-and-a-half of the season and because of the long road trips to other league cities were incurring expenses that the small revenues from home games could not cover. In early July, Omar Cabana announced that, because of poor attendance, he would not operate the team beyond July 15. The club did finish the season. Although Cabana owned the ballpark, the city owned the lights and would not turn them on. As a result, the Red Sox were forced to play late afternoon or twilight games before crowds that were frequently under two hundred. Granby finished the season attracting just over 31,000 fans, fourth in the six-team league. The Sherbrooke Canadians' problems came to a head late in July, when the Rochester ownership group sold the franchise to local investors, who quickly assured fans that the team would play out the season. The team did continue, remaining in last place, but did not finish the season, not having the money to pay the players for the last five games. The Canadians' final attendance of 25,576 was the lowest in the league.

1947. To no one's surprise, neither Granby nor Sherbrooke returned for the 1947 season. Omar Cabana relocated the Red Sox to Geneva, New York. When the Sherbrooke franchise was returned to the league, Tommy Gorman, who had recently resigned as general manager of the Montreal Canadiens hockey team, applied for a Border League team for Ottawa. With a metropolitan population of over 200,000, the nation's capital was not only the largest city in the league, it was also one of the largest in the lower minors. Gorman announced that he would adapt Lansdowne Park, home of the Rough Riders professional football team, for baseball games and have lights installed. He would not have to do without profitable Sunday dates, for he would get around the Ontario law that prohibited professional sports on Sunday by playing Sunday games across the river in Aylmer,

Quebec. He named as manager Paul "Daffy" Dean, the younger and quieter brother of Hall-of-Famer Jerome "Dizzy" Dean.

When opening day arrived, the Nationals' lineup indicated that this was not a typical Class C team. Seven of the nine players, including Bill Metzig, who had major league experience, were 26 years or older; seven had seen duty during World War II. The oldest was 40-year-old Walt Masters, who had played in the major leagues as well as the National Football League and who, later in the year, would coach the Ottawa Trojans semi-professional football club.

The two Canadian teams opened their seasons on May 14. Ottawa, playing an afternoon game (the lights would not be ready until early June), defeated Ogdensburg 6–3. In Kingston, just over 1,000 shivered through a cold, damp night game, watching the Geneva Red Birds win 5–2. The Nationals got off to a fast start, winning six of their first seven games, while the Ponies stumbled out of the gate, playing just under .500 ball. During June, Ottawa won 20 and lost 13 to solidify their hold on first place, while Kingston won 15 and lost 14 to retain fourth. In July, Ottawa held on to first place, fighting off the Watertown Athletics, who finished the month just two games behind the Nationals. During August, the Nationals increased their first-place lead over Auburn from two to eight games, while Kingston slipped badly, with only 11 wins against 18 losses. The Ponies slipped to fifth place 10 games out of the fourth and final playoff spot. Ottawa finished the season 12 games ahead of Auburn, while the Ponies managed to escape the cellar by one game. The Nationals' final record was 82 wins, 42 losses; Kingston's 49 wins and 77 losses.

Six Ottawa Nationals made the league all-star team. Catcher Al Grefe, whose .336 average was fourth in the league; third baseman Charlie Russian, whose .328, was fifth; and second baseman Bill Metzig, whose .317, was seventh. In addition to these three, Bob Sanborn made the all-star team as the best utility man, Charlie Shupp, with 16 wins and a 2.72 ERA, the league's second best, was one of the all-star pitchers, and Paul Dean was the manager. Jim Heximer, with a .317 batting average the only Kingston Pony to hit over .300, was an all-star outfielder. The two Canadian clubs' success or lack of it was reflected in the regular season attendance figures. Ottawa's 62,607 was second-best in the league, while Kingston's 52,268, down eight thousand from last season, was last in the league.

The Ottawa Nationals won the first round of the playoffs, defeating Auburn in four straight games. They won the first two games of the finals against Ogdensburg, before losing two. Then, as the team prepared to travel to Ogdensburg for game five, manager Paul Dean announced that he was leaving the club and turning managerial duties over to second baseman Bill Metzig. Dean, it appeared, had signed a contract to manage only until September 15, and, when playoffs continued beyond that date, pressing business concerns required that he return to Arkansas. The Nationals won game five in Ogdensburg 13–7 and returned to Ottawa the next night to win the championship with an 11–2 victory over the Maples.

1948. Each player in the Ottawa Senators' (they had changed their nickname during the winter) opening-day starting lineup was a returnee. The two youngest members of the team, who had seen limited duty in 1947, were 23-year-old Doug Harvey, who had just finished the first season of what would prove to be his Hall-of-Fame career with the Montreal Canadiens of the National Hockey League, and 21-year-old Pete Karpuk, who, last fall had played for the Ottawa Rough Riders of the Canadian Football League. Bill Metzig, who had led the Nationals to their victory in the 1947 playoffs, was the player-manager.

The Kingston Ponies began the season with only four returnees: pitchers Stan Stenhoff and Art Cook, outfielder Jim Heximer, and infielder Bill Meara. Newcomers included Chuck Tanner, a 19-year-old first baseman who would become a very successful major league manager, and catcher Del Crandall, who would be one of the mainstays of the Milwaukee Braves teams of the 1950s.

On June 4 Ottawa moved permanently into first place. Their lead until early September was never more than five games. Their final win-loss percentage was .622. There were two particularly bright spots in the season. Lefty Seamon won 21 games and posted a 2.00 earned run average, both tops in the Border League. Doug Harvey's .340 final batting average was fourth in the league and his 17 home runs, second. Seamon and player-manager Metzig were named to the all-star team. Attendance increased by over 13,000 to 76,299.

The Kingston Ponies did win their opening game, 1–0 at Geneva, but then stumbled, taking only one game in a 10-game stretch. By the beginning of June, they were in fifth place, where, except for a couple of brief excursions into the cellar, they remained for the rest of the season. Only two regulars, Bill Meara at .313 and Jose Perez at .308, were above the .300 level at the plate. Bill Reardon, who led the league with 24 home runs, provided some power. Art Cook earned an all-star berth with his 21 and 9 won-loss record. Attendance dropped for the second season in a row, from 52,000 to 41,000.

Lansdowne Park, home of the Ottawa Rough Riders of the Canadian Football League, served as the home field of the Ottawa Senators of the Border League from 1947 to 1950 and the Ottawa Giants/Athletics of the International League from 1951 to 1954 (courtesy City of Ottawa Archives, 31978–93 CA 1797).

As the Ottawa Nationals were leaving for their semi-final series against Ogdensberg, they learned that Len (Lefty) Seamon, who had not felt well for a month, had been taken to the hospital for the removal of a malignant tumor. The Nationals lost the first two games, 4–1 and 4–2, before responding to manager Bill Metzig's appeal to win this one for Lefty, taking game three 6 to 5 in 11 innings. However, they lost the next two games and the series. Seamon never left the hospital and he died in mid–October.

During the regular season, the attentions of Border League team executives were taken away from the field by two controversies. The first concerned Quebec's Provincial League, an independent circuit not bound by the National Association's rules and restrictions and therefore able to raid other minor league teams with impunity. Arnie Jarrell, Norm Dussault, and Joe Lay, all the property of the Kingston Ponies, were lured to Granby of the Provincial League with the promise of higher salaries.

The second issue concerned speculation about how the Ottawa Senators could maintain a roster with so many experienced and talented players. In early June, Kingston Ponies owner Nelles Megaffin charged that Ottawa was exceeding the monthly salary ceiling by $750 and threatened to withdraw his team from the Border League. The results of a private investigation into the matter were not revealed, but the Ponies did not withdraw.

1949. Ottawa built its 1949 squad around a core of returning veterans; Kingston announced it had started another rebuilding program. The Ponies hired a new playing manager, Zeke Bonura, whose experience and power at the plate were expected to lead the Ponies into the playoffs. Two of the newcomers, Gideon Applegate and Wally Williams, were the first African Americans to play for Kingston.

Ottawa occupied first place for the first two weeks of the season before being overtaken by the Geneva Robins. The Senators could not put together a significant win streak to overtake the Robins. They finished in second place, 6.5 games behind the leader. Five Senators were named to the all-star team. Doug Harvey, who led the league with a .351 batting average and a .562 slugging average, was named an outfielder. Manager Bill Metzig, whose .338 average was third in the league, was the second baseman, and Pete Karpuk, who hit .332 and compiled an 8–1 record on the mound, was named shortstop and MVP. The Senators' other all-stars were catcher Bill Kivett and pitcher Walt Balash, who ended up with an 18–8 record. Attendance increased by two thousand to 78,577.

In the opening game of Ottawa's semi-final series against Auburn, Doug Harvey's walk-off home run in the bottom of the ninth gave the Senators a 2–1 victory. Auburn took the next three contests, before Ottawa won two to even the series. The Cayugas took the seventh game 2–0 to advance to the finals. A few days after the Senators' final game, Pete Karpuk suited up for an Ottawa Rough Riders football contest and Doug Harvey reported to the fall training camp of the Montreal Canadians.

If the 1948 Kingston Ponies stumbled out of the gate, it could be said that the 1949 edition of the team never left it. The Ponies did win their opening game, 6–5, in Auburn. But by the end of the month, they had won only four more while losing 15. Bonura resigned on August 19, with the team 11.5 games out of fifth place. Catcher Hal Leach was named interim manager. However, the change did not help and as August progressed the Ponies entered a 10-game losing streak. Their final .295 won-lost percentage was the lowest in the four-year history of the Border League. Surprisingly, in spite of the Ponies' dismal showing, home attendance was only 2,000 less than in 1948.

1950. Ottawa opened the 1950 season with much of their 1949 lineup intact; Kingston initiated another rebuilding program. The Senators' opening day lineup featured six returnees, including all-stars Metzig, Kivett, and Russian. The Ponies hired Barney Hearn, a 31-year-old career minor leaguer who had managed Auburn to three playoff appearances in four years, as their new manager.

Ottawa won its opening game 9–8 at Ogdensburg, while Kingston lost their opener 6–2 to Watertown. The Ponies proceeded to drop their next three, but then won five straight. At the end of May, the Ponies and the Senators were tied for first place, but in June Ottawa moved into a 6.5 game lead over Watertown, while Kingston, with just 13 wins in 33 games, sank to fourth place.

The Senators slumped during July and their first-place lead shrank to 1.5 games. Then on the early morning of July 31 tragedy struck. No longer able to play Sunday games in nearby Quebec, Ottawa had to travel to the parks of the nearby New York clubs to play Sunday games and start for home in the late evening. Pitcher Bob Larkin, who had won 12 games, was driving one of the cars the Senators still used for their road trips when a truck crossed the center line, killing him and seriously injuring the four passengers. The Senators lost six in a row and yielded first place to Ogdensburg. However, the team then won seven straight and captured the pennant on the last day of the season. Kingston, in the meantime, had won 34 of its last 57 games, finishing in third place and earning a playoff berth for the first time since 1946.

Ottawa placed two men on the all-star team. Playing manager Bill Metzig, whose .318 average was seventh in the league, was selected at second base, while Johnny Russian, who hit .336, third highest, was selected at third base. The Nationals' top pitchers were Don Bryan (17 wins and eight loses) and Ed Flanagan (16 wins and 10 losses). Kingston's Harry Pilarski, whose 19 wins was tied for tops in the league, earned a spot on the all-star team. Bill Haschak led the Ponies with a .328 batting average. Manager Barney Hearn's .316 average marked the seventh consecutive season he had hit over .300. Both the Senators and the Ponies drew more fans than they had in 1949. Ottawa increased by 18,000 to 97,091; Kingston by 14,000 to 52,493.

With four of the Border League's top six winning pitchers on their rosters, the best-of-seven semi-final series between the Senators and Ponies shaped up as a succession of pitcher's duels. In games one, two, four, and five, the Nationals scored a total of eight runs to the Ponies' six. The Ponies won the opening game before the Senators took four straight to enter into the finals against the Ogdensburg Maples.

Unfortunately, in the finals the Ottawa bats fell silent as Ogdensburg jumped into a two-game lead with 5–1 and 3–0 wins. The Senators evened the series with 3–2 and 11–10 wins to tie the series. In game five, Ottawa was again shut out, 5–0. They lost game six and the championship by a score of 7 to 6. That game would be the last played by the Ottawa Senators. In 1951, the Jersey City Giants of the International League would relocate to Canada's capital city.

1951. When the New York Giants agreed to move their International League to Canada's capital city, Tom Gorman announced that he would transfer the Senators to Cornwall, an eastern Ontario city of just over 16,000 which hadn't had a professional baseball team since 1939. Shortly after Gorman made his announcement, a powerful November gale devastated the area, including the park where the new team, to be called the Canadians, was to play. This was the first of many misfortunes that would beset the club. By early April, only makeshift repairs had been completed. The new lighting was inadequate, as were rest room facilities. There were no club houses, and a wire fence surrounded the outfield, giving passersby a free look at the ballgame.

With crowds of less than 200 attending the games, Gorman issued a demand to the Border League: he wanted all the Canadians' home games to be played on the road until mid–June. When that ultimatum drew no responses, he withdrew his financial backing of the team. The league agreed to support the club for a few days and, when a search for local owners proved unsuccessful, decided to operate the Canadians as a road club. On June 23, Cornwall and Geneva withdrew from the league. However, except for their first Sunday home game, which drew 1,200 fans, Cornwall had attracted a total of only 3,800, last in the league.

The Kingston Ponies won their opening game, 9–7, over Watertown, before 547 home fans. However, by May 23, they had a 5–8 record and were in fifth place. By the end of June, the Ponies had moved into second place, two games behind Cornwall Canadians.

For the next two weeks, the games on the field, when they were played, were of secondary importance. Border League president John Ward, along with officials of four remaining Border League teams, was struggling to find a way for the organization to survive. Late June discussions about a possible merger with the Canadian-American League produced no results. On July 3, it was announced that both Watertown and Auburn were in severe financial difficulties. On July 16, the Border League announced that it was suspending operations for the rest of the 1951 season but hoped to return in 1952. It did not.

WESTERN INTERNATIONAL LEAGUE (Class B):
Vancouver Capilanos and Victoria Athletics (1946–1951)

The Western International League, a class B circuit that had suspended operations after the 1942 season, resumed play in 1946. The Vancouver Capilanos were one of the four returning clubs and the Victoria Athletics, one of four new clubs. Vancouver, Canada's third largest city, with a population of close to 400,000; Spokane, with a population of 125,000; and Tacoma, with a population of just over 110,000, were the largest cities in the league. Victoria had a population of close to 80,000, while each of the other cities had less than 30,000.

The two Canadian teams had a long history in professional baseball. Vancouver had fielded teams in Northwestern League and its successors the Pacific Coast International, Northwest International, and Western International League between 1905 and 1922, and had been part of the WIL when it was reformed in 1938. Victoria had been a member of the New Pacific League in 1896 and the Northwestern League in 1905 and from 1911 to 1915 and 1919 to 1921.

The Vancouver and Victoria teams were a study in contrasts. The former was owned by Emil Sick, a beer baron, who owned breweries in both Seattle and Vancouver, and who had named the two baseball teams he owned, the Seattle Rainiers and the Vancouver Capilanos, after those companies. The Capilanos were run by Bob Brown, an American who had come to Vancouver before World War I and had been an owner, executive, manager, and player for many of the Vancouver clubs. The Victoria Athletics were formed by a group of prominent local businessmen who had little baseball experience but a great deal of civic pride. Running the business side of the new enterprise was Reg Patterson, who

Victoria's Royal Athletic Park, which was built within the confines of a city block, was the home of the Athletics/Tyees of the Western International League from 1945 to 1954 and to several amateur soccer teams. The center field wall was just 331 feet from the plate, while the right field foul pole was just over 450 feet. The north sideline of the soccer pitch extended from left field along the outfield wall to right field and into right field foul territory (courtesy City of Victoria Archive, CVA 0731).

had been active in Vancouver Island senior amateur baseball during World War II. Laurel Harney, who had played amateur baseball in Edmonton, Alberta and, during the War, had managed senior teams in Victoria, was hired as field manager.

Both the Capilanos and the Athletics played in what could, at best, be described as "quirky" ball parks. Athletic Park, the Vancouver team's home grounds, had been in use since 1913. The left field foul pole was 383 feet from home plate, right field 232, the left field power alley 395, the right field alley 318. A low fence running in foul territory beyond third base protected players from tumbling down a steep slope leading to a railroad right-of-way. Royal Athletic Park in Victoria also had unusual dimensions. The left-field wall was 352 feet from home plate. From there the fence angled back for a few yards before turning sharply and heading due east to the right field pole, which was 452 feet from the plate. Dead center was 331 feet away from home plate.

1946. There would be no shortage of available players for the 1946 season. Returning service men, wartime replacement players who were being shunted from higher to lower classifications, and rookies were in abundance. Each team in a Class B league was allowed to carry 16 players (which could include a playing-manager) and could increase the number by adding up to four returning servicemen. Over the 1946 season, 21 of the 33 players to play for Vancouver were returning servicemen, and 22 of 43 in Victoria.

For Bob Brown in Vancouver, putting together a roster was relatively easy as he could draw from the Seattle Rainiers' large pool of players. The first gift from the Rainiers was manager Syl Johnson, who'd played in Vancouver in 1920 and gone on to pitch 19 years in the major leagues. Two of the Capilanos' most interesting acquisitions were Canadians. Victoria native Reg Clarkson, who joined the team after completing his year's studies at the University of British Columbia, batted .333 in his rookie season. The other Canadian was Alberta native Charlie Mead, who had played during World War II for the New York Giants. One of the most popular players on the Capilanos, he played in Vancouver for the next five seasons.

In late June, with Vancouver in a 10-game losing streak, Syl Johnson resigned his position as manager, was replaced briefly by Ed Carnett, a wartime major league replacement player who had started the 1946 season pitching for Seattle, and then by Bill Brenner, who'd broken into professional ball with the Capilanos in 1941 and spent four years in the service. He would pilot the Vancouver team for the next four years. The managerial changes did not appreciably alter the team's performance. The team remained in seventh position until mid–August before moving up to sixth place where it finished the season, 20.5 games behind pennant winner Wenatchee.

At the beginning of the season, Victoria Athletics manager Laurel Harney predicted that the club would finish in the first division. After 10 days, the fourth-place team had a 5–6 record, but on May 10, the Athletics began a 10-game losing streak that dropped them into eighth place, a position they would hold for the rest of the season. At the end of May, Harney, who was clearly out of his depth in the professional game, resigned as manager and was succeeded by Ted Norbert, a veteran Pacific Coast League player. Sixteen games out of first place at the beginning of June, the Athletics finished in eighth place, 38.5 games out of first. Pitcher Robert Jansen led the league in strikeouts with 296.

1947. Only four members of the Victoria Athletics returned, including manager Ted Norbert. But they had acquired an important affiliation—with the New York Yankees. The Yankees did not send any future major leaguers to Victoria in 1947, but of their 12 players who did arrive at Royal Athletic Park, four would advance to Triple A. Victoria did, however, acquire a future major leaguer, 19 year old Jack Harshman, who was optioned by the San Diego Padres to the Athletics just before the season opened. During May and June, the Athletics roster also included Frank Lucchesi, a weak hitting middle infielder who, in 1970—his twentieth year as a manager—became the pilot of the Philadelphia Phillies. Bob Brown decided to build the 1947 Capilanos around a core of returning players that Vancouver owned, among them manager Bill Brenner and Charlie Mead.

By early May, Spokane was in first place, two games ahead of Vancouver and 2.5 games ahead of Victoria. At the end of the month, Spokane and Victoria maintained first and third place respectively, but the Vancouver Capilanos had slipped to five games under five hundred and dropped to sixth place. By the end of June, Vancouver was once again above five hundred, and was tied for fifth place with Victoria. But the Caps once again nose-dived during July, losing 20. Victoria had moved into fourth place. The Athletics' Jack Harshman was sending the ball over Victoria and other league fences at an amazing clip. By July 8, he had tallied 23 home runs.

In August, the Capilanos earned 30 victories, while losing only six games and, on August 29, tied Salem for second place, one-half game behind league leading Bremerton. Vancouver won the pennant finishing .001 percent ahead of Spokane.

Vancouver's tremendous stretch run was a tribute to many members of the club. Frank Mullens, who batted .321 and hit 33 home runs, was named an outfielder on the all-star team. In all, five Capilanos, led by Charlie Mead, whose .354 average was third best in the league, hit over .300. Pitcher Jim Hedgecock earned a league high 21 wins.

The Victoria Athletics' first baseman Jack Harshman and outfielder Bill White were named to the all-star team. Harshman won the home run crown with 36. For the 1947 season, in which each team had 154 rather than 144 games scheduled, overall league attendance increased by nearly 220,000. Vancouver drew 119,303; Victoria 129,862.

1948. Victoria enjoyed its best season since joining the league, finishing in third place. Although the Athletics, guided once again by Ted Norbert, never seriously challenged for the pennant, they ended up a respectable 6.5 games out of first. The club dominated the all-star team: Vic Buccola at first base, Lauritz Jensen at second, Archie Wilson in the outfield, and Joe Blankenship on the mound. Blankenship's 25 wins were the most in the league. Wilson led the league in batting at .369 and RBIs, with 132.

The defending Vancouver Capilanos fared poorly in 1948, dropping into the second division in the middle of May and staying there for the rest of the season. Their final record of 66 wins, 80 losses, left them 12 games out of the first division and 25.5 behind pennant-winning Spokane. Catcher Jack Warren led the club with a .344 average and earned a place on the league all-star team.

League attendance fell: 108,000 fewer fans watched games than had in 1947. Victoria gained 13,000 for a total of 143,081; Vancouver's attendance dropped by 2500 to 116,722. No doubt many early season rainouts contributed to the overall league decline. However, it may be that the post-war novelty of having a hometown professional team was beginning to wear off, particularly in the league's smaller cities.

1949. Vancouver started the season with several returning players, including manager Bill Brenner. It was an old team for Class B ball, with three players over 30 and 10 between the ages of 25 and 29. At 20, rookie K Chorlton was the youngest member of the squad. In Victoria, manager Ted Norbert would not be surrounded by many old and familiar faces. With an average age of just under 23 years, Victoria was one of the youngest teams in the league. Twenty-three of these youthful players were New York Yankee farmhands, including 21-year-old infielder Gil McDougald who, in 1951, would begin a 10-year career with the Yankees.

Vancouver and Victoria started the season slowly—on May 1, they were sixth and eighth respectively. However, Vancouver picked up the pace in May and by the month's end occupied second place, five games behind Yakima. The Capilanos would remain in second the rest of the year, only once moving to within 4.5 games of the league leader. Vancouver won the playoffs, defeating fourth place Spokane three games to one and then defeating the regular season champions, the Yakama Bears, in three straight games.

Victoria meantime remained in the cellar. In late July, at the insistence of the New York Yankees, manager Ted Norbert was fired and replaced by Earl Bolyard. The change proved somewhat effective. During July, the Athletics moved up to fifth place, where they would stay for the remainder of the season. In September, the Yankees announced that they would not renew their affiliation with the Athletics.

During the regular season, several players from the two Canadian clubs turned in strong performances. Vancouver's Bob Snyder tied for the most wins with 22 while Vernon Kindsfather earned 18 victories. Dick Sinovik with a .369 average and Bob Sheely, at .348, placed second and sixth in the batting race. Sinovik, an outfielder, was named to the league's all-star team. Victoria's Jim Propst won 17 games and lost 5 and was named an all-star. Gil McDougald hit .344 on his way to a position as second baseman on the all-star team.

Vancouver's attendance increased from 117,000 to 138,000, while Victoria's dropped from 143,000 to 115,000. League attendance dropped by 92,000. During the summer several newspapers carried reports that three franchises were in precarious financial situations: Wenatchee, Bremerton and Salem. During the winter, the struggling Wenatchee and Bremerton franchises were relocated: Wenatchee to Tri-City (Richland, Kenewick, and Pasco, Washington), and Bremerton to Wenatchee.

One piece of good/bad off-field news affected the Vancouver Capilanos. During the summer, government officials announced that Athletic Park would have to be vacated at the end of the season in order to make way for an approach ramp for the soon to be constructed Granville Street Bridge. The team was given extra time to erect a new stadium, which it would move into in June 1951.

1950. Vancouver pretty much followed the pattern of previous seasons, rehiring playing manager Bill Brenner and 11 other members of the 1949 squad. Two of the team's best performers were both graduates of the University of British Columbia: Reg Clarkson and pitcher Sandy Robertson, a graduate of the university's Faculty of Engineering who had such a good day job as an engineer that he was only able to play home games.

The Athletics took the first step toward solving their problems by hiring a new manager: Marty Krug, who'd played briefly in the major leagues and had managed several seasons in the Pacific Coast League. The team he assembled included five returnees, along with castoffs from the Vancouver Capilanos: Edo Vanni, K Charlton, and Jim Hedgecock, and Saskatchewan native and former major leaguer Lefty Wilkie. Also on the roster was John Marshall, a pitching workhorse, who, when his career ended in the mid–1950s would have spent 13 seasons with a total of 6 WIL teams.

Neither the Capilanos nor the Athletics were in contention during the season. The two teams would move back and forth between seventh and eighth until early July, when Victoria advanced to fifth place. The Capilanos, who, at the end of June, vowed not to shave until they had moved from eighth place, did so the next day, and by the beginning of August were only a game and a half behind fifth-place Victoria. At the end of the season, each was in a virtual tie for fifth place, 26 games behind Yakama and 14 behind fourth place Wenatchee.

There were highlights for each club. Sandy Robertson won his first 12 games for Vancouver and ended up with a 12–3 record. Reggie Clarkson was the team's top hitter, with a .326 average and 13 home runs. For the Athletics, outfielder Gene Thompson finished fourth in the league with a .344 average and second among home run hitters with 24. Both Thompson and Marshall, who won 15 while losing 13, made the all-star team.

League attendance was down by 13,000 from 1949. Spokane dropped by 70,000, Vancouver by 41,000, and Victoria by five thousand. Salem was reported to have lost

Nat Bailey (left) and Bob Brown stand before their plaques at the B.C. Sports Hall of Fame. Bailey was instrumental in keeping the Mounties in the Pacific Coast League from 1957 to 1962 and from 1965 to 1969. Brown was president of the Vancouver Capilanos of the Western International League (BC Sports Hall of Fame, 7559.2).

$50,000 and was rumored to be moving to New Westminster, British Columbia. Late in the autumn, officials of the Victoria Athletics announced that the club had lost more than $30,000 over two years and appealed to the public for financial support.

1951. With their new stadium scheduled to open in late spring 1951, the Vancouver Capilanos did not want to have a second consecutive losing season. Accordingly, in the off season, they jettisoned Bill Brenner, who had managed the team for four and a half years, replacing him with Bill "The Rooster" Shuster, a wartime major league replacement player who had most recently served as a player-coach for the Seattle Rainiers. Also gone was power hitter Reg Clarkson, who had retired. Still, many of the old familiar faces remained, most notably pitchers George Nicholas, Sandy Robertson, and Bob Snyder, a trio which, in 1950, had won a combined 44 games, over half the Capilanos' victories. Among the newcomers was veteran catcher John Ritchie who had broken the Pacific Coast League's color barrier in 1948.

The Victoria team, which had signed a working agreement with the Portland Beavers of the Pacific Coast League, opened the season with eight returning players, six of whom were 27 years of age or older. Promising young newcomers included infielder Don Pries, catcher Milt Martin, and infielder Jim Clark. The Athletics had a new manager, their sixth in as many seasons: 44-year-old Dick Kewpie Barrett, a wartime replacement player in the major leagues and a Pacific Coast League veteran who was expected to take a regular turn on the mound.

Vancouver won its opening game 9–4 in Wenatchee and returned home with an 8–1 record, two games ahead of Spokane. In late May, the Capilanos enjoyed a 15-game winning streak and on the morning of June 15, the day the new stadium was to be opened, the first-place team enjoyed a 6.5 game lead over Spokane.

Built in just over nine months, Capilano Stadium was nestled at the base of Little Mountain in a picturesque park a few miles south of Vancouver's downtown. Built at a cost of $550,000, it seated 7,500. Clarence Rowland, Pacific Coast League president and one of the visiting dignitaries at the opening ceremonies, remarked that, had Vancouver built such a park right after the war, it would probably now have had a Pacific Coast League team. An overflow crowd estimated at 8,000 watched the home team win its first game at the new park, a 10–3 thumping of Salem.

The Capilanos maintained their first place standing until August 1, when the Spokane Indians, who had occupied second all season, moved ahead of them by .003 points. Vancouver would remain in second place, finishing the year one-half game behind the Indians.

In spite of the disappointing finish to the season, individual Vancouver players performed well: Bob Snyder led the league with 27 wins and 303 innings pitched, both all-time WIL records; catcher John Ritchie won the batting championship with a .346 average; outfielder Dick Sinovic was close behind at .342. All three made the all-star team.

The Victoria Athletics lost their first game, 6–2, to the Wenatchee Chiefs, returned home in sixth place, 4.5 games out of first place and spent the rest of the year in the second division. In late June, Barrett was released and replaced by former major league ballplayer Bobby Sturgeon. Barrett did not leave quietly: he successfully sued the Athletics for the balance of his salary and, when the Yakima Bears, with whom he had caught on, came to Victoria, he engaged in a fist fight under the stands with Victoria general manager Reg Patterson.

Vancouver led the WIL in attendance with a total of 164,026, an increase of nearly 67 over 1950. Five teams showed decreases at the gate, with each of these drawing a total of under 70,000 fans. Victoria was one of these, with a final attendance figure of 67,850, a decrease of over 42,000 from the previous season.

CANADIAN-AMERICAN LEAGUE (Class C): Quebec Alouettes/Braves and Trois-Rivières Royals (1946–1950)

Formed in 1936, the Class C Canadian-American League, which had fielded teams in Massachusetts, New York State, Ontario and Quebec, suspended operations after the 1942 season. When it resumed action in 1946, the league was an eight-team affair that included Trois-Rivières and Quebec City, Quebec; Pittsfield, Massachusetts; Oneonta, Amsterdam, Gloversville-Johnston, and Schenectady, New York.

The two Canadian teams shared similar histories and played in very similar stadia. Each had been a member of the Eastern Canadian League in the early 1920s and the Quebec Provincial League in 1939 and 1940. Each played in a concrete and steel stadium that had been built in the late 1930s, was called Municipal Stadium, and measured 317 feet down the lines and 372 to dead center. The main difference was that Quebec City's ballpark held 7,500 spectators, 1,500 more than that of Trois-Rivières.

1946. The Trois-Rivières Royals were owned and operated by the Brooklyn Dodgers and served, in a way, as a farm team for the major league club's Class B Nashua Dodgers and Triple A Montreal Royals. The roster included two former members of the Negro Leagues, two Double A (which was changed to Triple A after the 1945 season) veterans, and one from Single A. Six players were rookies. The Quebec Alouettes had a working agreement with the Chicago Cubs. Eleven players were rookies.

The Alouettes won their first three games, but by early June had descended into eighth place, a position they would occupy for the rest of the season. No one on the team hit above .300 and, in future seasons, only one player would advance beyond Class A level. For seven players, including four of the six rookies, the 1946 season would be their last in professional baseball.

The Trois-Rivières Royals lost their season's opener 8–7 at Schenectady, but by the end of the third week, were in first place. They won the pennant, but not without having to face a late season surge by Pittsfield Electrics who finished only .007 percentage points behind the Royals. Trois-Rivières went on to defeat the Rome Colonels four games to three in the semi-finals and Pittsfield, four games to one in the finals, making them one of seven Brooklyn Dodger farm teams that year to win either or both of their league's regular season and playoff championships. Manager "French" Bordaragay was also one of the best players on the team. One of five regulars to hit over .300, he won the Canadian-American League batting championship with a .363 average and was named the circuit's most valuable player.

Two of the leading contributors to the Royals championship were pitchers Roy Partlow and John Wright, who had both played in the Negro Leagues. Wright won 12 and lost eight; Partlow won 10 and lost one. In the playoffs, Partlow won the second, fourth, and seventh games of the semi-finals and was four for 14 at the plate, with two RBIs and a stolen base. He went on to pitch another win in the finals and won two more by driving in the winning runs as a pinch hitter. Wright lost one game in the semi-finals but won two in the finals.

The presence of two African Americans on the Trois-Rivières roster caused some anxieties in the Canadian-American League. On March 30, 1946, just over a month before the start of the Canadian-American League's season, the *Quebec Chronicle-Telegraph* printed, on page seven, this statement from the Quebec Alouettes' administration:

> We want the Three Rivers club to understand that the Alouettes will accept the presence of colored players on the Three Rivers team only on the condition that all clubs of the Canadian-American consent to allow these players to play against them. And we know that at Three Rivers last February certain clubs in the Can-Am were solidly against allowing Negroes on the teams of the Houghton circuit.

Trois-Rivières finished second in the attendance standings, drawing 72,000 fans compared with the Amsterdam Rugmakers' 79,000. Quebec's Alouettes, in spite of their dismal showing on the field, attracted 66,000, third-best in the league.

1947. As the 1947 season approached, officials of the Quebec Alouettes announced that there would be changes for the better. They no longer had a working agreement with the Chicago Cubs, they had hired a new manager, Rene "Buck" DeSorcy, and only two members of last year's team would be returning. Over half of the 29 people who would play during the season would be rookies. The team's inexperience quickly became evident. The Alouettes lost their first seven games, suffered seven consecutive rainouts, quickly descended into last place, and, at the beginning of June, announced that Tony Ravish, who'd been signed earlier that day as a catcher, would replace DeSorcy as manager. The change didn't help, and the Alouettes finished the season 40.5 games out of first place. Surprisingly, given both the dismal showing of the team and the worst spring weather the Northeast had experienced in many years, the Alouettes drew 86,000 fans, third highest in the league and 20,000 more than in the previous year.

The Trois-Rivières Royals also began the season having undergone many changes. Manager French Bordaragay and six members of his championship team had moved upward in the Dodgers system. The new manager, Lou Rochelli, assembled a club that was much younger than the 1946 one—the average age was 21.8. Seven of the players were rookies and six had been promoted from Class D teams.

The Royals lost the first game they played. By May 15, they had lost only one more and enjoyed a half-game lead over the Amsterdam Rugmakers. By the end of May they had won 14 games and lost five, with 12 of their 30 May games rained out. The club retained hold of first place throughout June, but in early July, dropped into in second place. By July 24, they had dropped to fourth, 16.5 out of first. By mid–August, the Royals found themselves in fifth place, half a game out of the first division and a playoff berth. At season's end, the Royals were 3.5 games out of a playoff berth. Lou Rochelli was named shortstop on the all-star team. The loss of 18 home dates, six of them Sundays, resulted in an attendance decline of 12,000 to 59,961.

1948. During the autumn of 1947, the Quebec Alouettes made a major change, one that was expected to put an end to the club's dismal performances. The team was purchased by a group of local businessmen; manager Tony Ravish was rehired and arranged a working agreement with the New York Giants. The Alouettes' principal owner, Ulysse Ste-Marie, purchased a new bus and, during the late winter and early spring, funded his manager's scouting and recruitment trips to the United States. Less than two weeks into May, the team occupied last place in the standings. They remained in the cellar until mid–June, moved up to seventh place until early August, and then dropped back into the basement. Only John Lewandowski, a Giants farmhand who had been sent down from Class B, hit above .300, posting a .308 average. Pitcher Al Belinski's 17 loses were tops in the league. However, attendance rose by 58,000 to 144,150, just two thousand less than that of Schenectady.

Although the Trois-Rivières Royals had more than adequately fulfilled their role as a developer of talent in the Dodger system, the team's poor showing in 1947 had adversely affected attendance and the Dodgers lost money on the operation. If Brooklyn was to recoup the losses, a more competitive team needed to be fielded.

In mid–April, Brooklyn assigned a freshman manager to the Royals, Ed Head, who had been a war-time replacement player in Brooklyn. Only four members of the 1947 team returned, and of these, only two, pitcher Michael Munsinger and third baseman Frank Powaski, saw regular duty. Only three members of the team, which had an average age of 22.1, had played professional baseball for more than two years.

The Royals floundered in the early weeks of the season and at the beginning of June were in seventh place. However, by July 1 the Royals moved into fourth place, 5.5 games behind league-leading Oneonta. They would stay close to Oneonta in July and, during August, to the new league-leaders, Rome. By September 2, Rome and Trois-Rivières were tied for first place with 76 wins and 56 losses apiece. However, the Royals finished in second place, two behind Rome and faced fourth place Pittsfield in the semi-finals. The Massachusetts team defeated Trois-Rivières four games to one. In spite of their early exit from the playoffs, the Royals' season had been much more successful than the prior one. They attracted 21,000 more people to the ballpark, 80,747. Three players hit over .300: Walt Kowalski, whose .352 average earned him a spot on the all-star team, Frank Powaski (.322), and Wiley Williams (.321). Mike Munsinger had 20 wins against three defeats for a league-high .870 percentage. Bill Mosser, who won 13 while losing nine, was named to the all-star team.

1949. During the off season, Quebec club directors changed the name of the team from Alouettes to Braves and the manager from Ravish to Frank McCormack, a 13-year major league veteran. Then, they decided that they would sign their own players instead becoming a farm team of a major league club. During the winter and early spring, McCormack and general manager Rene LeMyre used owner Ulysse Ste-Marie's very large bank account to assemble a very experienced team. In addition to McCormack, Pete Elko, Garland Lawing and Alex Mustaikis had appeared in big league games. There were Triple and Double A veterans, but no rookies.

The newly named Braves won the first two games of the 1949 season and played .500 ball for the first two weeks of the season. Then they took off, winning 15 and losing five and moving into first place. By August 4, they had a commanding 8.5 game lead over Oneonta and clinched the pennant 10 games before the end of the season. The Braves not only won the regular season championship but also set a Canadian-American League record for wins with 90. In addition, the club drew 177,779 fans, which would become an all-time Canadian-American League record and would be the seventh highest attendance total recorded by a Class C team between 1946 and 1952. Individual Braves had outstanding seasons as well. Pete Elko and Garland Lawing finished first and second in the league with .348 and 342 averages respectively. Hal Erickson won a league-leading 21 games, while Alex Danelishen earned 18 victories. Erickson and Lawing (outfield) were voted to the league's all-star team.

In Trois-Rivières, there was a complete turnover in management and player personnel. The team that new manager George Scherger, in his fourth year of piloting in the Dodger chain, assembled included six rookies, one second-year player, and nine third-year players. The Royals performed well, although they weren't in the hunt for the regular season championship as they had been in 1948. They remained firmly in the second division until mid–August when they moved into third place. They finished fourth and faced Quebec in the first round of the playoffs, losing to the Braves in fourth straight games. Several Royals enjoyed impressive seasons. George Clark, in what would be his only season in professional ball, hit .301, stole a league-leading 49 bases, and was named to the all-star team. Ed Umstead compiled a .317 average, eighth-best in the league. Thomas McMullen and Jay Vercrouse each won 16 games.

The Quebec Braves continued their dominance in the finals against the Oneonta Red Sox. It was a matter of the age and experience of Quebec City against the youth (twenty Oneonta players were under 20) and relative inexperience of the Red Sox. Braves pitchers turned in four consecutive complete games, two of them shutouts, and Quebec outscored Oneonta 14–7 to win the championship in four straight games.

1950. When the 1950 season opened, the Quebec Braves' roster included 13 members of the previous season's championship team, including pitchers Al Belinsky, Al

Danelishen, John Nansteel, and Hal Erickson, who among them had accounted for over 80 percent of the club's victories. However, there had been two significant changes made during the winter. Ulysse-Sainte-Marie, having fulfilled his goal of bringing a championship team to Quebec City, sold the club to Dr. J.A. Bellemare, who promised to spend as liberally as his predecessor. But when contract negotiations with Frank McCormack dragged into February, the Braves signed George McQuinn to lead the club. This would be the first managerial job for the 12-year major league veteran, who would lead the Braves for five seasons, winning two regular season and four playoff championships.

By mid–May, the Braves were in first place two games ahead of the Schenectady Blue Jays. Except for a couple of days, the team would spend the rest of the season leading the league. The Braves' pace slowed in August, as they won 14 and lost 13, and it wasn't until Friday, September 8, two days before the end of the season, that Quebec City clinched the pennant. The Braves final record: 97 wins (a new league record) and 40 losses.

The Braves marched through the semi-finals almost as convincingly as they had in 1949. Quebec City defeated Oneonta four games to one. The Amsterdam Rugmakers, managed by Mayo Smith, who nearly two decades later would lead the Detroit Tigers to the World Series championship, were no match for the Braves, who swept the finals four games to none, plating 34 runs to the Rugmakers' 14.

It had been a banner year for the Quebec City Braves. Five players turned in performances that earned them berths on the league all-star team. Outfielder Garland Lawing won the triple crown, with a .347 average, 19 home runs, and 168 runs batted in and was named the Canadian-American League's most valuable player. Bill Sinram's defensive play resulted in his being named all-star third baseman. Three pitchers also made the all-star team: Al Belinsky (22 wins), Hal Erickson (20 wins and a league-leading 205 strikeouts), and John Nansteel (13 wins).

For the Trois-Rivières Royals, the season had been as dark as the Braves' season had been bright. As usual the Brooklyn Dodgers sent very young players. Only four had more than two years' experience, four were rookies. One of these rookies was the youngest member of the team; George "Red" Witt, a 16-year-old pitcher who had been signed immediately after his graduation from high school.

By mid–May, they held fifth place, but by mid–June had sunk into the basement, eighteen games behind Quebec City. From mid–July to mid–August, the Royals won only eight games while losing 29. The Trois-Rivières' final record was 46 wins, 90 losses, putting them 43.5 games out of first place.

During the 1950 season rumors frequently surfaced about the future of the Canadian-American League. Poor weather, which caused the cancellation of many early season games and reduced attendance at others, caused a sharp decline in attendance. By season's end, a total of 228,000 fans fewer than in 1949 had attended league games. All teams lost money. The American teams laid much of the blame for the problem on the two Canadian teams. Going to Canada increased the American teams' travel by 10,000 miles each year. The six United States clubs would not be that unhappy to see a Canadian-American League without Canadian teams. The Royals and Braves also had problems. Road trips to the United States totaled 25,000 miles for each team. Attendance had dropped 53,000 in Quebec City and 31,000 in Trois-Rivières.

During the fall, Quebec strengthened its position by entering a working agreement with the Boston Braves in which the major league club would supply the Braves with twelve players. But in November, the Brooklyn Dodgers announced that they would not run an operation in Trois-Rivières. Then, when the administrators of the Schenectady team announced that they had received a franchise in the class A Eastern League, the Canadian teams' situation became even more precarious. With the largest American team having departed, there would be no way that the smaller towns would want to make the expensive Canadian road trips. At the Minor League winter meetings in early December, the Class C Provincial League announced that Quebec City and Trois-Rivières would become members for the 1951 season.

3

Mexican Jumping Beans, Hockey Players, and Negro Leaguers

Quebec's Provincial League

Perhaps the most unusual minor league ever to operate in Canada, if not in all of professional baseball, the Provincial League of Quebec had operated as a semi-pro and independent league before World War II and, in 1940, was a Class B league in the National Association. In 1947, after Granby and Sherbrooke had withdrawn from the Border League, it reconstituted itself as an independent professional league. In 1950, it again became a member of the National Association, operating as a Class C league until the end of the 1955 season, at which time it withdrew from Organized Baseball and returned to semi-professional status.

In 1947, the league consisted of eight teams: Saint-Hyacinthe, Granby, Sherbrooke, Drummondville, St. Jean, Farnham, Acton Vale, and Lachine. All, with the exception of the Montreal suburb of Lachine, were located south of the St. Lawrence River in the south western part of Quebec. None of the cities represented in the league was big. Sherbrooke, the largest, had a population of 35,965; Acton Vale, the smallest, had a population of 2,366.

Because, until 1951 when Quebec and Trois-Rivières joined the league, the cities were all close together, teams played single games against each other, rather than two or three game series. On Sundays, split double headers would be played: two teams would have an afternoon game in one city and an evening one at the other. With two exceptions, the ball parks were fairly standard pre–World War II facilities. Drummondville and Saint-Hyacinthe were different: games there were played on the infields of horse racing tracks. The seats along the home stretch formed the grandstand, backstops were erected at the infield edge of the tracks and light standards back of the foul poles.

Particularly between 1947 and 1949, the Provincial League drew many its players from sources different from those of most minor leagues. Many players came from the ranks of senior amateur and minor professional hockey leagues and a few from the National Hockey League. Many hockey players used baseball as a means of keeping fit and earning money during their off-season. The most famous of these hockey players was Maurice "The Rocket" Richard, who, in 1947, played briefly for the Drummondville Cubs, who were managed by long-time minor league goalie Jerry Cotnoir. The league also recruited African American players. With integration of Organized Baseball just beginning and the American and National Negro Leagues experiencing serious financial difficulties, Canadian teams provided talented Black athletes opportunities to play for reasonable salaries and in welcoming environments.

A third talent pool consisted of players who had been suspended by the Commissioner of Baseball for breaking their contracts in order to play in the outlaw Mexican League. At the end of World War II, many major and minor leaguers who had played during the war found themselves either being offered what they considered inferior salaries or being demoted to lower leagues. Disgruntled, a large number signed lucrative offers from Jorge Pasquel who was attempting to develop the Mexican League into an organization that would rival the major leagues in talent level. The players, sometimes referred to as "Mexican Jumping Beans," were suspended from playing in the major leagues or with National Association teams. However, over the 1946 and 1947 seasons, when the promised remunerations were not forthcoming and the living and playing conditions in Mexico had proved to be far less than had been described, the players left Mexico. The Provincial League offered these players, desperate for somewhere to play, contracts the values of which were reported to be above minor league maximums.

1947. Creating an account of the Provincial League's 1947 season is difficult: statistical records are incomplete and newspaper accounts sketchy. During the season, the league certainly deserved the nickname that had frequently appeared in newspaper stories: "Disorganized Baseball." Teams hired local umpires, resulting in great variations in the quality of officiating. Bad weather plagued the beginning of the season; after three weeks, 32 games had been cancelled because of rain, wet grounds, or cold. A large number never seemed to have been made up. The underfunded Lachine club, suffering from poor attendance, ceased operations in mid–July. At the end of the season, there was an enormous disparity in the number of games the seven surviving teams played. Granby appeared in 89 games, Sherbrooke 82, and Drummondville 74. The other four teams played less than 70 games: Farnham and Saint-Hyacinthe 68, St. Jean 66, and Acton Vale 65.

Until late July, the league lead was held by either the Drummondville Cubs or the St. Jean Braves. After that the Granby Grand-Bs took over, finishing with a record of 54 wins and 35 losses. St. Jean, Farnham, Saint-Hyacinthe, Sherbrooke, and Drummondville rounded out the top six. Only seventh-place Acton Vale did not make the playoffs. Underdog Drummondville defeated Granby four games to one in a semi-final round. St. Jean and Saint-Hyacinthe, who had beaten Sherbrooke and Farnham respectively in preliminary rounds, met in the other semi-final with the Braves defeating the Saints. St. Jean then won the championship over Drummondville, four games to two.

During the regular season, Farnham's Fred Morehead won the batting title with a rather low .322 average. Roger Vaillancourt of Granby lead the league with 14 wins, while Louis Poliquin of Drummondville had the best won-loss percentage with .867 (13 wins and two losses). Attendance figures (as sketchy as many of the other statistics) indicate that 302,000 fans came to the home games of the seven clubs that played the entire season. Drummondville had the top attendance, with 79,000, while Acton Vale (which would not return in 1948) had the lowest, just under 13,000.

1948. During the 1948 season, the Provincial became a less disorganized league, but a more outlaw one. The increasing "outlaw" dimensions of the league related to player signings. During the season, a representative of the National Association visited

Provincial League officials warning that hiring "Mexican Jumping Beans" and poaching on other minor leagues would jeopardize the careers of other Provincial League players who later might seek to sign contracts with National Association teams.

When the season opened on May 2, the Farnham team, which had taken the nickname Black Sox, fielded an impressive lineup that included playing manager Roland Gladu and pitcher Adrian Zabala, former major leaguers who had played in Mexico, Negro Leaguer and "jumping bean" Lauro Pascual, and Jorge Torres, who had reached the Triple A level before going to Mexico. During May the team got stronger, and, by June 1, they occupied first place, 1.5 games ahead of Saint-Hyacinthe. They stayed in first for the rest of the season, finishing six games ahead of the second place St. John Braves. Saint-Hyacinthe finished third.

Playing manager Roland Gladu and Claro Duany, a former Negro Leaguer, were the Sherbrooke Athletics' leading hitters, with .368 and .365 averages respectively. Gladu hit 28 home runs, Duany 17. Other .300 hitters included pitcher Adrian Zabala (.352 in 125 at bats), Francisco Coimbre (.312), and Jorge Torres (.305). Zabala won 18 games while losing eight, Paul Calvert, signed out of Triple A, won 11 and lost one, and major league veteran Ralph McCabe won 10 and lost five.

The St. John Braves were managed by Montreal-born J.P. Roy until near the end of the season, when, his suspension for his flirtation with the Mexican League having been lifted, he returned to Organized Baseball. Their lineup included Bobby Estalella, who had played 672 games in eight major league seasons before heading to Mexico, and two Negro League veterans, Buzz Clarkson and Terris McDuffie, also "jumping beans." Roy and McDuffie led the league with 19 wins each (McDuffie lost eight and Roy nine). Seven Braves hit over .300, led by Clarkson (.408, along with 31 home runs) and Bobby Estalella (.374, with 24 homers).

Saint-Hyacinthe Saints were, relatively speaking, much more of a home-grown team. They had no Negro Leaguers or Mexican "Jumping Beans." Eight team members were born in Quebec. Former major leaguer Connie Creeden hit .430—best in the league. Granby, now called the Red Sox, settled into fourth place in mid–June, and, except for a few days in July when they were displaced by the Drummondville Cubs, stayed for the rest of the season. The club had only one former major leaguer (Otto Huber, who, in 1939, had appeared in 11 games for the Boston Braves), no "Jumping Beans," and no Negro Leaguers.

The Drummondville Cubs spent from June onward in fifth place and finished 8.5 games behind Granby. The team featured three refugees from the Mexican League, Danny Gardella, Roy Zimmerman, and Quebecer Stan Breard. All three had major league experience. By the end of May, Farnham Pirates had won only three games, while losing 16. During June their record improved slightly as they won six and lost only 14, and rumors circulated that the team was in financial difficulties and might not finish the season. They did but ended in sixth and last place. The Pirates provided a welcome home for seven former Negro Leaguers, including Joe Atkins, who finished third in the batting race with a .384 average, and tied for second in home runs with 31, and Davie Pope, who would later play for the Cleveland Indians (.365 average and a league-leading 37 home runs).

All six teams entered the post-season playoffs. Sherbrooke defeated Granby five games to two in one semi-final, while Saint-Hyacinthe (who had defeated Farnham three games to two in one quarter final) won the other semi-final three games to two over St.

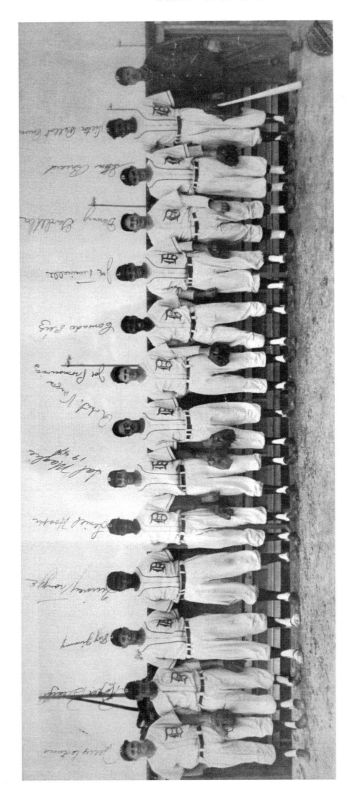

The Drummondville Cubs, winners of the 1949 Provincial League championship, signed players with a variety of backgrounds. For example, Jerry Cotnoir (far left) was a professional hockey player; Quincy Trouppe (fourth from left) a veteran of the Negro Leagues; Sal Maglie (sixth from left) a former and future major leaguer who had been banned from the major leagues for jumping to the Mexican League; and Vic Power (far right) a rookie from Puerto Rico who went on play in the major leagues for 12 seasons (courtesy Daniel Papillon).

Jean (which had won its quarter-final against Drummondville in three straight games). After falling behind four games to two in the finals against Saint-Hyacinthe, Sherbrooke won three straight and the Provincial League championship.

(No attendance figures are available for the 1948 season.)

1949. The 1949 season, the last in which the Provincial League operated outside the framework of the National Association, was undoubtedly the one for which it is most remembered. Each of the six teams returned and, as in the two previous seasons, rosters included a few hockey players playing baseball as their summer job, some aging professionals, a few of whom had spent short periods in the major leagues, and several former Negro leaguers. But the most notable members of the rosters were 10 "Mexican Jumping Beans." In the spring of 1949, ten of the exiled players readily accepted invitations and large salaries to play in Quebec. Lou Klein (St. Louis Cardinals), Red Hayworth (St. Louis Browns), and Alex Carrasquel (Washington Senators), joined the St. Jean Braves. Henry Feldman (New York Giants) and Fred Martin (St. Louis Cardinals) became Sherbrooke Athletics, along with Adrian Zabala (New York Giants), who'd been with the team in 1948. The Drummondville Cubs signed four of the "outlaws." Three were from the New York Giants: Danny Gardella, Sal Maglie, and Roy Zimmerman. Max Lanier was the Cubs' biggest catch, a nine-year major league pitcher who had won 74 games for the St. Louis Cardinals.

The salaries of these three teams, and perhaps of the other three in the Provincial League, certainly exceeded the monthly limits of the lower minor leagues of Organized Baseball, which were $2,600 at Class D, $3,400 at Class C, and $4,000 at Class B. In *Baseball's Pivotal Era,* William Marshall noted that Lanier was reported to have received $11,000, with special subscriptions from prominent citizens and from businesses supplying much of the amount. He also received a free room, a food allowance, and was showered with clothes and other gifts. Gardella received a reported $7,000 and Maglie $5,000. After the season was over, reports circulated that Drummondville's total salary was close to $100,000, over $30,000 more than that of the Triple A Montreal Royals.

At the end of May, Drummondville, with a 10–3 record, occupied first place, 1.5 games ahead of St. Jean. Granby, Farnham, Sherbrooke and Saint-Hyacinthe followed in that order. Then, on June 5, the makeup of the various teams was threatened. Commissioner Happy Chandler, apparently worried that major league baseball might lose one or more of the suits that had been filed by some of the Mexican Jumping Beans, announced that the suspensions against them had been terminated. Over the next few weeks, many of the high-priced recruits to the Provincial League returned to Organized Baseball: Red Heyworth, Alex Carrasquel and Lou Klein departed from St. Jean, Henry Feldman, Fred Martin and Adrian Zabala from Sherbrooke, and Max Lanier from Drummondville. Gardella, Maglie and Zimmerman decided to remain with the Cubs.

Playing only .333 ball at the time of Chandler's announcement, the Sherbrooke Athletics improved greatly, winning 47, losing 35 and finishing in third place. St. Jean did drop in the standings, from second to fourth, playing well under .500 ball for the rest of the season. Drummondville, however, maintained its lead, winning the regular season championship by eight games. Gardella contributed 15 home runs and Zimmerman 22; Maglie, who, it was rumored, was offered $15,000 by Molini to finish the season with the Cubs, led all pitchers with an 18–9 record.

Former Negro League players dominated the final batting statistics. Al Armour of

Farnham turned in a league-leading .348 average, three points ahead of Drummondville's Vic Power; Sherbrooke's Sylvio Garcia had 126 hits; Claro Duany of Sherbrooke, 99 RBIs, and Quincy Barbee of St. John belted 26 homers. Davie Pope of Farnham tied Al Zimmerman of Drummondville for second place in the home run derby; each had 22.

Each of the league's six teams qualified for the post-season playoffs. Drummondville faced sixth place Saint-Hyacinthe in one semi final. The other would be between the winners of the St. Jean-Sherbrooke and Farnham-Granby quarter finals. St. Jean and Farnham each took its series four games to two. Farnham then defeated St. Jean to enter the finals. Drummondville defeated Saint-Hyacinthe five games to four. Farnham, another second division team, also proved to be a difficult opponent for Drummondville. The best of nine final series was tied at two, three, and four games apiece before Sal Maglie won the deciding game. Maglie had contributed five of Drummondville's playoff victories and saved another in relief.

In spite of the contributions of fans, businesses, and others, there is no doubt that the 1949 season was a costly one for Provincial League teams, and it was decided to seek entry into the National Association, which had strict salary guidelines. In December 1949, Provincial League President Albert Molini tentatively accepted an offer for the Provincial League to join Organized Baseball as a Class C league.

(No attendance figures are available for the 1949 season.)

1950. The Provincial League's first season since 1940 as a member of the National Association, was, in many ways, similar from that of 1949. There was a sprinkling of former major league players, 18 players from the Negro Leagues, seven of them over 30 years old, a collection of minor leaguers from the lower classifications, along with former semi-pro and senior amateur players from Quebec and a few hockey players, such as Sherbrooke's Norm Dussault, the Montreal Canadiens' forward.

Sherbrooke, with veterans Silvio Garcia, Roland Gladu and Lou Shapiro returning, were favored to win the championship. By the end of May, thanks to an eight-game win streak, the Athletics occupied first place—but by only a half game ahead of Drummondville. The two teams battled for top spot for the next two months. However, during August, St. John moved from fifth place to first place. Entering the final week of play, six games separated the top five teams. St. Jean finished 1.5 games ahead of Sherbrooke. Farnham finished third, three games out and Drummondville fourth, four out. Saint-Hyacinthe and Granby, at fifth and sixth, did not qualify for the playoffs. Individual performance bests were dominated by the league's older players. Louis Shapiro, at age 35, won 18 while losing four games. Twenty-nine-year-old Leniel Hooker's 2.53 ERA for Drummondville led in that department. At 35 years old, Sherbrooke's Silvio Garcia enjoyed his finest season, winning the Triple Crown: batting average, .365; runs batted in 116; and home runs, 21.

The St. Jean Braves easily dispatched Farnham, four games to one in its semi-final series, while the Sherbrooke Athletics defeated Drummondville, four games to two. The final series went to the limit: after five games, the Athletics held a two-game edge over the Braves. However, St. Jean came back with 2–1 and 15–6 victories to take the championship. The most notable player in the post season was Ray Brown, a 42-year-old former Negro League pitcher whom Sherbrooke had acquired early in August. Although Brown posted a poor 1–5 regular season record, his turned in amazing playoff performances. He pitched 32 innings, won three and lost two, and batted .353.

Attendance figures suggested that the Provincial League's return to Organized Baseball was a successful one. A total of 524,855 fans attended regular season games, an average of over 87,000 per team. Drummondville drew 110,350 people. Only four teams of the 116 in Class C leagues had higher attendance figures. One of these, Quebec City, had a final total of 123,352. However, although the attendance figures were encouraging, rumors circulated shortly after the season that every team had lost money and that Farnham and Sherbrooke were in danger of not returning for the 1951 season.

1951. During the summer of 1950, Provincial League president Albert Molini had been contemplating the possibility of attracting Quebec City and nearby Trois-Rivières, members of the Canadian-American League, into his organization. In a late-December league meeting in Granby, Quebec City and Trois-Rivières were admitted.

In 1951, the Provincial League, with an average age of 28.2, up from 27.5 the previous year, was the oldest of all Class C leagues. The rosters of Farnham, Sherbrooke, Granby, and Drummondville had average ages of over 30. There were three players over 40, with Farnham's playing manager Sam Bankhead, the first African American manager in Organized Baseball, the oldest, at 45. There were, as well, several younger black players, two of whom would enjoy extended big-league careers. Saint-Hyacinthe's Hector Lopez would play 1450 games for the New York Yankees and Kansas City Athletics. St. Jean's Ruben Gomez would pitch in 289 games for the New York and San Francisco Giants, Cleveland, and Minnesota. Lopez would appear in five World Series for the Yankees, Gomez in one for the Giants.

During the first few weeks of the season, Granby, Drummondville, Sherbrooke, and Quebec City, the four clubs that would eventually make the playoffs, took turns occupying first place. Never did any team hold more than a game and a half lead. At the end of June, Drummondville began a nine-week period as the league's best team, at one time holding a four-game lead.

At the beginning of July, the Sherbrooke Athletics, who would become the regular season champions, occupied fifth place, with a 28–28 record. During the rest of the season, the Athletics won 45 while losing 22. On September 6, Sherbrooke defeated St. Jean to finish first, ahead of Granby by .001 per cent. Drummondville finished third .002 points behind. Joseph Montiero of Granby earned the league batting championship with a 353 average, while Frank Gravino of St. Jean hit 42 home runs. Granby's John Andre was the league's only 20-game winner, while Quebec's Carlton Willey, with a 15–5 record, had the best winning percentage, .750.

The Sherbrooke Athletics defeated the Drummondville Cubs four games to two in one semi final series, while the Quebec City Braves dispatched the Granby Red Sox four games to one. The Athletics took the finals, four games to one over the Braves. That night, after Sherbrooke had won, 3,219 fans who had attended the game had gone happily home and the players had celebrated the team's victory, the Athletics' stadium burned to the ground. Earlier in the year, authorities had banned the sale of peanuts at games, claiming that the discarded shells posed a serious fire hazard. The ban had not been strictly enforced, and a burning cigarette butt that had slipped between the planks of the stands and landed on shells was believed to have started the blaze.

The 1951 season also marked the end of the line for Farnham. During the season, reports surfaced that the Pirates, who were owned by a pool hall operator, the postmaster, an insurance agent, and a minister, were in deep financial difficulties. The team's costs for the season were estimated at $45,000 and to make that amount, the club needed to attract 750 paying customers a game. They didn't. Attendance was down by 29,000. The Pirates were not alone; the attendance for the original six teams dropped by 112,000, with only Sherbrooke showing an increase—6,000. Quebec City, whose 103,712 total was the sixth-highest among all Class C teams, was 20,000 less than the Braves had attracted in 1950. Surprisingly, attendance for eighth place Trois-Rivières rose by 23,000.

Clearly, the Provincial League could no longer continue to operate as a series of independently operated teams responsible for the salaries of nearly all of their players. Sherbrooke's victory was the last hurrah of teams composed of former Negro Leaguers and aging white players. In 1952, five of the six returning clubs would have affiliations with major league organizations.

PART II

1952–1977
The Lean Years

From 1952 to 1963, the attrition of minor leagues and teams and the decline in attendance continued. In 1952, 40 minor leagues, down from 59 in 1949, operated; attendance fell from 42 to 25 million. By 1963, there were only 18 minor leagues and attendance was under 10 million. From 1964 to 1977, the number of leagues ranged from 18 to 21 and annual attendance was around 11 million.

Canada's minor league teams seemed to be more vulnerable than their American counterparts. In 1952, 12 teams played in four leagues in three provinces. By 1967, the number had dropped to two teams in two leagues in two provinces. The Ottawa Athletics left the International League after the 1954 season, the Montreal Royals after the 1960 season, and the Toronto Maple Leafs after the 1967 season. In the Western International League, Victoria and Calgary folded in the middle of the 1954 season. Hamilton disbanded shortly after the beginning of the 1956 PONY League season. Vancouver and Edmonton were dropped when the WIL ceased operations after 1954. The Provincial League disbanded a few weeks before the start of the 1956 season. Vancouver joined the Pacific Coast League in 1955, dropped out after 1962, returned three years later, and departed after the 1969 season. The Winnipeg Goldeyes joined the Northern League in 1954 and departed after the 1964 season. The team returned in 1969 but was relocated in 1970 after the troubled Buffalo franchise of the International League relocated to Manitoba, where they played until the end of the 1951 season. The Eastern League had franchises in four Quebec cities between 1971 and 1977.

What caused this incredible downward spiral? First, and most obviously, many of the towns that had fielded teams were simply not large enough to support minor league baseball. Those without an affiliation with a major league team were the most vulnerable as they had to assume payment of all players' salaries.

The increase in the number of television stations and of the number of television sets in homes that began shortly after World War II and accelerated during the 1950s had a major and complex influence on the decline in the minor leagues. Television offered an alternative source of entertainment and the money spent on purchasing sets drastically reduced the amount of cash available for movie or baseball tickets. As major league teams began to telecast their games and then to increase the number of games telecast and the number of stations carrying their games, people with television sets had a chance to watch, for free and at home, baseball of much higher caliber than they would see at the local minor league ballpark.

As improved roads and highway systems developed, people had other outdoor options than going to the nearest ballpark. Lakes and the seashore became, especially for the growing number of people buying power boats, increasingly attractive destinations. And, with the growth of Little League baseball, parents who wanted to watch baseball could walk or drive a few blocks to the park where their children were playing.

Officials of the National Association, along with officials of minor leagues and teams, asked the major leagues for help. The major league's first response came in the summer of 1956, when Baseball Commissioner Ford Frick announced the formation of a "Save the Minors" committee, whose job would be to establish a $500,000 account, funded equally by the 16 major league teams, from which to distribute money to needy minor league clubs, usually from the lower minors. Then, in 1959, the major leagues developed a new plan, a "player development and promotional program," in which every Triple A team that completed the season would receive $25,000. The amount decreased by classification to $3,000 for Class D teams.

The two plans were band aid solutions. By the beginning of the 1962 season, the situation was dire: there didn't seem to be any end in sight to the shrinking of the minor leagues. Major league teams worried that, with not enough minor leagues operating, there wouldn't be enough teams to develop players to stock their own teams.

In May of that year, Frick announced a new plan to stabilize the minor leagues. The first step involved restructuring the categorization levels of the minor leagues. Triple A would remain the same and would include the American Association and the Pacific Coast and International Leagues. Double A would become a combination of the present Double and Single A leagues. Classes B, C, and D would now become Class A. There would also be a rookie league classification. Each major league team was committed to have affiliations with at least five minor league teams, one each at the AAA and AA levels, and three at the lower levels. The survival of the minors was guaranteed; there would be at least one hundred teams, with more added when the major leagues again expanded.

The minor leagues may have been saved and stabilized, but over the next 14 years they operated in what was, in many ways, a survival mode. The number of leagues remained around 20, and attendance fluctuated between 10 and 11 million. But the makeup of the leagues was in constant flux. In many instances, the off-season's major problem was finding enough teams to form a viable league for the upcoming season. The relocation of the Milwaukee Braves to Atlanta in 1966 and the Washington Senators to Dallas-Fort Worth in 1972, along with the granting of expansion franchises in Seattle and San Diego in 1969 seriously impacted on the Triple A leagues, where there were frequent franchise shifts. Class A and Rookie leagues often fielded only four teams.

4

International
League Departures

The International League began the 1952 season with three Canadian teams: the Montreal Royals, the Toronto Maple Leafs, and the Ottawa Athletics. By the beginning of the 1968 season each of these teams had been relocated to the United States and the league was international in name only. At the end of 1954, Ottawa departed for Columbus, Ohio, an example of the fate of a team without adequate major league player assistance which had been relocated in a city without a large enough population to support baseball at the Triple A level. The Montreal Royals' demise after the 1960 season was a result of the Los Angeles Dodgers, who owned the club, making the Spokane Indians of the Pacific Coast League their number one Triple A affiliate. For the Toronto Maple Leafs, under the ownership of Jack Kent Cooke, the quest was for a major league franchise. When that didn't happen, he, along with increasingly large numbers of fans, lost interest in the Leafs, who moved to Louisville after the 1967 season.

1952. As the 1952 International League season opened, Ottawa hoped to move up from the previous year's seventh-place finish and to increase attendance from the 1951 level. In Toronto, flamboyant owner Jack Kent Cooke wanted his team not only to make the playoffs for the first time since 1945, but also to finish in first place. He also hoped to attract over half a million fans. In Montreal, the fans and the parent Brooklyn Dodgers wanted more of the same: a crop of future major leaguers leading the team to league playoff, and Junior World Series championships.

During the off-season, the Philadelphia Athletics took over ownership of the Ottawa franchise. Using some of the players inherited from the Giants, a half-dozen prospects from their Class A Savannah team, and whatever old Triple A players they could find, Philadelphia cobbled together a Triple A roster for the renamed Ottawa Athletics. The Athletics opened the season with an eight-game losing streak. Except for a few days in June, when the club reached fifth place, the team spent the season in seventh or eighth place. It finished in seventh, 29.5 games behind first-place Montreal.

The Athletics could not hit. The team average was .237, second worst in the league. The pitching staff was somewhat better: Marion Fricano finished with a 2.26 ERA, tops in the league. In spite of its poor performance and extremely cold and rainy weather early in the season, the club drew 48,000 more than in 1951. Many observers believed that, had the Athletics been able to play Sunday home games, the figure would have been higher.

In Toronto, Jack Kent Cooke had the phrase "First in 1952" printed on the club's stationery; he also predicted that the team would have an advance sale of $300,000 and a total attendance of over half a million. He spent lavishly on player procurement, signing free agents and purchasing older or marginal players from major league teams. But spending money did not guarantee on-field success. By the end of May, the team had settled into fourth place, a position it would maintain for the rest of the season. On July 14, what Cooke considered the team's underachievement cost manager Joe Becker his job. He was replaced with Burleigh Grimes, the legendary spitballer who had managed the Maple Leafs to a regular season championship in 1943. The change had little effect; when the season ended, the team had won only two more games than they had lost. However, they did make the playoffs and prepared to meet the Montreal Royals in the semi-final round. Third baseman Ed Stevens, who led the league in RBIs with 113, was named to the all-star team.

In the stands, Cooke enjoyed greater success. Giveaways that included cars, television sets, and household appliances, along with fireworks when the team scored, encouraged fans to flock to the ballpark. The final figure of 446,000, while well below the number predicted by Cooke, was the highest among the 24 Triple A teams.

The Montreal Royals started the 1952 season with the core of the 1951 pitching staff back: Bob Alexander, Hampton Coleman, Mal Mallette, and Tommy Lasorda had a combined total of 54 wins in 1951. Also returning were 1951 rookie of the year Jim Gilliam and Don Hoak, both highly rated Brooklyn prospects. Among the newcomers was 19-year-old Johnny Podres, who would become the star of the 1955 World Series.

The Royals, who would spend only three days out of first place the entire season, began to move away from the rest of the International League pack at the end of July and finished the season eight games ahead of the second-place Syracuse Chiefs. Jim Gilliam opened the season with a 16-game hitting streak, followed soon after by another of eight games. Mal Mallette ran up a nine-game win streak. Ed Roebuck at one point turned in 31 consecutive scoreless innings and, in 53 innings, allowed only three earned runs. At the end of the season, four regulars posted batting averages of over .300: Carmen Mauro (.327), Frank Marchio (.307), Tim Thompson and Jim Gilliam (301). On the mound, Tom Lasorda posted 14 wins, Mal Mallette, with 13 wins and two losses, had the league's leading won-loss percentage, and Ed Roebuck had the club's best earned run average at 2.29. The Royals dominated the International League all-star team: Gilliam at second, Jim Pendleton at short, Mauro in the outfield, Tim Thompson behind the plate, and Mallette on the mound. Gilliam was also named the league MVP. Attendance was a major disappointment for the Royals: 313,160 came to Delorimier Downs, a drop of over 21 percent. Twelve games were postponed, four of them on Sunday and one on a holiday.

In the league semi-finals, Montreal defeated Toronto in seven games. The Royals then faced the Rochester Red Wings, who had enjoyed eight off days after having defeated Syracuse in four straight. The tired Royals lost the finals to Rochester four games to two.

1953. The watchword for the International League's three Canadian teams in 1953 was "improvement." The Ottawa Athletics wished to move into the first division and to attract more than the 153,152 fans they had in 1952. The Toronto Maple Leafs wanted to go beyond the first round of the playoffs and to become the first minor league team to draw over half a million fans during the regular season. For the Montreal Royals, winning the league championship and advancing to the IL finals was not enough; nothing less than a Junior World Series victory would please the hometown fans.

Seven members of the previous year's team returned to the Ottawa Athletics. Early in the season, the team occupied fourth place, only 5.5 games behind the league leading Montreal Royals. Much of their success was due to the pitching of Bob Trice, a former Negro League player who, by the end of June, had posted a seven-game winning streak, and the hitting of Taffy Wright, whose batting average, which hovered around .400, was the best in the International League. However, by early July, the team had dropped into seventh place. In mid–August, Ottawa had moved up into sixth place, where they remained for the rest of the season, finishing 26 games behind the eventual regular-season leader Rochester. Attendance at home games did not improve; 3,933 fewer fans watched the Athletics at Lansdowne Stadium than had in the previous season.

During the offseason, Jack Kent Cooke had announced that the Maple Leafs would operate as an independent team in 1953. In January, he stated that he was aiming for a regular season attendance of 600,000. He again spent a great deal of money procuring ball players. In December he purchased Cliff Mapes, Bob Hogue, and Stubby Overmire, all former major leaguers for a combined total of $32,500. When the team got off to a slow start, he authorized another big money purchase, paying out $30,000 for former major leaguers Lou Sleater and Forest Main. Just before the season began, he made public his desire to buy Maple Leaf Stadium, saying that ownership of the facility was the only way to increase seating and attract a major league club.

The lineup that manager Burleigh Grimes fielded on opening day in Springfield was both familiar and old. Six of the players were among the 15 that were returning from 1952.

A month into the season, the Maple Leafs were in first place, one half game ahead of Buffalo. But by July 9, the team had fallen to fifth place, a position they would occupy for the rest of the season. Only one player, Lew Morton hit above .300. Don Johnson, who won 15 games and led the league in strikeouts and earned run average, was named to the all-star team. The season's attendance of 382,462 was the best in all of minor league baseball but represented a drop of over 62,000 from the previous year.

Montreal manager Walt Alston began the season without four of the Royals' 1952 All-stars. Junior Gilliam and Carmen Mauro had graduated to the Dodgers, along with Johnny Podres. Jim Pendleton had been traded and Mal Mallette had retired. However, Don Hoak, Tommy Lasorda, Ed Roebuck, and all-star catcher Tim Thompson were back. New to the club was Sandy Amoros, a 23-year-old Cuban who possessed blazing speed in the outfield and power at the plate.

The Royals won their road and home openers, both to Rochester, and by

Hall of Fame manager Tommy Lasorda spent nine seasons pitching for the Montreal Royals. During the 1950s, he played in only eight games for the Brooklyn Dodgers, but appeared in 251 games for the Royals, winning 108 and losing 57 (National Baseball Hall of Fame and Museum, Cooperstown, N.Y., 2600–68WTa_HS_NBL).

mid–May occupied their familiar first-place position, which they held until mid–July, when a seven-game losing streak dropped them into second. They would briefly regain the lead in early August before dropping to third, partly because of another seven-game losing streak. Although they returned to second in the final week of the season, they finished seven games behind Rochester

The Royals again dominated the International League all-star team. Sandy Amoros, who won the batting title with a .353 average and hit 23 home runs, earned one of the outfield spots. Rocky Nelson, who had a .308 batting average and belted 34 home runs, was named the International League's most valuable player and all-star first baseman. Tommy Lasorda won 17, lost eight and posted a 2.81 earned run average to be named one of the all-star pitchers. For the second year in a row, unsung catcher Tim Thompson was named to the all-star team.

The Royals defeated the third place Buffalo Bisons in seven games and, for the second year in a row, faced Rochester in the finals. The Red Wings, who had needed seven games to win their series against Baltimore, were no match for the rejuvenated Montreal team, who swept the finals, outscoring the Red Wings 27 to 13 in the four games. On October 2, the Royals opened the Junior World Series at home against the American Association champions, the Kansas City Blues. The Royals took the first three games in Montreal, lost game four in Kansas City before winning their third Junior World Series with a decisive 7–2 victory in the fifth game.

1954. During the off-season, the geography of the International League changed radically and, in the process, became more international. When the St. Louis Browns moved to Baltimore, the International League Orioles relocated in Richmond, Virginia. The bigger move came when Springfield relocated to Havana. The league now stretched over 1,400 miles, from Canada to Cuba.

In 1952 and 1953 the Ottawa Athletics had incurred losses of $63,000 and club officials stated that an attendance of 231,000 would be necessary to keep the team in the capital city. The fact that Ottawa laws kept the team from playing Sunday baseball cost the team between $15,000 and $20,000 in travel expenses to other league cities for Sunday games. Bad weather during the first few weeks of the season kept crowds hovering around the one thousand mark. Except for one week in May and four in late July–August, when Ottawa occupied seventh place, the Athletics spent the season in the cellar. The final attendance figure of 93,982 was nowhere near the break-even number. Ottawa's chances of remaining in the league looked dim, especially after mid–October, when the Philadelphia Athletes franchise was sold and moved to Kansas City. The new owners established the team's Triple A affiliate in Columbus, Ohio.

In November 1953, the Dodgers named Walter Alston as their manager and replaced him in Montreal with Max Macon, who had played for Brooklyn during World War II and later had managed in the Dodger system. One of the newcomers when the 1954 season began was Roberto Clemente, a 19-year-old rookie from Puerto Rico, who had received a $10,000 signing bonus. The amount meant that, by the end of the 1954 season, Brooklyn would have to either place him on its 40-man roster or risk losing him to another team. Clemente only appeared in 87 games, had 155 plate appearances, hit .257, and hit two home runs. His surprisingly low statistics may have been a result of his inexperience. But it was rumored that Montreal was hiding him, playing him in situations where he could not adventitiously display his talents, thereby lessening the chance of other major league teams taking him at the end of the season. If this were the strategy, it didn't work. After the 1954 season was over, Branch Rickey, who had built the great Brooklyn teams of the post World War II era and was now running the Pittsburgh Pirates, drafted Clemente, who in 1955, began an 18-year Hall-of-Fame career with the Pirates.

The Royals started slowly and after three weeks were in fifth place. Then reinforcements arrived: Rocky Nelson, Sandy Amoros, and Gino Cimoli returned. After the trio's arrival, the team gradually improved and, within a month, had moved into third place, a position it would occupy until early September, when it moved into second, where it finished, nine games behind Toronto. Pitcher Ken Lehman (18 wins and 10 losses), and third baseman Chico Fernandez (.282) and first baseman Rocky Nelson (.311 and a league-leading 31 homers) were named to the all-star team. Final home attendance was 195,896, a drop of 90,000.

In Toronto, Jack Kent Cooke's quest to provide hometown fans with a pennant winning team continued. His first major acquisition was a new manager, Luke Sewell, who came to Toronto with a 10-year career as a major league manager. Sewell led an experienced club; during the off-season, Cooke had purchased several players with major league experience, including Archie Wilson (30 years old), Fred Hahn (25), Loren Babe (26), and Jack Crimian (28). In all, during the season, 22 players who had played a total of 3,209 major league games wore Maple Leaf uniforms. One of the youngest players was 25-year-old Elston Howard, the property of the New York Yankees, who wanted to turn the outfielder into catcher and had optioned him to Toronto where he could be mentored by Sewell, who had been a major league catcher.

The Leafs began the season with six wins and eight losses, but by the end May they occupied first place, a game ahead of Rochester. A nine-game win streak on the road, kept them in first place in June and, after a brief mid-season slump that saw them spend two weeks in second, they regained the lead, and held it for the rest of the season, finishing nine games in front of second place Montreal. The star of the team was Elston Howard. His .330 average was second-best in the league; his 22 round trippers put him in a tie for fourth. He was named league MVP and all-star catcher. Loren Babe at third and Sam Jethroe in the outfield were also named all-stars. The final attendance figure of 408,876 represented a 7 percent increase over 1953.

The Leafs were strong favorites to defeat fourth place Syracuse in the first round of the playoffs. However, after winning the opener 8–0, the Leafs would win only one of the next five games and Syracuse moved on to the finals against Montreal, who had defeated Rochester four games to two in the other semi-final series. Syracuse, the underdog, defeated the Royals four games to three to win the International League championship.

1955. In the early fall of 1954, Toronto was mentioned as a possible relocation site for the financially strapped Philadelphia Athletics. When the A's did locate to Missouri, it was suggested that Toronto was not chosen because the city did not have a large enough stadium for major league baseball. To overcome this obstacle, the Toronto City Council authorized the expenditure of $1.75 million to enlarge the capacity of Maple Leaf Stadium to 38,790, which would, it was hoped, be completed in time for the 1956 season. This never happened.

As the 1955 season opened, both the Maple Leafs and the Royals were favored to either win the regular season pennant or finish second. During the winter, Cooke bought or re-signed many veteran players, while the Brooklyn Dodgers sent to Montreal a mix of young prospects, including 18-year-old future Hall of Famer Don Drysdale, and seasoned veterans.

In early May both teams had settled into the positions they would trade between each other for the rest of the season. The Royals held first place, 1.5 games ahead of the second-place Leafs, who had won nine and lost six. The Canadian teams switched positions in early June and Toronto maintained the lead until late July, at one time enjoying a 5.5 game edge. The teams again traded positions in early August. Montreal maintained a narrow lead—never more than a game and a half—and won the regular season championship, finishing only .003 percentage points ahead of the Leafs.

The Canadian teams dominated the International League's all-star team voting. Hector Rodriguez (shortstop), Archie Wilson (outfield), Lou Berberet (catcher), and Jack Crimian (pitcher) were Leaf members of the team. For the third straight year, Montreal's Rocky Nelson (first base) was named to the all-star team, along with outfielder Gino Cimoli and pitcher Ken Lehman, who led the league with 22 wins. Nelson, who won the triple crown with a .364 average, 37 home runs, and 130 RBIs, received his second most valuable player award. Toronto's Jack Crimian, whose 2.10 ERA was the best in the league, was named the top pitcher. With 350,742, Toronto once again led the league in attendance, although 58,000 less than 1954 showed up. Montreal's 205,134, third highest in the league, marked an increase of just over 10,000.

The Royals faced fourth-place Rochester in one semi-final series, while the Leafs met third-place Havana in the other. The Royals, who had won their last nine regular season games, lost the first two to Rochester, won one, and then went down to defeat in the next two games. Toronto won two out of three home games against the Sugar Kings and, when the series moved to Cuba, took the final two, to move on to the finals. Heavily favored to win the championship, the Leafs were in for a surprise. Rochester swept the series, four games to none.

1956. In the fall of 1955, Toronto manager Luke Sewell accepted a position as pilot of the Pacific Coast League's Seattle Rainiers and was replaced by Bruno Betzel, who had managed in the minor leagues for a quarter of a century. Jack Kent Cooke spent the offseason orchestrating the Maple Leafs' buying and selling of players, one of whom, Jack Crimian, he sent to Cincinnati for a price of $60,000 along with two players, certainly a fine return on the $12,500 he had invested in the pitcher before the 1954 season. Just before the season opener, Cooke purchased Lynn Lovenguth from the Philadelphia Phillies, Archie Wilson from the St. Louis Cardinals, and Carl Sawatski from the Baltimore Orioles. The owner confidently predicted that these acquisitions would lead to Toronto's winning not only the regular season pennant, but also the playoffs and the Junior World Series.

The Brooklyn Dodgers promoted several Montreal players to the major league club, including Ken Lehman, Roger Craig, Glen Cox, Pete Wojey, and Don Drysdale, who among them, had accounted for 65 of the Royals' 95 regular season wins in 1955. Also called up were Gino Cimoli and Charlie Neal. Tommy Lasorda was traded to Kansas City. The Dodgers' prospects catcher Johnny Roseboro and infielder George "Sparky" Anderson came to Montreal.

Three weeks into the season, Toronto was in first place and Montreal was tied for fourth. However, by the end of May, Montreal had taken over first and Toronto had slipped to second. In spite of no-hit games pitched by Don Johnson (seven innings) and Lynn Lovenguth (nine innings), Toronto was playing only .500 ball by June 21, while

Montreal had pulled three games ahead of second place Rochester. In late July, the Leafs, who in just under a month had won 26 while losing only seven, climbed into first place, while the Royals had slipped to fourth place, six games behind the leader. They remained in fourth place for the rest of the season. During the last six weeks of the season. Toronto maintained its first-place position, but never held more than a 4.5 game lead. On the second to last day of the season, Toronto defeated Rochester to clinch the regular season pennant, its second in three seasons. Toronto's final attendance total of 315,161 was the best in the International League and the third-best in Triple A, but it represented a drop of over 35,000 fans from 1955. Montreal's attendance dropped by 13,000 to 191,624.

Between them, the Toronto Maple Leafs and Montreal Royals captured most of the International League's player honors. Montreal's Clyde Parris won the batting championship with a .321 average and was named all-star third baseman. Bobby Wilson, who batted .306, was named one of the three all-star outfielders, and Fred Kipp, who won 20 while losing seven was named rookie of the year and one of the all-star pitchers. Toronto's Lynn Lovenguth, whose league-leading 24 victories was the most ever by a Maple Leaf, was named pitcher of the year and a member of the all-star team. Archie Wilson, in the outfield, Carl Sawatski behind the plate, and Mike Goliat at second were also selected as all-stars. Goliat was named the league's MVP.

The two Canadian rivals faced each other in one the semi-final series. Toronto took the opening game and Montreal the second. Toronto easily swept the next three games. The Rochester Red Wings, who had defeated Miami four games to one in their semi-final series, and the Leafs split the first two games of the finals, both played in Toronto. In Rochester, Toronto took the third game, Rochester the fourth and Toronto the fifth. Back at home, the Leafs lost both games six and seven and with them the series.

1957. Several changes occurred soon after the Maple Leafs' season ended. Carl Sawatski was sold to Milwaukee Braves and Lynn Lovenguth to the St. Louis Cardinals. Ed Blake was drafted by Kansas City and traded to Detroit; Archie Wilson was traded to Charleston of the American Association for Bob Tiefenauer, a relief pitcher. Ed Stevens was sold to Charleston and Lou Limmer to San Diego. Manager Bruno Betzel was let go and replaced by Dixie Walker, a Brooklyn Dodger favorite of the 1940s who, in September 1956, had managed the Rochester Red Wings to their playoff victory against the Leafs.

In Montreal, the main question during the winter was whether Brooklyn would send their bright young prospects to what had been their number one farm club. In late February, Walter O'Malley announced that the Dodgers had purchased the Los Angeles Angels Pacific Coast League franchise and Los Angeles' Wrigley Field. When the 1957 season began, Don Demeter, Norm Larker, Norm Sherry, and Stan Williams, future Dodger regulars headed to St. Paul; Sparky Anderson, Tommy Lasorda, and Larry Sherry were assigned to the Los Angeles Angels.

Montreal won its opening game in Havana but came home from a 13-game road trip in sixth place, with a five wins eight losses record. They ended May in eighth place, 10 games behind Richmond, and, except for a few days in seventh place, remained in the cellar all season. The Royals' final record, 68–86, left them 20.5 games behind the pennant winning Maple Leafs. It was the first time the club had not made the playoffs since 1944 and their first last-place finish since 1907. The final home attendance figure of 176,137 (which included 19,299 for six games played in Quebec City) represented a drop of 15,000 over the previous season and was Montreal's lowest since 1940.

The Leafs opened the season with a 3–3 13-inning tie at Miami and returned home with a 7–5 record and fourth place in the standings. At the beginning of August, Jack Kent Cooke opened his wallet, purchasing former major leaguer Carl Abrams from Miami and Archie Wilson from Charleston of the American Association. The Leafs went on a three-week tear in August, winning 12 and losing three, moving into first place, one half game ahead of Buffalo. However, by August 29, they had dropped into second, 1.5 games behind. The pennant would not be decided until the last day of the season, when the Leafs edged Rochester to take their third regular season pennant in four seasons. Toronto had no .300 hitters. Mike Goliat, who was named all-star second baseman, was the top Leaf batter with .296. Don Johnson, who finished with a 17–7 record, was named the league's pitcher of the year.

The Miami Marlins, who had finished three games below .500 in the regular season, were the Leafs' first round opponent. The teams split the first two games, played in Toronto. The series moved to Miami for games three, four and five. In game three, which the Marlins won 7–4, Satchel Paige, who was believed to be 51 years old, controlled the Leafs for six innings, before leaving the game in the seventh. Toronto came back to even the series, but Miami moved ahead on an 8–4 win in game five, and then, with the series back in Toronto, took the semi-finals, with a 2–1 victory.

Hall of Fame manager Sparky Anderson played only one season in the major leagues—512 games in 1959 for the Philadelphia Phillies. He played for the Montreal Royals and Toronto Maple Leafs before accepting his first managerial position with the 1964 Maple Leafs (National Baseball Hall of Fame and Museum, Cooperstown, N.Y., 5192_71_HS_NBL).

1958. If Montreal fans had been anxious about the status of the Royals before the 1957 season, they were undoubtedly more so in October 1957 when Brooklyn Dodgers owner Walter O'Malley announced that he was moving his team to Los Angeles. (During the summer the New York Giants had announced their planned move to San Francisco.) The PCL's Los Angeles franchise moved to Spokane, Washington, and remained a Triple A Dodger farm team. Because the Spokane Indians were so much closer to Los Angeles than was Montreal, there was a question of how much good talent the Royals would receive. Worried about the team's future in the city, team president Butch Bouchard, a former hockey great with the Montreal Canadiens, tried, without success, to form a local group to buy the franchise from the Dodgers.

The Dodgers sent four of their top prospects—Jim Gentile, Larry and Norm Sherry, and Maury Wills—to Spokane and three more—Don Demeter, Ron Fairly and Stan Williams—to St. Paul. To Montreal, they sent such experienced veterans as Sparky

Anderson, Tom Lasorda and Sandy Amaros. Tommy Davis, a 19-year-old rookie, who would enjoy an 18-year major league career, would appear in 19 games for the Royals.

The Toronto Maple Leafs enjoyed a relatively quiet off-season. Jack Kent Cooke resigned manager Dixie Walker to a two-year contract and set about assembling a team whose payroll would be $200,000, an unheard-of figure for minor league teams of that era. Sixteen of the 28 men to play for Toronto during the season would be over 30 years old, with Sam Jethroe, at 41, Pat Scantlebury at 40, and Hector Rodriguez at 38 the oldest. Many of the old and familiar faces—Lew Morton, Rocky Nelson (who had become a Maple Leaf in 1957), Mike Goliat, Archie Wilson, Rodriguez, and Don Johnson—were in the opening day lineup.

The Montreal Royals started hot, occupying first place on May 1 with a 12–3 record, and remained in first place the rest of the way, clinching the pennant on the final Friday of the season. Their final lead was 2.5 games against the Maple Leafs. Veteran Tom Lasorda, who led the league in wins with 18 against six defeats, was named to the all-star team and voted pitcher of the year. Joining him on the all-star team were Sparky Anderson at second base and Solly Drake in the outfield. Clay Bryant was named manager of the year. In spite of the fact that rain forced the postponement of 11 games, attendance rose by 37,000 to 213,475.

Toronto did not reach second place until June 5, although not through any fault of knuckle-balling reliever Bob Tiefenauer or slugger Rocky Nelson. By May 28, Tiefenauer, appearing only in relief, had an 0.86 earned run average. Nelson's home run total had reached 16. The club finished in second place, 2.5 games behind Montreal. Rocky Nelson won the triple crown, with 43 home runs, 120 RBIs, and a .326 batting average. He was named the league MVP for the third time and all-star first baseman. Former Montreal all-star Tim Thompson was the all-star catcher. Attendance at Maple Leaf Stadium dropped by 60,000, although the final figure of 281,971 was second highest in all of the minors.

In the semi-finals the Maple Leafs easily defeated Rochester Red Wings, four games to one, while the Montreal Royals defeated the Columbus Jets four games to three. After two rainouts, the Royals won the first two games of the finals against the Leafs. When the series moved to Toronto, rain caused the cancellation of game three, and the next day, the Maple Leafs easily beat the visitors 9 to 3. Montreal won the next two to earn a berth in the Junior World Series.

Montreal's opponents in the Royals' eighth trip to the Junior World Series and first since 1953 were the Minneapolis Millers, a farm team of the Boston Red Sox. Led by player-manager Gene Mauch, the Millers had finished the regular season in third place but had won seven straight playoff games in their march to the American Association post-season championship. The Royals fell to Minneapolis in four straight games and managed only seven runs against the Millers.

1959. The goal of both the Montreal Royals and the Toronto Maple Leafs was to improve on the strong seasons each had enjoyed in 1958. In Montreal's case that meant receiving more top prospects than had been the case in 1958, when 17 of the players on the roster had been over 30. Neither team was successful in achieving these goals. Tommy Davis and Maury Wills went to the Dodgers' Spokane team, while Jim Gentile and Larry Sherry showed up in St. Paul. In Toronto, Sam Jethroe (41 years old) and Lew Morton (37) were gone, along with mainstays Bob Tiefenauer and Rocky Nelson. However, when the season opened, a lot of the old and familiar faces were still around: Ed Blake (33), Jack Crimian (33), Mike Goliat (37), Don Johnson (32), Stan Jok (33), Hector Rodriguez (39), Pat Scantleberry (41), Tim Thompson (35), and Archie Wilson (35).

By early June, it became apparent that neither the Royals nor the Maple Leafs were improvements over last year's teams; in fact, they were decidedly inferior. Montreal, who couldn't seem to win on the road, was in seventh place, while Toronto, who won only six of 28 games over a four-week period, was in eighth. The Royals were in contention for fourth place and a playoff spot until late August. They finished sixth, four games out of the playoffs. Toronto spent nine of the final fifteen weeks of the season in last place and finished seven games out of the playoffs. It was the first season since 1940 that no Canadian team participated in the post season. Two Royals, second baseman Curt Roberts and outfielder Sandy Amaros, were named to the league all-star team. The Leafs' Clay Bryant was named manager of the year. Not surprisingly, attendance dropped drastically in both cities: Montreal by 77,000 and Toronto by 74,000.

While those fans who did attend games in Toronto didn't have much to cheer about when they watched play on the field, they were excited by a major off-field event. On July 27, 1959, it was announced that a third major league, the Continental League, had been formed and would begin play in 1961. Included in the list of teams were New York City, Minneapolis-St. Paul, Denver, Houston, and Toronto. The Toronto entry would be owned by Jack Kent Cooke. The league never became a reality and Toronto remained in the International League.

1960. After the 1959 season, the International League faced significant questions relating to five of its eight teams. With their lease at Delorimier Downs expiring at the end of the 1960 season, would the Los Angeles Dodgers continue to operate a franchise in Montreal? If the Continental League began play as scheduled in 1961, what would happen to the Toronto Maple Leafs' and Buffalo Bisons' franchises? Would the financially struggling Miami Marlins operate during the 1960 season? Finally, and most important, would the Havana Sugar Kings continue to operate or would the franchise have to be relocated? With the outbreak of the Cuban Revolution and Fidel Castro's assumption of power in 1959, teams began to worry about the safety of their players when they played in the Caribbean Island. These worries became real fears after a game on July 25, 1959, when shots were fired by members of an exuberant crowd and Frank Verdi, a coach of the Rochester Red Wings, was grazed by a bullet as he stood in the third base coaching box. Nonetheless, the 1960 season opened with the Sugar Kings a member of the league. However, situations became so dangerous that by July, the International League moved the Havana franchise to Jersey City.

In Toronto, Jack Kent Cooke quickly began to take steps to make the Maple Leafs a better team. He signed a working agreement, the club's first major league affiliation since 1952, with the Cleveland Indians. Shortly after, Mel McGaha, who had managed Cleveland's Double A Memphis club, was hired. Even though Cooke expected to receive several good players from the Indians, he continued buying players, reportedly spending over $100,000 during the winter and into the first few weeks of the season. His most notable acquisitions were pitcher Al Cicotte from Cleveland for $12,000; pitcher Steve Ridzik from Chicago Cubs for $15,000; and Sparky Anderson from Philadelphia Phillies for $25,000.

Montreal had 11 returning players, most notably Mike Goliat (who had been acquired from Toronto during the 1959 season) and Tom Lasorda. Only 24-year-old

Ron Perranowski would go on to a significant career with the Dodgers. The best young Dodger prospects—this year, Willie Davis, Ron Fairly, and Frank Howard—wound up with the Spokane Indians of the Pacific Coast League.

Three weeks into the season, it was apparent to all, especially the seven other teams in the league, that the Toronto Maple Leafs were the best in the circuit. By mid–July their league-lead had extended to 12 games. When the season ended, the Leafs were 17 games ahead of the second place Richmond Virginians. Although the Leafs won the championship with no regulars hitting over .300, they possessed one of the most dominating pitching staffs in the club's history. Al Cicotte won the triple crown of pitching, leading the league in wins, 16; earned run average, 1.79; and strikeouts, 158. Bob Smith and Steve Ridzik each had 14 victories. The entire staff posted a league-leading 2.82 earned run average and shut out the opposition a total of 32 times. Sparky Anderson, at second base; Jim King, in the outfield, and Cicotte and Smith on the mound were named to the all-star team. King was named MVP, Cicotte pitcher of the year, and Mel McGaha manager of the year.

Surprisingly, attendance at Maple Leaf Stadium dropped by nearly four thousand to 203,700. Some of this was caused by the fact that cold weather, rain, and fog had forced the cancellation of eight games by the end of May. Were fans annoyed that Jack Kent Cooke declared he would apply for United States citizenship, that he was more interested in pursuing a Continental League franchise, or that, after late July 1960, when plans for the third major league were destroyed by the major league's announcement that they would expand by four teams within the next two years, he decided to pursue an American or National League expansion team?

The Maple Leafs breezed through the International League playoffs to win their first playoff championship since 1934. Buffalo fell in four straight games, and Rochester won only one game in the finals against Toronto. The Leafs met Louisville in the Junior World Series. The Colonels, who'd finished the regular American Association season in second place before beating Houston four games to one and Denver four games to two, humbled the Leafs 4–1 in the opener. The Leafs took the next two before losing three in a row and the series.

Although the Montreal Royals opened the season with an 8–6 road trip and returned home in third place, they quickly descended into the International League cellar. Between May 12 and June 9, they won only five games while losing 20. A relatively strong showing in July saw them move to within 2.5 games of fourth place and a playoff berth. However, during the last four weeks of the season, the team won only 10 while losing 26. The Royals were eliminated from playoff contention on August 17. Their final record, 62 wins and 92 losses, left them in eighth place, 38 games out of first. First baseman Joe Altobelli, who led the league in RBIs with 105 and home runs with 31, was named to the all-star team. Attendance for the team's final three home games was 3,647, to bring the season's total to only 111,911.

Less than a week after the close of the season, the Los Angeles Dodgers announced they were relinquishing ownership of the Royals. A Canadian group, bolstered by the Dodgers' promise of player aid, attempted to purchase the franchise. When its bid failed, a community group made an unsuccessful attempt to raise funds to buy the team. On the January 29, 1961, the International League announced that the franchise had been sold to a group that planned to operate a team in Syracuse. The Montreal Royals, who had formed one of the great post-war minor league dynasties, were no more. Montreal fans would go without professional baseball until 1969, when the National League awarded an expansion franchise to the city.

1961. During the 1961 season the Toronto Maple Leafs, the Vancouver Mounties of the Pacific Coast League, and the Winnipeg Goldeyes of the Northern League were the only minor league teams operating in Canada. The year would see major changes in professional baseball. In the American League, the Washington franchise would move to the Minneapolis-Saint Paul region, displacing the two American Association franchises there, and Washington, D.C., and Los Angeles would be granted expansion franchises. The National League announced its intentions to expand to New York and Houston in 1962.

As usual, most of the off-season baseball news in Toronto focused on Jack Kent Cooke. In 1960, he sold all of his Canadian business interests except the Leafs, moved to California and became an American citizen. He applied unsuccessfully for American and National League expansion franchises, was rumored to be interested in buying the Cincinnati Reds and moving them to Toronto, purchased a minority interest in the Washington Redskins football team and tried unsuccessfully to buy a minority share of what would become the New York Mets. He would later become owner of the Los Angeles Kings of the National Hockey League, the Los Angeles Lakers of the National Basketball Association, and the Washington Redskins of the National Football League.

As 1961 spring training neared, the Toronto front office announced that it was severing its relations with the Cleveland Indians and would once again operate as an independent club. Johnny Lipon, whom the Indians had assigned to manage Toronto, retained this position. During the season, the Leafs fielded 15 returnees, most notably Sparky Anderson, Rip Coleman, Steve Demeter, and Ron Negray. They also received four players on option, three from expansion clubs Los Angeles and Washington, and one from Cincinnati. When a rash of injuries hit the club in mid- and late season, the lack of an affiliation proved a detriment, as major league teams had tied up their better players with their own minor league clubs.

The Leafs opened the 1961 season in San Juan, Puerto Rico, where the financially struggling Miami Marlins team had relocated. (On May 19, the league would move that team to Charleston, West Virginia.) They lost the first game of the season, but won six in a row, returning to Canada in second place. But a devastating 10-game losing streak in May, plunged the team into seventh place, where they remained for a month, before edging into sixth place. The club was five games out of the playoffs with five weeks to go. Lipon was fired and replaced as manager by a long-time Leaf, the popular catcher Tim Thompson. Under Thompson's leadership, the Leafs moved into fifth place, two games out of the playoffs and a week later they were in forth, two games ahead of Rochester. The two teams ended in a tie for fourth and Rochester won the tie-breaker game 12–11. No doubt because of the team's dismal showing during a large part of the season, attendance dropped to 150,960—52,000 less than in 1960.

1962. During the offseason, Jack Kent Cooke stepped down as president of the Maple Leafs, retaining the title of Chairman of the Board. In December, the Leafs became an affiliate of the Milwaukee Braves, but the fact that Milwaukee's top farm team was the Louisville Colonels of the American Association suggested that the Braves' best prospects might not be coming to Canada. The other major winter news was the hiring of one time Brooklyn Dodger manager Charlie Dressen as Toronto manager.

The Leafs opened the season with a generous helping of returning veterans—notably Sparky Anderson, Steve Demeter and Steve Ridzik—along with a surprisingly strong array of talent supplied by the Milwaukee Braves. Most notable of these was Bobby

Knoop, a young prospect who would go on to a solid major league career with the Los Angeles Angels. During the season, the Braves transferred Neil Chrisley, who would earn an outfield berth on the all-star team, from Louisville and sent Dennis Henke, who would become a mainstay of the Braves' teams during the later 1960s, down from the big club. The Leafs also signed two veterans: Rockey Nelson was purchased from Pittsburgh during the off-season, and Jim Constable, who would win 16 and lose four, post a league leading 2.56 earned run average and be named to the all-star team.

The Maple Leafs began the season with games in Columbus, Richmond, Jacksonville and Atlanta, winning only four while losing seven. They arrived home in early May in fourth place, moved up to third in late May and then to second in late June, a position they maintained the rest of the season. From June 21 until the last two weeks of the season, Toronto was never closer than 7.5 games behind the league leading Jacksonville Suns. Then, with 12 days remaining, they made a pennant race of it, winning 13 while only losing two. However, Jacksonville held on to win the regular season championship by 2.5 games. The Leafs won the first two games of the semi-finals against Atlanta, but then they slumped, losing four straight to their Georgia rivals. Unfortunately, few Torontonians seemed that interested in the series; just under seven thousand fans attended the three games at Maple Leaf Stadium, certainly a disappointment to the front office considering that during the regular season 192,956 people had attended games, an increase of 41,000 over the previous year.

1963. In January, it was announced that Bill Adair, a career minor league manager and occasional major league coach, would be replacing Charlie Dressen as the Leafs' manager. Rumors circulated that Lou Perini might buy the Toronto Maple Leafs and move the Milwaukee Braves to Toronto. Neither happened. It was also rumored that this might be the last year of operation for the Toronto Maple Leafs, who held only a one-year lease on Maple Leaf Stadium.

The major off-season news was the complete restructuring of minor league baseball. The existing leagues were reorganized into five classifications: Triple A, Double A, High Single A, Low Single A, and Rookie. Each of the twenty major league clubs sponsored five farm clubs, one at each level. One of the casualties of the restructuring was the Triple A American Association which had operated with only six teams in 1962. Indianapolis and Little Rock joined the International League, bringing it to 10 teams. This realignment lasted only one year. Toronto threatened to leave the league should it continue in 1964. Indianapolis and Little Rock then joined the Pacific Coast League.

As usual, the Maple Leafs started the season with many old and familiar faces. Eight members of the 25-man roster were over 30. Fourteen players were returning from the previous year. By mid–May the team has settled into fifth place in the Northern Division, a position it occupied until late July, when the club began an amazing turnaround. During the last seven weeks, they won 36 games while losing 20 and, on the penultimate day of the season, clinched second place and a play-off berth. Two players, both acquired after the start of the season, were named to the all-star team. Outfielder Lou Jackson posted a .315 batting average and belted 31 homers, second best in the league. Catcher Jim Coker had a .309 average. In the opening round of the playoffs, the Maple Leafs faced the Atlanta Crackers, second-place finishers in the southern division, and made a speedy exit, losing four straight. In spite of the amazing turnaround that began in July, attendance was only 119,596, a 73,000 drop from the previous year and the lowest since 1941.

1964. During the winter, seeking to strengthen their roster, the Maple Leafs signed a working agreement with the Washington Senators, now in their third year as an American League expansion franchise. However, the American League team had little to offer in the way of talent. The agreement was not renewed after the 1964 season.

In early January, Jack Kent Cooke sold the Maple Leafs for a reported $50,000 to a group of Toronto businessmen. The new management announced that $100,000 would be used to make much-needed renovations to aging Maple Leaf Stadium. Shortly after the sale, Sparky Anderson, who would be 30 years old on opening day, was named the manager. A veteran of 10 minor league seasons, he had appeared in 152 games for the 1959 Philadelphia Phillies, posting a .218 batting average.

When the season opened in mid–April, Toronto and Syracuse were listed as the favorites for the championship of the International League, which had returned to a one-division, eight-team format after the transfer of Little Rock and Indianapolis to the Pacific Coast League. When Toronto began the season, there were only six returning players on the roster. The Leafs won their opener 5–2 and, when they opened at home, their 9–3 record made the pre-season optimism seem valid. They occupied first place throughout May and for the first two weeks in June. But then the club began losing and by early July was in fifth place, where they would remain for the rest of the season, although they remained close to fourth place and a playoff berth until the final day of the season. The one really bright note to the season was the performance of pitcher Ron Piche, a native of Verdun, Quebec, who posted the league's best winning percentage, with a 14–3, .824 record. He won six straight games at the end of the season, to keep the Leafs in playoff contention. The fact that the team drew over 25,000 more fans than in 1963 would have been encouraging if the number had not been 100,000 less than the number club officials said they needed to break even. Losses for the season were reported to be over $50,000.

1965. Shortly after the end of the 1964 season, Maple Leaf officials announced that they would not renew their working agreement with the Washington Senators. Nor would they continue their relationship with the Milwaukee Braves. In November, it was announced that Sparky Anderson's contract would not be renewed. It was believed that he lacked the experience to manage at the Triple A level. Anderson would manage the next year at the Single A level, and in 1970, he would take over leadership of the Cincinnati Reds, beginning a 26-year major league managing career that would earn him a place in the Hall of Fame.

Toronto signed an affiliation agreement with the Boston Red Sox. Instead of owning several players and receiving others from the parent club, Toronto would own no players— all would be the property of Boston. The object was not to assemble a team that would win a championship, but rather to provide a suitable environment in which to develop players so that they could perform at the major league level. In 1965, seven members of the team played for both the Leafs and the Red Sox. In 1966, seven played for both clubs, and, when the Red Sox played in the 1967 World Series, their roster included nine former Toronto Maple Leafs.

One of the most important people contributing to the success of the Leaf players was the new manager, Dick Williams. He, like Sparky Anderson, would begin his managerial career at the Triple A level. After he finished a 14-year major league playing career, including a three-year stint with the Red Sox, Boston gave him the job of leading Toronto in January 1965. So successful did he prove in his two seasons with the Leafs that he became the Red Sox manager for 1967 and began a 21-year major league managerial career that would lead him, like Anderson, to the Hall of Fame.

The Leafs spent early May in third place, but then came alive, winning 15 of 16 games, including nine in a row, and at the end of the month occupied first place. But in June, they won only 14, while losing 22. They dropped into and stayed in third place, finishing a respectable 3.5 games out of first place. Pitcher Jack Lamabe (11 wins and three losses) earned a berth on the league all-star team, as did Joe Foy, a 22-year-old rookie third baseman who won the league batting championship with a .302 average (the only .300 average in the International League that season) and was named both MVP and rookie of the year.

In the semi-finals, the Leafs defeated the favored Atlanta Crackers in four straight games, outscoring the Georgia team 15 to seven. They then opened the finals with three consecutive shutouts, lost the fourth game, and then won the fifth to win the Governor's Cup.

A success on the field, the Toronto Maple Leafs were in trouble off it. In spite of their being involved in a thrilling pennant race and a marvelous post season, attendance dropped by 26,000 during the regular season. Just over 11,000 came to four playoff games. It was estimated that the season's losses would exceed $50,000 for the second straight year and rumored that officials from the city of Richmond, Virginia, had made a very favorable offer to move the franchise to Virginia. In December, the Toronto Board of Control awarded a civic grant (mainly in the form of tax relief) of $30,000 to the ball club. The Leafs were alive—at least for another year.

1966. The Leafs began the 1966 season as one of the International League's teams deemed most likely to win the pennant. Fourteen members of the Governor's Cup team, along with five members of Pittsfield's Eastern League pennant-winning team, were on the roster. However, the Maple Leafs got off to a struggling start, winning two and losing seven on their opening road trip. At the end of May, they found themselves in eighth place, nine games behind first pace Columbus. At the beginning of June, Toronto began an amazing comeback, one that would see them win 69 while losing 43 the rest of the season and contending for the regular season pennant until the last day of the season. The Leafs ended the season in a tie for second place with the Columbus Jets.

What had happened to a team that just over three months earlier had been setting records for futility? First, Reggie Smith learned to hit Triple A pitching and ended up with a .320 average, the best in the International League. Second, Gary Waslewski, who had been deemed expendable early in the season, enjoyed a six-game winning streak in mid-season and finished with 18 wins, tops in the league. Smith and Waslewski were both named to the all-star team. Two months into the season, the Leafs acquired three veteran pitchers from other International League teams: Galen Cisco from Jacksonville and Julio Navarro and Ed Rakow from Syracuse. By mid–July, the trio had either won or saved 20 games for Toronto. Also contributing to the team's resurgence was Tony Horton, who batted .297 and hit 28 home runs after being sent down from Boston in mid–May.

Toronto took the best-of-five semi-finals three games to two from Columbus. Reggie Smith was the hero of the series with nine hits, including three home runs, and 10 RBIs. The Leafs opened the finals at home against the Richmond Braves in a best-of-seven series. Toronto quickly jumped into a two-game lead, split games three and four, and then won its second consecutive Governor's Cup in a come from behind 6–5 victory. The Leafs' achievements earned manager Dick Williams and players Mike Andrews and Reggie Smith promotions to the Boston Red Sox 1967.

1967. Although the Leafs had won the 1966 championship, there was little joy in the front offices during the following days and weeks. Regular season attendance had dropped by over 21,000 to 96,918, while four home playoff games drew an average of just under 2,500. Maple Leaf Stadium needed extensive renovations. The city's three daily newspapers were giving the team minimal coverage. An attendance drop of 21,392 had seriously reduced the club's income. Toronto City Council approved some relief, which amounted to $33,000, only eight weeks before opening day. However, the Leafs began the season owing the city $33,000 in back taxes and the Toronto Harbour Commission, owners of the stadium, $37,000 in rent and other charges.

The Leafs began the season in Toledo with another first-year manager, Eddie Kasko, who, the previous season, had finished a 10-year playing career as a utility infielder for the Red Sox. The roster included nine returning players and several promising newcomers, one of whom was Sparky Lyle, a 22-year-old left-handed pitcher who, later in the season, would begin a 16-year major league career in which he never started a game but amassed a total of 238 saves.

After the first week of the season, Toronto was in second place. But by early June, largely because of a hot streak in which the team won nine of 10 games, they found themselves in second place. Unfortunately, cold weather, along with fan apathy, kept attendance down. During the first 10 home games, the number of paying spectators averaged under one thousand. The team spent June in second place, but in July the team dropped to fifth. Attendance figures of less than a thousand a game became the norm. The baseball team regained its form in August and for three weeks occupied third place. However, the club hit a slump, winning only five and losing 12 over a two-week period, and ended the season in sixth place, two games out of a playoff berth.

The Leafs finished the season with four games over the Labor Day weekend, once one of the top-drawing three days of the season. On Saturday, 404 people watched them win a 13-inning thriller 2–1 against Syracuse. A Sunday doubleheader, which they split with the Chiefs, drew 1,215. On Labor Day, September 4, 1967, only 802 watched what was the final game for a team that had been playing in Toronto since 1912.

Although shortly after the season there were reports that the Maple Leafs hockey club of the National Hockey League was interested in purchasing the team, nothing came of that. In mid–October president Bob Hunter announced that the club would be sold to American interests for around $60,000 and moved to Louisville, Kentucky. Although the team was gone, the financial bad news continued. The Harbour Commission wanted to collect $52,000 for rent, taxes, and work done on the stadium. In late November, the club declared bankruptcy. It owed $134,000 to 86 Canadian creditors and $50,000 to 44 U.S. companies. In December, uniforms, bats, office furniture, a public address system and other items were auctioned off, bringing in just over $5,000, which was put toward paying off some of the debt. In February of 1968, the Harbor Commission asked for bids for demolition of Maple Leaf Stadium and by the summer piles of rubble marked the spot where one of the greatest of all minor league teams had played its games.

In 1975, Toronto would at long last be granted a major league baseball franchise which would begin play in 1977. In the interim Toronto's baseball fans had to live on memories and hopes.

5

Vancouver's Pacific Coast League
Mounties Come and Go ...
and Come and Go

In late August 1955, toward the end of Vancouver's first summer since World War II without professional baseball, local baseball fans heard news that many of them had been waiting for years to hear: Vancouver would be getting a Pacific Coast League franchise. Brick Laws, owner of the Oakland Oaks, who played in a deteriorating ballpark to a constantly decreasing number of fans, would be moving to the greener pastures of Capilano Stadium in 1956. The move would mark an important step in the PCL's goal of achieving major league status. In 1952, it had been upgraded from Triple A to "Open Classification" status, a position between Triple A and the major leagues. Two of the conditions for maintaining the new status were that league cities have an aggregate population of at least 10 million and that annual total attendance would be 2.5 million or more. Vancouver, with a metropolitan population of over 650,000, was at least 200,000 larger than Oakland; the team would most likely have an attendance considerably higher than Oakland's 1955 figure of just over 141,000; and the city had a five-year-old stadium that could easily be expanded beyond its present 6,600 capacity.

During the fall, owner Brick Laws predicted that the Mounties, as the team had been renamed, would outdraw all other clubs in the league. But events during the winter cast considerable doubt on these statements. First, city law prevented professional sports from being played on Sundays. As General Manager Cedric Tallis speculated, without Sunday home games, attendance could be lowered by 100,000. By mid–March, it was announced that there had been only $35,000 worth of advanced sales—an alarmingly low amount.

1956. In the fall of 1955, the Mounties announced that they had signed a working agreement with the Baltimore Orioles, who would provide four players on option (that is, subject to recall), and other player assistance if possible. But in March 1956, manager Lefty O'Doul, the former major league star now in his twenty-second year as a PCL manger, announced that Vancouver was in great need of more player help if it was to field a competitive team.

When the Mounties began their season on April 10, with a 6–3 loss at San Francisco, the opening day roster included six holdovers from the 1955 Oaks. Most notable of these were 35-year-old George Metkovich, who had won the 1955 batting championship with a .335 average; 36-year-old Spider Jorgensen, who'd played for the Montreal Royals and had had brief stints with the Brooklyn Dodgers, and 32-year-old George Bamberger, who'd enjoyed a cup of coffee in the majors. Only six members of the 1955 edition of the

Orioles AA farm team, the San Antonio Missions of the Texas League, were promoted to Vancouver.

Opening on the road, the Mounties won four and lost nine games, returning home solidly entrenched in eighth place. The team lost its home opener on April 24, 2–1, to the San Francisco Seals. A crowd of 8,149, the largest to watch a professional game in Vancouver, showed up on the chilly, moist evening. Even though the weather improved, the Mounties didn't. When the season ended, the Mounties still held onto their eighth and last place position. Although their team batting average, .258, was lowest in the league, and their top hitter, George Metkovich, only had a .294 average, the Mounties' pitchers turned in yeoman performances. Charlie Beamon won 13 and lost eight 8, Rhyne Duren was 11 and 11, while George Bamberger won nine while losing 14.

If there was a bright spot in an otherwise disappointing season, it occurred on August 7 when the Vancouver City Council passed, four votes to two, a law legalizing Sunday afternoon professional sport between the hours of 1:30 and 6:00. The Mounties scheduled three Sunday afternoon doubleheaders during the remainder of the season. Thanks, in part, to attendance at these doubleheaders, the club ended up with a total paid attendance of 152,823, which was, nonetheless, second poorest in the league and nearly 250,000 less than Laws had predicted.

1957. In November 1956, Nat Bailey, the very popular and successful owner of Vancouver's White Spot restaurant chain, announced the formation of a committee to raise money to buy the Mounties from Brick Laws. In January, $50,000 was paid to Laws and the new owners assumed the club's $100,000 in debts, which were paid off by mid–March. The Mounties entered spring training with $80,000 in operating capital.

The Mounties scheduled 11 Sunday doubleheaders for the 1957 season. Tickets to the Sunday games could be purchased only until midnight on Saturday. Over 47,000 came to the Sunday games on the date of the first Sunday double header, May 5, Vancouver police, responding to a complaint by the Lords Day Alliance, took the names of General Manager Cedric Tallis and his assistant Bill Sayles. The two were delivered a summons to appear in court in June. The matter dragged on through the summer, and it was not until mid–October that the court announced that the Mounties club, along with Tallis and Sayles, was guilty of violating the Lord's Day Act. The club was fined $150, $50 for each of the first three double-headers. The two men had to pay three dollars each, one dollar for each offense.

During the season, the Mounties received limited player assistance from the Baltimore Orioles. The opening day starting lineup contained only four players sent down from Baltimore. Two, Buddy Peterson at 32 and Joe Frazier at 34, were old; a third, Kal Segrist, at 26 had played the last of his 10 major league games in 1955. Only 24-year-old Lenny Green could be deemed a prospect. The rest of the lineup included 26-year-old Mike Marshall, 29-year-old Jake Crawford, 32-year-old Lenny Neal, 37-year-old Spider Jorgensen, and 33-year-old George Bamberger.

The Mounties had a very strong beginning to their season. By May 30, they had won 29 and lost 17 and were in first place two games ahead of Hollywood. But on June 11, the San Francisco Seals moved ahead of Vancouver and occupied first place for the rest of the season. Nonetheless, the Mounties did not fade; they remained close to the Seals, never dropping more than four games out of first. San Francisco clinched the pennant with only three games to go. Vancouver's total of 97 wins was 30 more than in 1956.

Charlie Metro, who had replaced Lefty O'Doul as the Mounties' manager, was named manager of the year. Shortstop Buddy Peterson (.298) was named to the all-star team, as were outfielder Lenny Green (.311), who was also named PCL rookie of the year, and pitcher Morrie Martin, who led the league with a 1.90 ERA. The Mounties led the league in attendance—306,145.

After the season, the Pacific Coast League faced major challenges. Early in the fall, the Brooklyn Dodgers and New York Giants officially announced their relocation to Los Angeles and San Francisco respectively. With its two biggest markets lost, the PCL's goal of becoming a third major league was destroyed. During the off season, league directors agreed to return to Triple A classification. Moreover, PCL would have to find new cities to host what had been the Los Angeles Angels, the Hollywood Stars and the San Francisco Seals. The Angels moved to Spokane, the Stars to Salt Lake City, and the Seals to Phoenix.

The Mounties still faced the problem that Sunday afternoon baseball was illegal. However, when the City of Vancouver held a plebiscite on the matter during the December elections and the vote was 62,000 to 34,000 in favor of Sunday sports, it was expected that the provincial government would agree to revise the Vancouver Charter. In anticipation, the Mounties announced that they would sell tickets for Sunday games on Sunday. The process moved slowly. It wasn't until mid–June that the British Columbia Court of Appeals voted three to two to make Sunday sports legal.

1958. The Mounties' opening day starting lineup included five returning players—all over 30 years old. The grandfather of the team, pitcher Joe Hatten, was 40; Barry Shetrone, who in 1957 had won the Class C Arizona Mexico League batting championship with a .371 average, was the youngest at 19. At the end of their first home stand, the Mounties were in first place, half a game ahead of Portland. The club dropped briefly into second place, then regained the league lead which they held until late July. Vancouver's success was mainly due to the performance of their pitchers. By mid–June, the mound corps had earned 13 shutouts and at one point turned in 48 consecutive scoreless innings. The Mounties cooled down during July dropping into third place, but at the end of the month had returned to first, half a game ahead of Phoenix. But after that they won only 14 while losing 26, finishing in third place, nine games out of first. The bright spot was the pitching of Bamberger, who ended the year with 15 wins and, at 2.45, the league's best earned run average. He was named to the all-star team. But the team's hitting was very weak. Charlie White was the best batter with a .291 average; the club average of .251 was the worst in the league. The final attendance figure of 245,755, was a drop of 60,000, which was attributed to extremely poor weather at the beginning of the season and the Mounties' collapse at the end of it.

1959. The Mounties opened the 1959 season with four highly touted young prospects on their roster. Barry Shetrone, age 20, returned for a second year in center field. Twenty-five-year-old Marv Breeding, a third-year pro, started at second base; Shortstop Ron Hansen, age 21, was starting his fourth year as a professional. And Jim Pagliaroni, age 21, a $65,000 bonus baby, handled the catching duties.

The Mounties got off to a slow start, winning only four of their first twelve games and occupying eighth place before the Baltimore Orioles sent help: George Bamberger, who had started the season in the major leagues, was coming back to Vancouver along with Brooks Robinson, a 22-year-old veteran who'd spent parts of four seasons in the

Although he had already played parts of four major league seasons with the Baltimore Orioles, Brooks Robinson was sent to the Vancouver Canadians in 1959 to work on his batting skills. In 42 games, the future member of the Hall of Fame posted a .331 average and dazzled Pacific Coast League fans with his fielding abilities (National Baseball Hall of Fame and Museum, Cooperstown, N.Y., 1022.64_Act_NBL).

major leagues. The future Hall of Famer played 42 games for Vancouver, turning in a .331 batting average and amazing everyone with his outstanding play at third base.

The club rebounded in June with an amazing 15-win and five loss record during June and moved into second place. The Mounties would remain in second—except for occasional days in first—for the rest of the season, never dropping more than three games behind the leader and finishing 1.5 games behind the Salt Lake City Bees. The rainout of three games over the Labor Day weekend, injuries and the late season call-ups of such players as Robinson, Barry Shetrone, and Joe Taylor may well have cost the club a chance to win the pennant. Three individuals turned in noteworthy season's performances. Marv Breeding led the league in stolen bases with 27, while Chuck Estrada finished second in the league in the number of strikeouts with 177. Outfielder Joe Taylor, the club's leading hitter with a .292 average, was voted to the league all-star team.

The Mounties posted a final attendance figure of 238,970, a drop of 6,628 from 1958. The club had lost $80,000 in the season. Without the $50,000 the Mounties had received from Major League Baseball for its invasion of Pacific Coast League territory and $22,500 from the Major League assistance fund, the situation would have been much worse. The executive quickly moved to trim expenses. A new general manager was hired. Bob Frietas, a veteran minor league administrator, accepted a salary $9,000 less than his predecessor. When manager Charlie Metro would not accept a $4,000 pay cut, he was replaced by George Staller for the amount refused by Metro. Expenses were further reduced by cutting $10,000 from the spring training budget.

1960. To avoid financial losses in the upcoming season, the Mounties would have to increase attendance. To do that, they needed both a competitive team and good summer weather. Prospects for the former were dimmed when the Baltimore Orioles announced that they would be sending their top minor league talent to their International League farm team, the Miami Marlins.

The 13 pitchers listed on the Vancouver roster at the beginning of the season won a combined total of only 47 games. Chet Nichols had 18 of them, tops in the league, along with a league-leading winning percentage of .750 and was named to the all-star team. The 11 pitchers who joined the club during the season won 21 while losing 43. The position players fared better. Chuck Oertel averaged .313 over 101 games, Ray Barker, .311 in 151 games. Howie Goss, while only hitting .262, belted in 29 round-trippers.

The Mounties lost their opening game, 10 to 9 at Sacramento, and returned home in last place. Their record did not improve. Moreover, by May 20, five home games had been rained out. They struggled through the rest of the season, spending most of June in sixth place before settling into seventh place, where they finished—23.5 games out of first place. Bad weather and a disappointing team kept the fans away. The final attendance of 144,278 represented a drop of 94,000. The club's debts were reported to be nearly $80,000.

1961. In early November 1960, the Mounties faced a new crisis: league president Dewey Soriano ordered them to pay all their outstanding debts, by November 15, 1960, or relinquish the franchise. A new local ownership group was formed and agreed to pay the debt and supply $40,000 operating capital.

The Mounties began the season with a new affiliation, the Milwaukee Braves, and a new manager, former major leaguer Billy Hitchcock. The began the season with several old and familiar faces on the roster including George Bamberger (age 37), Charlie White (33), Jim Dyck (39), and Bobby Balcena (35). The roster also included three very young and very promising players, 20-year-old bonus baby Dennis Menke; Manny Jimenez (22) and Denny Lemaster (22).

The club played winning ball during the first five weeks of the season, occupying second place behind the Seattle Rainiers. However, during late May and early June, they lost 18 games while winning only four and dropped to fifth place. In late June, the club climbed into third place and spent the rest of the season in either second or third place. They ended up 10 games out, in second place, with a record of 87 wins and 67 losses.

Although the team failed to capture the pennant, several individual Mounties enjoyed strong years. Ron Piche, sent down from the Braves at the beginning of June, won 14 and lost seven, led the league with a 2.26 earned run average, and earned a spot on the all-star team. Outfielder Howie Goss, who slugged 27 home runs, and third baseman Ed Charles, who posted a .305 average, made the all-star team, as did bonus baby Dennis Menke who had a .293 average and hit 15 home runs. Attendance rose by 55,000 to 200,143.

1962. Even though the team had shown a substantial attendance increase during 1961 and had made a profit of $19,000, the first one in the club's six years of operations, the team was over $45,000 in debt. The Mounties' board agreed to reorganize and continue running the team and began gathering funds for the upcoming season. They had to find a new affiliation as the Braves had decided not to operate a farm team in Vancouver. With Milwaukee's assistance they negotiated a full affiliation with the Minnesota Twins.

The team Minnesota sent to Vancouver couldn't hit. The team's final batting average, .240, was the worst in the league. Minnie Mendoza led the club with a .260 average. The two best pitchers, Al Schroll and George Bamberger, each won 12 games, but lost 12 and 13, respectively. The club lost the first game of the season and never reached the .500 mark, spending most of the season in seventh or eighth place, although twice they enjoyed a few days in sixth. Their final record of 72 wins and 79 losses put them in seventh place. Before the season, club officials had said that without a competitive team and reasonable weather, Vancouver could not attract enough fans to survive in the PCL. Not only was the team mediocre, but also the Pacific Northwest experienced the coldest and rainiest spring and summer in several years. Twelve of Vancouver's home dates were rained out. The season's total attendance, 88,075 represented a drop of 111,712 from 1961.

The Mounties' fate was decided, not just by their woeful financial condition, but by a major restructuring of minor league baseball that took place in the fall of 1962. Each of the 20 major league clubs agreed to have a working agreement with a Triple A club. That meant there could only be 20 Triple A teams. When the American Association disbanded and its five clubs relocated to the International and Pacific Coast leagues, there would be twenty-one teams at the Triple A level, one without an affiliation. When Minnesota decided not to renew its agreement with Vancouver, the Mounties were the odd one out. Canada's third largest city would be without professional baseball in 1963.

The PCL's acceptance of the Dallas American Association franchise proved unsuccessful. During the 1964 season, its second, the Texas club posted a 53–104 record, finished 42.5 games behind the division leader, and drew only 39,391 fans. In November, the Dallas Rangers applied for and received permission to withdraw from the league. The officials of the Mounties were ready. The directors had quietly been paying down the debts and loans the team had accrued and elected Nat Bailey as president. He, with Lew Matlin, a former Hawaii front office official who had been recently appointed the Mounties' General Manager, arrived at the Pacific Coast League winter meetings where they successfully applied for the Dallas franchise.

1965. The Mounties signed an affiliation agreement with the Kansas City Athletics who would supply players and a manager and would pay for the manager's salary and the amount of each player's salary that exceeded $700 a month; they would operate and pay for spring training, pay for the team's transportation from the spring training site to the site of the opening game, and foot the bill for transportation home for all players and the manager at the end of the season. That left the club responsible for players' base salaries, transportation to away games, and all operational expenses. The Mounties reported $45,000 in pre-season ticket sales. Some $20,000 of this money was put toward paying down more of the club's debt and another $20,000 to refurbish Capilano Stadium.

The team that arrived at Capilano Stadium on April 17, 1965, for the opening day-night doubleheader against the Spokane Indians was a young team lead by a young manager. Haywood Sullivan, who had been a not-very-successful bonus baby signed by the Boston Red Sox in the 1950s, was only 34 and in his second year as manager. Only seven members of the 20-man opening day roster were 25 or over. Over a third of the team would spend time in both Vancouver and Kansas City. Call-ups were frequent, with one of the first being manager Sullivan who took over as the Athletics' manager. Two of the most significant promotions occurred near the end of July, when two of Vancouver's top pitchers, Jack Aker and Lew Krausse, moved up to Kansas City. At the time, the Mounties, who were in the thick of the divisional pennant race, went into an eight-loss tailspin. They managed to recover and were only eliminated on the second to last day of the season. Their record of 77 wins, 69 losses put them in third place of the PCL's West Division. The relatively strong showing of the Mounties can be credited to the pitching staff, which posted a 3.28 earned run average, second-best in the league. At the plate, the team was relatively weak, with a .249 batting average and only 73 home runs. Though attendance was much better than the Mounties' in 1962 and Dallas' in 1964, Vancouver drew only 124,048 to Capilano Stadium.

1966. The Vancouver Mounties had a new manager, Mickey Vernon, long-time star of the Washington Senators and later a major league manager and coach. Only ten players returned from the 1965 squad and seven were promoted from Double A Birmingham of the Southern League. Overall, the roster remained much more stable during the season than had been the case the previous year. Only 32 players took the field for the Mounties, and of these, only six played parts of the season in Kansas City. The club's average age was up a few months from 1965, but at 25.1 years, it was still the youngest in the league.

After making a nearly 5,000-mile flight from their training camp in Bradenton, Florida, to Honolulu, the Mounties lost their season's opener to the Islanders 6–4. Four days later, they flew to Vancouver with a one win and three losses record, won their home opener and three of the next four home games before going into a deep slump. By May 24, the club was in sixth place in the West Division, ten games below .500. At the beginning of June, the Mounties found the winning touch. Victors of 13 games against two defeats, they climbed back to the .500 level and, in mid–June, took over second place, a position they would hold the remainder of the season. They finished the year with 77 wins and 71 losses, six games behind the Seattle Angels. The total season's attendance dropped slightly, to 121,482.

1967. The 1967 season followed a pattern that was now becoming familiar to Vancouver fans. The Kansas City A's supplied the manager and players and frequently called some of the better players up to the big league team. The Mounties, who once again featured strong pitching and average hitting, remained in contention for the West Division championship until the closing days of the season, and the attendance, though up from the two previous seasons, was disappointing.

Mickey Vernon returned to the Mounties for his second season as manager. Along with him came nine players from 1966. Eight others had graduated from Mobile, Kansas City's Double A farm club. The most notable of these was third baseman Sal Bando, who would in the early 1970s become a mainstay of the Oakland Athletics' three World Series championship teams.

The Mounties won their opening game 8 to 4 in Seattle but were victors in only four of their next 11 starts and finished April in sixth place in the West. For the rest of the season, however, they played consistently above .500, remaining in the thick of the pennant race, and for three weeks in August held a very slight lead over Spokane and Portland, the other contending teams. In the morning of Sunday, September 2, they held a 1.5 game lead over the other two contenders. Then they collapsed, losing three straight games to Spokane and finished in third place with a record of 77 wins and 69 losses.

Roberto Rodriguez led the pitchers with 12 wins against four losses. The team's earned run average of 2.90 was second best in the PCL, as was the strikeout total of 977. None of the batters reached the .300 mark. Sal Bando's .291 average was the best for a Mountie during their three years of affiliation with Kansas City. Warmer weather and the close pennant race resulted in a 22,000 increase in attendance to 143,541.

1968. Kansas City renewed its affiliation with Vancouver, although by the time the season opened, the Athletics had moved to Oakland. The Mounties performed acceptably during the first month and a half of the season, playing at or above .500 ball. But at the beginning of June, they began their descent toward the West Division cellar. On July 17, they owned a 37–52 record and were in sixth place, 16 games behind league leading Spokane. They managed 21 more wins and 36 more losses by the end of the season. Their sixth-place finish placed them 27.5 games behind division leader Spokane.

The team's problem was obvious. It couldn't hit. The batting average of .236 was the second lowest in the league, the home run total of 46 the worst. No regular batter reached the .250 mark. Over the season, the Mounties were shut out 22 times. The pitching, which had saved Vancouver's weak hitting teams in the past, had also slipped. Their 3.74 earned run average was 10th in the league. Not surprisingly, attendance plummeted. The 82,028 total was the second lowest among all Triple A teams.

1969. During the 1968 season, the major leagues had announced that they would be expanding by four teams: San Diego and Montreal would enter the National League and Seattle and Kansas City, the American. The Oakland Athletics terminated their working agreement with Vancouver and Mountie officials announced that the team had entered into a full working agreement with the new Seattle Pilots. During the winter, the Montreal Expos, who wanted to establish a presence across Canada, also announced that they would send players to Vancouver.

The relationship between the Mounties and the Expos and the Pilots was much different than the one they had with the Kansas City/Oakland A's. The A's had sent the top prospects in their farm system to Vancouver, along with experienced veterans, most of whom had had some major league experience, to be members of a taxi squad to be called up as needed. Being first-year expansion teams, the Expos and the Pilots did not have extended farm systems filled with advancing prospects. The majority of their players had been signed in the expansion draft and were, at best, over the hill or marginal major leaguers. One of the most notable of these players was Jim Bouton, one time New York Yankee pitching star, who, during the 1969 season hoped to make a successful comeback and who, unbeknownst to his teammates, was gathering material for his book *Ball Four*, one of the first behind-the-scenes exposés of the lives of major league players. Bouton pitched in 10 innings over seven games with the Mounties, compiling a no win and one loss record, before being recalled to Seattle.

In spite of the constant changing of the Mounties' roster—only three position players appeared in over 100 games and only five pitchers threw over 100 innings—the Mounties performed well during the first six weeks of the season and creditably the rest of the way, playing around .500 ball the rest of the season. When the season ended, the Mounties and Spokane Indians were tied for second 14 games behind Tacoma. Greg Goossen, with a .298 average, and 18 home runs, was the Mounties' top hitter. Bill Ferrell and Carl Morton, three of the 24 pitchers the club used, each won eight games.

While the club's on-field performance was considerably better than that of the 1968 team, attendance was much worse. Because of extremely bad weather, an average of only 784 per game showed up in April. By late June, the figure had crept up to 990 a game; in late August, with the team well out of contention, crowds were generally well below the 1,000 mark. On August 30, on what would be the final PCL game to be played in Vancouver until 1977, 1,101 people paid to see the Mounties win against Hawaii. The total season's attendance of 62,666 was the second worst of the 20 Triple A clubs.

In mid-summer, the Seattle Pilots, who were covering the baseball-related expenses for the Mounties, expressed displeasure with the poor attendance in Vancouver and intimated that they might place their top farm team in Portland the next season. Montreal made it clear that they would like a team closer to home. On October 8, officials of the Vancouver club terminated the lease on Capilano Stadium, and the Mounties became the Salt Lake City Bees.

Canada's Border League Teams Go South

Western International League, Provincial League, PONY League, Northern League

The greatest attrition in the minors occurred in classes A, B, C, and D. In addition to facing increased competition for people's entertainment dollars with the growth of television, teams were faced with a decreasing number of affiliations or working agreements with major league teams. In 1953, there were 13 Canadian teams in the lower minor leagues. After the Hamilton Red Wings withdrew from the PONY League in May 1956, only one Canadian team operated from Class A to D: the Winnipeg Goldeyes of the Class C Northern League. It operated until the end of the 1964 season.

WESTERN INTERNATIONAL LEAGUE (Class A): *Vancouver Capilanos and Victoria Tyees (1952–1954), Calgary Stampeders and Edmonton Eskimos (1953–1954)*

The Western International League entered the 1951–52 off season with five of its eight teams in financial difficulty. One of them was the Victoria Athletics. At its January meeting, the league advised the club that unless it could reduce its high debt and generate enough operating capital to make it through to the spring, the franchise would be moved elsewhere. In January and February, club officials organized a fund drive which raised enough money to save the club.

The most amazing off-season news was the league's decision to move from Class B to Class A, a "promotion" that would increase the monthly salary ceiling from $4,000 to $5,200. It was, officials explained, a move designed to prevent under the table payments to players that had contributed to several clubs' monetary difficulties.

1952. After being notified in February that the club was officially back in the league, Victoria officials made a series of moves to rebrand the team, make it more effective on the field, and increase attendance. First, the team was renamed the Tyees, after a particularly fierce fighting salmon. Second, team officials reaffirmed their working agreement with the Portland Beavers of the Pacific Coast League. Third, they hired Cec Garriott, as playing manager. A Pacific Coast League veteran, who had played a few games with the

Chicago Cubs in 1946, he would bring his baseball knowledge, along with a strong bat and outfield skills, to the team.

The Tyees opened the season in Yakama, eking out a 14–13 win over the Bears and returned home a week later with 6–1 record, half a game ahead of Spokane. Over the next three months, the club steadily increased its lead and, by the beginning of August, it had grown to 13.5 games. The Tyees clinched the pennant on September 8, the beginning of the final week of the season. Ben Lorino won 24 games, and former Negro Leaguer Jehosie Heard won 20 games and hurled a no-hitter. Bob Moniz's .330 average was fourth-best in the league and manager-outfielder Cec Garriott's 17 home runs, the best. Garriott, Lorino, and shortstop Jimmy Clark were named to the league all-star team. The final Victoria attendance total was 105,948, an improvement of 36,000 over 1951.

In Vancouver, the Capilanos, who couldn't hit the long ball—only 26 homers for the entire season—settled early into third place and finished the season there, 18 games behind the Tyees. One time Negro Leaguer, veteran catcher John Ritchey hit .343, second best in the league and was named to the all-star team. Although attendance dropped by 44,000, the total of 119,533 was still the best in the league.

1953. Shortly into the offseason, it became clear that the WIL was in a crisis state. Five teams saw significant attendance decreases. Salem and Vancouver reported $35,000 operating losses, Wenatchee had debts of $16,000. And Victoria, in spite of its stellar season both on the field and at the turnstiles, had accounts payable of $19,926.87.

To meet the crises that threatened to destroy the WIL, league owners and officials proposed two major solutions. The first was to replace the two weakest teams, Tri-City and Wenatchee, with teams in Calgary and Edmonton, Alberta. The second was to add these two Alberta cities to the existing eight. Both Alberta cities had metropolitan populations of over 200,000, booming economies, and strong fan support for their senior amateur teams. League directors chose the second option; Calgary and Edmonton each paid an expansion fee of $25,000.

What WIL team owners didn't seem to have considered fully were the facts that the Alberta cities were a long way from any of the other league cities (the distance from Edmonton to Salem, Oregon, was 1008 miles), that the weather could be very cold and even snowy until the middle of May, and that, like Vancouver and Victoria, Edmonton and Calgary did not allow the playing of professional sport on Sundays.

The league also decided to adopt a split-season format, with the winners of each half meeting for the league championship. It was hoped that if teams who had performed poorly in the first half had a strong second half, their attendance might increase.

During the offseason, the league made an appointment of historic dimensions when it hired African American Emmett Ashford as an umpire. He was outgoing and quickly became a fan favorite. The next year he began a 12-year career in the Pacific Coast League and, in 1966, signed a contract with the American League, becoming the first African American to umpire in the major leagues.

Although Victoria opened the season with Cec Garriott again the playing manager and with 13 other members of the 1952 championship squad back, the Tyees finished the first half in sixth place, began with the second half with seven straight losses, and ended it in tenth place. Only outfielder Granny Gladstone, whose .348 average earned him a spot on the all-star team; Don Pries, at .329; and Milt Martin at .307 gave the Tyees some punch at the plate. The pitching was a disappointment. None of the regulars had an earned run average under four. The most successful pitcher, hometown Victoria boy Bill Prior, won 15 games, but lost 16 and posted an earned run average of 4.64.

But much of the news about the team concerned its worsening financial condition. The club started the season with no working capital and by late May, poor play and bad weather had limited attendance to less than 850 a game. In early August, in order to raise badly needed cash quickly, the Tyees sold their best player, shortstop Jimmy Clark, to the Vancouver Capilanos. Then, in the last week of the season, the alarm bells again rang. General manager Reg Patterson announced that unless 8,000 fans attended the Tyees' last four home games, the team would not be able to meet its final payroll and would not be able to return for the 1954 season. Only 2,601 paid to see these games, enough to enable to club to pay the players, but not enough to insure Victoria's continued participation in the WIL. Final attendance was 55,352, a drop of over 50,000 from 1952.

The Vancouver Capilanos started the season with only six holdovers from the previous season. Their general manager, Dewey Soriano, who would later become the president of the Pacific Coast League and then owner of the major league Seattle Pilots, was new, as was their manager Harvey Story, a 36-year-old veteran of 13 Pacific Coast League seasons. He was, as well, the team's top player, finishing fourth in league batting with a .343 average, and was named all-star third baseman. Pete Hernandez led the team with 18 wins and had a league best ERA of 3.06. The club finished the first half in fourth place, 6.5 games behind Salem, and spent most of the second half four or five games behind the leaders before a late-season eight-game winning streak brought them to within 2.5 games of Spokane. Attendance dropped by 43,000 to 75, 877, fifth highest in the league.

The new Calgary entry, the Stampeders, was owned by oil man Bud Lacey. It would play its home games in Buffalo Stadium, built by Calgary Brewing Company for its amateur baseball team. Before the season began, the park's seating was expanded from 2,500 to 4,000. Gene Lillard, a long-time Pacific Coast League player, was hired as manager and began to gather players. Five players he signed had spent the previous season in Class C ball, and seven were 23 years old or younger.

On opening day, the Stampeders won a double header in Salem, Oregon, but spent the rest of the first half playing under .500 ball and ended up in tenth place. They finished the first two weeks of the second half with a 7–7 record, but then won only seven of their next 20 games and ended the second half of the season in seventh place. Veteran Charlie Mead, a native of Vermillion, Alberta, was the club's top hitter, with a .328 average. He led the league with 31 home runs and 116 RBIs. Joe Orrell was the Stampeders' best pitcher, with 13 wins and 13 losses. Only 40,106 paying customers, the lowest number in the league, showed up at Buffalo Stadium.

The biggest story of the Stampeders' season was Buffalo Stadium itself. Built for amateur baseball teams to play in, the deepest part of the park was only 336 feet from home. During the first home stand of 12 games, home and visiting teams hit a total of 48 home runs. A six-foot-high chicken wire fence was constructed above the wooden outfield fence, but this did little except stop low line drives. At the end of the season, the Stampeders led all teams in Class A baseball with 146 home runs, most of them hit at home.

The Calgary Stampeders' northern neighbors, the Edmonton Eskimos, fared much better, both on the field and in the stands. The drive for a professional team for Alberta's capital city was spearheaded by John Ducey, known affectionately around the town as "Edmonton's Mr. Baseball." He had been a player and umpire in his earlier days, had been in charge of several senior baseball teams, and, in his several decades in the game, had made many valuable contacts in the baseball world. Ducey gathered 24 Edmonton businessmen to invest in the team, attended baseball's winter meetings to find a manager and acquire players, and successfully petitioned the City Council for $45,000 for upgrades to Renfrew Park, which had been constructed in 1933.

Ducey and manager Bob Sturgeon put together a far more experienced team than the one that had been assembled in Calgary. In addition to one former major leaguer

Like many former Negro Leaguers, Leon Day, who was elected to the Hall of Fame in 1995, finished his career in the minor leagues. Here (left) he congratulates an unidentified player of the Edmonton Eskimos (Western International League), with whom he played in 1953 (courtesy City of Edmonton Archives, EA-254–53).

(Sturgeon), there were six regulars with Triple A experience; a one-time Negro Leaguer and future member of the Hall of Fame, Leon Day; and a handful of Class A veterans, the most notable of whom was pitcher John Conant. The Eskimos started the season slowly, not reaching the .500 mark until early June. However, they caught fire during June, winning 25 and losing nine, but were edged out by Salem by one game for the first half title. The second half was not so successful, as the club finished in fifth place. The Eskimos' top performers were two class A veterans, outfielder Clint Weaver and Conant. Weaver's .354 average was second best in the WIL; Conant's 24 wins was tops in the league. Both were voted to the league all-star team. The final attendance figure was only 92,758, the best in the WIL, but nonetheless a disappointment. Two factors, neither under the club's control, accounted for this lower figure. May was colder and damper than usual and in August, the city of Edmonton endured a plague of mosquitoes, which made attending games painful.

1954. Shortly after Labor Day, 1953, the WIL entered into what was becoming its annual off-season of discontent. Financial problems had been reported from Victoria, Salem, Wenatchee, and Spokane. In the final week of the season, a report from Calgary noted that the Stampeders were expected to lose $72,000. The Spokane Indians, Vancouver Capilanos, and Victoria Tyees, playing in three of the league's biggest markets, saw a combined attendance drop of 123,000. However, by January 1954, all 10 teams confirmed that they would be operating.

As spring training approached, several directors of the Calgary Stampeders announced that they were unwilling to invest more money in the club. And then, on April 2, manager Gene Lillard reported from Porterville, California, home of the team's spring training camp, that there were no uniforms, equipment, or money. In early May, the WIL took over the franchise from the ownership group because it had neither submitted the required performance bond nor sent the players meal money. The Stampeders were permitted to remain in the league when Lacey sent the necessary funds.

By the end of May, the Spokane Indians were also in financial trouble. Owner Ray Hotchkiss turned his franchise over to the league. In addition, the Salem and Lewiston and Tri-City franchises were in trouble and the first two were threatening not to make upcoming road trips to Alberta. In Calgary, in early June, a mid-week, day-night double header at Buffalo Stadium drew only 125 spectators. It was also reported that the Stampeders' bank account was down to sixty-two dollars.

Victoria was the club most hurt by the collapse of the two teams. Under their rookie manager 27-year-old Don Pries, a four-year veteran of the team, they were just managing to meet their payroll and other expenses. They had been unable to play four home games in mid–June when a strike of city workers shut down operations at Royal Athletic Park and forced their series with Vancouver, always a popular one with fans, to move to the mainland. Then, when the WIL hastily revised a schedule for the last three weeks of the first half, another home series was switched to an away series. The Tyees finished the first half of the season in last place (in the now eight-team league) 12 games behind the Vancouver Capilanos.

The Vancouver Capilanos were a much different team from the one that finished the 1953 season. General Manager Dewey Soriano had been promoted to the same position with the parent Seattle Rainiers; manager Harvey Story had been let go; and their top pitcher Pete Hernandez (18 wins and 10 losses) was promoted to the Double A Texas

League a few weeks into the season. Their roles were taken over by one person: Bill Brenner. The former Vancouver catcher turned pitcher became the new general manager, field manager and a part of the starting rotation. The club won its opening game but stayed in the middle of the pack until May 12, when it took over first place, a position it would occupy for the remainder of the first half of the season.

Heading into the season, the Edmonton Eskimos' general manager John Ducey wanted a contending team, a stable situation in Calgary, and decent weather. The team he assembled, along with returning manager Bob Sturgeon, included some of the best players from the 1953 squad. He fought hard for Calgary to remain in the league, lending a financial hand, agreeing to switch home dates with the Stampeders so that the struggling Calgary team would be able to open its home season in warmer weather. The Eskimos won more than they lost during the first half, but finished in third place, 6.5 games behind Vancouver. The early cold weather and the uncertainty of the Calgary situation (along with worry that a Stampeders collapse might force Edmonton out of the league) hurt attendance. By June 21, the day of Calgary and Spokane's departure, only 13,098 fans had attended Eskimo home games.

Officials of the WIL teams greeted the opening of the second half of the 1954 season with cautious optimism. The Victoria Tyees hoped to sell enough second half season tickets at $12.50 apiece and to field a competitive enough team to attract more single game spectators in order to raise the cash to make it to Labor Day. The Vancouver Capilanos hoped to continue their winning ways and not to be too badly hurt at the gate during the first week of August when the British Empire Games, an international multi-sport athletic festival, was in town. Edmonton hoped to win more games, stay in contention until the last day of the season and to avoid a mosquito infestation like that of 1953.

The Tyees' hopes were not realized. They did start the second half on a winning note. On July 18, their 5–3 record was enough to put them into first place by one game. But there followed a disastrous nine game losing streak. On August 2, only 327 showed up to Athletic Park. The team didn't have enough money to make an upcoming 10-day road trip. On August 3, the board of directors made the decision to return the franchise to the league. When the team disbanded, it had drawn 28,651 fans.

The Edmonton Eskimos got neither the mosquitoes nor the wins. Their 29–35 second half record put them in fifth place, 12 games behind Lewiston. However, they did attract the fans. Even though the Eskimos' final attendance figure of 67,746 was a drop of 25,012 from 1953, it was still the best in the WIL.

For the Vancouver Capilanos the second half was a disappointment on the field and at the box office. They finished in fourth place, 5.5 games behind Lewison, and their final attendance total of 55,217 was their lowest since before World War II. The British Empire Games had captured sports fans' interest and entertainment dollars as well as nearly all of the space in the sports pages. After the conclusion of the Games, their attention turned to the exhibition games and first league game of the British Columbia Lions, an expansion franchise in the Canadian Football League. The Capilanos led the league in placements on the all-star team. Bill Brenner, whose 21 wins was best in the WIL, was named pitcher; Marv Williams, a 34-year-old former Negro Leaguer, led the league with a .362 average and was named all-star second baseman; K Chorlton, the league's number two hitter with a .349 average, was an all-star outfielder, while Jimmy Clark was selected as the all-star shortstop. The Capilanos won the best-of-seven championship series four games to none against Lewiston for its third WIL pennant of the post World War II era.

The game was also the last to be played in the WIL. Within days officials of the Lewiston Broncs and the Tri-City Braves announced that they wanted Vancouver and Edmonton out of the league. John Ducey, Edmonton's general manager, refused to leave the league and threatened to take legal action if the Eskimos were driven out. And so, on September 26, the American directors voted to disband the WIL. Soon after, they formed a new Class B league, the Northwest League, composed only of American teams. Vancouver would be without a professional team for only a year when the Oakland Oaks of the Pacific Coast League were transferred to British Columbia. Victoria would field a team in the Northwest League for three years in the late 1970s, and, in 1977, Calgary began the first of eight seasons in the rookie level Pioneer League. Edmonton did not have another professional baseball team until 1981, when the Ogden (Utah) A's became the Edmonton Trappers of the Pacific Coast League.

PROVINCIAL LEAGUE (Class C): Drummondville Cubs/Athletics (1952–1955), Granby Phillies (1952–1953), Quebec Braves (1952–1955), Sherbrooke Indians (1953–1955), Saint-Hyacinthe Athletics (1952–1953), St. Jean Canadians (1952–1955), Trois-Rivières Yankees/ Phillies (1952–1955), Thetford Mines Mineurs (1953–1955)

1952. The Class C Provincial League opened the 1952 season with six teams returning from the previous year. The Sherbrooke club was taking a year's leave while a new stadium to replace the one that had burned down the night the Athletics had won the 1951

The infield of LaFramboise Park racetrack served as the baseball field of the Saint-Hyacinthe Saints of the Provincial League. Notice the players' benches near the foul lines and, to the far right, the horse stables (courtesy Daniel Papillon).

championship was being built. Farnham, which played in the smallest city in the circuit, had withdrawn.

Although there were no new teams in the league, it had a very different look on the field. Only 10 players were returning to the teams they had played for in 1951. The average age had dropped from 28.2 to 23.6. Of the 19 who were over 30, six were playing managers. The change was a result of the league becoming essentially a farm team league, developing players for the major league teams whose nicknames they bore. Five would eventually make the major leagues, the most notable being 19-year-old rookie Ed Charles of Quebec City, who would finish his career as a member of the "Miracle New York Mets," the 1969 World Series champions. He would play with the 1961 Vancouver Mounties of the Pacific Coast League, and make his major league debut in 1962 with the Kansas City Athletics.

Quebec City, the only club with a major league affiliation in 1951, once again had an agreement with the Boston Braves. Saint-Hyacinthe was affiliated with the Philadelphia Athletics and Granby with the Philadelphia Phillies. St Jean had a working agreement with Pittsburgh and Drummondville with Washington. Only Trois-Rivières was without a full major league hookup, although it did receive player help from the New York Yankees.

For big league clubs, Quebec's well-deserved reputation of being hospitable to African American players made the Provincial League an ideal destination for its young black prospects. Seventeen black players performed in the league in 1952, and one of them, pitcher Bob Trice, would, in 1953, become the first African American player for the Philadelphia Athletics.

Provincial League fans enjoyed watching two very close races during the season: one for first place and the other for fourth place and the final playoff berth. Third place belonged to St. Jean from July 7 onward. The Granby Phillies took permanent possession of sixth and last place by late May. Quebec City Braves and Saint-Hyacinthe Athletics traded first and second places regularly until early August, when Saint-Hyacinthe moved into first place for good. The regular season championship was decided when the two faced each other on the final day of the season, with Saint-Hyacinthe the winner over Quebec City. The Athletics' Al Pinkston, a veteran of the Negro Leagues, won the triple crown with his .360 batting average, 30 home runs and 121 RBIs. Teammate Bob Trice had a league-best .842 win-loss percentage. He was tied with teammate Stan Wotychowisz, John Wingo of Trois-Rivières, and Thomas Smith of Drummondville for the most wins, with 16.

The Trois-Rivières Yankees, who had been mired in fifth place since late June, went on a streak of 11 wins and two losses as the season wound down, beating Drummondville on the second to last day of the season to pass the Cubs and take fourth place.

Attendance for the regular season dropped by 186,000 from 1951. Well over half of that was a result of the fact that Sherbrooke, which had drawn over 100,000 fans in 1951, was sitting out the season. Granby and Drummondville suffered losses of 43,000 and 47,000, respectively. Poor weather—there were 72 rainouts during the season—cut into the attendance of all teams. Quebec led the league with 111,800 paying customers.

In the semi-finals, Saint-Hyacinthe spotted St. John a two-game lead before coming back to take four consecutive games and earn a berth in the finals. Quebec City had a more difficult time in its series with Trois-Rivières. The Braves lost three in a row, before taking the next four. Saint-Hyacinthe won the first three games of the finals, but the Braves once again came back with four straight victories to win the championship.

1953. During the off-season, the Provincial League expanded to eight teams. After a one-year absence, Sherbrooke returned. The Indians were owned by the Cleveland Indians who supplied the front office staff, manager, and players and covered all operating expenses of the club. Thetford Mines, a city of 25,000 in the center of Quebec's asbestos mining country, was also granted a franchise. Nicknamed the Mineurs, they were affiliated with the St. Louis Browns. Four of the returning clubs maintained their major league working agreements from the previous year. The Washington Senators dropped Drummondville as a farm team and the club, under completely new local ownership and management, was renamed the Royals. The Brooklyn Dodgers provided a manager, Al Gionfriddo, and some players. The New York Yankees again provided some player help to the Trois-Rivières Yankees. There were few returning players, 26 in all, with seven of Quebec City's championship club back. The number of players over 30 dropped to 10, five of whom were playing managers.

By the middle of the season, it became clear that two clubs would not be challengers for first place. The Saint-Hyacinthe Athletics, who had lost their two major stars, Bob Trice and Al Pinkston, were two games below .500 and in fifth place. They would drop to seventh by the end of the season. Drummondville lost 12 straight early in the season and dropped deep into the cellar, where it remained for the rest of the season.

Until early August, three clubs were in the race for first place: the Sherbrooke Indians, Granby Phillies, and Quebec City Braves. Then the Indians won 30 of 40 games during August, winning the regular season championship with an 11.5 game lead over Granby, and 12.5 over Quebec City. Thetford Mines earned fourth place and the final playoff spot by edging out Trois-Rivières by a half game and St. Jean by a game.

John Waters of Sherbrooke won the batting championship with a .348 average; his teammate Robert Diers hit 26 home runs, tops in the league. Thetford Mines' William Diemer and Saint-Hyacinthe's Mike Munsinger led all pitchers, each with 20 wins. (In later years, Munsinger would achieve minor notoriety when his then ex-wife, German-born Gerda, became enmeshed in a sex-spy scandal involving a cabinet minister in Canada's federal government.) The attendance crown once again went to Quebec City, whose 115,943 paid admissions represented an over 4,000 increase from the previous year. However, five teams had a combined attendance drop of 137,219.

In spite of its fine regular season record, the Sherbrooke team lost its semi final series four games to one to the Quebec City Braves. Granby defeated Thetford Mines four games to two. Granby quickly jumped to a three-games-to-none lead over the Quebec City Braves in the finals. However, again the Braves won four in a row to repeat as Provincial League playoff champions.

1954. The playoffs over, league officials entered an off-season not unlike that of many other leagues in the lower minors: dealing with the financial crises facing some of the franchises and working to make sure that there would be enough teams "alive" in the spring to form a viable league. In late October, the Cleveland Indians announced that they did not intend to operate a franchise in Sherbrooke, citing poor attendance and losses of $25,000 However, by mid–November, they reversed their decision. Once Sherbrooke was back in, the league announced that Saint-Hyacinthe, whose finances had been devastated by the 28,000 drop in attendance, had asked for a year's leave and that there would be six teams for 1954, Quebec City, Sherbrooke, Trois-Rivières, Thetford Mines, Drummondville and either St. Jean or Granby. Granby officials decided to return the franchise to the league. The Philadelphia Athletics shifted their affiliation from Saint-Hyacinthe to Drummondville. The Philadelphia Phillies would now send players to Trois-Rivières instead of Granby. In addition to the Sherbrooke-Cleveland tie up, the Quebec City would remain with the Milwaukee Braves, Thetford Mines with the (now) Baltimore Orioles, and St. Jean with Pittsburgh. As in 1952 and 1953, the 1954 season featured many new young players, 27 of whom were under 20 years of age. Only seven, including three playing managers, were over 30.

By mid–May, after 16 playing dates, only 24 games had been played, the rest having been cancelled because of rain. By June 4, 45 games had been postponed. In the first 10 days of June, Drummondville and Thetford Mines managed to get in seven games; St Jean, six; Sherbrooke, five; and Quebec City and Trois-Rivières only four.

By mid–June, Quebec City and Sherbrooke were in a battle for first place, Drummondville and St. Jean were close behind, while Trois-Rivières held fifth place and Thetford Mines occupied sixth place. As the season progressed, the Mineurs sank lower and lower into the cellar, finishing 37 games out of first place. After the games of July 1, four and a half games separated first-place Sherbrooke and fifth-place Trois-Rivières. In late August, the Quebec City Braves took over first place and won the regular season championship by 4.5 games over Sherbrooke. Trois-Rivières was third, eight games behind, while Drummondville finished fourth, 20.5 games out of first. In the semi-finals, Drummondville defeated Sherbrooke four games to three, as did Quebec City against Trois-Rivières. Quebec City defeated Drummondville four games to two to take its third consecutive playoff title.

Quebec City dominated the annual awards: Mike Fandozzi, all-star second baseman, won the batting championship with a .331 average; Matthew Peoplis had the best earned run average, 2.34, and was one voted to the all-star team, as were shortstop Julio Palazzini and manager George McQuinn. Sherbrooke outfielder Bill Williamson, who hit a league-leading 27 home runs, and teammate Robert Stevens, first baseman, also made the all-star team. The Indians' John Luthern had a league-high 20 wins. Trois-Rivières placed three players on the all-star team: third baseman David Kiley, catcher Eddie Sack, and pitcher Paul Beitz, whose .783 win-loss percentage was the league's best. Drummondville placed outfielders David Shea and Bill Stuifbergen, who tied for league lead with 118 RBIs, on the team.

Once again, the Provincial League's teams experienced extreme drops in regular season attendance. Only Drummondville, who attracted 1,100 more fans than in 1953, showed a gain. The combined losses of the other five clubs totaled 62,982. Quebec City was once again the top draw, with 105,269 paying spectators.

1955. During the off-season, the big question in the Provincial League was how many and which teams would be back. During the fall of 1954, officials of the Philadelphia Athletics announced that the major league team would be relocating to Kansas City, Missouri, and that it would no longer operate the Triple A franchise in Ottawa, or the Provincial League one in Drummondville. The Cleveland Indians had also announced that they would no longer run the Sherbrooke franchise, having lost over $14,000 during the 1954 season. If a local ownership group would take over the club, the Indians would enter into a full working agreement and supply 16 players and a manager. A local group raised enough money to save the Sherbrooke franchise. The Kansas City Athletics formed a working agreement with a new franchise in Burlington, Vermont. Quebec City remained with

Milwaukee, Trois-Rivières with the Philadelphia Phillies, St. Jean with Pittsburgh, and Thetford Mines with Baltimore. Drummondville, without an affiliation, left the league.

During the first two months of the 1955 season, the Quebec City Braves and St. Jean Pirates traded first and second place. And by mid–July, the questions were: which of the two would win the pennant; would Burlington or Trois-Rivières finish third; and would either Sherbrooke or Thetford Mines end up with worst record? St. Jean took over first place at the end of July and remained there, finishing the season five games ahead of Quebec City. Burlington finished third, 20.5 games out of first, and Trois-Rivières fourth, 24 out. Sherbrooke was fifth, 8.5 games out of the playoffs, and Thetford Mines occupied the cellar, 44 games behind the leader. In the playoffs, Quebec City defeated Trois-Rivières, four games to two. Burlington surprised league champion St. Jean, winning four games to one. In the finals, Quebec City lost the first game to Burlington before reeling off four straight victories, to win its fourth-straight Provincial League pennant.

For both the Sherbrooke Indians and Thetford Mines Mineurs, on-field performance and in-the-stands attendance were so dismal that, in early July, both clubs requested an emergency meeting of the Provincial League to discuss the possibility of adopting a split-season format, hoping that with a fresh second-half start, they might perform better and in doing so draw more fans and lessen their financial woes. The other members of the league rejected the request. However, an emergency meeting was held at the end of the month to determine whether the Indians, deep in debt, could finish the season. With league assistance, they were able to do so.

On the field, although the Quebec City Braves' all-star outfielder Bill Robinson won the batting championship with a .342 average, St. Jean players dominated the individual awards. Bill Causion belted a league-leading 24 home runs; Dean Lakatosh posted a 17–3 record and Ramon Salgado had a 2.21 earned run average. Salgado and five other members of the club—Francis Glamp (third base), Walter Hardy (shortstop), John Wrye (outfield), Frank Washington (outfield), and Valmy Thomas (catcher)—were named to the all-star team.

In the stands, attendance dropped again. Sixty-three thousand fewer fans came to games than had in 1954. Each of the five returning teams had a decline in attendance. Trois-Rivières showed the largest decline, with 47,000 fewer fans than the previous year. Quebec City's 101,695 was again tops in the league.

In October, the league reported that St. Jean, Thetford Mines, Quebec City, and Trois-Rivières would operate next season. Burlington, which had sold several players to balance its books, also confirmed that it would be back. By late winter, it was clear that Sherbrooke would not be back. Sorel, Quebec, was accepted to fill the vacancy, but, in early April, Provincial League officials announced that the city did not qualify for membership. In the meantime, neither St Jean nor Trois-Rivières, both of whom were in financial difficulties, had acquired a working agreement with a major league club.

In April, Quebec City, Thetford Mines, and Burlington, teams that had renewed their affiliations with Milwaukee, Baltimore, and Kansas City, respectively, began training at those major league teams' minor league camps. But, without six teams, all with affiliations, the Provincial League could not function. On April 17, the decision was made to suspend operations for the 1956 season. It became one of six leagues (two each at the Class B, C, and D levels) for which 1955 was the last season. Professional baseball would return to the province of Quebec in 1969, when the Montreal Expos entered the National League as an expansion team. Two years later Quebec City and Trois-Rivières would become members of the Class AA Eastern League.

PONY LEAGUE (Class D): Hamilton Cardinals/Red Wings (1952–1956)

1952. The Hamilton Cardinals had always been one of the most financially stable clubs in the PONY League. The circuit's largest city, it regularly led the league in attendance. The 1951 season had been a disappointing one: the Cardinals finished in fourth place and were eliminated in the first round of the playoffs; attendance had dropped 30,000. But 1952 promised to be a better year. Under new manager Hal Contini, the club was predicted to be a serious contender for the league crown.

The club was in a tight race all season and won the regular season championship on the final day of the season. Three Cardinals made the all-star team: third baseman and rookie of the year Hal Miller, outfielder Mike Trapani, and pitcher Bob Umfleet, who joined the club three weeks into the season and then won 23 while only losing four. The team entered the playoffs without power hitter Pidge Brown, who was gravely ill, and lost the first round four games to one against the Hornell Dodgers. Attendance of just over 82,000 was 20,000 more than in the previous year.

1953. Poor weather and mediocre on-field performances put a damper on the opening weeks of the 1953 season. Although the Hal Contini–led club was only seven games behind Jamestown at the beginning of July, a dismal 10 wins and 21 losses in that month basically knocked it out of contention for first. The team finished third, 19.5 games behind Jamestown, and won a playoff berth. Hamilton swept Bradford in three games but lost in the finals four games to one against Jamestown. Perhaps the brightest spot in Hamilton's 1953 season was the pitching of Robert Rauber who was named an all-star for his 15 wins and 11 losses performance. Also named to the all-star team was outfielder Robert Kosis, who belted 18 of the team's 49 homers. The final attendance of 53,291, best in the league, was nearly 30,000 fewer than in 1952.

1954. The season opened under a metaphorical cloud: rumors circulated that, unless attendance increased significantly, the St. Louis Cardinals would no longer operate the Hamilton club. Injuries and poor pitching plagued Hamilton during the first month of play, and by the end of May it was in seventh place. Attendance was averaging only 735 a game. Then in June, pitcher Marty Kutyna was sent to Hamilton from Class C Fresno of the California League. He pitched 17 complete games, had a 10-game winning streak, compiled a 17–8 record and was named to the all-star team. Outfielder Arthur Remsa was also named to the all-star team. The club finished in sixth place, 4.5 games out of the playoffs. The lackluster season and the opening of Hamilton's first television station caused a drop of nearly 12,000 in attendance. The final figure was 41,379.

1955. At the end of September 1954, the St. Louis Cardinals announced that they would no longer sponsor (which basically meant covering all expenses) their Hamilton affiliate. The major league had lost over three quarters of a million dollars in running their farm system and decided to cut back on the number of Class D affiliates. Hamilton civic leaders set about creating a community owned club to which St. Louis would send players.

The 1955 season would be Hamilton's best since it had returned to the PONY League in 1946. The team won its opening game and by the end of the first week was in first place, a position it never relinquished. The Cardinals finished eight games in front of second place Bradford, with an outstanding 82–43 record. Four players, including all-stars

Walter Brown (catcher) and Arthur Barrett (third base), batted over .300. Gary Geiger, an 18-year-old pitcher who won 20 and lost 7 and hurled 25 complete games including a no hitter, as well as playing 41 games as a position player, also made the all-star team. He would go on to a 12-year major league career—as a position player. Player-manager Eddie Lyons was also named to the all-star team.

Geiger did not get to display his pitching talents in the playoffs. He was suffering from bursitis and, along with Bufort Cloer, was sent to St. Louis for medical examinations. Also absent from the playoffs were pitcher David Lutz (16 wins and four losses) and infielder Eugene Mirandi; both were schoolteachers who had to report for work. Even without these players, the Cardinals dominated the playoffs, defeating Wellsville, two games to one before taking the finals in three straight against Corning.

But in spite of the on-field success and the aggressive promotions at home games (including bingo nights and giveaways, one of which was a mink coat), the Hamilton Cardinals faced an uncertain future. Attendance increased by 12,000; but the team lost $15,000. In September all but one of the directors resigned and St. Louis announced it would not renew its working agreement with the team.

1956. One of the Hamilton directors, Tony Tatti, became team owner. He hired his Jean Marini, his niece, and Jean Hodge (who had worked in baseball front offices in Ottawa, Galveston, Texas; and Winston-Salem, North Carolina) to run the team. The women, both 21 years old, pooled their resources to purchase majority interest in the club, which they renamed the Red Wings. They hired Cart Howarton, a career minor leaguer, to his first managerial position and then placed ads in *The Sporting News* seeking players.

The team the Red Wings fielded at the beginning of May was, to say the least, inexperienced. Of the 23 players on the roster, 15 were rookies, 13 of whom would be playing in their only professional season. During the first 18 days of May, the Red Wings won six and lost eight games. Highlights included one game in which Hamilton pitchers walked 19 men and another in which the team lost 22 to 4. Seven games were rained out. Only 1,459 attended the first five home games and, on May 17, for a game played in 35-degree weather, only 63 showed up. By this time, Tatti, who owned a construction company, had been sentenced to six months in jail for attempting to bribe a government official.

On May 14, Jean Marini announced that the Hamilton franchise had been returned to the league. At the same time, the Bradford team was also in serious financial difficulties. On May 18, both teams folded. The Red Wings had debts of $14,000. Hamilton, the largest city in Class D baseball, was without a franchise and would be until 1988, when another team named the Cardinals and also affiliated with St. Louis would rejoin the league, now called the New York Pennsylvania League.

NORTHERN LEAGUE (Class C/Class A): Winnipeg Goldeyes (1954–1964)

In the early 1950s, Winnipeg, Manitoba, which had the fourth largest metropolitan population (over 350,000) in Canada, did not have a professional baseball team and had not had one since the Northern League temporarily suspended operations in 1942. However, in 1953, two events took place that led to the lack being rectified. First the city decided that the newly built Winnipeg Stadium, created for the Blue Bombers Canadian Football League team, should be modified to include a baseball field and grandstand behind what would be home plate. Winnipeg "Sportsmen" applied for a franchise in the American Association but were turned down. They then purchased the Sioux Falls Canaries of the Class C Northern League (which had teams in Minnesota, Wisconsin, and North and South Dakota).

At the same time, the St. Louis Cardinals, the major leagues' most southerly team, had decided to racially integrate. Winnipeg, whose teams in the semi-pro Mandak League were racially integrated, would be a hospitable place to send their young black players. The Cardinals signed an affiliation agreement with the Winnipeg team in January 1954.

1954. The Winnipeg Goldeyes (named after an area fish) were a mix of rookies and second- and third-year players. Mickey O'Neill, who had played nine major league seasons and been a minor league manager for 11, was in charge of the 1954 team, which averaged 21.9 years old, second youngest in the league.

The Goldeyes' first six games, all on the road, were cancelled: five because of rain, one because of snow. The team then won two games before returning home only to have the home opener cancelled. The Goldeyes split a day-night double header on May 8. The day game drew 2,580; but only 965 showed up in the evening. Attendance remained low during the first six weeks of the season as the team sank into sixth place. The weather remained cool and, on May 31, Winnipeg's first television station went on the air. However, by mid–July, the team's performance, the weather, and attendance had improved. The club moved into the first division and in one week, 17,000 fans turned up at Winnipeg Stadium. The Goldeyes finished the season in third place, with a record of 73 wins and 60 losses, before losing in the first round of the playoffs, two games to one to Fargo-Moorhead. The team was not strong offensively, posting only a .261 team batting average. Pitching was very strong, with Leverette Spencer (14 wins, seven losses) and William Smith (17 wins, eight losses) named to the all-star team. The Goldeyes' attendance of 100,458 was tops in the Northern League.

1955. Although the Goldeyes finished in the first division, thus qualifying for the playoffs, and led the Northern League in attendance (84,668 and 64,459), their 1955 and 1956 seasons were relatively lackluster. Under new manager Al Kubski, they finished the 1955 season in third place, 12 games behind league leading Eau Claire, and, in the first round of the playoffs, were defeated by St. Cloud in two straight games. The team hit an anemic .255. The pitching was steady with William Howard (12 wins), all-star Cliff Savage (13 wins), Carlos Thorne (12 wins), and Bob Whitaker (14 wins) accounting for 71 percent of Winnipeg's victories. The attendance drop of nearly 16,000 was attributed to poor early season weather, the team's uninspiring performance, and a law prohibiting the playing of professional baseball on Sundays.

1956. The season saw the introduction of the third Goldeye manager in as many years: Vern Benson, a five-year major league veteran, but a rookie manager. The season opened with bad weather: the first game was rained out and when it was played, the temperature at the end of the contest was 33 degrees fahrenheit. Three games in the first home stand were postponed and by May attendance was down by three thousand. The Goldeyes stayed close to first place through the season, but finished in second, five games behind Eau Claire. They then lost a one game playoff against Aberdeen. Outfielder Pedro Cardinal, with a .315 average, best on the team, was named to the all-star team, as was catcher Bob Rikard. Attendance declined by 20,000.

1957. The directors of the Northern League decided to operate 1957 as a split season, with the winners of each half meeting in the championship series. Returning Winnipeg manager Vern Benson was enthusiastic about the Goldeyes' season. St. Louis had dropped one Class A and one Class B affiliate, and it was expected that several players from the two higher classifications would be sent to Manitoba. Five were sent down from Class A and another two from Class B.

At the end of May, Benson's optimism seemed well-founded: the Goldeyes shared first place with Fargo-Moorhead. But a late June slump resulted in a fourth place first-half finish. The slump continued in the early weeks of the second half. However, when several injured players returned to action, the team's bats, along with the weather, warmed up, and by mid–August Winnipeg was in first place. The Goldeyes clinched the second half title with three games to go. First baseman Walt Matthews (.322 batting average and a league-high 100 RBIs) and outfielder Don Brown (.301) both made the all-star team. A total of 86,214 fans—an increase of nearly 22,000 over 1956—watched Winnipeg enjoy its most successful season since rejoining the Northern League. The Goldeyes defeated the Duluth Superior White Sox in three straight games to win the championship.

1958. Their performances earned ten members of the Goldeyes' 1957 championship team, along with manager Vern Benson, promotions to higher classification teams in 1958. Only two regulars returned in 1958. Five of the newcomers (Julio Gotay, Jimmie Schaffer, Dick Hughes, Ray Sadecki and Bob Sadowski) would go on to play in the majors. Former major leaguer Al Unser was the new manager.

After one year, the Northern League abandoned the split-season format: the top four clubs would meet in the playoffs. The Goldeyes played well above .500 and by mid–June were in first place. They held this position until early August, when eight losses in an 11-game span dropped them into second. They ended the season tied with Minot for third place and then lost a one game playoff with regular season leader St. Cloud. Three Goldeyes were named to the all-star team: Julio Gotay at second base (.323 average and a league-best 24 homers); catcher Jimmie Schaffer (.309, 19 home runs), who was also named most valuable player, and pitcher Gary Willison, who topped the league in wins with 19. Attendance increased by 47,000.

1959. In 1959 and 1960, the Goldeyes won both the regular and post-season championships. Under new manager Chase Riddle, the Goldeyes started the 1959 season slowly: by the middle of May, the club was in eighth place. But a month later, a 22–5 streak under their belts, they occupied first place. They never relinquished the lead and clinched the pennant with nearly two weeks to go. Winnipeg completely dominated the regular season. The team batting average, .287, topped the league and five players hit over .300. Three of these, catcher Roberto Herrera (.303), outfielder Rogers Robinson (.323), and shortstop Chico Suarez (.313) were named to the league all-star team. William Carpenter, another all-star, led the league in wins (19), won-lost percentage (.826) and earned run average (1.59). The only disappointing statistic was the attendance: 79,847, down over 11,000 from the previous year. While the local television station's carrying the major league game of the week on Saturdays may have caused some of the decline, the real culprit was he weather: 11 games had been postponed by August 20.

The Goldeyes won the single game semi-final against Fargo-Moorhead, and then defeated Aberdeen two games to one in the final, the two wins being played as a Sunday doubleheader, the first Sunday professional baseball games to be played in Winnipeg. The crowd of 6,734 was the largest for the team in five years and gave hope to the team's owners and fans who believed the figure would bolster the quest for an American Association team for the Manitoba city. (It didn't.)

1960. Although the 1960 Goldeyes' roster was filled with rookies, new manager Whitey Kurkowski got them off to a fast start. By mid–May, the Goldeyes were in first place. The team then bounced between second and fourth before ending July with a seven-game win streak that put them back in first. The Goldeyes won the regular season championship, edging out the Duluth-Superior Dukes on the second to last day of the season—their final record: 72 wins and 51 losses. The close race helped raise attendance by just over 3,000 to 83,014. The Goldeyes defeated Aberdeen in a one game semi-final before taking two straight from Duluth-Superior to claim their second consecutive playoff crown.

Two second-year pros contributed greatly to the team's success: Joe Peterson posted a .311 average, while Johnny Lewis led the league in RBIs, with 104, and home runs, with 10. Both outfielders were named to the all-star team. Dal Maxvill, who would become a member of the great St. Louis Cardinals teams of the 1960s, joined the club in June. Although his average was only .257, his fielding at second base added strength to the infield.

1961. The Goldeyes' next four seasons were disappointing. Winnipeg finished sixth (in a six-team league), then seventh (of eight teams), followed by two fourth place finishes in a six-team league. As the Goldeyes made no post-season appearances in these seasons, fans had little to capture their interest in the late weeks of summer. Early in the 1961 season, Winnipeg found itself in fifth place. In an unusual move, the St. Louis Cardinals sent beleaguered manager Grover Resinger to the Billings Mustangs of the Pioneer League and brought Mustangs manager Owen Friend to Winnipeg. The Goldeyes went on to win only eight of the last 37 games of the season for a final record of 46 wins, 77 losses. A total of 45,874 showed up at Winnipeg Stadium, a drop of 3,000. Outfielder Carlos Dore, a future major leaguer, posted a .307 average and made the all-star team. Other future major leaguers included returnee Dal Maxvill (who was called up to Triple A Charleston in mid–June), Tom Hilgendorf, George Kernek, and Jeoff Long.

1962. The Northern League added two teams for the 1962, Bismark and Minot, and, after a year without post-season games, resumed the four-team playoff system. During the season, the Goldeyes fielded eight returning players, the parent Cardinals giving their younger prospects more time to develop. One of these, pitcher Tom Hilgendorf, earned a spot on the league all-star team, posting 11 wins against nine losses and a 2.66 ERA. Newcomers included future major leaguers Elrod Hendricks, Larry Jaster, Tommy Matchick, and Chuck Taylor.

Grand Forks maintained first place throughout the season, with six teams, including Winnipeg, in the hunt for a playoff berth. The Goldeyes lost six of their last seven games and finished seventh, four games out of a playoff spot. Surprisingly, final home attendance was 83,645, up over 37,000 from 1961.

1963. During the winter of 1962–63, minor league baseball was completely restructured: Classes B, C, and D, were abolished and the surviving leagues in those categories, one of which was the Northern League, were reclassified as Class A. The purpose of the reorganization was to cut expenses for the major league clubs, who would now be required to sponsor only five or six teams. The Northern League once again became a six-team league. With the exception of Winnipeg, all the teams in the league had experienced considerable financial difficulties. The Goldeyes, whose 1963 attendance of 61,377 was 21,000 higher than that of the next-best-drawing club, were virtually carrying the league.

The Goldeyes opened the season with nine returning players and manager Fred Koenig and resumed where they had left off at the end of the previous season: in a prolonged slump. They won only two of their first fourteen games. They ended the season in fourth place, 21.5 games out of first. There were no playoffs that year. The league instituted what were called the Baukol Playoffs (named after league president Brooks Baukol), in which each of the last 30 games a club played counted in both the regular season standings and a special August-only set of standings. The idea was to increase interest and attendance during the last four weeks of the season by giving all clubs a second chance. It didn't work: overall attendance was down by 25,000; Winnipeg's dropped by 22,000. The Goldeyes, by the way, finished fifth in the Baukol standings. The bright spot of the season was the performance of future major leaguer Coco Laboy, who led the Goldeyes with a .292 average and 21 homers.

1964: The Goldeyes' season opened with a home loss, followed by five rainouts, nine losses and three wins. By mid–June, Winnipeg had moved up to .500, but was stuck in fourth place, where they remained until the beginning of August, at which time they began their annual tailspin, winning seven and losing 19. Surprisingly, they managed a fourth-place finish, 17 games out of first. Because of their August performance, the Goldeyes finished last in the Baukol "playoffs." The Goldeyes did well at the gate, attracting 85,425. It was not because of the team on the field, but because of an aggressive marketing campaign which included special season ticket rates for families and

In 1964, his rookie season, 19-year-old Steve Carlton appeared in 12 games for the Winnipeg Goldeyes of the short season Class A Northern League. He struck out 79 batters in 75 innings and, the next year, began his 24-year Hall of Fame career, debuting with the St. Louis Cardinals (National Baseball Hall of Fame and Museum, Cooperstown, N.Y., 443-67 NBL).

students, special nights at the ballpark, and several giveaways. All-star outfielder Felix DeLeon had a .338 average with 27 home runs and 96 RBIs. In mid–June, a young rookie and future Hall-of-Famer named Steve Carlton joined the club. Used sparingly, he won four and lost four, but struck out over a batter an inning.

After the season, general manager Terry Hind made the decision to end the Goldeyes' affiliation with the St. Louis Cardinals and began an unsuccessful search for a new affiliation. Meanwhile, the league made major changes. In 1965, it would become a short-season league, beginning in June after college students and recently graduated high schoolers had been drafted by big league clubs. In early January, Grand Forks withdrew from the league, leaving St. Cloud, which was 400 miles from Winnipeg, as the closest Northern League team. Soon after, Goldeye officials announced that Winnipeg was dropping out of the league. It would return in 1969, but then only for a year.

Struggling to Survive in the 70s

Northern League, International League, Eastern League, Northwest League, Pioneer League

By the beginning of the 1970s, the main purpose of the minor leagues was the development of players. The major league clubs covered spring training expenses and the salary of a manger, supplemented salaries at the Triple and Double A levels (anything above $450 and $150, respectively) and paid all salaries at Single A and Rookie levels. Owners of minor league teams had to pay many on and off field expenses: uniforms, equipment, stadium rental, team travel, front office salaries, along with insurance, utilities, and office expenses. With the increased availability of televised major league games as well as other options potential fans had for spending their recreational budgets, it was not an easy task to operate a minor league franchise successfully. From the late 1960s to 1976, yearly attendance in the minor leagues averaged just under 11 million fans. During the first seven years of the 1970s, individual Triple A teams drew over a quarter of a million fans only 18 times. However, 30 times teams at this level drew under 100,000. In the lower classifications, there were over 100 times that clubs averaged less than a thousand fans a game during a season. Much of the offseason business in the minor leagues involved searching for new cities in which to relocate failing franchises and often to find enough teams to create viable leagues.

Between 1969 and 1977, Canadian cities hosted two major league franchises (Montreal, which joined the National League in 1969, and Toronto, which joined the American in 1977), two Triple A clubs (Winnipeg and Vancouver), four Double A teams (Quebec City, Trois-Rivières, Sherbrooke, and Thetford Mines), two short season Class A clubs (Winnipeg and New Westminster), and three rookie level squads (Lethbridge, Calgary, and Medicine Hat).

NORTHERN LEAGUE *(Short Season Class A): Winnipeg Goldeyes (1969)*

1969. In 1969, Winnipeg returned to the Northern League, now a short-season Class A circuit, as an affiliate of the Kansas City Royals, who were beginning their first year as an American League expansion team. Acquiring a franchise in the Northern League may have been intended by media mogul Randy Moffatt as the first step toward acquiring a franchise in the Triple A American Association, which had resumed operations in 1969. In 1970, it was slated to expand by two teams and Winnipeg, with a metropolitan population of over half-a-million, was mentioned as a possible location for an expansion franchise. With the Goldeyes now back in Organized Baseball, Moffatt's chances of entering the American Association in 1970 seemed good.

The team that manager Spider Jorgensen opened the season with was young and inexperienced: the 11 players who appeared in the Goldeyes' first game had never played a professional game before. Throughout the season nearly all of the Goldeyes were rookies, making the Winnipeg club the most inexperienced in the league. The results bore witness to that fact. The Goldeyes lost the opening game at Sioux Falls, came home with one win against five losses, played consistently below .500 ball throughout the season and finished in sixth and last place. Four of the 29 players did make the major leagues, the most notable being 19-year-old pitcher Doug Bird, who appeared in 432 major league games over 11 seasons. Fans' response to the on-field product was as cool as the early summer weather had been: 18,077 attended games.

During the off-season, Goldeyes officials, along with Winnipeg civic leaders, and with the support of the Montreal Expos, who'd entered the National League in 1969, applied for an expansion franchise in the American Association. The bid was rejected and the Expos placed a Triple A team in Buffalo. Goldeyes officials began preparing for the 1970 Northern League season.

INTERNATIONAL LEAGUE (Triple A): Winnipeg Whips (1970–1971)

1970. In early June, shortly before the scheduled opening of the Northern League season, it was announced that the Buffalo Bisons of the International League were relocating to Winnipeg. The Expos' Triple A franchise was in serious financial difficulty. A mediocre team, playing in an aging ballpark located in an increasingly dangerous neighborhood, was deep in last place and attracting only 300 fans a game. The International League revoked the local owners' franchise, which it turned over to the Expos, to locate wherever they wished. Because the nearest club to Winnipeg was in Toledo, Ohio, over 1,600 miles to the east, visiting teams had to fly to Manitoba and the Expos agreed to pay the airfare from Toledo. They also purchased the Goldeyes from Randy Moffat and transferred them to Watertown, South Dakota.

Renamed the Whips, the eighth-place team, which was seven games behind seventh place Louisville, was greeted enthusiastically by the public, the media, and civic leaders. An opening day parade and a chamber of commerce luncheon were held on June 19, followed by a game at which 7,021 spectators watched the new home team defeat Syracuse 4–2. Although much appreciated by local fans, the team did not improve appreciably after its relocation, although the Whips did manage to slip into seventh place on the last day of the season. The Whips had no .300 hitters. Ernie McAnally, who in 1971 would begin a four-season career with the Expos, won 12, lost 13 and struck out 178. It was an expensive season for the Expos, who spent close to a half-million dollars operating a Triple A team. The combined attendance for games in Buffalo and Winnipeg was 89,901, second lowest among the 24 Triple A teams.

1971. The Montreal Expos and Winnipeg Whips approached the 1971 season with cautious optimism. If they could field a competitive team and if the weather were neither too cold nor too rainy, the attendance might be large enough to cover the expenses. Neither of these "ifs" materialized. The early season weather was brutally cold. The opening game drew 1,958, the next two just over 300 each. At the end of the season just under

96,000 had showed up at Winnipeg Stadium. The figure would have been much lower had an overflow crowd of 15,187 not attended a pony giveaway night in mid–June.

Much of the cause for the low attendance was a result of the club's poor showing on the field. The 43 men who appeared in a Whips uniform in 1971 were a motley bunch of career minor leaguers, players who'd had very brief major league careers, young players who had been rushed up to Triple A before they were ready, and a taxi squad (nine players shuttled between the Expos and the Whips over the spring and summer). The one young player who would enjoy a long and successful major league career with the Expos was Steve Rogers, who had been drafted out of college in June and assigned directly to the Whips, where he compiled a 3–10 record.

The Whips quickly established themselves as the weakest team in the International League; a seven-game losing streak in May left them in seventh place. By the end of June they were in eighth, a position they solidified with a 12-game losing streak in July. The club was weakened by loss of several players because of injuries and call-ups. The Whips were mathematically eliminated from contention for the regular season championship on August 8. Their final record of 44 wins and 96 losses left them 42 games out of first place.

Signed out of the University of Tulsa in 1971, Steve Rogers spent his rookie year at the Triple A level with the Winnipeg Jets. Two years later, he began a 13-year career with the Montreal Expos (courtesy waybackwinnipeg.com).

It became increasingly apparent that the only way the Whips could survive would be by having the franchise transferred to the American Association, whose teams were located in cities closer to Winnipeg. The other International League clubs did not want Winnipeg in the league, and the American Association was not interested in exchanging one of its more eastern franchises to the International League for the Whips. On November 1, 1971, the Expos announced that the next season, they would operate their highest-level minor league team in Hampton, Virginia. It would be over two decades before Winnipeg would again be the home of a professional baseball team. In 1994, the Winnipeg Goldeyes joined the independent Northern League.

EASTERN LEAGUE (Double A): Quebec City Carnavals/Metros (1971–1977), Trois-Rivières Aigles (1971–1977), Sherbrooke Pirates (1972–1973), Thetford Mines Pirates/Mineurs (1974–1975)

1971. Montreal's desire to place many of their farm teams in Canada led to the return, in 1971, of two Quebec cities to professional baseball. The Double A Eastern League had been granted two expansion franchises and, when the Expos announced their intentions of operating a club in Quebec City in 1971, the league decided to place the other expansion franchise in nearby Trois-Rivières, where it would be stocked by the Cincinnati Reds. With a population of over 170,000, Quebec City was the largest city in the league, while Trois-Rivières, with a population of 55,000, was bigger than all the American Eastern League cities except Reading, Pennsylvania. The Quebec Carnavals and the Trois-Rivières Aigles (Eagles) would play in the stadiums that had been built in the 1930s and had been used by the Trois-Rivières Royals and Quebec Braves when they had played in the Canadian-American and Provincial leagues in the early 1950s.

The fortunes of the 1971 Carnavals and Aigles reflected their being affiliates of the Expos and Reds respectively. Montreal, as a major league expansion franchise, was just beginning to assemble a farm system and had few prospects. By contrast, the Cincinnati Reds entered the 1970s having developed a farm system that supplied players for what was known as the "Big Red Machine," winner of six division titles, four National League pennants, and two World Series championships. Two weeks into the season, the Quebec Carnavals were in fourth and last place of the National Division of the Eastern League, a position they held until the end of the season. Their final record of 64 wins and 75 losses placed them 15 games out of first place. The Aigles caught fire a month into the season, winning 20 and losing 13 in June and going from third to first place. They won 78 games and lost 59 to take the National Division championship by six games over Reading but lost the league championship series three games to one to Elmira. Trois-Rivières placed two players on the all-star team, batting champion and league MVP Gene Locklear (.323 average), and pitcher Mike Ruddell, whose 186 strikeouts and .667 winning percentage topped the league. Aigles manager Jim Snyder was named manager of the year. Although shortstop Pepe Frias and outfielder Pepe Mangual of the Carnavals made the all-star team, no Quebec player hit above .300 and the team average was an anemic .231. Trois-Rivières led the league in attendance (109,346), while Quebec City was second (99,688).

1972. The Eastern League relocated the Waterbury (Connecticut) Pirates, farm team of the Pittsburgh Pirates, to Sherbrooke. Competition in the National Division was tight throughout the season: each team finished with a .500 plus won-loss record and the three Canadian clubs took turns occupying first place during the final two weeks of the season. Heading into the final day, only .002 percent separated Trois-Rivières and Sherbrooke. The Aigles won their last game, while the Pirates lost theirs. For the second consecutive year, Trois-Rivières headed to the league championship series, which it lost in three straight games to the American Division champions, the West Haven Yankees.

The Canadian clubs dominated the league all-star team: Trois-Rivières outfielder Ken Griffey (Senior) and first baseman Dan Driessen, who posted .318 and .322 averages respectively, and pitcher Will McEnaney (11–6); Quebec City's shortstop, Larry Lintz who stole 96 bases, a league record, and catcher Barry Foote, and Sherbrooke's third baseman Fernando Gonzales, who led the league in hitting with a .333 average and was also the league MVP and outfielder David Augustine. Quebec City and Trois-Rivières enjoyed great success at the gate. The Carnavals led the league in attendance with 148,818, the highest attendance figure in the Eastern League since 1950. Trois-Rivières was second with 119,751, while Sherbrooke finished a disappointing third. The city of Sherbrooke experienced exceptionally cold and wet early season weather; the home opener was postponed five times. Given the frigid temperatures, one of the club's early promotional giveaways was appropriate: instead of bat day, the Pirates held hockey stick day! During the season only 66,101 showed up to watch the Pirates.

1973. The Trois-Rivières Aigles and the Sherbrooke Pirates traded first place frequently during the first four months of the season, with Sherbrooke in first place in mid–August. However, the Pirates lost a six game home series to the Reading Phillies, who went on to win the pennant on the final day of the season, edging out Sherbrooke by .004 percentage points. Trois-Rivières and Quebec City finished 9.5 and 10.5 games, respectively, out of first. Sherbrooke placed three players on the all-star team: third baseman Luther Quinn (.294, 16 home runs), shortstop Mario Mendoza (.268), and outfielder Dave Arrington (.311, 14 home runs). Pirates pitcher Kent Tekulve had the league's top winning percentage, .750. Neither Quebec City nor Trois-Rivières placed a player on the all-star team. However, two members of the Carnavals would later achieve fame playing for the Montreal Expos: nineteen-year-old catcher Gary Carter, a future Hall of Famer, and pitcher Steve Rogers. Attendance dropped by 32,000 in Quebec City and 29,000 in Trois-Rivières. Sherbrooke's attendance rose by 4,300 to 70,457. However, the increase in Sherbrooke was not sufficient to prevent a second successive money-losing season. Early in the off-season, it was announced that the club had been sold to new owners and would move to the small Quebec mining city of Thetford Mines, where a new 2,000 seat ballpark would be built at a cost of a quarter of a million dollars.

1974. The Quebec City Carnavals spent the first two and a half months of the 1974 season in third place in the National Division. Then, a 14 win, four losses surge in late June and early July vaulted them into first place, where they stayed. The club won the division championship, edging out Thetford Mines on the last day of the season. Their record of 76 wins and 64 losses put them .007 percent ahead of the Pirates. Trois-Rivières Aigles, finished fourth, 10 games behind the Carnavals. Quebec City lost its semi-final series against Pittsfield two games to none. The Thetford Mines Pirates swept their semi-final against Bristol and the championship series against Pittsfield, both two games to none. The Carnavals' regular season success indicated that the Montreal Expos' fledgling farm system was becoming stronger. Twenty-year-olds Larry Parrish, a third baseman, and outfielder Warren Cromarte made the all-star

Hall of Fame catcher Gary Carter divided 1973, his sophomore professional year, between Peninsula of the International League and Quebec City of the Eastern League. At the end of the 1974 season, he made his debut with the Montreal Expos (National Baseball Hall of Fame and Museum, Cooperstown, N.Y., 16–78–HS–NBL).

team. Cromarte's .336 batting average was second-best in the Eastern League. Thetford Mines dominated league batting statistics. The team batting average of .266 was number one, as was the home run total of 108. Ken Macha had a career year at the plate, with a league leading batting average of .349, along with 21 homers and 100 RBIs. He was named league MVP and all-star catcher. The Pirates also led the league in stolen bases, with 200. Nineteen-year-old Willie Randolph, who would later star with the New York Yankees, accounted for 38 of these.

Eastern League attendance dropped by 154,000 in 1974, with seven teams showing decreases from 1973. Trois-Rivières drew 5,000 fewer fans and Quebec City 34,000. Thetford Mines drew 47,000 less than had watched games in Sherbrooke a year earlier. The Thetford Mines' final total of 22,516 was the lowest in the Eastern League since it had achieved Double A status in 1963.

1975. The Eastern League abandoned its two-division structure in 1975, playing instead a split season, with winners of each half meeting for the championship. The three Canadian teams fared poorly in the first half. Thetford Mines, now affiliated with the Milwaukee Brewers, finished fifth, 14 games out of first; Quebec City sixth, 14.5 out; and Trois-Rivières eighth, 16.5 out. Things didn't improve in the second half. Quebec City was fifth, 10.5 games behind first place Bristol; Trois-Rivières, sixth, 15 behind; and Thetford Mines eighth, 16.5 games behind. Outfielder Gary Roenicke of Quebec City (who had a league-leading 74 RBIs), and second baseman Len Sakata of Thetford Mines were named to the all-star team. Trois-Rivières drew 31,000 fewer fans than in 1975, Quebec City 26,000 fewer, and Thetford Mines 6,000 fewer. The Mineurs' final figure of 16,360 was the second lowest of all-full season minor league clubs. The franchise was moved to Williamsport, Pennsylvania, after the season.

The biggest news regarding the Canadian teams occurred in late May, when the Eastern League revoked the franchise of the Quebec City Carnavals, which had outstanding debts of nearly a quarter-of-a-million dollars. The parent Montreal Expos refused to offer financial aid and the league seized the team's assets. A group of local businessmen quickly put together an ownership group which began selling shares at $100 each. The club, which hadn't missed playing any games, was renamed the Metros.

1976. The Eastern League dropped the split-season format and returned to a two-division structure for the 1976 season, with Trois-Rivières and Quebec in the North Division. The two Canadian teams began the season with cold weather, as usual, and slow starts. Quebec's opening home series was snowed out and when the Metros finally had opening day, on May 5, the temperature was only 38 degrees Fahrenheit. Just under 400 people turned out. Trois-Rivières occupied second place until early June, when they moved into first ahead of Berkshire. In late June, Quebec City replaced Berkshire as the second-place club. Trois-Rivières maintained its lead over its provincial rival for the rest of the season, finishing 4.5 games ahead of the Metros. South Division champion West Haven swept the Aigles in the best-of-five playoff.

Trois-Rivières placed three players on the all-star team, third baseman Ron Oster, outfielder Steve Henderson (.312, 17 home runs) and pitcher Paul Moskau (13–6, 1.55 ERA). Manager Roy Majtyka was named manager of the year. Quebec City's Gerald Hannahs, who won 20 games, was also named to the all-star squad. Quebec City was one of the three places where future Hall-of-Famer Andre Dawson played during the season.

The 21-year-old, who had spent the previous year with the Expos' rookie-level team in Lethbridge, Alberta, started the season with the Metros, posting a .350 batting average with 20 home runs, before moving to Triple A Denver and then, in early September, to the Montreal Expos. Attendance for the Canadian teams dropped again: by 1,438 in Quebec City and by 8,219 in Trois-Rivières.

1977. In 1977, the two Quebec teams became members of the Canadian-American Division and once again found themselves making long road trips to the home of their division rivals, Jersey City, 520 miles away, and Reading, 600. By the end of April, Trois-Rivières had established a three-game lead over second-place Quebec City, a lead that grew to 16.5 games by mid–August. The Aigles finished the season with a 76–62 record, 10.5 ahead of its intra-provincial rival. In the championship final, the Aigles faced the Southern Division West Haven Yankees for the third time in seven years, and, for the third time, lost in three straight games. "The Little Red Machine," as Trois-Rivières was dubbed, a reference to its powerful major league parent, led the Eastern League with a .279 batting average, even though only one player, Harry Spilman, the batting champion (.373), all-star first baseman, and league MVP, was above .300. Aigles third baseman Tim Doerr, shortstop Rafael Santo Domingo, and designated hitter George Weiker also made the all-star squad. Second-place Quebec City placed one player, second baseman Terry Bernazard, on the all-star team. Although finishing a distant second to Trois-Rivières, the Quebec City Metros showed an attendance increase of 6,463, while Aigles drew 9,728 fewer than in 1976.

At the end of the regular season, the Montreal Expos announced that they were dropping their affiliation with Quebec City, and a few days later, Cincinnati ended its agreement with Trois-Rivières. Cold early season weather, increased travel expenses, and attendance figures that were tens of thousands below the peak year of 1972 were no doubt major factors in the two major league clubs' decisions. Until 1986, when the Toronto Blue Jays established a farm club in the New York Pennsylvania League, all of Canada's minor league baseball teams would be located in the western provinces of Alberta and British Columbia. Minor league baseball would not return to the province of Quebec until 1999, when les Capitales de Quebec joined the independent Northern League.

Northwest League (Short Season Class A): New Westminster Frasers (1974)

In 1974 New Westminster, British Columbia, hosted a team for the only time in the city's history. The team was notable for its miserable failures both financial and on the field, the unusual story about how it was formed, and the fact that, decades later, it become the subject of a book and a musical. The Frasers, named after the river that flowed by the southern edge of the city, played in the Northwest League, which had been formed in 1955 after the collapse of the Western International League. The circuit, which had teams in Washington, Oregon, and Idaho, had two recurring problems. The first was finding enough cities to form a viable league; from 1966 to 1969 it fielded four teams, and from 1970 to 1973, six. The second problem was finding major league affiliations for its teams. By the end of the 1973 season, teams in Bend (twice) and Portland operated as independent clubs, recruiting their own players and covering all salaries and expenses. Lewiston,

Seattle, and Tri-City (Washington) were coop teams, made up of players who were left over when major league organizations had assigned their better players to their own farm teams. The Walla Walla Rainbows were a farm team for the Hawaii Islanders of the Pacific Coast League.

Fourteen of the 30 players to perform for the Frasers were rookies, undrafted high school and college players for whom being a Fraser represented the first chance at creating a professional career. For 18 players, their playing careers ended after the season. The Frasers lost their opening game against the Seattle Rainiers, won their second, and at the end of the first week were in second place in their division. But a two wins, 10 losses streak dropped them into last place, where they remained for the rest of the season. Their final record of 34 wins and 50 losses left them 18 games out of first place. A crowd of 2,123 people showed up for the home opener, but only a total of 8,416 for the rest of the season.

While the on-field story of the Fraser's dismal season is similar to stories that could be told about many failing teams, the story of how the club was formed is different. In 1973, Dean Taylor, a graduate of Claremont College in California and now a master student in Ohio University's Sports Administration program, began creating a business plan for a hypothetical team in a short season league. When he and his fellow student Mike Manning heard that the Northwest League was intending to expand, he arranged financing with his father-in-law, visited several smaller northwest cities, chose New Westminster as the best city in which to locate a team, made a presentation to the league, and, for a $500 fee, was granted a franchise.

Taylor had estimated that attendance of 50,000 would raise enough revenue to cover the $80,000 budget and perhaps yield a small profit. When nothing came of his quest for an affiliation with a major league team, he was faced with not only meeting game expenses and salaries, but also the cost of holding tryouts and running a training camp. Financial worries increased when the New Westminster city council refused to grant the rights to sell signage on the outfield walls of Queens Park Stadium until it was too late to line up potential advertisers. Nor were the Frasers permitted to sell beer at games. For Taylor, the Frasers' 1974 season was an expensive, but ultimately profitable learning experience. He went on to serve as a front-office leader for other minor league teams before becoming the general manager of the Milwaukee Brewers and later vice president of baseball operations for the Kansas City Royals.

The story of the Frasers might have been forgotten if it hadn't been for Ken McIntosh and Rod Drown, two New Westminster baseball fans. They gathered newspaper reports and interviewed as many of the players and officials as they could locate and wrote a book titled *The New Westminster Frasers Baseball Club*, published in 2010. The book served as the basis of a play, "Burning Up the Infield," which had one local performance.

Pioneer League (*Advanced Rookie Classification*): *Lethbridge Expos/Dodgers (1975–1977), Calgary Cardinals (1977), Medicine Hat A's (1977)*

The Montreal Expos' desire to increase national awareness of the team led to Lethbridge, a southern Alberta city of 45,000, becoming a member of the Pioneer League in 1975. Founded in 1939, with teams in Montana, Utah, and Idaho, the circuit had become a short season advanced rookie level league in 1964. From 1972 to 1974, it had operated with only four franchises. In the fall of 1974, when the Pioneer League announced that the Ogden team was available for relocation, the Expos agreed to form an affiliation if it were moved to southern Alberta. In late November 1974, it was announced that for first time since 1910, Lethbridge would host a professional club.

1975. On June 25, 1975, the Lethbridge Expos lost their opening game 8–7 to Great Falls, playing before 1,467 fans in Henderson Stadium, which had been built in the early 1960s as a home for semi-pro teams. Playing against Great Falls and Billings, Montana, and Idaho Falls, Idaho (a 540-mile bus ride away), the Expos remained in the race for the pennant until the middle of August. However, a record of seven wins and 13 losses during the last two weeks of the season knocked them out of contention and they finished third, with a record of 35 wins and 37 losses. They did, however, lead the four-team league in attendance, with a final figure of 31,719.

"Baby," the surname of one of the Lethbridge players, could have been applied to nearly all members of the team. One was 17 years old, four 18, and five 19. Several had signed their first professional contracts just a few days before reporting to the Alberta city. Even the manager was young: Van Kelly, a career minor leaguer who had spent parts of two seasons with the San Diego Padres, was 29. It was his first, and last, managerial assignment. Only two Lethbridge players made it to the majors. One, Steve Ratzer, pitched a total of 21 innings for Montreal. The other began his Hall-of-Fame baseball career at Henderson Stadium. Andre Dawson led the team with a .330 batting average, and the league in hits (99), and home runs (13). He and fellow Expos outfielder Andrew Dyes (.324) were named to the Pioneer League all-star team.

1976. The 1976 Lethbridge Expos were the same average age, 19.9, as the 1975 team, but they did not have anyone who would make it to the major leagues. Their most promising player, John Scoras, who won the triple crown with a league leading average of .370, and home run and RBI totals of 13 and 63, respectively, played four seasons and made it only to Double A ball. Led by manager Walt Hriniak, who'd played for Montreal Expos farm teams in Winnipeg and Quebec City and managed in Jamestown and Peninsula, the young Expos struggled from the opening day. The team lost its first game and won only two of its next seven. By late July, it had settled into fourth place, where it would remain for the rest of the season. The dismal 22 wins and 36 losses record affected attendance, which dropped by 12,000 from 1975.

1977. Shortly after the conclusion of the 1976 season, Lethbridge president and general manager Reno Lizzi announced that the Los Angeles Dodgers would be the new parent team. In October, the Pioneer League announced that it would be placing expansion franchises in Medicine Hat (a small city east of Lethbridge) and Calgary, a booming city of over half a million people. The expansion was part of the general expansion of the minor leagues necessitated by the addition of Toronto and Seattle to the American League in 1976. Medicine Hat would be owned by Alberta television magnate Bill Yuill (who would later buy baseball teams in Florence, South Carolina; Tucson, Arizona; Fort Myers, Florida; and Chattanooga, Tennessee) and would play in Athletic Park, which would undergo $15,000 of renovations to bring the playing surface up to professional standards. The Oakland Athletics would supply players to the team. Calgary was owned by Russ Parker, a local businessman, and John Elick, owner of the local semi-pro baseball team. The city would donate $40,000 to update the Foothills Stadium and the playing field and the St. Louis Cardinals would send their young rookies to Alberta. "We'll break all minor league attendance records," Elick enthusiastically pronounced.

The three Canadian teams opened the season at their home parks, where they were successful both on the field and in the stands. The Calgary Cardinals defeated the Idaho Falls Angels before 2,722 fans at Foothills Stadium; the Lethbridge Dodgers topped the Great Falls Giants before a Henderson Stadium crowd of 1,495; and the Medicine Hat A's beat the Billings Mustangs in front of 2,040 fans. By the third week of July, only two games separated the top five teams in the league. Lethbridge held a one-game lead over Great Falls, Medicine Hat was a half-game behind Great Falls, and Calgary a half-game back of Medicine Hat. Lethbridge managed to remain just ahead of Great Falls the rest of the way, winning the championship on the last day of the season with a 44 wins 26 losses record. Calgary's 34–36 record earned it fourth place, 10 games behind Lethbridge, while Medicine Hat won 29 and lost 41 to end up in fifth place, five behind Calgary. There were no playoffs. Lethbridge's second baseman Don DeJohn and catcher Jesse Baez made the all-star team, as did third baseman Ty Waller and shortstop LeRoy Grossini, both of Calgary, and outfielder Jim Bennett of Medicine Hat. Twelve players from the Canadian teams made it to the major leagues, the most notable being Lethbridge's Ron Kittle (843 games over 10 seasons) and Mitch Webster (1,265 games over 13 seasons) and Calgary's Jim Gott, who pitched in 554 major league games over 14 seasons.

Calgary did not attract the record crowds Elick had enthusiastically predicted: 27,774 fans, second best in the league, attended Cardinals games. Medicine Hat drew 26,665, Lethbridge 24,423.

PART III

1978–2020

Boom and Bust II—
Independence and Survival

In 1978, the beginning of the era referred to in Baseball America's *Encyclopedia of Minor League Baseball* as "The Revival," 13,012,727 fans watched games in 121 minor league parks (these figures do not include attendance for games played by rookie teams in spring training complexes or by teams in Mexican leagues). The total was the highest since the 1958 season. By 1990, the total had reached 25,244,569. During these thirteen seasons, clubs in the higher minors exceeded 500,000 in annual attendance 30 times. In 1982, Louisville, playing in a converted football stadium, attracted 1.1 million fans; for three straight seasons, beginning in 1988, the Buffalo Bisons, playing in a 19,000-seat stadium that had been built to attract (unsuccessfully) a major league team, drew over 1.1 million. During these bakers-dozen years, the operators of minor league franchises had made coming to the ballpark more than just an opportunity to watch a game. Group picnics, between-innings entertainment and contests, souvenir giveaways, appearances by cartoon-like mascots, visits to souvenir stands and in some cases to in-stadium restaurants made a day at the ballpark a social or family experience, of which the game on the field was only one—although the largest—element.

During the period, the value of minor league franchises increased steadily. One of the most famous examples of how much minor league franchises had grown in value involved longtime baseball owner Joe Buzas. In the 1970s, as a favor to the Eastern League he purchased the financially struggling Reading Phillies for one dollar. In 1987, he sold the club for one million and one dollars. "I wanted to show my friends what kind of a return you could get from a one-dollar investment," he told me in a 1998 conversation. In another famous example, Miles Wolff and his friends pooled a few thousand dollars to buy a franchise in the Class A Carolina League. They placed their team in a very small and very old ballpark in Durham, North Carolina, called it the Bulls, marketed the club very skillfully, had a Hollywood movie named after it, and, in 1990, sold it for $4 million.

Officials of Major League Baseball, as well as big-league team owners, were not unaware of the growth of interest in minor league teams and the concomitant rise of minor league franchise values. For nearly three decades, the majors had subsidized the minors, keeping leagues and teams going so that there would be places for prospective major leaguers to develop their talents. Now, they wanted to have expenses shared equally between farm teams and their parents. A new financial arrangement was embodied in the 1990 Professional Baseball Agreement, the document that delineates the relationship between the major leagues and the National Association. Major league teams would pay salaries of players, coaches, and trainers, along with meal money, while minor league affiliates would pay travel expenses. In addition, the National Association was to pay Major League Baseball $750,000 in 1991, with the figure rising to $2 million in 1994.

Equally as important as the new financial arrangements outlined in the agreement were the sections dealing with facility standards. The majority of the minor league ballparks were very old. Many playing fields were in deplorable condition—lumpy, rocky and, in some instances, swampy. Lighting was inadequate, club houses were cramped, spectator seating uncomfortable, and washrooms dark, dirty, and damp. Major league teams did not want their prospects honing their skills under such conditions. Minor league franchise owners, many of whom had paid seven figure prices for their teams and who were facing rising operating costs, needed facilities conducive to generating needed income. The 1990 PBA contained a list of park standards and specifications that had to be met by the beginning of the 1994 season (the deadline was later extended by a year). Included in the list were specifications for lighting, height of outfield walls, dugout and clubhouse sizes; number of parking spaces, number of lavatories, locations of concession stands, and handicapped accessibility and seating.

Teams could meet these specifications by making costly and extensive modifications or by finding money, either public or private, to build a new park. Teams that cold not fulfill the stadium requirements could move to cities where a suitable stadium would be built. The cities that were left behind had two choices: do without professional baseball or place a team in one of the many independent leagues that began to spring up in the 1990s. These organizations, which were affiliated with neither Major League Baseball nor the National Association, did not have to adhere to the standards of the new PBA. The first two independent leagues, the Northern and Frontier, were formed in 1993. The Northern morphed into the American Association in 2006; the Frontier League still operates. By the end of the century, thirteen more had been formed, only three of which, the Northeast League, (later called the Canadian-American League), the Atlantic League, and the Texas-Louisiana League made it into the twenty-first century. Since 2001, a dozen more independent leagues formed—most soon disappeared.

Two things remained constant after the implementation of the 1990 agreement. Attendance at minor leagues games continued to rise—to over 37 million by 2000 and to over 41 million by 2012. Franchise values also increased. In 1996, Jim Paul, who purchased the El Paso Diablos 10 years earlier for $1,000, sold the club for $4 million. Eight years later it was sold for $9.8 million and moved to another city. In 2003, the owners of the Tacoma Rainiers, who'd bought the club for $5.5 million in 1991, sold it for $11 million. As a result of major league expansion by four teams in the 1990s, 16 new minor league franchises had to be created. In 1994, a Triple A expansion franchise cost $4.8 million; in 1998, it had risen to $7.5 million.

While the 1990s marked the beginning of what the *Encyclopedia of Minor League Baseball* termed "The Boom Years," it marked the beginning for Canadian minor league baseball of what could be called Exodus II, as teams moved to American cities, lured by promises of lavish, facility-complaint stadiums. None of the minor league Canadian teams that played during the 1990s would be around after 2007. The departures began after the 1993 season when Hamilton relocated to rural New Jersey and London moved to Trenton, New Jersey. The year after that Welland moved to Erie, Pennsylvania. After the 1998 season, a second wave of relocations began: St. Catharines to Brooklyn and Lethbridge to Missoula, Montana (1999), Vancouver to Sacramento (2000), Medicine Hat to

Helena, Montana (2003), and Calgary to Albuquerque (2003). The Edmonton Trappers departed for Round Rock, Texas, after the 2004 season. The Ottawa Lynx's departure for Lehigh Valley, Pennsylvania, occurred in 2008. Since 2009, the Vancouver Canadians of the short season Class A Northwest League have been Canada's only affiliated minor league team. Since 1993, 16 Canadian cities have hosted independent teams playing in 10 different leagues. Of these teams, the Winnipeg Goldeyes and les Capitales de Quebec have been the longest-operating (after the 2019 season, 26 and 21 years respectively) and the most successful.

8

Another Minor League
Boom in Canada, 1978–1990

Pacific Coast League, Northwest League, Pioneer League,
New York–Pennsylvania League, Eastern League

After Quebec City and Trois-Rivières departed from the Eastern League follow-ing the 1977 season until 1986, when St. Catharines joined the New York–Pennsylvania League, all of Canada's minor league teams played in Alberta or British Columbia.

PACIFIC COAST LEAGUE (Triple A): Vancouver Canadians (1978–1990), Edmonton Trappers (1981–1990), Calgary Cannons (1985–1990)

In the late fall of 1977, after a seven-year absence, the Pacific Coast League returned to Vancouver. Portland, Oregon, and the British Columbia city were awarded expansion franchises created after the major leagues had awarded teams to Toronto and Seattle. The Vancouver franchise was awarded to Harry Ornest, an expatriate Canadian living in Los Angeles who had made his fortune in the vending machine business in western Canada.

During the ensuing months, Ornest, who paid $70,000 for the franchise, would have to negotiate a lease with the city for the use of Capilano Stadium (which would be renamed Nat Bailey Stadium before the opening of the 1978 season) and finance many of the renovations necessary to bring the aging ballpark up to Triple A standards. Ornest had purchased the franchise to acquire for himself professional baseball rights for the Vancouver area. If the major leagues expanded again, Vancouver was considered a prime expansion city, and Ornest had a strong chance of becoming a major-league owner.

Ornest hired Fred Whitaker, the highly successful general manager of the Hawaii Islanders, as his general manager, and announced that he, himself, would be a "gentleman owner." However, Whitaker resigned before the opening day because Ornest had become a "hands-on" (i.e., interfering) owner. During the season, several other experienced front office employees would resign because of his high-handed meddling. He entered into an affiliation agreement with the Oakland A's, whose owner, Charlie Findley, was another hands-on person. The Vancouver team became one end of the shuttle service Oakland operated during the season. Twenty-two players who appeared on the Vancouver roster would also play for the major league team in 1978.

On Valentine's Day of 1978, Ornest announced that the team would be called the

Canadians and that their colors would be red, white, and blue. He made reference to his proud Canadian heritage. However, others cynically noted that the name, the colors, and the style of lettering bore a very close resemblance to the flagship product of Molson Breweries, which had acquired the marketing and promotional rights to the team.

1978. The Canadians, managed by Jim Marshall, performed creditably, spending most of the season in contention. They entered the last two weeks of the season only three games out of first place in the West Division. However, when they won only eight of their final 19 games, they finished in third place, seven out of first. Jerry Tabb, playing his last year of professional ball, led the club with a .357 batting average and 18 home runs; career minor leaguer Craig Mitchell had 12 wins and a 3.60 ERA. The attendance of just under 124,000 was 62,000 more than had attended Mounties games during the 1969 season, but only half of what Ornest had called the break-even number.

1979. Shortly after the end of the season, Ornest began looking for a working agreement with a different major league team. Late in the fall, the Canadians announced that they would be affiliated with the Milwaukee Brewers. In 1978, 37 players had appeared on the Canadians' roster; but only five position players had appeared in more than 100 games. In 1979, only 27 were on the roster, but 10 position players appeared in more than 100 games.

In 1979, the Pacific Coast League played a split-season and arranged the teams in new divisions, North and South, with the Canadians in the North Division. Under John Felske, a former major league player and future major league manager, the Canadians got off to a strong start and, at the beginning of June, were in first place; however, they cooled down quickly, winning only six of their next 16 games and finishing the first half in third place in the North Division. During the second half, they were out of first place for only a few days and finished first. They faced the Hawaii Islanders in the North Division play-offs, losing two games to one. Two players were named to the league's all-star team, second baseman Len Sakata (.300) and pitcher Mark Bomback, who led the league in wins (22) and earn run average (2.56). Poor May weather kept early season crowds low; however, at the end of the season, attendance had increased by 8,000 to 131,367.

1980. Bob Didier, another former major leaguer, replaced Felske as manager for 1980. The Canadians finished the first half in second place, four games behind Hawaii and then, as they had done the year before, dominated the second half, finishing with a 7.5 game lead over Spokane. Once again, the Canadians and Hawaii Islanders faced each other in the North Division finals, and once again, Hawaii took the series two games to one. Bobby Smith led the Canadians with a .316 batting average; pitcher Rickey Keeton had the most victories, ten. Attendance increased to just over 150,000, in part because fans were now able to purchase beer at the stadium.

At the same time as the baseball team was clinching the second half North Division championship, Harry Ornest sold 49.9 percent interest in the club to Nelson Skalbania, a free-wheeling flipper of business and residential properties, who, a few months earlier, had signed then 17-year-old Wayne Gretzky to his first professional hockey contract— with the Indianapolis Racers. During the summer, Skalbania had been on a buying whirl-wind, purchasing, among other sports teams, the NHL's Calgary Flames and the Western Hockey League's New Westminster Bruins.

1981. In October 1980, the Pacific Coast League added its second Canadian franchise, as the Ogden A's were moved to Edmonton. One of the league's "vagabond" teams, the A's during the 1970s had moved from Seattle, to Eugene, Oregon, to Sacramento and then San Jose, California, and then to Ogden, where, in 1980, they had drawn only 76,000. The deal was engineered by Mel Kowalchuk, an Edmonton advertising executive and minor league aficionado. When he learned that the franchise was available, he approached Peter Pocklington, owner of the Edmonton Oilers, at a hockey game, arranged a meeting with him, and sold him on the idea of buying the team, which cost $200,000 (U.S.) and the assumption of $200,000 in debts. The team would play at aging Renfrew Park (soon to be renamed John Ducey Park), which hadn't hosted professional baseball for 27 years, and would be called the Trappers—a reference to both the first baseman's mitt and the western Canadian frontiersmen who harvested animal furs.

Neither of the Canadian teams, both playing in the six-team North Division, distinguished themselves during the 1981 season, although the Trappers were slightly better than the Canadians. Playing as an affiliate of the Chicago White Sox and managed by Gordie Lund, now in his seventh season as a minor league skipper, the Trappers won 31 and lost 33 in the first half and 31–41 in the second, finishing fourth in both halves. However, three members of the team earned league all-star honors: Gary Holle, with a .327 average and 26 home runs, as designated hitter; Jay Loviglio, who stole 40 bases, as second baseman, and Rich Barnes (13 wins and eight losses) as left-handed pitcher. The team attracted 187,000 fans, no mean feat considering that the Oilers hockey team was engaged in the Stanley Cup playoffs until mid–May.

The Canadians, now in their third year of affiliation with the Milwaukee Brewers, were managed by Lee Sigman, who, at 30 years of age, was not much older than several of his players. The team, which had the lowest batting average in the league at .256 and hit the fewest home runs, at 60, finished in sixth and fifth place in the first and second halves. Attendance dropped by 23,000. During the off-season, Harry Ornest sold his controlling interest in the team to respected Vancouver businessman Jim Pattison.

1982. The Canadians and Trappers performed at best adequately. Vancouver spent all the first half in second place in the North Division, finishing 4.5 games behind Tacoma. In the second half, the Canadians dropped to fourth, 9.5 games out of first. The Trappers started their first half dismally, suffering a 10-game losing streak in early May, and finished third, 7.5 games off the pace. They started the second half hot and were in first place later in July, before enduring a three-week slump in August. Their final second half record of 35–38 placed them one game ahead of Vancouver and again put them in third place, this time 8.5 games out of first. The two clubs were a study in contrasts. The Canadians had the lowest team batting average in the league, .269, but the second-best ERA, 4.19; only one regular, Kevin Bass (.315), had an average above .300. The Trappers by contrast led the league in home runs with 162 and had the second-best team batting average, .295. Five regulars, led by Lorenzo Gray at .358, had averages above .300. Their abysmal 5.78 earned run average was the worst in the league. The highlight of the season was the power hitting of Ron Kittle, who set a modern PCL record of 50 home runs, the last of which was sent over the left field wall in the eighth inning of Edmonton's final game on September 1. The next day, Kittle made his major league debut with the White Sox in Chicago. Kittle and Gray, who had a 40-game hit streak during the season, were named as outfielders on the all-star team. In the fall, *The Sporting* News named Kittle the minor league player of the year. Both Vancouver and Edmonton showed attendance increases: 31,606 and 45,543 respectively.

1983. During the off-season, Jim Pattison bought out Nelson Skalbania, gaining complete control of the Vancouver Canadians. With rumors of troubled major league franchises considering relocating and the possibility of major league expansion, Vancouver, whose domed stadium was scheduled to open in the summer of 1983, was a prime candidate for a big-league team. With complete ownership of the Pacific Coast League team and, with it, professional baseball rights for the greater Vancouver area, Pattison could well have made a very good business investment. In other off-season news, the Edmonton Trappers signed an agreement to become the California Angels' Triple A farm club. Over the next 10 years, northern Alberta baseball fans would see the home team, stocked with many future major leaguers, make the playoffs three times and win one championship.

Led by such future major leaguers as Gary Pettis, Dick Schofield and Mike Brown, the Trappers stayed close to division-leading Tacoma Tigers throughout the first half and, although they won only three of their last five games, Tacoma won only two out of six, the Trappers won the first half pennant. The club finished the second half four games behind the Portland Beavers, to whom they lost the division finals three games to one. Mike Brown (whose .355 average was third-best in the league) was named to the all-star team as an outfielder; Dick Schofield (.284) was named shortstop. The Vancouver Canadians' season was a dismal one as they finished fifth in the first half and forth in the second, with an overall record of 60 wins and 80 losses, worst in the league. Manager Dick Phillips was replaced in mid-season after a nine-loss, one-win streak and was replaced by future major league manager Tom Muser. Third baseman Randy Ready (329) and catcher Bill Schroeder (.286) were named to the all-star team. Edmonton showed a modest increase at the gate: 11,778. Vancouver's attendance figures rose by 20,000. However, that is only because, on August 12, 41,875 people attended a Canadians game at the newly opened B.C. Place. It was the first indoor professional baseball game played in Canada.

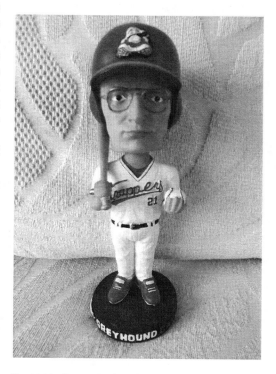

In 1982, Ron Kittle of the Edmonton Trappers became the last minor leaguer to hit 50 or more home runs in a single season. The day after he hit his fiftieth, he made his major league debut with the Chicago White Sox. A bobble head doll of his likeness was one of the Edmonton Trappers' most popular give-away items (courtesy Gary Tater).

1984. Shortly before the opening of the 1984 season, Molson Breweries announced that it had purchased the Vancouver Canadians, along with professional baseball rights for Vancouver, from Jimmy Pattison for a reported $3 million. The brewery joined Canada's other two major breweries in the baseball business. Labatt had a majority interest in the Toronto Blue Jays, while Carling O'Keefe had a major sponsorship agreement with the Montreal Expos. Molson executives stated that they would aggressively continue the quest to acquire a major league franchise for Vancouver.

The words "average" and "mediocre" could be used to describe the Vancouver Canadians and Edmonton Trappers during the 1984 regular season. The former's overall regular-season record—71 wins and 71 losses—was fourth in the league while the latter's 69 wins and 73 losses was seventh-best. Vancouver finished both halves of the season in third place in the North Division. Edmonton finished first—with a 35–35 record—in the first half to win a berth in the playoffs, while sinking to fourth in the second half with 34 wins and 38 losses. The Canadians, who had only one .300 hitter, all-star outfielder Doug Loman (.324), had the league's third lowest batting average (.264), but the second-best earned run average (3.90). Catcher Jamie Nelson (.276) made the all-star team. Rick Steirer, with 12 wins and 4 losses, was the team's best pitcher. Edmonton, by contrast, had three .300 hitters (Chris Clark led the team at .335) and the league's second-best team batting average, .298. The Trappers' earned run average was abysmal, 5.10—second worst in the league. In spite of competition from the Edmonton Oilers who played many home games en route to winning the Stanley Cup and even though they had such an abysmal August record, the Trappers' attendance dropped by only 16,000 fans; Vancouver's, without the benefit of playing any games in the domed stadium, dropped by 31,000.

Coming into the playoffs, the Edmonton Trappers were certainly not favorites—they had won only 13 of their last 32 regular season games. However, two events regarding their opponents gave them an advantage: the Salt Lake City Bees were locked out of their stadium for non-payment of rent and had to play their semi-final series in Edmonton and the Hawaii Islanders had been unable to book home playoff dates at Aloha Stadium and had to play their semi-final games in Las Vegas and the finals in Edmonton. The Trappers took the semi-finals three games to two against the Bees and were leading two games to none in the finals against Hawaii, when September rains descended on central Alberta and the remaining games had to be cancelled. Edmonton was declared the winner and became the first Canadian team to win a Pacific Coast League championship.

1985. Midway through the 1984 season, the Salt Lake City Bees, playing in an aging stadium before diminishing crowds, were sold for just under one million dollars to Russ Parker, owner of the Pioneer League Calgary Expos. The City of Calgary agreed to spend $1.5 million to increase the seating capacity of Foothills Stadium from 2,500 to 7,500 and to bring the stadium, lighting, and playing field up to Pacific Coast League standards. The Cannons (Parker owned a business supply and equipment company) opened the 1985 season on the road, returned home with a 6–2 record, and were snowed out for three consecutive days.

The three Canadian teams, Calgary, Edmonton, and Vancouver, dominated the North Division. The Calgary Cannons, who were affiliated with the Seattle Mariners, won the first half of the split-season, but it wasn't easy. After a fast start, the Cannons won only one in 13 games. Vancouver occupied first place till early June, when Calgary won seven of eight games, overtaking the Canadians and winning the first half Northern Division championship on the final day. The Cannons started the second half with six straight wins; however, a few days later, they lost first place to the Edmonton Trappers, who had finished the first half in fifth place with a dismal 29 wins and 42 losses record. In mid–August, the Trappers, in turn, were overtaken by the Canadians, who won 15 of their last 21 games to take the second half title. Edmonton finished in second place. The Cannons finished in fourth, four games below .500. Calgary entered the North Division finals without Danny Tartabull, the league-leading home run hitter with 43, who had been called up by the parent Seattle Mariners. They were dispatched in three straight games by the Vancouver Canadians, who went on to win the Pacific Coast League pennant, sweeping the Phoenix Firebirds three games to none.

Five players on the Canadian teams were named to the PCL all-star team: Calgary's Danny Tartabull (.300/43 home runs) and John Moses (.321) at short and outfield, respectively; Edmonton's Jack Howell, league batting champion with a .373 average, at third; and Vancouver's Carlos Ponce as designated hitter (.320) and Mike Felder (.314) as an outfielder. Tartabull was named league MVP and would go on to enjoy a 14-year major league career. Calgary, in spite of the early season cold weather, had a final attendance of 272,322, second-best in the league. In Edmonton, where the Oilers played many home playoff games from early April to mid–June on their way to their second consecutive Stanley Cup championship, the Trappers attracted one thousand more fans than the year before. Vancouver's attendance increased by 52,000, but the Canadians' total was just below 200,000.

1986. The Vancouver Canadians dominated the North Division during both halves of the 1986 season, finishing 8.5 games ahead of Calgary in the first half and three ahead of Tacoma in the second. The team's total won-loss percentage of .616 was the best of all 26 teams playing at the Triple A level. Five regulars batted over .300, including all-stars Glenn Braggs (outfield), who hit a league leading .360, but didn't have enough official at bats to win the championship, and catcher B.J. Surhoff (.308). Reliever Chris Bosio, who earned 17 saves and posted a 2.28 ERA, also made the all-star team. The Calgary Cannons, who led the league in home runs with 143, had the second-best team batting average, .288, but were last in the league on the mound, with a 5.36 ERA. After finishing the first half second to Vancouver, with a record of 36 wins and 35 losses, they collapsed during the second half, with a 30–42 record and a fifth-place finish. Mickey Brantley (.318), who led the club with 30 home runs, was named an all-star outfielder. The Edmonton Trappers finished fifth during the first half and climbed to third in the second half. Shortstop Gus Polidor (.300) and designated hitter Mark Ryal (.340) made the all-star team. Vancouver faced off for the North Division championship against the Tacoma Tigers, whose .500 won-loss record was the overall second-best in the division, and took the series in three straight games before going on to face Las Vegas for the league pennant, which they lost three games to two. Each of the Canadian teams showed an increase in attendance: Edmonton a modest 670; Calgary nearly 16,000; and Vancouver 32,000, which brought their season's attendance to over 200,000 for the first time.

1987. Before the start of the season, the Vancouver Canadians ended their eight-year affiliation with the Milwaukee Brewers and became the top farm club of the Pittsburgh Pirates. Vancouver fans found themselves watching a team that had no returning players, while Edmonton fans watched 19 returning players, Calgary fans 15 players.

The Calgary Cannons were the best of the three Canadian teams during the season,

Edgar Martinez played part of four seasons with the Calgary Cannons before becoming a full-time member of the Seattle Mariners. The future member of the Hall of Fame was named Pacific Coast League all-star third baseman in 1987 and 1988 (National Baseball Hall of Fame and Museum, Cooperstown, N.Y., 390996_Bat_NBL).

finishing second to Tacoma by only .006 points in the first half and dominating the second half, ending up 7.5 games ahead of the rest of the pack. They had the best team batting average, .287, and the most home runs, 120. Edgar Martinez, a future Hall-of-Famer, finished second in the league with a .329 average and was named to the league all-star team. Pitcher Mike Campbell won 15 games while losing only two and posted a 2.66 ERA, second best in the league. He was named the league's most valuable player and a member of the all-star team. Other Calgary all-stars were outfielders Jim Weaver and Dave Hengel. The Cannons came back from a two-game deficit to win the North Division playoff three games to two over Tacoma. However, they lost to Albuquerque three games to one in the championship finals.

Vancouver finished third in the division during both halves, while Edmonton twice finished fourth. However, each placed players on the all-star team: Trappers outfielder Jim Eppard, who won the batting championship with a .341 average; and Vancouver's second baseman Jose Lind (.268) and catcher Mickey Sasser, who played most of the season in Phoenix. Vancouver led the league in attendance with 338,614 fans watching a team that played only .500 ball; Calgary finished second, with 304,897. The Edmonton Trappers drew just under 230,000.

1988. The Vancouver Canadians started the 1988 season with another completely new team. Stocked with top prospects and minor league veterans from the Chicago White Sox organization and led by former Vancouver player and future White Sox manager Terry Bevington, the team spent most of each half of the split-season in second place in the North Division behind the Portland Beavers. However, in the last three weeks of each half, they overtook the Beavers, finishing on top both times by 4.5 games. Although Vancouver had only a .272 batting average, seventh in the league, the pitching staff was the best in the league with a 3.64 ERA. Second baseman Mike Woodward, with the team's best batting average of .332, was named to the all-star team. The Canadians defeated Portland three games to none to win the North Division championship, but lost the championship series to the Las Vegas Stars, three games to one. For the fourth season in a row Vancouver's attendance rose; the regular season figure of 386,220, was over 57,000 above 1987's and was the best in the Pacific Coast League.

The Calgary Cannons finished in third place during the first half of the season, nine games behind the Canadians and again in third during the second half, this time eight games out. Although the Cannons led the league in homers, with 122, and were second in team batting with a .289 average, their pitchers posted a dismal 4.84 earned run average. Edgar Martinez, in his last minor league season, won the league batting championship with a .363 average and was named all-star third baseman. Attendance increased to 304,897, second best in the PCL. It was a dismal year for the Edmonton Trappers, who finished fifth and then fourth and were out of contention by the mid-point of each half-season. The team had no .300 hitters, but had a team earned run average of 5.04. A total of 243,419 fans watched the Trappers play in aging John Ducey Park.

1989. The Vancouver Canadians continued their winning ways during the first half of the season, capturing their third consecutive divisional split-season title. They climbed into first place after the first two weeks of the season and finished the first half 2.5 games ahead of Tacoma. The second half was a completely different matter. They played consistently below .500 and ended up fifth and last in the North Division, 9.5 games behind Calgary. The Cannons were in last place throughout the first half and finished 12.5 games behind Vancouver. But in the second half, they were in first place from the opening week to the end of the season. The Canadians recovered their winning ways for the playoffs, defeating Calgary three games to none to advance to the finals, where they defeated Albuquerque three games to one, winning their second championship in five years.

Vancouver had strong pitching (a league-leading 3.44 ERA), highlighted by Tom Drees's three no hitters, two of them pitched in consecutive starts. However, their batting average, .248, was the lowest in the league. The Cannons' team batting average of .289 was second best in the league, but the team ERA of 5.20 was the worst. Calgary outfielder Bruce Fields won the league batting championship with a .351 average and was named to the all-star team, as was designated hitter Jim Wilson, who drove in a league-leading 133 runs. The Edmonton Trappers suffered their fourth season without a winning record in either half, finishing each half in fourth place in the North Division. Fans and local reporters questioned whether the Trappers should continue their association with the California Angels. Club general manager Mel Kowalchuk speculated without a new ballpark to replace small (5,000 seating capacity) and aging John Ducey Park, the team might have to relocate in a few years. Already there had been at least one offer to buy and move the franchise.

Attendance for the three clubs dropped: Vancouver's by over 10,000 (eight rainouts and a dismal on-field second-half), Calgary's by 16,000 (a very cold spring and a poor first-half showing), and Edmonton's by 12,000 (continuing on-field mediocrity).

1990. For the Edmonton Trappers, the first half of the 1990 season was similar to the previous six half-seasons. The club finished once again losing more than it won and well out of first place. However, they dominated the second half, posting a 47–25 record and finishing 12.5 games ahead of second place Portland. The team had adequate hitting, although only one regular, Dan Grunhard, had an average above .300 (301). However, the mound corps posted a league-best 3.97 ERA. The Trappers defeated Tacoma three games to two in the North Division finals but lost the championship to Albuquerque in three straight games.

Vancouver, after falling out of first place on the last day of the first half, experienced a 10-game losing streak in July and ended the second half in fourth place, 15 games behind Edmonton. They did, however, place two men on the all-star team, catcher Jerry Willard (.279/20 home runs) and pitcher Grady Hall (13–8/4.24 ERA). The Calgary Cannons finished third in the first half and fifth in the second. The club's brightest spot was first baseman Tino Martinez (.320/17 HR), who made the all-star team, was named *USA Today*'s Minor League Player of the Year and the next season began a 16-year major league career. Other Cannons to make the all-star team were second baseman Todd Haney (.339) and designated hitter Tom Dodd, who led the league with 114 RBIs. Attendance was down slightly for the three Canadian teams: 400 in Vancouver, 1,200 in Edmonton, and 4,200 in Calgary. Cold, snowy April weather contributed to the decreases for the Alberta teams.

Shortly before, during, and after the 1990 season, several stories appeared in Edmonton newspapers raising doubts as to whether the Trappers would remain in Edmonton after 1990. In March, Sam Katz, a concert promoter from Winnipeg, where the Trappers had played two regular season games in each of the 1988 and 1989 seasons, made an unsuccessful offer to purchase the Edmonton club. Then in August, Mike Nicklous, owner of the Memphis Chicks of the Southern League, reached an agreement to purchase the team for a reported five million dollars. He withdrew his offer in October because the Pacific Coast League refused to ratify the offer before the date he'd specified. Throughout the season, there were reports that the more-than-50-year-old John Ducey Park needed extensive renovations and considerable enlargement. As the fall wore on, members of the city council would not consider allocating funds for necessary work on the city-owned ballpark and the future of the Edmonton Trappers remained as uncertain as ever. In other off-field news, Molson Breweries sold the Vancouver Canadians to Japan Sports Systems for a reported $5 million.

NORTHWEST LEAGUE (Short Season Class A): Victoria Mussels/Blues (1978–1980)

By the late 1970s, nearly all teams in the short season Class A and rookie leagues had affiliations with major league clubs. A notable exception was in the Class A Northwest League. Between 1976 and 1980, Portland, Seattle, Grays Harbor, Salem, Boise, and, from 1978 to 1980, Victoria hosted independent, non-affiliated teams. These clubs were responsible for signing and paying their own players, who included mostly undrafted high school and college athletes and players who had been released from major league organizations after a few seasons.

1978. After the 1977 season, when the Pacific Coast League moved into Portland, displacing the Mavericks, a highly successful independent team, the Northwest League needed to find a new city so that the league could operate with an even number of clubs. The City of Victoria (British Columbia) Parks Division applied for and was granted an expansion team for 1978 and, a few weeks later, announced that it would be owned and operated by Van Schley, a maker of television documentary films who had recently owned a team in the Lone State League, which had been made up of only independent teams.

Victoria's club would be called the Mussels and would play at Royal Athletic Park, which had been rebuilt after a fire destroyed the original grandstand in 1964. It would share the playing field with Victoria Budget, the Canadian national fastball champions, and various soccer teams. Just over a month after the city had announced the return of professional baseball, Schley withdrew his offer, stating that he'd been unable to reach an acceptable lease with the city. The league scrambled to find new owners and, at the end of April, less than seven weeks before the opening of the season, announced that Don Rogelstad of Burnaby and Jim Chapman of Victoria, both of whom had had a few years playing minor league baseball, would be running the new team. The price of admission to the league was a $10,000 bond insuring that the club would finish the season.

The club, managed by Chapman, was made up of undrafted rookies, recently released pros, local senior amateur standouts, and in one case, a former major leaguer—Dan Cheadle, a 26-year-old pitcher who had appeared in two games for the Atlanta Braves and wanted one more kick at the can. For one of the undrafted players, Dale Mohorcic, playing for the Mussels marked the first step toward the realization of his dream. His 2.02 earned run average earned him a berth on the league all-star team and a contract in the Toronto Blue Jays organization. He would go on to pitch for the Texas Rangers, the Montreal Expos, and the New York Yankees. By contrast, third baseman Danny Gans, who played only one season of pro ball, went on to a long and distinguished career as a standup Las Vegas comedian.

Both on and off the field, the Mussels' inaugural season was a failure. The club finished in fourth place in North Division, 17.5 games out of first place. Only 10,103 fans showed up at Royal Athletic Park. Rogelstad estimated the year's losses at $30,000. The city said it lost $5,000 in maintenance and salary expenses. One of the highlights of the Mussels' season took place during a road game played in Greys Harbor, Washington, where the home team, the Loggers, run by Schley, fielded a player who would later become a major motion picture and television star. Bill Murray coached at first base for six innings and batted in the seventh. It was all filmed as one of the features to be shown during the winter on the TV show *Saturday Night Live*.

1979. The Mussels' second season was more successful—on the field. Van Schley agreed to provide a manager and 16 players, along with their salaries, provided he could retain the rights to sell any of these players during or after the season. Off the field, the lease arrangements remained the same, although the team acquired a sponsorship with Labatt Brewery and a license to sell beer at the games—in a specially designated area referred to as a "lounge." The team finished .002 points out of first place and would have had a chance of winning the pennant had the league agreed to reschedule two of the Mussels' rained out games. Two Mussels made the all-star team: first baseman Emil Drzayich (.284) and pitcher Ed Koziol, who led the league in wins, nine, and strikeouts, 104. On July 20, midway through the season, Tom Candiotti, an undrafted pitcher from Saint Mary's College of California, joined the team and enjoyed the first of his five wins (against one loss) for the season. Four seasons later, he would begin a 16-year career in the major leagues.

In spite of the Mussels' much-improved on-field performance, attendance dropped to 8,073, lowest in the league. Van Schley announced after the season that he would not return to support the team as director of personnel and financial benefactor. Jim Chapman announced that the 1979 losses amounted to $10,000 and that the team would be available to any individual or group (preferably local) that would agree to assume the Mussels' debts.

1980. A local group headed by Victoria contractor Bob Peden assumed these debts and the ownership of the team, renamed the Blues, no doubt in recognition of Labatt Blue, the flagship beer of the club's major sponsor. Not only the name was new: player manager Jim Gattis and all but two of the players were new. Fifteen were rookies appearing in their only professional season. The club finished strongly, only three games out of first place in the North Division. Ken Klacza, a rookie pitcher, led the league in wins, with 11 and was named to the all-star team. Shortstop Rod Murphy (.258), one of the returnees, was named all-star shortstop. Although attendance improved by over three thousand, to 11,127, it was still the lowest in the league.

At the beginning of the 1980 season, the new principal owner had confidently announced that the team would be in Victoria for many seasons to come. However, Victoria, along with Greys Harbor, did not return to the Northwest League for the 1981 season.

PIONEER LEAGUE (Short Season Advanced Rookie): Lethbridge Dodgers (1978–1983), Calgary Expos (1978–1984), Medicine Hat Blue Jays (1978–1990)

Unlike the Victoria Mussels, who acquired all of their own players, Calgary, Lethbridge, and Medicine Hat, the Alberta clubs in the short season, advanced-rookie level

Pioneer League, consisted of just-drafted or second year pros from big league organizations. The Pioneer League players were much younger than those of the Mussels, with an average age of all players between 1978 and 1980 just under 20, as opposed to the Mussels' 23. Only two members of the Mussels ever reached the major leagues. Thirty-seven members of the three Alberta teams during the same three years went on to become major leaguers.

1978. None of the three Canadian teams was in playoff contention during the season. The Calgary Cardinals finished third, 13.5 games behind league and playoff champion Billings; the Lethbridge Dodgers, fifth, 17 games out; and the Medicine Hat Blue Jays, in their first year of affiliation with the Toronto Blue Jays, seventh, 22 games behind. There were some bright spots. Two Calgary players made the all-star team: catcher Dennis Delany (.333) and pitcher Axel Vega (3–4/4.05 ERA); one Lethbridge player: third baseman German Riviera (.313); and one from Medicine Hat: Lloyd Moseby, a first-round draft choice and future Toronto Blue Jays star (.304/10 home runs). Of the 11 future major leaguers to play for the Canadian Pioneer League teams, the most recognizable names, along with Moseby, include four Lethbridge players: Mike Marshall, and Dave and Steve Sax (future Los Angeles Dodgers), and Candy Maldonado (a member of Toronto's 1992 World Series championship team). None of the Alberta teams were close to averaging a thousand fans a game during the 35-game home season. Calgary attracted 25,000 paying customers, Medicine Hat 17,000, and Lethbridge 14,000.

1979. The fortunes of Lethbridge and Calgary (which had become a Montreal Expos affiliate during the offseason) improved in 1979. The Pioneer League had split into two divisions, North and South, and Lethbridge dominated the North division, finishing five games ahead of second place Calgary, and then defeating South Division champion Helena two games to nothing for the league championship. Lethbridge pitcher Rick Rodas dominated the league, winning 12 games without a loss, posting a league-leading ERA of 1.12, and striking out 148 batters, also best in the league. He, first baseman Greg Block (.356 batting average and 16 home runs) and manager Gail Henley were named to the all-star team. Calgary placed two on the all-star team: third baseman David Perez (.272) and outfielder Fernando Marin (.250/ 19 home runs). Virtually unnoticed on the Expos' roster was 18-year-old Andres Galarraga, who hit an anemic .214, but would go on to a stellar 19-year major league career, most notably with the Montreal Expos and Colorado Rockies. The fourth-place Medicine Hat Blue Jays, who finished 11.5 games out of first, did manage to place two on the league all-star team: shortstop Fred Manrique (.300) and second baseman Julio Paula (.288). Pitcher Mark Eichorn, who would be on Toronto's 1992 and 1993 World Champion clubs, turned in a workman-like seven wins and six losses record. Calgary's and Lethbridge's winning ways resulted in attendance increases, the Expos by 12,000 and the Dodgers by 6,500 (but only for a total of 20,000); Medicine Hat's gate totals dropped by 3,600 to just over 13,000.

1980. Although the 1980 Lethbridge Dodgers had no notable draft choices on their roster and none of the four players who went on to the majors had significant big-league careers, the team posted an amazing 52 wins and 18 losses record, to win the North Division championship. However, even though their won-loss percentage was .743, they finished only three games ahead of the Great Falls Giants. The team went on to defeat

Billings, two games to one for their second consecutive league championship. Four members of the team were named all-stars: first baseman Greg Smith (.364), designated hitter Audie Cole (.335), pitcher Curtis Reade (3–2/2.17 ERA), and manager Gail Henley. Calgary finished a dismal third, 28.5 games out of first in the North Division, and Medicine Hat an even more dismal fourth, 35 games out of first. Calgary's attendance dropped by 11,000, while Lethbridge's rose by 6,300, and Medicine Hat's increased by 2,500.

1981. The Calgary Expos won 26 of their last 37 games to dash Lethbridge's hopes of winning three straight North Division titles. Led by all-stars third baseman Tom Fittig and outfielder Glen Stacheit, who each hit 10 of the team's league-leading 41 home runs, and pitcher Barry Branam, whose league-leading 10 wins earned him an all-star berth, the Expos finished three games ahead of the Dodgers, but were defeated by Butte three games to two, in the championship final. Second place Lethbridge's all-star pitcher Sid Fernandez, who would go on to a 15-year career in the major leagues, led the league in strikeouts with 128 and had the best earned run average, 1.54. The Dodgers' manager, Gary LaRocque, was named manager of the year. Medicine Hat, which finished in third place, four games above .500, placed three on the all-star team: outfielder Herman Lewis (.298/14 home runs), catcher Bill Pinkham (.300), and pitcher John Cerutti (8–4/3.03 ERA). Each team posted significant attendance increases: Medicine Hat 17,000, Calgary 12,000, and Lethbridge 10,000.

1982. The Medicine Hat Blue Jays won the North Division title and, for the only time in the team's history, the championship finals. Posting a record 44 wins and 26 losses, the club was out of first place only a few days during the season but was never more than one game ahead of the second-place Great Falls Giants. They went on to defeat Idaho Falls three games to one in the finals. The parent Toronto team had sent nine of its first 10 draft choices to Medicine Hat, including Pat Borders, Jimmy Key and David Wells, who would later be members of the 1992 World Champion Toronto club. Blue Jays outfielder Kash Beauchamp (.318) and pitcher Daniel Gorden (6–1/2.10 ERA) were named to the all-star team. Lethbridge and Calgary tied for third place in the division, each with 25 wins and 45 losses. The Calgary Expos placed second baseman Armando Moreno (.338) and catcher Steve Ramier (.303) on the all-star team. Medicine Hat achieved a new attendance record of 51,236, while that of Calgary and Lethbridge dropped by 13,000 and 15,000, respectively.

1983. After trailing the Lethbridge Dodgers during the first six weeks of the 1983 season, the Calgary Expos won 26 of their final 38 games to win the North Division championship. They started out the championship series against the Billings Mustangs the victims of a no-hitter and ended up losing three games to one. The team had considerable power, posting a .289 batting average and leading the league with 61 homers, 20 of which were hit by all-star first baseman Tom Krupa (.335). Outfielder William Moore (.362) and catcher Michael Rupp (.326) also made the all-star team. The pitching was less than stellar, with the squad's 5.25 earned run average the second poorest in the league. The second place Dodgers placed two members on the all-star squad: second baseman Ken Harvey (274) and shortstop Jeff Hamilton (.335). Derrick Lee led the league with a 9–1 record. Medicine Hat dropped to fourth place; for the Blue Jays, who had a 33–34 record, it was the first of 10 consecutive losing seasons. The Jays' attendance also dropped by 1,400, the

Along the top of the outside walls of Medicine Hat's Athletic Park are displayed the names of players for the Pioneer League Blue Jays who went on to star for the parent Toronto Blue Jays (author's photograph).

first of eight consecutive declines which bottomed out in 1990 when only 13,350 paid to see the club's home games. Lethbridge's dropped by 2,400, while Calgary's rose to 41,000. The 1983 season marked the last in the Pioneer League for the Lethbridge Dodgers as Los Angeles switched their affiliation to Great Falls.

1984. Both the Medicine Hat Blue Jays and the Calgary Expos played below the .500 level throughout the season, finishing third and fourth respectively in the North Division. The two teams had the worst earned run averages of the league's eight teams: Medicine Hat's hurlers turned in a 5.99 average and Calgary's a 6.42 average. Surprisingly, each team placed one player on the all-star team: Expo pitcher John Dodd, who won nine while losing two, and Blue Jay outfielder Darryl Landrum (.237), who belted a league-leading 17 home runs. Despite Medicine Hat's poor on-field performance, an all-time Blue Jay high of 51,401 watched home games; Calgary's attendance was off by 9,000. The 1984 season was the last for Calgary in the Pioneer League. During the off-season, Expos owner Russ Parker purchased the struggling Salt Lake City franchise of the Pacific Coast League and moved it to Alberta.

1985–90. From 1985 to 1990, the Medicine Hat Blue Jays' record was, mildly speaking, disappointing. In 1985, they finished in third place in the North Division, 28 games out of first place. In 1986, when the league had only six teams and one division, they finished in sixth place. And then from 1987 to 1990, they finished fourth and last in the North Division, 19.5, 36, 31, and 27 games out of first place. Attendance plummeted: twice by over 10,000, twice by over 4,000, and once by over 3,000. Only outfielder Brian Morrison

(.238) and catcher Greg David (.234)—both in 1985—and first baseman Greg Vella (.265)—in 1988—were named to the league's all-star team. Of the 23 future major leaguers who passed through the Medicine Hat ranks, only four enjoyed big-league careers of over 10 seasons: Randy Knorr, Mark Whiten, Geronimo Berroa and Mike Timlin (who would become a member of the 1992 and 1993 World Series champion Toronto Blue Jays).

What caused the Medicine Hat Blue Jays to experience so many very bad seasons? In the lower minors, particularly the short season Class A and rookie leagues, the strength of a team depended on the quality of players acquired by major league teams in recent drafts and how many of the better draft choices were assigned to a team in a specific year. From 1981 through the 1985 season, the Medicine Hat Blue Jays had been Toronto's only short season farm team. However, in 1986, St. Catharines, Ontario, acquired a franchise in the short season Class A New York–Pennsylvania League and the new team replaced Medicine Hat as Toronto's top lower minor leagues farm team. In 1985, Toronto sent nine of its top ten draft picks to Medicine Hat. The next season, only three of the top ten picks (numbers three, nine, and ten) went to Medicine Hat, while numbers one, two, four, five, and six reported to the St. Catharines Blue Jays—who went on to win the division title and the playoff championship. In subsequent seasons, 21 members of the 1986 Medicine Hat squad did not progress beyond the High A level, as opposed to 13 for St. Catharines. The Medicine Hat Blue Jays had become a poor second-choice destination for Toronto's young hopefuls.

New York–Pennsylvania League (Short Season Class A): St. Catharines Blue Jays (1986–1990), Hamilton Red Birds (1988–1990), Welland Pirates (1989–1990)

The New York–Pennsylvania league had been formed in 1957 out of the ashes of the PONY League, which had disbanded at the end of the 1956 season. Since 1966, it had operated as a short-season Class A league, with teams in smaller New York and Pennsylvania cities. Although the rosters of the various teams were composed of young players, many of whom were rookies, the average age of teams tended to be older than the ages of clubs in the rookie level Appalachian and Pioneer Leagues. There were often more draftees with collage experience and some players who had had a year's experience at the rookie level.

In the fall of 1985, the Niagara Falls franchise was sold to the Toronto Blue Jays of the American League and relocated in St. Catharines, Ontario, a city of 125,000 on the Niagara Peninsula that had not hosted a professional baseball team since 1930. The parent club hoped to capitalize on the rapidly growing popularity of the major league team and to have its top young prospects located less than a two-hour drive away. The city of St. Catharines provided $168,000 to fund upgrades and renovations to Community Park.

1986. The Baby Jays (as the newspapers dubbed them) enjoyed a very successful first season, winning the Wrigley Division by 11.5 games over Erie, defeating Auburn in a single game semifinal and winning the finals two games to one over Newark. Managed by Cloyd Boyer, who, along with his younger brothers Ken and Clete, had played major league baseball, the club included 11 first-year players who had college experience, along with six with a year of professional experience. One of the rookies was future Toronto star, pitcher Pat Hentgen, who lost four games while winning one; another, Jimmy Kelly, a young Dominican, turned 16 during the season. Second baseman Oscar Escobar (.313), outfielder Barry Shifflett (.298), and manager Boyer were named to the league all-star team. A total of 42,125 attended the Baby Jays' home games.

1987. The second season was not so successful. St. Catharines' record slipped to 41 wins and 35 losses, only good enough for a fourth-place divisional finish. Members of the club included Derek Bell and Bob MacDonald, members of Toronto's 1992 World Series winning team. Second baseman William Suero, the team's leading hitter with a .316 average, and pitcher Alex Sanchez, who led the league with 116 strikeouts, were named to the all-star team. In spite of the slip in the standings, nearly 7,000 more people came to the Community Park, which had been extensively renovated before the start of the season.

1988–90. In 1988, the Erie Cardinals became the Hamilton Red Birds, giving the Steel City its first pro ball team since the Red Wings had folded a few weeks into the 1956 PONY League season. Before the season began, the team faced controversy. First, the local amateur club controlled the name Cardinals, which the pro team had wanted to use. Second, local residents tried unsuccessfully to stop the club from playing in Bernie Arbour Memorial Stadium, saying that increased traffic and large noisy crowds would disturb their quiet neighborhood. A year later, the Watertown (New York) Pirates located to Welland, where they played in a $3.6 million stadium built specifically to attract a professional team. The New York–Penn League now had three Ontario teams within an hour's drive of each other.

From 1988 to 1990, none of the three Ontario teams distinguished itself—all finished their seasons playing under .500, well out of playoff contention. Only pitcher Woody Williams (1988) and catcher Carlos Delgado (1990), both of St. Catharines, made the all-star team. Fans did, however, get to see 32 players who would become future major leaguers. Most notable were David Weathers, Woody Williams, and Carlos Delgado of St. Catharines, all of whom would play for Toronto's great teams of the early 1990s; and Tim Wakefield of Welland, who, after developing a knuckle ball, became one of the stars of the Boston Red Sox champions of the first decade of the twenty-first century. During the three seasons, St. Catharines' attendance dropped to well under 1,000 a game, while Hamilton drew close to 2,000 a game. In 1989 and 1990, Welland's attendance was just over 1,000 per game.

The business aspects of the three Ontario clubs indicated new trends that were developing in minor league baseball and that would accelerate in the next decade. Each of the teams had moved from smaller cities that had declining populations and aging ballparks to larger cities that had new or extensively renovated ballparks. None of the owners of the three Canadian teams was local. The Toronto Blue Jays owned St. Catharines, while the Hamilton Red Birds and Welland Pirates were owned by Americans.

Eastern League (Double A): London Tigers (1989–1990)

After the Quebec Metros and Trois-Rivières Aigles withdrew following the 1977 season, the Double A Eastern League operated in larger towns and smaller cities in Ohio, Pennsylvania, New York, and western New England. Most of the owners struggled constantly to attract enough paying customers to meet expenses. After the 1988 season, the local ownership group of the financially strapped Glens Falls Tigers decided to sell the franchise to a group of businessmen from London, Ontario.

The move seemed an auspicious one. The Detroit Tigers would have their Double A franchise nearby—London was a two-and-a-half-hour drive away from Tiger Stadium. Moreover, London, with a population of 270,000, was a comparatively large city, with a tradition of baseball going back to the nineteenth century. The parent Tigers had long had a strong fan base in the western Ontario city. It wouldn't be hard for the new London Tigers to exceed Glens Falls' 1988 attendance of 57,000. However, there were drawbacks to the London location. Western Ontario could have very poor April weather—cold, damp, and often snowy. And London was located far from other Eastern League teams. The owners of the London franchise were required to provide a total of $20,000 to help defray the increased travel expenses of visiting clubs. Another drawback was the fact that, although home games were played in Labatt Memorial Park, the name of which related the grounds to one of Canada's major breweries, provincial liquor regulations prohibited the sale of beer at the games. The club was deprived of an important source of revenue. (The regulation was overturned midway through the 1990 season.)

Labatt Memorial Stadium, the Tigers' home, is located on a site where baseball had been played since the 1870s. Next to the Thames River, it faces east toward downtown, and the city's skyscrapers loom above the trees that stand behind the outfield fence. Although it occupied an historical site, the stadium had to be modernized to meet Double A standards. Just under a million dollars were spent for 2,500 new seats, new clubhouses and lights, modernized restrooms and concession areas and a $120,000 state-of-the-art scoreboard. Twelve hundred season tickets were purchased. London's baseball fans were ready to watch the city's first professional team since 1941, when the Pirates played in the PONY League.

1989. The Tigers were managed by Chris Chambliss, a 17-year major league veteran, but a rookie manager. His team was the youngest in the Eastern League, averaging 22-and-a-half years of age. The inexperience showed: at the end of May, the club dropped below the .500 level and never recovered, finishing in sixth place, 28.5 games out of first. However, the 167,679 fans who attended home games did get so see 10 future major leaguers, eight of whom would play for the Detroit Tigers. The most successful of these was 20-year-old shortstop Travis Fryman (.265), who was named to the league all-star team and who, in 1990, would begin a major league career of 13 seasons, eight of them spent with Detroit.

1990. Chris Chambliss returned as manager, along with 12 members of the 1989 squad. An older and more experienced team, the London Tigers finished the season in second place, three games behind Albany-Colonie. All-star first baseman Rico Broga (.262) led the league in home runs, 21, and RBIs, 77; Rusty Meacham (3.13 ERA) tied for the league lead with 15 wins. The team caught fire in the playoffs, defeating Canton-Akron three games to two in the semi-finals and New Britain three games to none in the finals. Chris Chambliss was named manager of the year. A total of 15 more people watched the club than had the previous year. Eight members of the team would go on to play for the parent Tigers.

9

Canada's Minor League Teams Go South Again, 1991–2007

New York–Pennsylvania League, Eastern League,
International League, Pioneer League,
Pacific Coast League

The costly facility standards of the 1990 Professional Baseball Agreement (PBA), along with the rapidly increasing value of minor league franchises, had a great impact on the 10 Canadian minor league teams that played in the 1990s and into the twenty-first century. By 2008, all had relocated to American cities. The second great exodus began in Ontario in 1993, continued in Alberta and British Columbia after 1998, and ended with the departure of Ottawa after the 2007 season.

NEW YORK–PENNSYLVANIA LEAGUE *(Short Season Class A): Hamilton Redbirds (1991–1992), Welland Pirates (1991–1994), St. Catharines Blue Jays/Stompers (1991–1999)*

1991. Each of the three Canadian New York–Pennsylvania League teams experienced lackluster seasons in 1991. St. Catharines and Hamilton tied for fourth in the Stedler Division, 15.5 games out of first place; Welland was a distant sixth, 20.5 games out. There was only one all-star among the three clubs: St. Catharines' Rob Butler (.338/33 SB), a native of East York, a Toronto suburb, was named an all-star outfielder, most valuable player, and rookie of the year. Attendance was up by 5,800 in St Catharines and down by 4,800 in Hamilton and 145 in Welland.

One of the off-field stories in 1991 was about the St. Catharines Blue Jays. Ellen Harrigan-Charles, general manager; Marilyn Finn, assistant general manager, and Eleanor Bowman, secretary, were the business employees running the franchise, and the only all-female front office in minor league baseball. Attendance did increase and, after the 1994 season, when the team was sold, Harrington-Charles returned to the parent Blue Jays in an administrative post, moved on to the Baltimore Orioles and later to the Los Angeles Dodgers. The story was picked up by newspapers across Canada, and, a year later, *Sports Illustrated* ran a short piece about the three women.

1992. The Hamilton Redbirds dominated the 1992 season, compiling a .737 winning percentage, the highest of any farm team in St. Louis Cardinals history, and finishing

16.5 games in front in their division. (St. Catharines finished fifth, 22.5 games out, and Welland sixth, 25.5 games out). Catcher Jeff Murphy (.264); pitchers Jamie Cochran (5–0/1.04 ERA) and David Oehrein (10–1/2.61 ERA), and manager Chris Maloney made the all-star team. The Redbirds lost the one game semi-final playoff to Erie, 5–2. In spite of the team's amazing performance, attendance dropped by over four thousand to 65,584.

Running concurrently with stories of the Redbirds' amazing on-field performances were stories about the efforts of a group of Hamilton businessmen who were not affiliated with the team to acquire one of the two Double A expansion franchises that would begin operation in 1994. However, when the city council of Hamilton voted against funding for either the building of a new stadium or the extensive renovation of Bernie Arbour Stadium to bring it up to the new PBA standards, the group's bid was unsuccessful. Ron Hilliard, one of the American owners who had bought the team from other American owners before the 1991 season, initially announced the Redbirds' support of the application. However, after it was turned down, he expressed doubts that the New York–Penn team could continue operating in Hamilton. Shortly after the close of the season, the Redbirds' owners announced that the team would play the 1993 season in Glens Falls, New York, before moving to a new stadium in northwest New Jersey in 1994. As the New Jersey Cardinals, the club, in its first season, drew 85,000 more fans than it had in its last season in Hamilton. Although many people blamed the Redbirds' move on the City of Hamilton's failure to provide needed park upgrades, that was not the prime factor. In 2016, Robert Hilliard published *The Circus Is in Town: A Baseball Odyssey,* in which he stated that the group had bought the team with the intent of moving it to New Jersey.

1993–94. In 1993, the St. Catharines Blue Jays finished first in the six-team Stedler Division, capturing their first division title since 1986. However, they lost the one game semi-final to Niagara Falls, a wild-card team that had finished two games behind the Jays in the regular season. Blue Jay's third baseman Adam Melhuse (.256) and pitcher Adam Meinershagen, who led the league with a 1.88 ERA and an 8–1 record, made the all-star team, as did manager J.J. Cannon. Welland finished in fifth place in the division, 13.5 games behind the Jays. St. Catharines' success on the field had a positive effect on attendance, which increased by over 10,000 to 46,535; Welland's attendance dropped by 26,000. The next season, 1994, St. Catharines dropped back into the pack, finishing third in the division, while Welland finished fourth. Jays catcher Jeff Ladd (.325) made the all-star team. Attendance dropped by 14,000 for the Jays and 900 for the Pirates.

During the 1993 season, it became apparent that the Toronto Blue Jays had become disenchanted with owning a rookie league franchise. When it became known that the London Tigers of the Eastern League would be relocating to Trenton for the 1994 season, the major league team attempted to sell the St. Catharines franchise to a group from London, only to have the move vetoed by the New York–Pennsylvania League. Then word came out that former Toronto catcher Ernie Whitt and St. Catharines businessmen who had formed a group called "Home Innings, Inc." were interested in the club. In November 1994, the sale to the Whitt group was completed, for a reported $660,000 (U.S.). Meanwhile, Alan Levin and Ken Silver, the current American owners of the Welland Pirates, moved their team to Erie, Pennsylvania. They would play their 1995 home games in a 6,000-seat state-of-the art stadium that included six revenue-producing luxury boxes. More than 180,000 would watch the home games of the Seawolves, as they were now called, 147,000 more than had attended Welland games the previous season.

St. Catharines, Ontario's, Community Park, a city recreation field that was upgraded to meet professional standards, was the home of the St. Catharines Blue Jays/Stompers from 1986 to 1999. The team was sold to American interests and, in 2001, began play in a multi-million-dollar state-of-the-art stadium in Brooklyn (author's photograph).

1995. St Catharines would play five more seasons in the New York–Penn League before they, too, would be moved to an American city. But they played these seasons not as the Blue Jays but the Stompers. The new name was not only a reference to what hometown fans hoped the players would be in relation to their opponents, but also a reference to a traditional process in wine making and thus a tribute to one of the area's major agricultural industries. The rebranding was part of a plan to emphasize the fact that the team was now locally owned. Community Park, dubbed "The Stomping Grounds," was refurbished, with 300 new club seats, a new sound system, and a kids' play area. The rebranding proved successful. Over 50,000 people, the most for any Jays season to this point, showed up at the "Stomping Grounds," even though the club finished in second place, only one game above .500.

1996. The Stompers won their division by 1.5 games over Batavia and defeated Waterton two games to one in the semifinals before losing the finals two games to one to the Vermont Expos. Will Skeyt (.276) led the league in homers with 15 and earned an all-star berth at second base; Abraham Nunez (.279/ 37 stolen bases) was all-star short-stop and Ralph "Rocket" Wheeler, manager of the year. Attendance reached an all-time high of 56,546.

1997. The 1997 version of the Stompers was in the thick of the Stedler Division race until mid–August, when a prolonged slump dropped them into third place, 14.5 games off the lead. Three members of the club went on to extended major league careers.

Eighteen-year-old Vernon Wells (.307), whose signing bonus was $1.7 million and who made the all-star team, would play 12 of his 15 seasons with the Toronto Blue Jays. Michael Young played for 14 years, most with the Texas Rangers. Cesar Izturis enjoyed a long career with the Los Angeles Dodgers. Attendance dropped by three thousand.

1998. The Stompers were tied with Batava for first place with two weeks left in the season but lost their final five games to finish second in the Stedler Division. Although the team had set an attendance goal of 61,000, only 55,787 showed up, an increase from 1997 of just over 2,000, but not enough to meet expenses. The Stompers posted a $75,000 operating loss. Throughout the season, reports circulated that the Stompers' future in St. Catharines was uncertain and that the team might be moved to Brampton, a large suburb northwest of Toronto.

1999. Just before the beginning of the season, a rumor spread that the Stompers might move to Welland and then another that the Stompers' owners were negotiating with the New York Mets, who were seeking a New York–Penn franchise to relocate to the New York City area. In early July the team suffered a six-game losing streak, and, later in the month, one of nine games. Attendance was down by over 350 a game. By August, the Stompers were completely out of convention. They finished in fifth place, eight games below .500 and nine games out of first place in their division. The team batting average, .246, was fourth worst in the league; the earned run average, 4.49, the second worst. Attendance dropped by nearly 10,000 to 46,905.

In late September, the St. Catharines Stompers were sold to Brooklyn Baseball, a company linked to the New York Mets, for $2.4 million (U.S.), nearly $1.8 million more than Whitt and Home Innings had paid for it just under five years earlier. After a year as the Queens Kings, the team moved to a new stadium on Coney Island, where, as the Brooklyn Cyclones (named after a famous roller coaster in the amusement park), they drew 289,381 fans, at the time an all-time short season record.

Eastern League (Double A): London Tigers (1991–1993)

After setting a club attendance record and winning the Eastern League playoff championship in 1989, the London Tigers saw their fortunes diminish, both on and off the field during their last three years in the Eastern League.

1991. The Tigers posted a 61–78 record, finished in sixth place, 25.5 games behind Harrisburg, and posted a .251 batting average and 4.16 earned run average, both third-to-worst in the eight-team league. No member of the team batted above .271 and no one made the all-star team. Attendance dropped by 17,000 to 150,435, third poorest in the league.

1992. The 1992 version of the London Tigers fared slightly better, placing fifth, 12.5 games off the lead. First baseman Ivan Cruz (.273), who led the league in RBIs with 104, and designated hitter Greg Sparks, who hit a league-high 25 home runs, made the all-star team. Mike Lumley, a native of London, posted a team best 2.52 ERA. Although the Tigers improved slightly on the field, 36,000 fewer fans showed up. The final attendance

Labatt Memorial Park, which is on a site where baseball has been played since 1877, has recently been the home of the Eastern League Tigers (1989–1993), Frontier League Werewolves (1999–2001), Canadian Baseball League Monarchs (2003), and Frontier League Rippers (2012) (author's photograph).

of 113,735 was the lowest in the Eastern League and the-second lowest of the 26 Double A teams.

1993. The slight improvement of the 1992 season did not continue in 1993. The Tigers finished in sixth place, 31 games out of first. The club had barely adequate hitting—.259 average, and 64 home runs—and the poorest pitching in the league—a 4.32 ERA. Pitcher Felipe Lira, who won 10 and lost four and posted a 3.38 ERA, made the all-star team. Attendance, which dropped by just under 10,000, was, once again, the lowest in the league.

Before the 1993 season, it was rumored that a group of New Jersey businessmen were close to finalizing the transfer of the Tigers from Labatt Stadium, near the banks of the Thames River, to Trenton, New Jersey, where they would play in a new park being built next to the banks of the Delaware River. The deal was approved after the 1993 season, and, in 1994, the Trenton Thunder, playing in a city less than a third the size of London, attracted 318,252 fans, almost twice the number the Tigers had attracted in their best year.

INTERNATIONAL LEAGUE (Triple A): Ottawa Lynx (1993–2007)

In September 1991, the city of Ottawa was granted one of the two Triple A expansion franchises created because of the addition of two major league teams (the Colorado

Rockies and Florida Marlins). Ottawa and Charlotte, North Carolina (the recipient of the other expansion franchise) would begin play in 1993. Both would be members of the International League, which had been without an Ottawa team since the 1954 season and without a Canadian one since 1967. The acquisition of the Ottawa franchise was the culmination of a three-year quest by government officials and businessmen to bring a Triple A franchise to Ottawa. Howard Darwin, a successful area jeweler and part owner of the popular Ottawa 67s junior hockey club, was the sole owner of the team and guaranteed both the franchise fee of just under $5 million (U.S.), and $4 million in construction costs. Most of these funds would be raised through the sale of sponsorships of sections of the new park, fees for domain rights for soft drink and beer sales, and the sale of 20 to 25 luxury boxes, leased for $18,000 a year for a minimum of five years. Public funding would be provided by the city government's sale of nearby property and grants from the provincial government.

The franchise granted, the enormous amount of work to get the team ready for opening day April 1993 began. Construction on the ballpark, which didn't begin until June 1992, was delayed by bad weather and strikes. The day before the opener, it still resembled a construction site. Tom Maloney, who, for a year had been the general manager of the highly successful Denver Zephyrs of the American Association, was appointed general manager. The team name Lynx was chosen in a name-the-team contest that drew 35,000 entries, and the Montreal Expos announced that the new Ottawa team would be their Triple A affiliate. Sponsorship of the scoreboard went to Labatt for half a million dollars and Pepsi Cola acquired exclusive soft drink rights for the same amount.

1993. The Lynx opened the 1993 season in Charlotte, on April 9, defeating the home team 8–6. They returned home just over a week later to again face Charlotte, losing this time by a score of 4–3, in front of a crowd of 10,392, the first of 44 sellouts in the Lynx' inaugural season. After over two months hovering around the .500 mark, the team climbed into second place in the East Division behind the Rochester Red Wings. On the season's final weekend, the Lynx travelled to Rochester tied with the Red Wings for the division lead but lost their penultimate game and finished second. The Lynx' final record of 69 wins and 73 losses left them 1.5 games out of first. Ottawa faced Rochester in the East Division finals, losing three games to two.

The Lynx 1993 team was essentially a taxi squad for the parent Montreal Expos. Twenty-six of the 52 players who donned a Lynx uniform spent part of the season with the parent club, sometimes spending a few days with the Expos before returning to triple A. For manager Mike Quade, nearly every game represented a challenge as he tried to create a winning team with a constantly changing roster. Off the field, there is no doubt that the Lynx were a great success. The final attendance figure of 663,926 set a new International League season's attendance record.

1994. The 1994 season proceeded in a similar fashion to that of 1993. The new manager, Jim Tracy, dealt with a constantly changing roster—until August 12, when the beginning of the Major League baseball strike signaled the end of player call-ups from Ottawa to Montreal. There were 12 returnees from 1993 and 16 players who had spent all or most of the previous season with Harrisburg of the Double A Eastern League. The team opened at home and was snowed out, went on to lose seven of eight games in later April and lost five of six games in mid–May. However, the Lynx reached the .500 mark at the end of June and remained in contention for a playoff berth until the second to last day of the season, when they lost to Syracuse and finished in third place, eight games out of first. The Lynx' final record was 70 wins and 72 losses. Tim Laker, who hit a team-high .309, was named all-star catcher. Attendance dropped by 67,000 to 596,858, still tops in the International League.

1995. The season began with uncertainty. The start of the major league season had been delayed by three weeks because of the late settlement of the players' strike that had begun in August 1994. Rosters of minor league teams would remain fluid for the first month of the season until major league teams had settled their own rosters. During the season only four position players appeared in more than 100 games for Ottawa and only four pitchers threw over 100 innings.

After playing below .500 for the first half of the season, Ottawa, led by Pete Mackanin, the third manager in as many years, spent 28 days in July in first place in the East Division. In August after winning only nine of 23 games, and slumping to fourth place, they rebounded to find themselves in first place with a week to go. They finished in second place, two games above .500 but only one game behind Rochester. The Lynx defeathered the Red Wings three games to two in the division finals and went on to defeat the Norfolk Tides three games to one for the International League championship. There were no all-stars on the team, and no regulars batted .300 or higher.

None of the Lynx home games were sell-outs in 1995. The best crowd was 9,885, during the final weekend. The two games of the playoffs attracted 9,688 and 8,818. Season ticket sales were down by 1,800 from the inaugural year. And regular season attendance dropped by 114,706 for a total of 482,144. The "honeymoon period" was definitely over.

If the 1993 to 1995 seasons represented the Ottawa Lynx' "honeymoon," the next 12 seasons represented the slow death of the marriage between the franchise and its fans. During this period, the Lynx lost more games than they won in nine seasons and participated in the post-season playoffs only once. Attendance declined during nine seasons, with the lowest in 2006, when only 122,574 fans, 541,000 less than in 1993, attended home games. Much of the blame for the on-field failure must be placed on the Montreal Expos, the major league parent of the Lynx through the 2003 season. Talented young players were frequently rushed through the farm system to the major leagues. Nearly every year, the Ottawa Lynx had their most promising players called up to the parent club. A succession of Lynx managers had to form a cohesive team out of constantly shifting rosters. The falling attendance can be blamed on inept marketing of the team, frequent poor weather during the early weeks of the season, and the distraction of sports fans' attention by the fact that the Ottawa Senators were in the post season hockey playoffs every year but one (2005—when the NHL season was cancelled by a strike) between 1997 and 2008.

1996. Pete Mackanin became the first Lynx manager to return for a second season. The team played consistently below .500 and by mid-season had a record of 34 wins and 49 losses. The Lynx finished in fifth place in the five-team East Division, 18 games out of first. As distressing as the on-field performance of the team was the number of people in the stands. Opening day attracted a crowd of 4,909, less than 50 percent capacity; overall attendance was down by over 30 percent from 1995. Front office troubles and resignations, including reports that owner Howard Darwin and his sons were constantly overruling decisions of the experienced staff, along with poor promotions and giveaways, were presented as contributing factors to the attendance decline. Ten rainouts did not help either. The final attendance of 333,401 represented a decline of over 158,000 from 1995.

1997. Early in 1997, Howard Darwin warned that the team was in danger of moving unless more support (i.e., buying tickets and luxury boxes) was forthcoming from the corporate community and said that attendance would need to average 7,000 a game. The April weather turned out to be dreadful, with five home games postponed, and the team lost 31 of its first 42 games. New manager Pat Kelly's team was weak at the plate (the team average of .260 was seventh in the 10-team league and no Lynx regular posted an average of above .274). Pitching was even weaker, with the worst ERA in the league, 5.03. The final won-loss record of 54 wins 86 losses placed the club 28.5 games out of first place. The final attendance, 266,833, represented a drop of nearly a thousand fans a game. After the season, it was announced that the Lynx had a debt to the city of $300,000, a debt that might rise to $800,000.

1998. Before the beginning of the 1998, minor league baseball at the Triple A level underwent a major restructuring. Major league baseball had added two new teams, Arizona and Tampa, and accordingly two new clubs at each of the Triple and Double A levels. One of the Triple A franchises was awarded to Durham, North Carolina. Also, the American Association was dissolved and three of its eight teams were absorbed into the International League. With these additions, along with the Durham expansion team, the International League became a three-division, 14-team league. With Pat Kelly again at the helm, the Lynx improved their record to 69 and 74 and finished only 12 games out of first; however, they ended up in fifth place in the six-team North Division. The club's .255 batting average was the lowest in the league. There was one bright spot. Outfielder Allen Battle, who led the team with a .304 average and 11 home runs, was named to the all-star team.

Before the season had opened Howard Darwin announced that he would sell the team for $10 million if a new owner would pledge to keep it in Ottawa. He also said that he would need a per-game average of 5,000 fans to break even. Attendance sagged by nearly 43,000. Although an American who owned three minor league clubs located in the United States expressed interest in buying the team and visited Ottawa during the summer, nothing came of it. At season's end, Darwin said that his club was no longer for sale.

1999. Matters did not improve on or off the field in 1999. New manager Jeff Cox oversaw a team whose batting average of .255 was second lowest in the league. The Lynx finished in sixth place with a 59 and 85 record. Attendance woes continued. Attendance dropped to under 200,000, less than 3,000 a game. Darwin again announced that the club was for sale, but, again, only to an owner who would keep it in Ottawa.

2000. If the shrinking group of hardcore Lynx supporters thought that the 2000 team couldn't be any worse than the 1999 one, they were wrong. On April 6, the Ottawa home opener was snowed out; the next day the Lynx lost a double header in front of the smallest crowd in the team's history, 1,353, and by the end of April they had won only six and lost 12. The club never came close to playing .500 ball. In mid-season, Jeff Cox was replaced as manager by Rick Sweet. The season ended with the Lynx posting a 53–88 record, finishing sixth and last in the North Division, 31 games out of first place.

The team batting average of .258 was the worst in the league, as was the ERA of 5.26. The core of die-hard fans grew smaller: attendance dropped by 60,000.

Several months before the 2000 season had opened, Darwin announced that if he could not sell the team to someone who would keep it in Ottawa or if he could not negotiate a new stadium lease with the city, he would attempt to relocate it. He stated that he'd lost over $700,000 in 1999 and that he'd be willing to buy out his lease at $2.5 million if that would enable him to relocate. As it was, a new owner came forth. In June, Ray Pecor, a wealthy Vermont businessman and owner of a minor league team in the New York–Pennsylvania League, purchased 75 percent of the club for a reported $7 million (U.S.).

2001. During the 2001 and 2002 seasons, the Lynx fared better at the box office and on the field than they had for several years. However, attendance was not high enough for the franchise to avoid losses and the increased number of wins was not enough for the team to make the playoffs. Although the 2001 Lynx, managed by Stan Hough, were weak at the plate—the .248 team batting average was again the worst in the league—they had adequate pitching—the 3.89 ERA was the fifth best. The team played well above .500 ball and was a serious contender for the wild card spot in the playoffs. That was until mid–July, when, over a period of a couple of weeks, the Expos called up seven of the team's best players. Ottawa won only 16 of its last 51 games and finished 24 games out of first. The season's home opener drew 3,834, the largest opening day crowd since 1997. Then in June 10,067 showed up for a game, the most for a game since 1995. However, the final attendance count, 205,916, an increase of over 70,000 from 2000, was well below the breakeven number of 300,000.

2002. The Lynx had their best regular season record, in part because the roster that manager Tim Leiper had to work with stayed relatively constant throughout the spring and summer, with only 12 players shuttling between Ottawa and Montreal. The club was in contention for the wild card playoff berth until the last week of the season and won 80 games while losing 61, good for third place in the North Division. The team batting average of .281 was tops in the International League and the ERA of 3.54 fourth best. Both outfielder Endy Chavez, who won the league batting title with a .343 average, and first baseman Joe Vitiello, whose .329 average was third highest in the IL, earned berths on the all-star team. Tim Drew's 14 wins ranked second best in the league. Unfortunately, attendance dropped by over 14,000, much of the loss attributable to the fact that bad weather caused the postponement of nine home games. The final figure of 191,305 would have been considerably lower had the last two home games not attracted a total of 17,000 fans.

2003. After the 2002 season, the Lynx signed a working agreement with the Baltimore Orioles, an organization which was in the early stages of redeveloping its farm system. Shortly after the agreement was announced, rumors surfaced that after the 2003 season the Lynx would relocate to Maryland. This proved to be just another rumor. But, when the team drew only 747 fans to a mid–April home game, rumors of the team's sale or relocation were revived.

After a slow start, the Lynx, managed by Gary Allenson, spent much of the season in contention for either the division crown or a wild-card spot in the playoffs. On August 26, they had taken the top spot in the wild-card race and in late August clinched a wild-card berth in the playoffs. For the second consecutive season the Lynx finished above 500, winning 79 and losing 65. Although no regular batted above .300, the team itself had the league's best batting average, 281, and second-best ERA, 3.66. In the play-offs, the Lynx were defeated by Pawtucket three games to one. Once again, the season's attendance dropped, this time to 176,002, well below the break-even per game average of 4,000.

2004. Tim Leiper returned to manage the Lynx. Posting the ninth-lowest batting average (.265) and the league's third-highest ERA (3.65), the club played below .500 ball and finished fifth in the six-team North Division, 17 games behind first place Buffalo. Only 159,000 showed up for home games, over 16,000 fewer than in 2003.

2005. Things improved slightly—on the field and in the stands. Led by new manager Dave Tremblay, the club won three more games than in 2004, but still finished fifth in the division. Second baseman Bernie Castro, who led the team with a .315 average, was named to the all-star team. Attendance improved—but only by a total of 825. In early July, the *Ottawa Citizen* reported that the Lynx would move to Allentown, Pennsylvania, for the 2008 season. The Pennsylvania Legislature was considering funding a new stadium for the city and Craig Stein and Joseph Finley, the owners of the highly successful Reading Phillies of the Class AA Eastern League, were rumored to be investigating purchase of the Ottawa franchise.

2006. During the 2006 season, the penultimate for the Lynx and their last as an affiliate of the Baltimore Orioles, returning manager Dave Trembley led the club to its fifth .500 plus season in 14 years. The team got off to a slow start, both literally and figuratively. After winning the home opener before 2,132 chilly fans, the Lynx saw their next three games postponed, first rain, then a tarp frozen to the ground, and finally, an unplayable wet field. For the first two and a half months, the club played losing ball, but from mid-June onward, it hovered around the .500 mark and was in contention for the wild card playoff spot until midway through the last week of the season. The Lynx final record of 74 wins and 69 losses put them in fourth place. Attendance dropped by 38,000 to 122,574, the lowest in the club's 15-year stay in Ottawa.

2007. During the summer of 2006, there was much speculation about the future of the Lynx. In June, the Philadelphia Phillies announced that Ottawa would be their triple A affiliate for the 2007 season, and, as the 2006 season drew to a close, the Lynx informed the city of the club's intent to leave Ottawa after the 2007 season and, shortly after, the sale of the Lynx to the Stein group for a reported $14 million (US) was confirmed.

Under manager John Russell, the final version of the Ottawa Lynx performed dismally, posting the league's worst ERA (4.78) and finishing in sixth and last place in the North Division. The final attendance figure of 126,894, an increase of 4,320 over 2006, was reached only because 21,000 people showed up during the last home stand to say their farewells to what was Canada's last remaining Triple A team. The Vancouver Canadians, Calgary Cannons, and Edmonton Trappers franchises had already been sold and the teams relocated to the United States. In 2008, as the Lehigh Iron Pigs, the former Ottawa Lynx, the club attracted 8,362 fans a game (more than 6,500 more than the Lynx had in 2007) to their new stadium in Allentown, Pennsylvania.

What had happened to the Ottawa Lynx, who had attracted more fans during their inaugural season than the Iron Pigs would in theirs and had set what was then an International League record for attendance? Why had attendance dropped so low that, in

Ottawa's last season, only 24 of 120 full-season minor league teams drew fewer fans? Undoubtedly, the Lynx oversold the market during their initial season, as fans flocked to see the new show in town, a show that would feature many players who soon might be wearing the uniforms of the parent Montreal Expos. It was inevitable that attendance would decline after the honeymoon period—but certainly not so drastically. There were some serious marketing and public faux pas during the first season, notably, the decision (quickly rescinded) to make tickets for postponed games valid only for the next home game and the decision not to offer discounted tickets for children, students, and seniors. Second, the parent Montreal Expos were constantly calling up players and replacing them with unfamiliar faces. It became impossible for the team to coalesce as a unit and for fans to develop attachments to players who might soon be gone.

Perhaps most important, the Ottawa Lynx, like the Triple A teams in Alberta, Calgary and Edmonton, suffered literally and figuratively from "winter woes." Ottawa weather in April and much of May is, at best, "iffy." Snow, sleet, rain, and temperatures not many degrees above freezing caused many postponements, resulting in irrecoverable revenue losses. The second winter woe was caused by Canada's great winter sport, professional hockey. The Stanley Cup hockey playoffs, which ran from early April to mid–June, claimed the attention of sports fans across the nation. From 1997 to 2007, the Ottawa Senators were (except for 2005 when the playoffs were cancelled) in the playoffs every year.

PIONEER LEAGUE *(Advanced Rookie): Medicine Hat Blue Jays (1991–2002), Lethbridge Mounties/Black Diamonds (1992–1998)*

The facility standards detailed in the 1990 Professional Baseball Agreement left the Medicine Hat Blue Jays and, after they rejoined the Pioneer League in 1992, the Lethbridge Mounties particularly vulnerable to relocation. The parks in Medicine Hat and Lethbridge were small and needed much work. In addition, the teams in these cities faced another major difficulty—the great distance between them and most of the other teams in the leagues. For Medicine Hat and Lethbridge, the distance ranged from just over two hundred miles to Great Falls, Montana, to nearly 750 miles to Ogden, Utah.

1991. For the Medicine Hat Blue Jays, the 1991 Pioneer League season was similar to that of 1990. With the best of players recently drafted by Toronto going to the St. Catharines Blue Jays, the Alberta club finished fourth in the North Division, 21.5 games out of first place. The team's .261 batting average was second worst in the league, although designated hitter D.J. Boston, with a .280 average, was named all-star designated hitter. Less than 15,000 home fans watched the lackluster team perform, an increase of just under 50 a game from 1990.

1992. The Jays' on-field performance did not improve in 1992. Managed by former major league player Jim Nettles, the club finished again in fourth place, this time 29.5 games out of first, and owned the league's worst batting average, .226, with no regular hitting above .272. Surprisingly, total attendance increased by just over 2,000.

Lethbridge returned to the Pioneer League in 1992, as Dave Winter, owner of the Pocatello (Idaho) Pioneers, moved his team to the southern Alberta city. Taking the name Mounties, in honor of the historic police force that had had its beginnings in southern Alberta, the club operated during its first four seasons without a direct affiliation with a major league organization. Designated as a co-op team, its roster was filled with late-rounds draft choices who needed somewhere to play, higher draft choices who had performed poorly the previous year and needed a second chance, along with other young, unpromising players filling out the roster. During this period, just six players drafted during the first ten rounds wore a Mounties uniform. Only two players, Rodney Myers and Adrian Brown, would make it to the major leagues. Surprisingly, in 1992, the unpromising group of players won more games than Medicine Hat, finishing third in the North Division, 1.5 games ahead of the Blue Jays, but 28 games out of first. A total of 21,669 fans showed up at Henderson Park.

1993. During the 1993 and 1994 seasons, neither the Mounties nor the Blue Jays were in contention for the post-season playoffs. In 1993, Lethbridge finished fourth in the North Division, 19 games out of first place, while Medicine Hat finished in second, nine games out. Each club placed a player on the league all-star team: Lethbridge outfielder Willie Brown (.244), who led the league in home runs with 16, and Medicine Hat shortstop Jeff Patzke (.293). Attendance was up in both cities—in Lethbridge by 6,384 and in Medicine Hat by 8,275. The biggest off-field news of the season was the purchase in July of the Lethbridge Mounties by a group headed by southern California real estate developer Matt Ellis. He assigned day-to-day operations of the franchise to his son Mike, who had worked in the front offices of several minor league clubs.

1994. Lethbridge again finished fourth in the North Division, 21 games off the pace, while Medicine Hat finished a distant second, 14 games out. Mounties shortstop Mark Duncan (.330) and outfielder Chris Priest (.307), who tied for the league home run lead with 14, and Blue Jays pitcher Mike Toney, who led the league with 18 saves, were named league all-stars. Attendance rose to 30,038 in Medicine Hat and to an amazing 42,967 in Lethbridge—an increase of over 430 a game. The credit for the increase goes not to the on-field performance of the Mounties, but to the promotional efforts of Mike Ellis, Jr., who organized an imaginative array of game-night activities and giveaways.

1995. The Pioneer League introduced a split-season format, with the half-season winners of each division meeting in a semi-final series before facing the winner of the other division's playoff. In the case of one team winning both halves in its division, the team with the next best overall record in its division would win the other playoff spot. That is what happened in 1995. The Medicine Hat Blue Jays, who had finished third and second during the season and lost two more games than they won, faced the Billings Mustangs, winning the division playoff two games to one before losing the finals two games to none to Helena. Medicine Hat pitcher John Mitchell (11 saves) made the all-star team. Lethbridge finished fourth in each half, winning a season's total of 25 while losing 47. Medicine Hat's attendance dropped by over 10,000. Lethbridge's increased to 47,607.

During the 1995 season, Richard Dozer and Joe Garagiola, Jr., the president and general manager, respectively, of the Arizona Diamondbacks, a National League expansion franchise scheduled to begin play in 1998, visited Henderson Stadium in Lethbridge. Impressed with the front-office staff and the condition of the facilities—which had undergone $750,000 in renovations to bring them into PBA compliance—the Diamondbacks chose Lethbridge as the site for their advanced rookie farm team. After four years of fielding teams made up of wannabes and castoffs, Lethbridge would be a part of a major league's farm system.

1996. Renamed the Black Diamonds, Lethbridge's Pioneer League team were legitimate pennant contenders for the next and, as it would turn out, last three years of the franchise's presence in Alberta. The 1996 roster included three of the Diamondbacks' first 10 draft choices and five of the next ten. Two others were highly sought-after Cuban defectors, Vladimir Nunez and Larry Rodriguez. Seven would make it to the majors; and one of these, Rod Barajas, who hadn't been drafted, would become a member of the Diamondbacks' 2001 World Series championship team.

Led by long-time major league star Chris Speier, now in his first season as a manager, the 1996 Diamondbacks finished the first half of the season two games behind Helena, but went on a tear in the second half, winning 29 of 36 games and finishing nine games ahead of second place Helena. The club was loaded with power and pitching, leading the league with a .314 batting average and a 3.68 earned run average. Kevin Sweeney, one of six regulars to hit above .300, won the batting championship with a .424 average and was named to the all-star team and voted the league's most valuable player. Nunez won the triple crown of pitching, and an all-star berth, with 10 wins against no losses, 93 strikeouts, and a 2.22 ERA. In spite of the club's outstanding regular season achievements, the Black Diamonds lost the division final two games to nothing to Helena. Attendance was up by 1,517, to a Lethbridge record of 49,093. About the Medicine Hat Blue Jays, the best that can be said about their season was that attendance rose by 22,000 to 41,942. Their overall record was the inverse of the Mounties', 22 wins and 50 losses, and their batting average (.256) and their ERA (7.52) were the worst in the league. David Bleazard, who tied for the league lead in saves with 10, was named the relief pitcher on the all-star team.

1997. Although the Arizona Diamondbacks had a weaker draft in 1997 and sent only five top 20 picks to Lethbridge, the Black Diamonds again made it to the post-season. After finishing the first half of the season two games under .500, they came back in the second, beating Helena by half-a-game for first place. They lost the semi-finals to Great Falls, two games to none. The team batting average fell to .274, sixth in the league, and only one regular, Jamie Sykes (.305), reached the .300 level. No players were named to the all-star team and attendance dropped by 2,200.

The Medicine Hat Blue Jays performed slightly better than they had in 1996, finishing tied for second with Lethbridge in the first half, but winning only nine of 36 games in the second half, finishing fourth in the division. Amazingly, attendance increased by nearly 5,000 to a club record of 46,770. The reason: fans turned out to watch local boy Greg Morrison turn in one of the best individual season-long performances in Pioneer League history. Picked by the Los Angeles Dodgers in the 71st round of the 1994 draft, he was released after hitting only .254 in his sophomore professional season. The Toronto Blue Jays signed him so that they could have a local boy on their Medicine Hat roster. Morrison went on to win the triple crown, leading the Pioneer League in batting, .448; home runs, 23 (still a league record two decades later); and RBIs, 88. He was named an all-star outfielder and the league's MVP. He played two more years of organized ball before spending seven seasons with independent league teams. Only once after his record-setting season did he post a batting average over .300.

1998. During the 1998 season, the Medicine Hat Blue Jays had the best overall Pioneer League record: 46 wins and 28 losses. The team ERA, 4.36, was best in the league; the .286 batting average second best. Three players made the all-star team including league MVP and designated hitter Jay Gibbons, who became Medicine Hat's second consecutive triple-crown winner with a .397 average, 19 home runs, and 98 RBIs. However, the Blue Jays finished second twice: during the first half, 3.5 games behind Great Falls, and during the second, one game behind Lethbridge and so didn't make the playoffs. Four Blue Jays, including Gibbons, did make the all-star team: pitcher Scott Cassidy (8–1/2.43 ERA), shortstop Jorge Nunez (.319/31 stolen bases), and manager Ronaldo Pino. The Lethbridge Black Diamonds had had a miserable first half, winning 15 and losing 20, but rebounded in the second, with a 27 and 12 record. Outfielder Jack Cust (.345 average) made the all-star team. Lethbridge won the divisional playoffs, two games to one against Great Falls, before losing the league final, two games to one to Idaho Falls.

Both Lethbridge and Medicine Hat experienced significant drops in attendance: the Black Diamonds just under 6,000, the Blue Jays just over 12,000. The second straight year of large losses was enough for Black Diamonds president Mike Ellis. During the summer, he had been approached by businessmen and civic leaders from Missoula, Montana. They and others had acquired half a million dollars of pledges toward the building of a $5 million stadium in the Montana city. Expressing sadness and regret, Ellis announced two months after the season ended that he would be relocating his team to Missoula. The next year, playing as the Osprey, the team attracted 56,000 fans. Even though Medicine Hat's 1998 attendance drop was more drastic than that of Lethbridge, the Blue Jays' future was more secure. Local owner Bill Yuill did not wish to sell or move the club and Toronto was happy to send many of its young players to southern Alberta.

1999. The Medicine Hat Blue Jays looked like a real contender: the first six of Toronto's top 10 draft choices, along with numbers eight and 10, had been signed to Medicine Hat. However, on the field, they were less impressive. Alex Rios, the first-round pick, who had signed for $845,000, managed only a .269 average, while second choice Mike Snyder had a .209 average. The pitching staff was slightly better: Gustavo Chacin made the all-star team with a 4–3 record. The club finished the first half in third place, 12 games out, and the second half tied for second, 9.5 games out. Attendance was 26,852, a drop of 20,000 A few weeks after the close of the season, Bill Yuill sold the club to the Salt Lake City Elmore Sports Group, owners of six other minor league franchises. The new owners were obligated to keep the club in Medicine Hat until the end of the 2000 season, after which the lease on Athletic Park expired.

2000. While the Elmore group may have acquired an extremely valuable piece of paper, the Medicine Hat franchise certificate, it did not receive very good teams from the parent Toronto club. The 2000 season started out well, as the club finished the first half-season in first place in the North Division. However, the Blue Jays collapsed in the second half, winning only 13 while losing 25. The Jays fell to Great Falls, two games to one in the North Division final. Two members of the club made the all-star team: outfielder Jeremy Johnson, whose .376 average was second-best in the league, and pitcher Andrew McCulloch, who had a league-high 15 saves. Attendance increased—but only by 1,281.

2001. The next year was a disaster—two fourth place division finishes and a total of 20 wins against 56 losses. No Blue Jay made the all-star team and attendance dropped by 1,200.

2002. During the first half of the season Medicine Hat posted another losing record—18 wins against 20 losses—but finished in second place in the North Division. The second half was an improvement—of sorts. The Jays finished one game above .500, but dropped to fourth place, 3.5 games out of first. Scott Dragicevich, who led the club with a .303 batting average, was named all-star third baseman, while reliever Jordan de Jong, who led the league with 16 saves, was one of the all-star pitchers. Attendance increased by 355 to 26,285.

Medicine Hat's 26-year history in the Pioneer League ended abruptly two weeks after the end of 2002 season when the Toronto Blue Jays announced that they had terminated their 25-year relationship with the club. Soon after, the franchise shifted to Helena, Montana, where in 2003, the Helena Brewers attracted 47,493 fans, 21,000 more than the Medicine Hat Blue Jays had in their final season in Alberta.

PACIFIC COAST LEAGUE *(Triple A): Vancouver (1991–1999), Calgary (1991–2002), Edmonton (1991–2004)*

During the 1990s, the Calgary Cannons, Edmonton Trappers, and Vancouver Canadians, the three Canadian teams in the Pacific Coast League, faced three major challenges. Given the strict facility standards of the 1990 PBA, would there be limits to how long the three could operate in their aging, substandard, and, in terms of seating, small ball parks? Would they be able to establish strong affiliations with major league teams, many of whom could be put off by the distance from most other PCL teams and, during the early part of the season, by the poor weather, particularly in Alberta? And, finally, given the rapidly increasing value of Triple A franchises, would the owners sell out, allowing teams to move to other, almost certainly American markets?

1991. The Calgary Cannons, now in the eighth year of their affiliation with the Seattle Mariners, began the 1991 season slowly, at one time losing 16 consecutive road games and finishing the first half of the season in fourth place in the North Division, 13 games below .500. In the second half, the team got hot, taking over first place in mid–July and winning the second half division championship by 8.5 games. Former first-round draft pick Tino Martinez, now in his third professional year, the second with Calgary, posted a .326 average, hit 18 home runs, and was named all-star third baseman and league MVP. In late August, he was called up to the Mariners. Then during the semi-final series with Portland, which Calgary won in three straight games, pitchers Dave Burba and Gene Harris were called up. Calgary won the first two games of the championship series with Tucson and had intended to pitch Doug Fleming for the third game; however, he was called up before it was played. Tucson swept the final three games from Calgary. Attendance at regular season home games was 325,965, an increase of 13,000 over the previous year.

The Edmonton Trappers finished second in both halves of 1991, two games behind Portland and then 8.5 behind Calgary. Two members of the squad made the all-star team, outfielder Ruben Amaro, who posted a .326 average, and pitcher Kyle Abbott, who won 14 games while losing 10. The biggest on-field story related to Fernando Valenzuela, the one-time Los Angeles Dodgers star who had been let go by the Dodgers and had signed a minor league contract with the California Angels. He spent August in Edmonton and, in seven starts, he won three and lost three, while posting an ERA of 7.12.

Since the early 1990s, the humorous antics of costumed mascots have been among the many off-field attractions at minor league games. Homer, a giant baseball, was for years the very popular mascot of the Edmonton Trappers of the Pacific Coast League (author's photograph).

The major off-field story for the Trappers concerned the future of the franchise in Edmonton. Before the season, owner Peter Pocklington had held discussions about selling the club with groups in San Bernardino and Fresno, California, and with local Edmonton businessmen. Nothing came of these discussions. As the season opened, Trapper president and general manager Mel Kowalchuk stated that if there were no deal to either extensively remodel Ducey Park or build a new stadium, the team could be playing its last season in Edmonton. By the end of the season, the team's future was in limbo. The good news was that a record number of people attended Edmonton's home games: 252,813. There had been eight sellouts at the 6,200-seat park, four of them when Fernando Valenzuela was the starting pitcher.

The Vancouver Canadians under their new owners, the Canadian division of Japan Sports Systems, finished in fifth and last place in the North Division for both halves, winning a total of 49 games and losing 86. The team batting average of .261 was the worst in the league and the ERA of 4.88 ranked seventh. In spite of the club's dismal showing, 288,978 fans attended home games, the third-largest attendance in the team's history.

1992. During the first half of the 1992 season, the Vancouver Canadians went from worst to first. Sparked in part by an 11-game winning streak in May, the club had 48 wins and 28 losses and had won 28 of 30 home games to finish the first half on top of the North Division, two games ahead of the Portland Beavers, who would win the second half while the Canadians finished three games behind them. Vancouver defeated Portland in the division finals three games to two but lost the finals in three straight games to Colorado Springs. The Canadians were not a powerful team at the plate, finishing eighth in team batting with an average of .270. However, their team 3.54 ERA was best in the league. Pitchers Rod Bolton, who had 11 wins, nine losses, and Brian Drahman, who made 30 saves, best in the league, made the all-star team. Attendance increased by over 44,000 to 333,564.

The Edmonton Trappers finished third in the North Division for both halves of the season. Tim Salmon, who batted .347 (second in the league), hit a league leading 29 home runs and drove in a league high 105 runners, was named one of the all-star outfielders, the league MVP, *and Baseball America*'s Minor League Player of the Year. He was called up by the parent Angels in mid–August when the Trappers were fighting for first place. In spite of the cold, damp spring weather, attendance rose by just under 5,000.

This would be the final year of the Trappers' 10-year relationship with the California Angels. In May, Angels Vice-President Whitey Herzog visited Edmonton. Although impressed with the Trappers' front-office organization, he was not impressed with the distance between Los Angeles and Edmonton, the condition of Ducey Park, and especially the weather—there had been a rare mid–May snowfall while he was in town.

After the season, rumors of a move unless the park was extensively renovated or replaced continued. Serious and protracted negotiations for a new park proceeded through the spring and early summer, one of the chief stumbling blocks being how much of the funding would be provided by Trappers owner Peter Pocklington and how much by the city. In late July, it was announced that the city would pay $5.5 million and Pocklington $3.8 million to build a new park on the site of the old one. The Trappers would get all the revenue from naming rights to the stadium, concessions, and parking.

If Calgary Cannons owner Russ Parker was unhappy with the Seattle Mariners calling up key players during the second half of the 1991 PCL season and during the finals, he was probably equally or more unhappy with the major league club in 1992. Twenty-seven players shuttled back and forth between Seattle and Calgary. Only five position players appeared in more than 90 games for the Cannons, while 14 pitchers appeared in 10 or fewer games. The team finished in fourth place during both halves, 14.5 and 7.5 games respectively out of first place. Attendance plunged by over 48,000.

One of the brightest lights on the club was Bret Boone, whose father was Tacoma manager and whose brother Aaron would, a quarter of a century later, become manager of the New York Yankees. A second baseman, Bret Boone, who, along with third baseman Mike Blowers (.317), would be named to the all-star team, was batting .314 when he was called up to the Mariners in mid–August.

Like the Edmonton Trappers, the Calgary Cannons were experiencing stadium problems. The visiting team's clubhouse was a portable trailer, there was no front office building, and some of the bleachers were rotting. After inspectors from Major League Baseball visited, the Cannons were given until the start of the 1994 season to bring the facility up to PBA standards. Owner Russ Parker approached the city, requesting $2 million for upgrades and expansion of seating from seven to ten thousand. At the end of the season, the Cannons and the City of Calgary had not reached an agreement.

1993. Following the 1992 season, the Vancouver Canadians signed an affiliation agreement with the California Angels. The team included manager Max Oliveras and 13 players who'd been with the Edmonton Trappers the year before, and Vancouver fans frequently found themselves rooting for players they'd booed the previous summer. Edmonton signed an agreement with the Florida Marlins, who began their first season of play in

1993. The composition of the Trappers, the Marlins' first Triple A team, was very different from that of the Canadians; whereas many of the Angels' top farm hands had played together for at least a season, the Marlins' top farm team had been cobbled together from many sources. Twelve players had been acquired by the Marlins in the 1992 expansion draft. Another 18 were free agents who had not been resigned by their major league teams following the 1992 season, and another seven had been acquired in trades.

For the first time since 1982, none of the Canadian teams made the PCL's post-season playoffs. Vancouver finished tied for third and second in the first and second half of the seasons, 7.5 and 6 games out of first. Third baseman Eduardo Perez, who posted a .306 average, was named to the all-star team. Edmonton finished second and fifth, losing the competition for first half championship with three games to go. Outfielder Nigel Wilson (.292/17 home runs), a native of Oshawa, Ontario, and the Marlins' first pick in the expansion draft, and pitcher Dave Weathers (11 wins-four losses/3.83 ERA) made the all-star team. The Calgary Cannons, who maintained their affiliation with the Seattle Mariners, finished both halves of the season with 34 wins and 36 losses, records, good for a tie for third place and fourth place, respectively. Each team posted an increase in home attendance: 843 in Calgary, 4,215 in Edmonton, and 16,162 in Vancouver.

After the 1992 season, Calgary owner Russ Parker had announced that he had received inquiries from interested buyers in Portland, Oregon, and Fresno, California. But, in late August 1993 the city of Calgary and the Cannons seemed to be close to an agreement in which Parker, the City of Calgary, and the Province of Alberta would provide up-front money of $150,000 each for renovations, and Parker would pay the balance of renovation costs over several years.

The funding problem in Edmonton was more complex. In the fall, it was announced that the initial estimates for the stadium were too low: new figures added $1 million to the initial $8 million. Then, in June 1993, the city announced that there would be no deal until Peter Pocklington guaranteed his $4 million contribution to the cost and that all the initial bids for building the new park were $2 million over budget. Then in July, it was announced that Peter Pocklington had been unable to acquire a $4 million line of credit from banks. At the end of the 1993 season the National Association granted both the Cannons and the Trappers a year's extension on renovating or building. The two cities needed to have acceptable facilities by the beginning of the 1995 season.

Late in the winter of 1993–1994, Pocklington announced a deal whereby money for a new ballpark in Edmonton would come from a federal government program for funding infrastructure projects. However, when the deadline passed for Pocklington to provide his share of the funds, the Council gave him a new deadline: June 14, 1994. Finally, in early August, after a 13 percent tax on tickets had been authorized to help with the city's share of the deal, a final agreement was reached. On September 1, 1994, demolition began at John Ducey Park, the first step in a process that would see the new facility ready for the 1995 PCL season. In Calgary, the acquisition of federal infrastructure funds was necessary if planned renovations to Foothills Stadium were to be made. Cannons owner Russ Parker had contingency plans, having purchased one-year rights to place a Triple A franchise in Portland, which after the 1993 season had lost its team to Salt Lake City. Parker reached an agreement with the Calgary council in mid-season. The Cannons would pay $1.067 million and infrastructure funds would make up the balance of the necessary $2 million. The baseball team would pay $15,000 a year rental.

1994. Vancouver dominated the North Division during the 1994 season, winning both half championships, the first by half-a-game over Salt Lake and the second by 1.5 games over Calgary. They defeated Salt Lake three games to one for the North Division championship before losing to Albuquerque, three games to two, in the championship series. The Canadians led the league in pitching, with a 4.53 ERA. Andrew Lorraine, only in his second professional year, led the mound staff with a 12–4 record and a 3.42 ERA and was named to the all-star team. Calgary finished the first half in fifth place, but only five games behind Vancouver and finished second to the Canadians in the second half, 1.5 games out. Outfielder Marc Newfield, with a .349 batting average and 19 home runs, was named to the all-star team. During August, Alex Rodriguez, the top choice in the 1993 draft, who was playing his first professional season, appeared in 32 games for the Cannons, posting a .311 average, with six home runs. In spite of their first-place finishes, the Vancouver Canadians saw a 29,000 drop in attendance. Calgary's attendance rose by 20,000, and Edmonton attracted 272,631, the most people to come to Ducey Park in the 14 years of the Trappers' tenancy. The figure included 12 sellouts in the 6,200-seat stadium.

1995. During the fall of 1994, the Edmonton Trappers and Calgary Cannons announced affiliation agreements with two new major league teams. The two-year relationship between the Trappers and Florida Marlins had been a marriage of necessity— for each there were no other options. But the 3,000-mile distance between Edmonton and Miami, bridged only by two very long air flights, had limited the parent club's ability to quickly call up players from its Triple A affiliate. The Trappers new major league "parent," the Oakland A's, were a long plane flight away, but much closer than Florida. Calgary's 10-year affiliation with the Mariners ended when the Seattle club signed an agreement with the Tacoma Rainiers, only a long hour's drive from Seattle's Kingdome. Calgary signed with Pittsburgh. In Calgary, the Cannons received $500,000 from Burns Foods for the naming rights to the ballpark.

The Vancouver Canadians dominated the first half of the 1995 season, finishing seven games in front in the North Division. However, in the second half, they slipped to second, 3.2 games behind Salt Lake City. The team's diminished second half performance can in part be attributed to the fact that the California Angels, in serious contention for the Western Division American League pennant, called up or traded important Vancouver players. Just as the Canadians were preparing to meet the Salt Lake City Buzz for the division championship, three .300 hitters, Eduardo Perez (.325), Rod Correia (.303), and club MVP Orlando Palmero (.307), were called up. The Canadians lost the first round of the playoffs three games to two. Don Long was named manager of the year. Attendance at Nat Bailey Stadium dropped to 305,738.

The Edmonton Trappers, who finished fourth and third, were below .500 in both halves, 10 and 8 games out of first. Nonetheless, they placed two players on the all-star squad: catcher George Williams (.310/13 home runs) and shortstop Fausto Cruz (.281/11 home runs). Jason Giambi, who would go on to a long major league career, first with Oakland and then with the New York Yankees, hit .342 in 55 games before being called up to the A's. Edmonton opened their home season with a sellout crowd in their new, as-yet unnamed stadium (dubbed John Doe Park by sportswriters). It was the first of 15 sellouts for the year. The final attendance of 426,012 was second best in the PCL. Late in the season, Telus Communications obtained naming rights for the park.

Calgary fared poorly in its first year of affiliation with Pittsburgh, finishing fifth and last in the North Division for both halves. Although the team could hit—the .302 average was second-best in the PCL—the pitching was the worst in the league with a 5.32 ERA. A total of just over 279,000, a drop of 19,000, showed up at the refurbished Burns Stadium.

1996. The 1996 Edmonton Trappers won both halves of the regular season, finishing .001 points ahead of Tacoma in the first half and two games ahead of Salt Lake in the second. They went on to defeat Salt Lake City in the division championship, three games to one, and then Phoenix, three games to one, for the league championship. Second-year manager Gary Jones was named manager of the year. Although 26 players appeared on the rosters of both Edmonton and Oakland, the A's, who would finish in fourth place in the American League West, did not gut the Trappers' roster in August and early September: only pitcher Mark Acre (six wins and two losses), and Brian Lesher (18 home runs) left the Trappers late in the season. In spite of very bad April and May weather and a total of 10 cancelled games during the season, attendance increased by 37,672 to what would be an all-time Trappers record of 463,684.

The Calgary Cannons won 37 and lost 34 during each half-season but finished amazingly close to first place each time: 2.5 and 7.5 games behind, respectively. Losing seven of eight games in late August knocked them out of a wild card spot in the playoffs. Outfielder Jermaine Allensworth, with a team-best .330 average, and catcher Angelo Encarnacion, who hit .319, were voted to the all-star team. During the first half of the season, 10 games were lost to rain, snow, and/or cold weather, and, in late June, owner Russ Parker remarked that selling or moving the Cannons would be a possibility if attendance didn't improve. Although it did somewhat during the second half, the final total of 273,545 represented a decline of 5,500 over the previous season. In Vancouver, the Canadians finished third, 2.5 games behind the Trappers, during the first half, and then fourth, 11.5 games out. Their attendance improved by 2,000, to 334,800.

1997. Shortly before the Edmonton Trappers' 1997 home opener, General Manager Mel Kowalchuk stated that the record-breaking attendance figures of the previous year had not resulted in a cash bonanza for the team. The announced total of just over 463,000 counted all tickets sold, not people who had attended games. The actual attendance was 100,000 less and resulted in a loss of revenue from concessions, souvenir sales, and parking.

On the field, the 1997 Trappers became the first team since the 1982 Albuquerque Dukes to win two consecutive PCL championships. They finished the first half a game behind the Vancouver Canadians, and won the second by half a game over Tacoma. Manager Gary Jones was named minor league manager of the year by *Baseball America*. Although 23 players returned from the championship team of 1996, the roster was in a constant state of flux, with 96 transactions being enacted during the season. Just as the post-season began, Ben Grieve, one of Oakland's hottest prospects, who had posted a .426 average after being called up to Edmonton in the middle of the second half, was promoted to the parent club.

The Vancouver Canadians also experienced an incredible number of transactions, 86 in all, including losing all-star catcher Todd Greene to California mid-way through the season. They had barely won the first half championship over Edmonton, with 39 and 32 record, but slumped to fourth place in the second half, playing only .500 ball. Edmonton swept the series with Vancouver before defeating the Phoenix Firebirds, three games to one. Attendance dropped in both Vancouver and Edmonton by 31,000. Surprisingly, in Calgary, where the Cannons finished a dismal fifth during both half seasons, attendance rose by 18,000. Cannons outfielder Manny Martinez (.331/16 home runs) was voted to the all-star team.

Following the 1997 season, the American Association disbanded, with three of its eight teams being absorbed by the International League, the other five by the Pacific Coast League. In addition, two expansion franchises were granted: the Durham Bulls would enter the International League in 1998 and the Memphis Redbirds, the Pacific Coast League. The PCL now had 11 teams in cities east of the Rocky Mountains. The Edmonton Trappers, Calgary Cannons, Vancouver Canadians, and Tacoma Tigers formed part of the four-team West Division of the eight-team Pacific Conference. Winners of each of the four divisions would qualify for the playoffs with the winner of the finals meeting the winner of the International League playoffs in the "Triple A World Series."

1998. Calgary, Edmonton, and Tacoma were in a season-long fight for the championship of the West Division. During the off-season, the Cannons had ended their disappointing affiliation with Pittsburgh and hooked up with the Chicago White Sox. The Cannons started slowly and didn't reach the .500 mark until the end of May. In early July they took over first place, which they held the rest of the way, but only by slim margins over Tacoma, which finished in second place, 4.5 games out, and Edmonton, which was five games out in third. First baseman Mario Valdez led the team with a .330 average and 20 homers and was named to the all-star team. Calgary defeated the Fresno Grizzlies three games to two to advance to the league final for the third time in their history. For the third time, they were defeated, this time three games to two by the New Orleans Zephyrs.

In spite of having their best regular season since 1987, the Cannons drew just over 5,000 more fans than they had in 1997—the total was 296,047. These disappointing figures were part of the season-long story of the difficulty of the club to generate sufficient revenue to meet mounting expenses and make a reasonable profit while operating in a sub-standard facility. The Trappers entered the season with a new manager. Gary Jones, after his two consecutive pennants, had been promoted to the Oakland coaching staff, and was replaced by Mike Quade, who had piloted the expansion Ottawa Lynx in 1994. With the help of 18 returnees, many of whom stayed in Edmonton for most of the season, and, thanks to a limited number of late-season call-ups (only four in August) by the A's, he kept the team in contention until the last five games of the season. The Trappers finished in third place with a record of 76 and 67. Attendance dropped to 410,414.

In the front office of the Trappers, there was considerable concern about how the major financial difficulties owner Peter Pocklington was experiencing with his various businesses would affect the baseball club. The Edmonton Oilers and the Trappers, two of Pocklington's most successful and valuable assets, had been seized by the Alberta Treasury Branches, to whom he owed millions. In May 1998, it was announced that the Trappers were in receivership.

The Vancouver Canadians made little news during the 1998 season for their on-field play. They finished in fourth place in the division, 28 games behind Calgary; their final record of 53 wins and 90 losses was the worst in the league. Attendance had dropped to 284,935, a decrease of 38,000 over two years. Japan Sports Systems had become disenchanted with owning the Canadian team which had not generated the profits they had hoped for. When Art Savage, former CEO of the NHL's San Jose Sharks, approached them representing a group of California investors looking to purchase a team for a state-of-the art stadium planned for Sacramento, they listened—and then made a very profitable deal. Near the end of the season, what had been the most poorly kept secret in baseball for well over a year became a reality. The Vancouver Canadians would be moving to Sacramento, most likely after the 1999 season. The sale price, $8.5 million (U.S.).

1999. After the 1998 PCL season had ended, Calgary owner Russ Parker stated emphatically that he would not pay the estimated $4 million necessary to upgrade Burns Stadium to PCL standards. In Edmonton, the Alberta Treasury Branches, who held the Trappers as security against owner Peter Pocklington's debts, announced in October that the baseball club was for sale, with proceeds going to pay down some of the former owner's debts. Several groups, nine local, expressed interest in the club. In late January 1999, the new owner was revealed: the Edmonton Eskimos of the community-owned Canadian Football League team. The sale price, announced as $8 million Canadian (years later reported as $6.5 million), included a million dollars from the Eskimos, another million from 10 Edmonton businessmen/baseball fans, a bank loan of $3 million, and the assumption of $3 million of Pocklington's debts.

During the offseason, each of the Canadian teams entered into affiliations with different major league clubs: Vancouver with the Oakland A's, Edmonton with the Anaheim Angels, and Calgary with the Florida Marlins.

The Vancouver Canadians ended their 22-season run in the Pacific Coast League on a triumphal note. After a slow start during a very cold spring, they moved into first place in the West Division in mid–June, never relinquishing that spot and finishing 13.5 games ahead of second place Tacoma. Although their .282 batting average ranked 10th in the league and only two regulars, including all-star utility man Frank Menechino, with a .309 average, were above .300, they had the best ERA: 3.84. Brett Laxton, who led the mound core with 13 wins against eight losses and posted a 3.46 ERA, was also named to the all-star team. The Canadians defeated Salt Lake City three games to two in the semi-finals and then Oklahoma City three games to one to win their third Pacific Coast League championship. They faced the International League champion Charlotte Knights, whom they defeated three games to two to win the Triple A World Series.

The Edmonton Trappers had been in first place several times during the first two and a half months of the 1999 season but slipped into second behind the Vancouver Canadians in mid–June. As the weeks progressed, they slipped further and further out of contention. Their final record of 65 wins and 74 losses left them in third place 17.5 games behind the Canadians. Calgary had an even more disappointing season. The Cannons came home from their opening road trip with a one win and seven losses record and played the rest of the season well below the .500 mark. Their final record of 57 wins and 82 losses left them solidly in fourth place in the division, 25.5 games behind Vancouver. During the season, there were many rumors about a pending sale of the Cannons to a group of businessmen from Portland.

In part due to cold and often very damp weather, attendance in the three Canadian cities dropped by a combined total of 86,280. In spite of its winning season, fans of the Canadians, discouraged by the clubs' impending departure, stayed away. In Edmonton and Calgary, dismal on-field performances contributed to the decline. Edmonton drew 385,913; Calgary 269,002; and Vancouver 241,461.

2000. As the 2000 season approached, neither the Calgary Cannons nor the Edmonton Trappers had to worry about off-field matters. The Edmonton Eskimos had taken control of the Trappers, while Calgary owner Russ Parker announced he was ready to sign a five-year extension on the lease to Burns Field.

On the field, the Trappers started out cold—literally and figuratively. They won only two of their first seven games and four games of the first home stand were snowed out. The team hovered around the .500 mark until July 1, when it was in second place, after which it steadily dropped out of contention for a play-off spot. The Trappers finished third in the division with a record of 63 wins and 78 losses, 26 games out of first place. As had been the case for last year's manager Carney Lansford, new manager Gary Templeton had to deal with a constantly changing roster. There were 139 player transactions during the season and 60 different players appeared on the Trappers' roster. The constant parade of new faces, the poor performance on the field, and bad weather at the beginning and end of the season resulted in another drop in the season's home attendance, the fourth in a row. A total of 359,697 showed up at Telus Field.

After being swept in a late April four game series against Edmonton, the Calgary Cannons dropped into fourth place in the North Division and never left it. They finished the season with 60 wins and 82 losses, 29.5 games out of first. The brightest light of the season was Nate Rolison, who led the team with a .330 average and hit 23 home runs and was named PCL rookie of the year. Surprisingly home attendance rose—but only by 1,080, to 270,682.

2001. The question of whether the Cannons would be sold or moved resurfaced in November of 2000 when Russ Parker announced that a group from Albuquerque, New Mexico, wished to purchase the team. A few weeks later, Parker said that he would be signing a letter of intent to sell the franchise to a group led by Ken Young, owner of the Norfolk Tides of the International League. The sale was contingent on the passage of a bond allowing the city of Albuquerque to build a new stadium. It passed in late May, too late for a new park to be completed within a year. And so, the Cannons would remain in Alberta though the 2002 season.

In 2001, the Cannons, led by manager Chris Chambliss, improved over the previous year, spending nearly all season in second place. They finished one game above .500, 12.5 games out of first. The team could hit, leading the PCL in batting average, .292, and home runs, 187. All-star catcher Ramon Castro was the best on the club with a .336 average and 27 home runs. However, the pitching was weak: the 5.34 ERA was highest in the league. Nearly 27,000 fewer fans came to home games than in 2000. The final attendance figure of 246,991 was the lowest since Calgary had joined the league in 1985.

The announcement of the Cannons' impending sale to the Albuquerque group caused worry in the front offices of the Edmonton Trappers. Before the season, Mel Kowalchuk stated that Calgary's departure would increase his club's travel budget enormously. He noted that two yearly bus trips to Calgary had cost $1,000 each (Canadian funds), but that each trip to Tacoma, which would become Edmonton's closest rival, would be $10,000 each, payable in American funds.

During the off-season the Trappers announced that they had signed a two-year affiliation agreement with the Minnesota Twins of the American League. Edmonton lost its opening game 3–2 in Memphis and never reached the .500 mark the rest of the year; in late May, the Trappers sank to fourth place in the division, where they remained, finishing up with a 60–83 record, 24.5 games out of first. The final attendance of 372,244, which was 15,556 less than in 2000, marked the fifth straight season of declining attendance in Edmonton.

2002. The Trappers would start the 2002 season with several of the Minnesota Twins' top prospects, but without general manager Mel Kowalchuk. He had been instrumental in procuring the franchise in 1981, had guided it through the 1990s when its existence had been threatened because of owner Peter Pocklington's financial difficulties, and had overseen the construction of the new ballpark that, at the time, seemed to insure a long future for the team in Edmonton. The team's owners, the Edmonton Eskimos, did not name a replacement for Kowalchuk; long-time assistant general manager Dennis Henke oversaw day-to-day operations.

The Trappers spent the first half of the season in third and then second place, never more than four games off the lead, before taking over first place on July 3. They clinched the North Division championship on August 23, 10 games before the end of the season, and finished 10.5 games ahead of Tacoma, with a team record of 81 wins and 59 losses. The team's batting average of .287 was third in the league; three regulars posted averages over .300: Todd Sears (.310), Casey Blake (.309) and David Lamb (.309). The Trappers' 202 home runs, an all-time team record, led the league. Outfielder Mike Ryan's 31 round trippers were the most by a Trapper since Ron Kittle's 50-homer season in 1982. Four Trappers made the PCL all-star team: Ryan, catcher Javier Valentin (.286/21 home runs),

Winter weather in the early weeks of the season was a constant possibility for many Canadian baseball teams. In Edmonton, Alberta, the most northern city in professional baseball, a groundskeeper carefully shovels snow off the artificial turf at Telus Field (author's photograph).

outfielder Michael Restovich (.296/29 home runs), and pitcher Scott Randall, who won 12 and lost none. The Trappers moved through the playoffs with relative ease, defeating the Las Vegas Stars three games to one to win the Pacific Division championship, and then the Salt Lake City Stingers three games to one to win the championship.

In spite of the Trappers' superb on-field performance, attendance dropped once again—this time by 31,854 to 340,387. The main culprit was some of the worst spring weather in several years. The club's home opener on April 13 was played under partly cloudy skies before 7,307 fans. But the next morning, rains moved in, followed by heavy, wet snow. The remaining three games of the home stand were cancelled and, the field having been rendered unplayable, the next four home games against the Iowa Cubs were transferred to Des Moines.

The Florida Marlins provided the Calgary Cannons with a competitive and comparatively stable roster for the final season in the foothills city. The Cannons hovered around the .500 mark all season; their final record of 69 wins and 71 losses placed them in third place, 13 games behind the division champion Edmonton Trappers. Third baseman Jason Wood led the club with a .315 average and was named to the all-star team. Pitching let the team down: the 5.34 ERA was second highest in the league. A total of 182,831 fans watched games at Burns Stadium. The figure might have been higher had a four-game home stand been snowed out in early May and the next four games transferred to Omaha Nebraska because of the home field's unplayable condition. And it might have been lower had the final three home games, played against provincial rival Edmonton, not attracted 23,670, nearly one-eighth of the season's total. In 2003, playing as the Albuquerque Isotopes, the franchise would attract 576,867. During the team's first season in New Mexico, the front office was led by Mel Kowalchuk, who oversaw the construction of a new stadium and the assembling of sales, marketing, and game day staffs.

2003. Although the 2002 Edmonton Trappers had won the Pacific Coast League championship, the atmosphere in the Telus Field offices during the off-season was not always cheerful. The Twins had severed their relations with the ball club. In addition, the club suffered over $300,000 in operating losses in 2003, and had to go, hat in hand, to the city asking to be released from its obligation to pay $100,000 rent for 2003. In September 2002, the Trappers announced that they would be affiliated for the 2003 and 2004 season with the Montreal Expos, one of the least financially stable of the thirty major league teams. Before the 2002 season, Montreal had become the property of the 29 other major league clubs. Operating on a shoestring budget, the Expos were not expected to provide Edmonton with a competitive team.

In fact, however, they did. The Trappers were under the leadership of veteran minor league manager Dave Huppert, whose most interesting playing achievement had been catching 31 of 33 innings in the longest minor league game ever played: Rochester against Pawtucket of the International League on April 18, 1981. He led a mixed bag of rookies up from Double A, prospects about to make the jump to the majors, and aging veterans who formed a kind of taxi-squad for Montreal to the North Division championship. The Trappers played below .500 until the end of June. Then they took over first place, which they held for the rest of the season. With four days to go, they clinched the division crown. The Trappers had a league-leading .292 batting average, with Terrmel Sledge the top trapper with a .324 average. Named an outfielder on the all-star team, he also led the club in homers, with 22. The pitching was the worst in the league, with a 5.08 average. Attendance dropped by 6,500 to 333,792. There was only one sellout all season and nine rainouts. The Trappers were overwhelmed in the Pacific Conference playoffs by the powerhouse Sacramento River Cats, who won the semi-final series in three straight games.

In late October 2003, the Edmonton Eskimos held a press conference to announce what diehard Trapper fans had feared would happen sooner than later. The baseball team that the football team had purchased in 2000 for a price reported as $8 million and later $6.5 million Canadian had been sold to a Texas group headed by Hall-of-Fame pitcher Nolan Ryan for $10.5 million American. It would play the 2004 season in Edmonton before moving to Round Rock, a wealthy suburb of Austin, the capital city of Texas.

2004. For the 2004 season, both the Edmonton Trappers and their major league partner the Montreal Expos would be lame ducks, the former moving to Texas a year later and the latter to Washington, D.C. Fourteen members of the North Division winning 2003 Trappers returned in 2014, 15 players were promoted from Harrisburg, and 18 Trappers would also spend part of the season with Montreal. The Trappers got off to the best start in their history, winning 10 and losing six before they arrived in Edmonton for their home opener. Their won-loss record hovered around the .500 level until early August, when they won 10 while losing 17 and fell 11 games behind division leader Portland. The club finished in third place, 14.5 games out of first place. Outfielder Ryan Church led the team with a .343 batting average and was named to the league all-star team. So too was pitcher Scott Downs, who won 10 while losing six and who pitched a no-hitter, only the second in the club's history.

Partly because of seven home rainouts and party because of the club's lame duck status, attendance dropped by 81,235—to 252,557. One of the rainouts occurred on September 2, when the season's only sell-out crowd had gathered to watch the Trappers' final home game. Unfortunately, the weather made the playing field more suitable for real ducks than a lame-duck baseball team. After one inning, the game was cancelled and fans milled around waiting for it to get dark enough for the season-ending fireworks display. In 2005, the franchise, now the Round Rock Express, drew over 700,000 fans to its home games.

10

On Their Own

Canadian Teams
in the Independent Leagues

At the beginning of the 1990s, there were more cities, individuals, or groups looking to acquire minor league franchises than there were franchises available. Given the strictly controlled expansion of the National Association, an alternative was needed. That came with the creation of a number of independent baseball leagues that were not members of the National Association and were made up of clubs that were not farm clubs of major league teams. In June of 1993, the Northern League, with five teams in the upper Midwest and one in Thunder Bay, Ontario, and the Frontier League, with eight teams in southern Ohio and northern Kentucky, began operations. Over the next five years, 13 more leagues were formed. Only five of these, including the Northern and Frontier leagues made it into the twenty-first century; two didn't even make it through their first season. Between 2001 and 2014, another 11 began operations. Only six independent leagues competed in the 2019 season.

Many leagues and teams failed because owners and league officials lacked experience in running professional baseball operations both on and off the field; carefully thought-out business plans; sufficient startup capital; and playing fields and stadiums that met minimal standards. Canadian independent league teams faced these challenges and two other very significant ones: the problems of a late arriving spring with frequently very chilly weather and the fact that, during the early weeks of the season, most Canadian sports fans were focused on the National Hockey League playoff games that were shown nightly on television.

In this chapter, we shall trace the fortunes of 23 independent baseball clubs which, between 1993 and 2019, represented 14 Canadian cities in 10 independent professional leagues. The stories of Canada's most successful independent teams, the Winnipeg Goldeyes and les Capitales de Quebec, will be told in Chapter 11.

THUNDER BAY WHISKEY JACKS: Northern League (1993–1998)

The Northern League, which morphed into the American Association late in the first decade of the twenty-first century, was the brainchild of Miles Wolff, a veteran minor league owner and administrator who, in the 1980s, had made the Durham Bulls of the Carolina League one of the great success stories of the minor leagues and the subject of one of the most popular of all baseball movies. During the early 1990s, he scouted out several cities in the upper Midwest, looking for ones that had a baseball history but hadn't hosted professional teams for several years and had suitable ball parks and large enough populations to draw sufficient fans. He then recruited as owners experienced minor-league operators to form a professional league with no ties to the National Association or Major League Baseball. One of the six teams in the inaugural season was located in Thunder Bay, which was chosen to be a geographical partner to Duluth, Minnesota, 190 miles to the southwest. The city reluctantly allocated $250,000 for necessary improvement to a 42-year-old stadium. Team owner/general manager Rickey May, who had served as general manager for Wolff's Durham Bulls, began putting together on and off-field teams.

1993. With the exception of the Rochester, Minnesota, Aces, who played in a small park in a small market, the clubs in the Northern League's 1993 inaugural season enjoyed success. Teams were made up of undrafted college players, young and veteran minor leaguers released by major league organizations, and a sprinkling of former major leaguers, the most notable of whom were the Saint Paul Saints' Leon "Bull" Durham and the Sioux Falls Canaries' Pedro Guerrero. Much of the attention was focused on the St. Paul Saints, run by Mike Veeck, who orchestrated a game-day experience that included very good baseball, a trained pig who delivered baseballs to the home plate umpire, and a nun who gave massages at a station in the third base stands. The Saints won both halves of the split season and the playoff championship.

The Whiskey Jacks' roster included one major leaguer, Rodney McCray, who had appeared in a total of 67 games for the Chicago White Sox and New York Mets, and nine rookies, including two 19-year-olds from Japan. The season didn't begin well for Thunder Bay, which lost its first six games, all played on the road. When it returned to Canada, manager Dan Shwam, a long-time coach in the lower minor leagues, got the team turned around. The club finished the first half with a 19 wins, 16 losses record, good for second place, 1.5 games behind St. Paul. The second half was less successful, as the Whiskey Jacks finished in third place, two games below .500. Pat Tilmon posted a 2.38 ERA, which earned him a berth on the all-star team. The Whiskey Jacks drew 127,581 fans in just under three dozen home games.

1994. Manager Dan Shwam returned in 1994. However, only five of the previous season's players, including Pete Kuld, who would hit a league leading 27 homers, were back. Two of the leading newcomers were Rod Steph and Toronto-born Warren Sawkiw, both of whom had been released from major league organizations. Sawkiw hit .322 and Steph, who made the all-star team, had eight wins and one loss. Although the Whiskey Jacks posted a 22 wins, 18 losses record during the first half, they finished a disappointing fourth. The second half was a disaster: 12 wins and 27 losses. Total attendance increased by 5,000, but given that four games had been added to the home schedule, the per-game average was slightly down.

1995. During the off-season, Shwam left for a managing job in a different independent league, and the Whiskey Jacks hired Doug Ault, who had played four seasons with the Toronto Blue Jays and gone on to manage a number of teams in their farm system. The club won only 14 games while losing 28 in the first half, finishing sixth and last, and, although they were better in the second half with a 24–18 record, they finished second, seven games out of first place. The dismal on-field performance affected the gate profoundly: over 30,000 fewer fans attended than in the previous year, for a total of 100, 211, second-poorest in the league.

1996. Following the 1995 season, Rickey May sold the Whiskey Jacks to an American group headed by veteran minor league administrator Bill Terlecky. Jason Felice, a popular member of the 1993 squad, was hired as manager. The league added teams in Madison, Wisconsin, and Fargo-Moorhead, North Dakota/Minnesota, and was organized in two divisions. The Whiskey Jacks finished in fourth and last place in the East Division for both halves of the season. Felice was fired after compiling a 10 win–16 loss record and was replaced by Jay Ward, an experienced minor league manager who would lead the club for the rest of its tenure in the Northern League. The team's top player was Sean Hearn, whose .322 batting average and 20 home runs earned him a berth on the all-star team. Second baseman Casey Waller (.300) was also an all-star. Attendance dropped to just above 50,000.

1997. In Jay Ward's first full season as manager, Thunder Bay continued its losing ways, posting 18 wins, 24 losses for both halves of the season. Danny Lewis, a 1986 second-round draft pick for the Houston Astros, tied for the Northern League batting championship with a .358 average and led Thunder Bay with 24 home runs. One piece of bright news was that attendance rose by 12,000 to 62,496—still not enough for the organization to turn a profit.

1998. This was a make-or-break season for the Whiskey Jacks. If they could put together a winning team and draw decent crowds, they could perhaps continue operations. For the first time, the team finished on top of its division, posting a 22 win, 21 loss record for the first half. The Whiskey Jacks slumped in the second half, winning 18 and losing 24, finishing second. However, they had made the playoffs at last. They faced the St. Paul Saints during the first round, losing three games to two. Returning veterans Danny Lewis and Pat Tilmon led the way during the season with a .316 batting average and 17 home runs and an eight wins, six loses mound record respectively.

Even with the successful on-field season, attendance did not pick up. In fact, it dropped by 8,000 to 54,566, the lowest in the Northern League. The drop was not completely the club's fault. From mid–May to mid–June, the team was locked out of Port Arthur Stadium because of a strike of civic employees. Spring training had to be held in Grand Forks, North Dakota, an eight-hour drive away, and the first six home games were held in Grand Forks, Fargo, and Wahpeton, North Dakota, each game drawing less than 100 fans. Officials estimated the strike cost the Whiskey Jacks $200,000 in lost ticket, concessions, and other revenue. Shortly after the end of the season, the Whiskey Jacks ownership announced the sale of the franchise to a group from Schaumberg, a prosperous Chicago suburb that had built a state-of-the-art facility with the hopes of acquiring an expansion Northern League franchise.

Saskatoon Riot, Regina Cyclones: *North Central League (1994)*

During the summer of 1993, two Thunder Bay residents, Dave and Chris Ferguson, who, with their father Dave Sr., were part-owners of the local minor league hockey team, had been very impressed with the success of the Whiskey Jacks and the Northern League in general. "One day," Dave told me a few years later, "I was looking at a map of Canada and I realized that there weren't any Canadian professional baseball clubs between Thunder Bay and Calgary." He, his brother and his father began discussing the idea of locating an independent league team somewhere in this pro-baseball desert. They learned that George Vedder, a pharmacist who had unsuccessfully applied for a Northern League franchise, was considering forming a league that would operate in Minnesota and the Dakotas. They cast their lot with Vedder and established franchises in Saskatoon and Regina, Saskatchewan.

The caliber of the teams and the playing facilities were definitely at least a notch below those of the Northern League. Five of the parks were city-owned recreational facilities used by American Legion and other amateur teams; the sixth was the home of the University of Minnesota Golden Gophers. Regina played at Currie Field, which was also a soccer pitch and football field and had a ridge running from halfway down the first base line to deep left center field. Their clubhouse, a walk across two recreation fields, served in the winter as the headquarters for the local figure skating club.

1994. The Regina Cyclones roster included three members of the 1993 Thunder Bay roster: Jason Felice (player/manager), Tommy Griffith, and Dennis Hood, along with 13 rookies (most undrafted college players) and a sprinkling of released players from the lower minors. For eight players, this was the last season in professional ball; only two players made it back to major league organizations. The Saskatoon Riot roster was even less experienced. One player had briefly reached the triple A level and fifteen were rookies.

The Regina Cyclones dominated the regular season, winning the western division with a 44–25 record, best in the league. Player-manager Jason Felice won a triple crown with a .343 batting average along with 73 RBIs and 17 home runs; Dennis Hood had 93 hits; and he and Tommy Griffith scored 69 runs. Saskatoon's 32 wins, 38 losses earned them second place in the West Division, 12.5 games behind the Cyclones. Regina lost the playoff championship three games to two to the East Division leaders, the Brainerd Bears.

The Cyclones and the Riot led the North Central League in attendance, with 48,892 and 47,544, respectively, and ended the reason in relatively healthy financial condition. During the off season, the Fergusons became disenchanted with Vedder's leadership and, along with Greg Olson, owner of the Minneapolis Loons, began plans to form their own league. The North Central League folded a month into the 1995 season.

Brandon Grey Owls/West Man Wranglers, Moose Jaw Diamond Dogs, Regina Cyclones, Saskatoon Riot/ Smoking Guns/Stallions: *Prairie League (1995–1997)*

1995. The Prairie League that was formed by the Ferguson brothers and Greg Olson was one of 11 independent leagues—seven of them new—to start the 1995 season. Three leagues suspended operations early in their seasons; only two of the new leagues (the Northeast League and the Western Baseball League) survived into the twenty-first century. In addition to teams in Regina, Saskatoon, and Minneapolis, the Prairie League had franchises in Moose Jaw, Saskatchewan; Brandon, Manitoba; Aberdeen, South Dakota; and Bismarck and Minot, North Dakota.

Of the 142 players listed on the 1995 rosters of the four Canadian teams, 78 were rookies and only 21 had played High A level minor league baseball or above. One, Bryan Clutterbuck, who joined the Brandon Grey Owls during the season as player-manager, had pitched for two years in the major leagues. For 84 of the players, the inaugural Prairie League season would be their last in professional baseball. Only Shawn Wooten of Moose Jaw and Chris Coste of Brandon would make it to the major leagues.

The Moose Jaw Diamond Dogs, managed by Mike Brocki, won the Canadian Division, with 44 wins and 28 losses, finishing three games in front of the Regina Cyclones. Bryan Cornelius dominated batting statistics, with a league-leading .403 average; he also hit 20 home runs, fourth-best in the league, and was named to the all-star team. The team's other all-star, third baseman Sean Wooten, hit .373.

Jason Felice led the Regina Cyclones, on the bench and in the field, to a second-place finish in the division. He hit .394 and belted 23 home runs, earning him an outfield berth on the all-star team. Saskatoon and Brandon had dreary seasons. The Saskatoon Riot finished in third 17.5 games back of Regina. The Brandon Grey Owls won only 19 games while losing 51. Chris Coste, who joined the team after Brainerd of the North Central League folded, would play five years in the independent leagues, before being signed by the Philadelphia Phillies. He entered the big leagues in 2006.

In the league final, the Aberdeen Pheasants, who dominated the American Division with an amazing win-loss percentage of .812, met the Regina Cyclones, who had won their first round series two games to one against Moose Jaw. Regina won the finals three games to one.

Currie Field, Regina, home of the independent Prairie League Regina Cyclones, was also used as a field for amateur Canadian football teams. A ridge ran from left center field through the infield to first base (author's photograph).

Officials declared the Prairie League's inaugural season a success and announced that a total of 310,000 had attended regular season games. Moose Jaw, owned by Murray Brace, an almost frenetically energetic promoter, attracted 75,000 fans for 36 home games. Regina's attendance was up by a total of 800 to 49,223; Saskatoon's total of 38,711 was a drop of 8,000. Brandon averaged only 688 a game.

1996. The league began the season with eleven teams: seven of the previous year's clubs returned, with the eighth, Minneapolis transferring operation to Austin, Minnesota (where they became the Southern Minny Stars). In Saskatoon, the Riot became the Smokin' Guns. There were three new teams: the Green Bay (Wisconsin) Sultans, Brainerd (Minnesota) Bobcats, and Grand Forks (North Dakota) Varmints. The league now extended 1,200 miles, from central Saskatchewan to the shores of Lake Michigan.

During the regular season, Moose Jaw Diamond Dogs dominated the North Division, posting half-season records of 24 wins, 12 losses, and 26 wins 17 losses, finishing 5.5 and 5 games ahead of second place Grand Forks. Regina finished third in the first and second halves, 7.5 and 11.5 games out of first. Saskatoon and Brandon finished a dismal fourth and fifth. Grand Forks defeated Moose Jaw two games to one in the first round of the playoffs.

The Diamond Dogs, with 13 members of last year's team returning, dominated the all-star team: catcher Kevin Schula posted a .325 average; third baseman Randy Kapano hit .310 and belted 18 home runs; outfielder Brian Cornelius had a league second-best .388 average along with 18 homers and also earned the most valuable player award; pitcher Mike Toney earned 17 saves. Regina's player-manager Daryl Boston, a veteran of 11 major league seasons, led the Cyclones with a .352 average. The Saskatoon Smokin' Guns shot blanks most of the year, although Waune Weinheimer posted a .355 average, while manager Andre Johnson hit 15 home runs.

Off the playing field, the organizational and financial stability the league sought to achieve did not come. Less than three weeks into the season, the Brainerd Bobcats had drawn less than 300 fans a game, and the league shut the team down. Aberdeen was nearly suspended in a dispute with league officials, while league president and Smokin' Gun owner Dave Ferguson raised the ire of other league members when he refused to give them access to the league books. Although Moose Jaw drew over a thousand more fans than in the previous season, attendance in the rest of the league was down. The other three Canadian teams each drew 15,000 fewer fans than in 1995. After the close of the season, Green Bay was expelled for failure to pay long-outstanding dues and Dakota, after accumulating over $300,000 in debts, withdrew.

1997. During the off-season, Murray Brace announced that he was selling his very successful Moose Jaw Diamond Dogs team and moving 40 miles to the east to run the Regina Cyclones. As events of the next summer would prove, his decision marked the beginning of the end of the Prairie League. In 1997, the Diamond Dogs, under new ownership, attracted less than 14,000 fans and, in late July, unpaid players refused to go on a 10-day road trip. The team was disbanded. Shortly after, the Brandon club, which during the winter had acquired its third set of owners in as many years and had been renamed the West Man Wranglers, announced its intention to withdraw from the league; two days later the club recanted. In the meantime, the league suspended the Aberdeen Pheasants for several days for non-payment of dues.

As the dog days of August approached, Prairie League co-commissioner Mike Elgie resigned, citing personal reasons and an overwhelming workload. Murray Brace left his job as Regina general manager; and Mitch Zwolensky, the volatile manager of the Minot Mallards and the league director of player personnel, was suspended for the balance of the season when he kept his team off the field for an hour and a half, refusing to play a road game because the team's laundry was still damp. Although Regina's attendance rose to 47,000 and Saskatoon's to 28,000, attendance in the rest of the league was down. The West Man Wranglers attracted only 7,000 paying fans.

On the field, the Prairie League's last season was a good one for the Regina Cyclones and the Saskatoon Stallions (renamed by a new American ownership group). Regina won the first half of the season, Saskatoon the second. The Cyclones won the first round of the playoffs, two games to one against their in-province rivals, before losing the championship to Minot in three straight games. Regina's Randy Kapano, with a .383 batting average and 23 homers, was selected for the all-star team and voted the league's most valuable player. Teammate Thomas Taylor, who posted a 1.65 earned run average, was also named an all-star. Stallions named to the squad were shortstop Brian Giles (.360), a former major leaguer; outfielders Brian Cornelius (.320) and Andre Johnson (.358); and pitcher Ernesto Nieves, who had 10 wins against only one loss.

In the early fall, President Dave Ferguson returned to Thunder Bay saying that he would no longer continue administering the league. After three tumultuous summers, the Prairie League was dead.

WELLAND AQUADUCKS: *North Atlantic League (1995–1996)*

The North Atlantic League, another of the short-lived independent leagues of the mid–1990s, began the first of its two seasons with teams in four cities that had lost their National Association franchises: Nashua, New Hampshire; Newark and Niagara Falls, New York; and Welland, Ontario. The league was run by and all the teams were owned by Ed Broidy, a real estate operator who, a few years earlier, had tried unsuccessfully to form a minor professional hockey league in the American southeast. The Welland Aquaducks played their games in the Welland Sports Stadium, which had been built in 1989 to house the short season Class A Pittsburgh affiliate in the New York–Pennsylvania League.

1995. Of the 30 young athletes—the average age of the team was just under 22 years—to put on Aquaducks uniforms during the season, 27 were rookies. None of the players would make it into Organized Baseball and for 17, it was their only season as professional players. The Aquaducks performed creditably on the field, winning 32 and losing 27, good enough to finish second, 5.5 games behind the Nashua Barge Bandits. There were no playoffs. Three Welland players, shortstop William Bellanger (.297), outfielders Doug Shumway (.292) and Chris Neill (.337), along with manager Ellis Williams, made the post-season all-star squad. Total home attendance was only 2,563, lowest in the league.

1996. The Aquaducks were more experienced than last year. Thirteen players, including nine returnees, had played in independent leagues, while six had been member of affiliated teams in the lower minors. That greater experience did not help the team. Even though returning catcher Chris Hasty (.269) and outfielder Dan Dillingham (.356) made the all-star team, the club finished fifth in the standings, 23 games out of first. Attendance rose to just under 7,000, which was, again, the worst in the league.

Shortly after the close of the season, the team and the league ceased operations.

Surrey Glaciers: *Western Baseball League (1995)*

The Western Baseball League, which was conceived by Bruce Engel, a Portland timber magnate and former owner of independent league teams in Duluth, Minnesota, and Erie, Pennsylvania, opened its first season in May 1995. Three of the eight cities—Palm Springs, Sonoma Country, and Salinas—had hosted clubs in the California League, and three others—Bend, Oregon, and Tri-Cities and Greys Harbor, Washington—in the Northwest League. The two other franchises were located in Long Beach, California, and Surrey, British Columbia, a rapidly growing city with a population of over 300,000.

The Surrey Glaciers (the name related to the top-selling beer of a major sponsor) were owned by Engel and a group of local investors led by Stu Kehoe, a former general manager of the Vancouver Canadians of the Pacific Coast League. The team would play its home games at Stetson Bowl, a former rodeo grounds that would be extensively renovated for baseball with funds largely supplied by the local civic government.

Kehoe picked Dick Phillips, a one-time major leaguer and former manager and later front office official with the Vancouver Canadians, as his field manager. Phillips compiled a roster that included rookies and 17 players with minor league experience. For one of these former minor leaguers, 32-year-old Joe Strong, playing in an independent league meant having a second chance. After a 10-year career with affiliated teams, he had been released during the offseason. He was a workhorse on the mound for the Glaciers, winning eight while losing nine, but striking out 129 batters in 131 innings. He dropped out of baseball after 1995, later played in Korea and Mexico, and was then signed by the Tampa Bay Devil Rays. At age 38, he made his major league debut and, in two seasons, appeared in 23 games.

The Glaciers started well, finishing the first half in first place with a 26–16 record, but collapsed in the second half with only 12 wins against 36 losses. They were defeated two games to nothing in their semi-final against Salinas. The on-field melt-down was paralleled by one in the stands. During the first half, the Glaciers averaged 1,400 fans a game; during the second, under 800. The final attendance figure, 53,769, was the second lowest in the Western Baseball League.

Stories appearing in Vancouver newspapers in August and in the weeks after the season ended cast some light on why the team fared so poorly on the field and at the box office during the second half. The city of Surrey had, it was revealed, entrusted oversight for the renovations to the ball club, which ignored the process of seeking bids from contractors and even offered a contract to one of the Glaciers' minority owners. The cost of the renovations was over a million dollars above estimates and, when that was known, the city called in the $300,000 security pledge that the Glaciers had intended to use for operating expenses, including players' salaries. In the fall, it was also discovered that over $100,000 of the money provided by Surrey had been diverted to cover club expenses. As the story unfolded during August, disgusted local baseball fans stopped coming to Stetson Bowl.

After the season, it was discovered that the players hadn't received a full paycheck since mid–July and that players had helped each other with meal money. On one occasion, the bus driver refused to leave on a road trip because he hadn't been paid. In late September the mascot revealed that he was still owed $900. In October 1995, the Western Baseball League announced that the Surrey Glaciers had been officially decertified.

London Werewolves: *Frontier League (1999–2001)*

The Frontier League had begun operations in 1993 in small towns in southern Ohio and northeast Kentucky. In the following seasons, the league began placing franchises in larger centers in Pennsylvania, Ohio, Indiana, Illinois, Missouri, and, in 1999, Ontario. The London Werewolves had begun in 1994 as the Buffalos, playing in Newark, Ohio, a city of 47,000. The Buffalos became extinct after the 1995 season and were reborn as the Kalamazoo, Michigan, Kodiaks, playing to baseball fans from a metropolitan population area of 150,000. However, after three seasons, the Kodiaks became an endangered species, and morphed into the Werewolves, playing in London, which had a metropolitan area with a population over twice the size of Kalamazoo.

1999. The Werewolves were operated by the John Kuhns, Senior and Junior, who had bought the club while it was still in Kalamazoo. The younger Kuhn was a disciple of and had worked for Mike Veeck, whose promotional genius had made the St. Paul Saints of the Northern League a great success The team was named after "The Werewolves of London," a popular song from the late 1970s by Warren Zevon. The mascot, a werewolf named "Warren Z. Vaughn," entertained fans between innings with foolish and sometimes outrageous antics. Kuhn provided London fans with a variety of unusual, zany promotions, including Salute to Silly Putty Night to celebrate the 50th anniversary of the children's toy, and Bad Rug Night, when men with toupees got in for free. The team, which played in historic Labatt Park, drew 60,456, over 19,000 more than it had the year before in Kalamazoo.

Most of the players were fairly young. The Frontier League's 1999 roster regulations specified that every team's 24-man roster must include a minimum of 11 first-year players, a maximum of 8 players with one year of experience, and a maximum of three veterans. Moreover, every player had to be under the age of 27 at the beginning of the season. The roster assembled by Andy McCauley, who had never played professional baseball, but had begun an over two-decade career as a manager in the independent leagues the previous year in Kalamazoo, reflected these roster specifications. There were 13 rookies, nine players with previous independent league experience (including six from Kalamazoo), and three who had had brief careers in the affiliated minor leagues. Three players, rookies Jamie Pogue and Ian Harvey and second-year player Brett Gray, were Canadians.

The Werewolves ended the season with 54 wins against 30 losses, finishing first in the East Division, 6.5 games ahead of Chillicothe. London defeated Johnstown in the semi-finals and Chillicothe in the finals, two games to none in both series. Outfielder Rick Nadeau, the team's best hitter, with a .348 batting average, and shortstop Dalphie

Correa, with .344, were named to the all-star team. Scott Conner had a 10–5 record on the mound, and Brett Gray set a league record by striking out 125 batters. Andy McCauley was named manager of the year.

2000. Optimism ran high at the beginning of the 2000 season. Manager Andy McCauley and 10 members of the championship team, including Rick Nadeau and pitching stalwarts Scott Connor and Brett Gray, were returning. Gray's 2000 stay with the Werewolves was brief. In his first start, which was also the team's home opener, he struck out 25 batters and a few days later was signed by the Cincinnati Reds and sent to their Class A Midwest team, the Dayton Dragons. London finished second in the East Division, 1.5 games behind the Johnstown Johnnies, the team they'd beaten the previous year in the semi-finals, and then lost to them two games to none in the semifinals. Three Werewolves were named to the all-star team: shortstop Geoff McCallum (.295 average), designated hitter Chris Gavriel (.337—third highest in the league), and outfielder Rick Nadeau (.312 average and a league-high 19 home runs). Nadeau was also named the Frontier League's

A native of Sarnia, Ontario, pitcher Brett Gray opened the London Werewolves' 2000 season by striking out 25 batters. A week later he signed a contract with the Cincinnati Reds' organization, for which he played five seasons (photograph by Jeffrey Reed/LondonOntarioSports.com).

most valuable player. Attendance at Labatt Field dropped by a total of 1,700.

2001. During the off season, Andy McCauley left London to manage an expansion team in Kalamazoo, taking 10 Werewolves with him. His replacement, Bruce Gray, Brett's father, moved up from the role of pitching coach. It was a long and disappointing season that ended with the Werewolves in fifth place, with a 37–47 record, 14 games out of first place. One of the bright spots of the season was the batting of New Westminster, British Columbia, resident Ben Van Iderstine (one of six Canadians on the team). His .338 average earned him a shot at Organized Ball, where he would reach the Double A level.

During the season, rumors circulated that the Werewolves might be playing their last season in London. Attendance in 2001 dropped by 19,000. Given that the club's revenue was in Canadian dollars (which were worth less than seventy cents American) and that nearly all their travelling expenses, as well as league dues, were payable in American dollars, the income generated was far less than expenses. Late in the year it was announced that the team had been sold to a group of Canton, Ohio, businessmen. The Werewolves wandered south where, in 2002, they became Coyotes.

VICTORIA CAPITALS, KELOWNA HEAT, CALGARY OUTLAWS, LONDON MONARCHS, SASKTOON LEGENDS, NIAGARA (Welland) STARS, MONTREAL ROYALES, TROIS-RIVIERES SAINTS: *Canadian Baseball League (1993)*

In September 2001, Tony Riviera, a Seattle resident, announced the formation of the Canadian Baseball League. Riviera was joined in Vancouver for the announcement by Charlton Liu, his chief financial backer and a former Microsoft developer and executive, and the league's commissioner, Canadian-born Ferguson Jenkins, a member of baseball's Hall of Fame and now a permanent resident of Oklahoma. Riviera stated that 25 cities, including Vancouver, were being considered as franchise locations. In November, the Regina Storm, Saskatoon Yellow Jackets, Red Deer Outlaws, Lethbridge Dust Devils, Kamloops Critters, Kelowna Heat, Abbotsford Saints, and Nanaimo Navigators were named as the teams to play in the inaugural season, 2002. All the teams would be owned by the league, an arrangement which, Riviera explained, would reduce expenses.

During the fall of 2001, Riviera announced that the caliber of play would be similar to the Japanese leagues which had become an important source of talent for major league teams. The players selected, he said, would be major league free agents, former major leaguers, and six-year free agents (minor leaguers who after six years were not on a major league roster and could become free agents). Each team would be required to carry five Canadian players. He noted that the league would have a $12 million operating budget and that he expected there to be a minimum of 2,000 season tickets sold for each team. Sixty thousand dollars a month would be budgeted for salaries, with high profile players earning up to $7,000 and rookies just over $1,000 a month.

On February 12, 2002, the Canadian Baseball League issued a press release stating that, in order to be on sounder organizational footing, opening day was postponed from May of 2002 to May of 2003. Later in the year, the eight teams that would make up the league were announced. The Victoria Capitals and Calgary Outlaws would play in the Western Division, along with the Kelowna Heat and the renamed Saskatoon Legends. The Eastern Division would be comprised of the London Monarchs, Niagara Stars (Welland), Trois-Rivières Saints, and Montreal Royals. Attempts to find a home for the Montreal Royals failed and the team ended up playing some of its games in nearby Sherbrooke and the rest at the homes of their opponents. Jeff Mallett, who had grown up in Victoria and had become the CEO and President of Yahoo, became a major investor. Liu predicted that the league would become profitable in its first year.

The composition of the rosters of the CBL teams bore little resemblance to those of Double A or Triple A affiliated teams—something Riviera had said they would. Of the over 250 players appearing in 2003, there were nine former major leaguers whose careers had ranged from six to 196 games; another 10 players had reached the triple A level and seven double A. Fifty-four had labored in the lower minors and another 23 had experience in the independent leagues. One hundred and sixty-four were first year players. There were 70 players from Latin American countries, many of whom had been let go from major league organizations and couldn't get visas to play in the United States.

None of the 13 Japanese players had appeared in either of Japan's two major leagues. Most of the rookies were Canadians, but two other Canadians were former big leaguers. Thirty-one-year-old Victoria-born Steve Sinclair (45 major league games in two seasons) pitched for his hometown, compiling a no win–two loss record, with a 7.27 ERA. Toronto's Rick Potter (34 years old), who'd appeared in 86 major league contests over three seasons, posted a .277 average for the Niagara Stars.

The first game was played in London, on May 21. A crowd of just over 5,000 watched as Ferguson Jenkins tossed the ceremonial first pitch, the Snowbirds aerial team flew over Labatt Park, and the Monarchs defeated the homeless Montreal Royals, 13–3. The final game of the series drew only 545. In Welland, just over 500 showed up for an opener that had been postponed several times by rain. In Victoria, things were better: 3,623 attended the opener. Around the league, attendance dropped steadily. Only Victoria and Calgary were regularly drawing over 1,000 per game.

In early June, Mallett took over from Riviera as chairman and chief operating officer. Things did not improve and on July 18, he announced that the Canadian Baseball League would suspend operations after an all-star game to be held in Calgary, on June 23. The league stated that it would reorganize over the winter and, in the meantime, players' salaries for the rest of the year and all debts would be paid. Season ticket holders would receive refunds for the unpaid games. In early September the league, which had debts totaling over $1.7 million (including just over $150 to each of Welland's teenage bat boys), was placed in receivership. In December, an auction of the league's "belongings"—bats and balls, uniforms and hats, and even a batting cage—was held.

At the end of the truncated season, London topped the East Division with a .606 win-loss percentage; Calgary won the West with a .649 percentage. Because there were no playoffs, Calgary, with the better record, was "declared" the champion. Individual statistics were dominated by Latin players. Of the 10 players with a batting average of over .350, eight were Latin. One Galindo Gomez posted a .403 average. Canadian Ben Van Iderstine was runner up; his average of .401 was enough to earn him a contract in the affiliated leagues, where he reached the Double A level. The leading pitcher was Bienvenido Feliz of Saskatoon, with a 6–2 record.

When the season ended in late July, nearly 200 players found themselves with no baseball jobs and little chance of finding any during the rest of the season. For 150 players, their time in the shortened CBL season was their last in professional baseball. A poor business plan accompanied by unreasonable promises, virtually no local marketing, a fairly low level of play, an overabundance of Latin players and the relatively low status of the Canadian players, and unending, but deserved bad publicity surrounding the league from its inception to its demise guaranteed the failure of what, in more skillful hands, might have become a fairly successful professional sports enterprise.

CALGARY VIPERS, EDMONTON CRACKERCATS: *Northern League (2005–2007)*

In the autumn of 2003, three months after the Calgary Outlaws and the rest of the Canadian Baseball League teams had suspended operations and one day after the announcement that the Edmonton Trappers of the PCL had been sold and would move to Texas after the 2004 season, rumors were that the Alberta cities would acquire franchises in the Northern League, the very successful independent league that had begun play in 1993. During the winter, it was reported that two Edmonton and two Calgary groups would apply for franchises. Mel Kowalchuk, who had run the Edmonton Trappers for two decades and who had recently finished a very successful two years of setting up the Albuquerque Isotopes and leading them through a very profitable first year, and Dan Orlich, a Florida real estate developer, were one Edmonton group. The other included members of the Edmonton Eskimos administration and board. Russ Parker, owner of the PCL's Calgary Cannons, headed one of the Calgary groups, and two American and one Japanese businessmen the other. In April 2004, two expansion franchises were granted: Kowalchuk and Orlich would operate the Edmonton team; the American-Japanese group the one from Calgary. The entry fee to the Northern League would be $1 million each. In addition, each Alberta team would have to pay $50,000 annually to subsidize the league's other clubs' travel to Alberta.

Over the next several months, Kowalchuk went about the business of setting up the new team. He assembled an experienced front office staff, many of whom had worked for the Trappers, announced the team nickname, Cracker-Cats, a reference to the oil field operation of catalytic cracking, and hired Terry Bevington, one-time manager of the Chicago White Sox as manager. Meanwhile, in Calgary, the owners had done virtually nothing to transform their impressive business plan into a reality. In December 2004, the Northern League revoked their franchise, took over running the still unnamed team and began looking for owners. In mid–February, less than three months before the season opened, Jeff Gidney, a Winnipeg businessman, was named as the new owner. He hired Peter Young, a former Manitoba sports broadcaster, as president. A team name was chosen, Vipers, and a manager, Mike Busch, who'd had a very brief major league career, appointed. Renovations began at the somewhat run-down Burns Stadium.

2005. During the season, the Cracker-Cats fielded a total of ten rookies, one of whom, Edmontonian Aric Van Gallen, was drafted by the Seattle Mariners during the season. North Vancouver resident Scott Richmond would play three seasons for the Cracker-Cats before being signed by the Toronto Blue Jays and going on to play during four major league seasons. The two were among the 11 Canadians to play for the team. Another of the Canadians was Stubby Clapp, the only Edmonton player with major league experience (23 games during one season) and a member of Canada's national baseball team. Twelve players had experience with affiliated minor league clubs, including four at the Triple A level. Seven were veterans of other independent league teams.

The Vipers' roster included 31 players with experience in organized baseball, seven at the AA or AAA level. There were also two former major leaguers, Dan Reichert (124 games in five seasons), and Pedro Santana (seven games in one season). Five members of the team came from the Dominican Republic and seven were Canadians, one of whom, Greg Morrison, had won a triple crown while playing for his hometown Medicine Hat Blue Jays of the Pioneer League.

Neither of the two expansion teams made post-season play. Calgary finished second in the Northern Division for both halves of the season, 2.5 games out of first in the first half and 14.5 games out of first in the second. The Cracker-Cats finished fifth and third. Calgary's third baseman Carlos Duncan, with a .319 batting average and 20 home runs, and second baseman Pedro Santana, with a .288 average, were named to the league's all-star team.

Edmonton's and Calgary's final attendance figures of 107,987 and 55,066, respectively, were the two lowest in the league. While the Vipers' low turnout can be attributed in large part to the facts that the new owners had very little time to develop preseason marketing and ticket sales campaigns, Edmonton's was caused by more serious problems. In spite of the fact that Dan Orlich and his life partner and club vice-president Ericka Cruise had no previous experience running minor league sports franchises, they decided well before the season to become hands-on, some might say counter-productive, meddling, owners. On opening day, Cruise very loudly fired one of the ushers helping invited dignitaries to their seats. Then a few weeks later, she picked a fight with the Big River Prospects amateur team, the other tenant of Telus Field, restricting their use of seating and concession areas. Newspaper reports suggested that she was encouraging employees to spy on each other and that general manager Kowalchuk had to be talked out of resigning more than once. In mid–July, Kowalchuk was fired and his assistant general manager Fraser Murray resigned. Edmonton fans began staying away from the games in increasing numbers. The opening day had drawn 5,200 people and for the next several games had been in the mid to high two thousands. It dropped drastically over the next two-and-a-half months.

Shortly after the end of the season, four Northern League teams—the St. Paul Saints, Lincoln Saltdogs, Sioux Falls Canaries, and Sioux City Explorers—withdrew from the league to join the newly-formed American Association.

2006. The situation did not improve in either Calgary or Edmonton. The Vipers and Cracker-Cats played under .500 ball for both halves of their seasons. There was a bright spot on each club: Calgary's Manabu Kuramochi had emailed the Vipers from Japan requesting a tryout. He posted a .303 average, stole 29 bases, made the all-star team and was voted rookie of the year. Edmonton's Stubby Clapp raised his average by 36 points to .323 and was named all-star shortstop. In a not so illustrious highlight, Terry Bevington resigned as Cracker-Cats manager during the season in protest against an eight-game suspension meted out by the league after a major brawl between the Cats and the Vipers. He was replaced by pitching coach John Barlowe. Attendance dropped by 42,000 in Edmonton (with the per-game average 1,000 below the breakeven point) and by 50,000 in Calgary (to barely over 1,000 a game).

At the close of the season, Dean Hengel, who had been a member of the University of Alberta Athletics Department and who had joined the Cats' sales staff midway through the 1995 season and been named general manager at the end of it, was relieved of his duties. Al Coates, the team's radio broadcaster, was named to replace him. John Barlowe, who had been given a two-year contract at the end of the 2006 season, was informed during the winter that he would not be reemployed and that his job as manager would be given to pitching coach Frank Reberger. During the off-season, Calgary owner Jeff Gidney spent $800,000 to purchase over 2,000 new and more comfortable seats for the Calgary park.

2007. The Cracker-Cats entered the season without Stubby Clapp, the face of the franchise, who had retired to take a job as hitting coach in the Houston Astros' organization. However, Scott Richmond and Reggie Rivard, the mainstays of the pitching staff, were back. Joining them were three players with major league experience: Mike Johnson, an Edmonton native who had pitched for the PCL Trappers in 2004; Ryan Radmanovich, a power hitter from Calgary; and pitcher Lou Pote, who had played for the Trappers for two seasons at the turn of the century. Although the Cracker-Cats appeared stronger on paper, they proved not to be on the field: they finished both halves of the season in fourth (last place) in the Northern Division. Early in August, Frank Reberger was fired as manager and replaced with pitching coach Gord Gerlach. During the season Scot Richmond was the workhorse on the mound: winning 10 and losing nine, while striking out 110 batters over 145 innings. His performance earned him a contract in the Toronto Blue Jays organization and he appeared in his first major league game in July 2008. Terrence McClain, a five-year veteran of the independent leagues, now in his second season in Edmonton, led the club in batting with a .304 average. In spite of the poor showing on the field, attendance increased by over 16,000 to 82,414, still well below the break-even point of just over 140,000.

The Calgary Vipers finished the first half on top of the Northern Division with 29 wins and 19 losses. They slumped to third place in the second half, winning 21 and losing 27. They defeated Fargo-Moorhead in the semifinals before losing to Gary, three games to two in the finals. The Vipers dominated the all-star team. Darryl Brinkley, who won the batting championship with an amazing .399 average, was named one of the three outfield all-stars and league MVP. Carlos Duncan (.350), third base, Nelson Castro (.323), shortstop, and Jason Colson (.290), first base, comprised three-quarters of the all-star infield. Calgary attendance increased by 21,338 to just over 71,000, the best in the club's three years in the Northern League. But that figure was well below the breakeven point.

The Vipers and the Cracker-Cats would play baseball again next season. However, it would be in a new independent circuit, the lower-level Golden Baseball League.

CALGARY VIPERS, EDMONTON CRACKERCATS/CAPITALS, VICTORIA SEALS: *Golden Baseball League (2008–2010)*

As the 2007 Northern League season drew to a close, an uneasy peace existed between the two Alberta teams and the rest of the league. League executives were concerned with the financial losses incurred by the two teams and by the ongoing front-office instability of the Edmonton team. The Northern League feared that the Alberta clubs might either fold during mid-season or, as had been rumored, jump to the Golden Baseball League, which operated in California, Utah, Arizona, and Nevada. League officials demanded that the Vipers and Cracker-Cats each post a $500,000 letter of credit as security. The management of the Vipers and Cracker-Cats reacted angrily, and, late in the fall, they applied to and were accepted into the three-year-old Golden League, the caliber of play of which was reported to be slightly lower than that of the Northern League.

2008. During the winter, the Vipers and Cracker-Cats front offices began preparing for the upcoming season. In Calgary, manager Mike Busch, back for his fourth season, built a roster that included several of the mainstays from previous years. In Edmonton, it was chaos as usual. Team broadcaster Al Coates indicated that he did not wish to continue as the club's general manager. A few weeks later, the Capacity Group, a Calgary sports management firm, was hired to run business operations. Six weeks later, it withdrew from the agreement, citing "philosophical differences" with owner Dan Orlich. A general manager was hired six weeks before the opening of the season but resigned after the first four games. Brent Bowers, who had played a handful of major league games for the Baltimore Orioles and had managed in the independent Frontier League and for six winters in Columbia, became the field boss—the fifth in four seasons.

The two Canadian teams began their first season in the Golden Baseball League in Edmonton. The Cracker-Cats defeated the Vipers 8–7 before a crowd "announced" as 2,177. On the strength of a seven-game winning streak in June, Calgary won the first half, finishing four games ahead of Edmonton. Edmonton won the second half, with a very strong 29 wins, 15 losses record; Calgary was second 9.5 games behind. The Vipers won the North Division playoffs in three straight games before losing the league championship three games to two to Orange County. Attendance dropped drastically in both Alberta cities: in Edmonton by 35,000 to just under 47,000; in Calgary by 26,000 to just under 46,000. The Golden Baseball League was a hitters' league. The overall league batting average was an amazing .307. Just over 800 home runs were hit in league parks. However, the league earned run average was 6.45 a game. Led by major league veteran Felix Jose, who posted a .391 average, seven Calgary regulars were above .300. Six Cracker-Cats were above .300 with Carlos Arroyo tops at .377. It was another losing season financially. Calgary lost $300,000, while Edmonton's losses, which were not disclosed, were believed to be as great if not greater.

2009. During the offseason both Alberta teams underwent important changes. Mike Busch was replaced as Calgary manager by Morgan Burkhart, the team's hitting coach. In Edmonton, the changes were greater. In January 2009, Dan Orlich sold the Cracker-Cats to the Edmonton Oilers of the National Hockey League. Renamed the Capitals (Edmonton is the capital city of Alberta), they would have a front office run by a team of experienced professionals, seasoned by their work with the National Hockey League team and the highly successful Edmonton Oil Kings of the Western Hockey League.

During the off season, a third Canadian city, Victoria, British Columbia, was granted an expansion franchise for a $350,000 (U.S.) fee, as were Tucson, Arizona, and Tijuana, Mexico. It was hoped that the addition of Victoria to the league would be a significant step toward the creation of an all-Canadian division. Named the Seals, the team was owned by Russ and Darren Parker of Calgary.

Calgary dominated the North Division, winning both halves of the split season, each time finishing four games ahead of second place Edmonton. They went on to win the division playoffs three games to one over Edmonton before defeating the Tucson Toros, also three games to one, in the finals, giving the city of Calgary its first professional baseball championship. The Vipers had the top four of the top hitters in the league: shortstop and league batting champion Nelson Castro (.410), outfielders Calvin Moro (.376) Fehlandt Lentini (.366), and Alberta native Drew Miller (.364). Each was named to the all-star team. Mac Suzuki was named top right-handed pitcher and Morgan Burkhart, manager of the year. Castro was the league's most valuable player.

Second place Edmonton never really challenged the Vipers during the season. Seven players, including Edmonton native Mike Johnson, had major league experience. They also signed Darryl Brinkley, who had been *Baseball America*'s 2007 Independent Leagues player of the year while playing for Calgary. Third baseman Chris Ehrnsberger (.332) and pitcher Lou Pote (nine wins, three losses), one of the ex-major leaguers, made the all-star team. The expansion Victoria Seals were never in contention, finishing fourth and third in the North Division. Seals pitcher Isaac Hess won an all-star berth with his nine wins, two losses record. Sergio Pedroza, with a .325 average, along with 17 home runs, was all-star second baseman.

Both Calgary and Edmonton saw increases in attendance. Even with its championship team, Calgary's was a modest boost of 9,224 to a total of 54,910. Edmonton's, where the administration scheduled several after-game fireworks displays, concerts, and movies, increased from 46,000 to nearly 85,000. Victoria was a pleasant surprise: despite finishing far out of contention during both halves of the season, the Seals drew 93,691 fans, the second-highest total in the league, to Royal Athletic Park.

2010. The Golden Baseball League expanded, adding the Tijuana Cimarrones and the Maui Na Koalkaika (Fierce Warriors) of Hawaii. The Victoria Seals opened the season with eight returnees and two former major leaguers, but with a new manager, 14-year big league veteran Bret Boone. It was his first managerial job and, citing family matters, he resigned after five games. Although the team finished 11 games out of first during the first half and six during the second, there were several bright spots. Catcher and assistant coach Josh Arhart was named to the all-star team and posted a .352 average, with 17 home runs. Utility man Wilver Perez stole a league-record 64 bases and was also named an all-star, as was Brandon Villafuerte, a former major leaguer who won six games and earned 12 saves.

The Edmonton Capitals, who had stacked their roster with eight former major leaguers, finished second and fourth in the North Division. Larry Bigbie, a former major leaguer, had a league high .403 batting average and was named to the all-star team as an outfielder. Lou Pote earned an all-star berth with a 9–3 record. Capitals manager Brent Bowers resigned in August, after he had been suspended by the league for directing homophobic slurs toward an umpire.

Calgary, again managed by Morgan Burkhart, had a dismal first half, finishing third, nine games out, but won the second half with an amazing 30 wins against 15 losses and met the Chico Outlaws in the division final, losing in three straight games. Alberta native Drew Miller, back for his sixth season with the Vipers, was the club's only .300 hitter, posting a team high .353 average and belting 21 home runs. All three Canadian teams showed attendance increases. Victoria's was the largest, 23,181, for a total of 116,872, second-best in the league. Calgary drew just over 66,000, while Edmonton attracted just over 92,000.

EDMONTON CAPITALS, CALGARY VIPERS: *North American League (2011)*

Although in the North Division at least, the Golden Baseball League seemed to be on strong financial ground, Tijuana, Yuma, and St. George were struggling in the South. In addition, Tucson, the league's top draw, was scheduled to return to the Pacific Coast League in 2011. However, the biggest shock came in November 2010 when the Victoria Seals announced their withdrawal from the league. The problem was an untenable lease with the city of Victoria. Not only did they have to share the field with amateur softball and soccer teams, which meant that the outfield fence and its signs had to be removed and stored after every home stand, but also, the club had a concessions contract with the city which restricted the amount of income that could be generated. At around the same time, four members of the Northern League decided to join the American Association, leaving the remaining four teams to seek new homes. And in Texas, the United League lost its Amarillo franchise to the American Association and two other clubs went dark. Some of the survivors of the three leagues formed an uneasy and unwieldy alliance, the North American League, a 10-team organization (if it can be called that) that extended from the northern suburbs of Chicago in the east to Maui in the west and from Harlingen, Texas, in the south to Edmonton in the north.

Problems with the league's makeup started early, although they weren't apparent until July. The Lake County (Illinois) Fielders, travelled first to Maui and then all around the rest of the North Division for the first 32 of their scheduled 96 games. The club had no significant revenue (because of no home games) well into the season. In early July, they traded nine players and released 14 others. Soon after, the manager, Tim Johnson, retired by email, the replacement manager, Pete LaCock, quit after one game, and the radio play-by-play announcer "retired" on air in the middle of a game. In early August, the city of Zion presented the Fielders with a bill for $185,000 for a year-and-a-half back rent. The Fielders finished their schedule playing against an area semi-pro team.

The two Canadian teams dominated the Northern Division, with Edmonton finishing the season two games ahead of Calgary. Managed by Orv Franchuk, a one-time Edmonton area schoolteacher who had spent over 20 years coaching in the affiliated minor leagues, the team included only three returning members and was led offensively by former major leaguers returnee Enrique Cruz (.361 average and 14 homers) and Todd Linden (.355 average and 14 homers). Cruz was all-star shortstop and Linden one of the all-star outfielders and league offensive player of the year. Roy Shortell won 11 and lost four, while all-star relief pitcher Tom Boleska posted an incredibly low (for this league) 2.11 earned run average along with 11 saves. Calgary's leading hitters were Gary Perez and Jimmy Rohan, each with a .379 average. Rohan was named all-star utility man. For the third straight year, Edmonton's attendance increased, this time by just over 10,000 to 102,253; Calgary's dropped by just under 100 a game to 62,308.

The two Alberta teams met in the playoffs, with the Capitals winning the division championship four games to two. Edmonton went on to meet the southern division champion Rio Grande Valley (Texas) White Wings. And the 2011 North American League season ended with another bizarre twist. All games in the best-of-seven championship were played in Edmonton, with, it was rumored, the Capitals underwriting the major expenses for the Texas team. Fielding a full team to bring to Canada proved a challenge for the White Wings, as they were unable to acquire visas for several players. However, they acquired a handful of visa-eligible players from other Southern Division teams and showed up in Edmonton, where they lost the championship four games to one.

The 2011 season would be the last in the North American or any other professional league for both the Vipers and the Capitals. Shortly after the Calgary Vipers' elimination, President John Conrad resigned. By October 1, the website was down and reports were that some checks for players had bounced. The end for the Edmonton Capitals came nearly five months later. In February with only four teams definite starters for the 2012 North American League season, management decided to suspend operations.

OTTAWA RAPIDS/RAPIDES/RAPIDZ, TROIS RIVIERES AIGLES, OTTAWA CHAMPIONS: *Canadian-American League (2008, 2013–2019)*

After the 2004 season, the Northeast League, which had begun operations in 1995 and, from 1999 to 2002, had operated as the Northern League—East, changed its name to the Canadian-American League. The name change, which implicitly paid homage to the league that had operated from 1936 to 1942 and from 1946 to 1951, recognized the presence of a Canadian team, les Capitales de Ottawa, which joined the league in 1999.

After the 2007 season, the Ottawa Lynx' last in the International League, Miles Wolff acquired a lease for the now tenantless Ottawa ballpark and placed a Canadian-American franchise in it. The club would be known as the Rapids in English and Rapides in French and would be managed by Ed Nottle, who had spent 50 years in the minor leagues as either a player or manager. Under Wolff's direction the league would own the franchise for at least a year before seeking private, preferably local, ownership. However, less than a month before the opening game, Rick Anderson and Rob Hill, two Ottawa-area businessmen, bought the team for $750,000 and renamed it the Rapidz.

The Rapidz opened their season on May 22, before 4,246 fans, losing 6–0 to the New Jersey Jackels, but won the next evening. After that, it was all downhill. In early June, the team had a 2–14 loss record; they finished the first half of the schedule in eighth and last place, 18 games out of first place. The situation improved only slightly during the second half; they moved up to seventh place. Only two regulars, designated hitter Jabe Bergeron, with a .354 average and catcher Kyle Geiger, at .319, were above the 300 mark. Both were voted onto the league all-star team. Attendance was a respectable 101,073, just under 2,400 a game.

The season over, the owners began planning for next year. However, at the end of September, they announced that the club had debts of $1.4 million, that they had been unable to renegotiate their stadium lease, that they were bankrupt, and that they were returning the franchise to the league. Miles Wolff worked during the winter to reenergize the franchise, now named the Voyageurs, but in March announced that it would not operate during 2009.

With the exception of Quebec City, the Can-Am League struggled from 2009 to 2012. Six cities lost their franchises and in order to maintain a viable league, the league twice formed a travelling team and in 2012 began the first of three seasons that included an interlocking schedule with the American Association.

2013. The league's Canadian footprint again expanded. Miles Wolff, along with area businessmen and former major league star Canadian Eric Gagne, established Les Aigles (Eagles) de Trois-Rivières. The team would be the first professional team to play in Le Stade Fernand-Bedard, since 2003, when the Saints played in the ill-fated Canadian League. Built in 1938, the ballpark had hosted professional teams in the original Can-Am League, the Provincial League, and the Eastern League during the twentieth century. During the early years of the new century, a reported $8 million were spent on repairs, renovations, and updates.

In their inaugural season, the Aigles were managed by Pete LaForest, a native of Gatineau, Quebec, who had appeared in 68 major league games over three seasons and had spent the last four seasons with les Capitales de Quebec. The team got off to a slow start, winning only one of its first nine games, and never reached the .500 mark. The

Aigles finished in fourth place; their final record of 43 wins and 56 losses put them 13.5 games behind Quebec City. Two members of Trois-Rivières made the all-star team: out-fielder Steve Brown, who led the league with 19 homers, and pitcher Alex Burkard (nine wins and six losses). Cam Kneeland (.306) was named rookie of the year. The season's attendance, 71,568 was half that of Quebec City.

2014. If Trois-Rivières fans were hoping for better in 2014, they were in for a dis-appointment. The Aigles again started slowly in what was now a four-team league, win-ning only one of their first eight games. They ended up losing six more games than in their inaugural season, ending up in fourth place, their 37–59 record placing them 19 games out of first place. They had the lowest batting average (.249), the fewest home runs (66), and highest earned run average (4.72) in the league. There were no .300 hitters. Second base-man Jose Cuevas (.295), who had started the season with the New Jersey Jackals, made the all-star team. Matt Rusch, in the first of his five seasons with the Aigles, posted a 2.72 ERA and struck out 110 batters. Attendance rose by an average of just under 20 a game.

2015. In 2013, Ottawa civic officials conducted an active search for a tenant to fill the stadium that had been vacant since the departure of the Rapidz after the 2008 sea-son. The Eastern League wanted to move one of their weaker franchises into a larger mar-ket with a large, PBA compliant ballpark. But, alarmed by the financial outlay that would be required to host a Double A team, the city turned to the Canadian-American League and its president Miles Wolff, offering a franchise for the 2015 season. The city promised to put up $750,000 for renovations and the Can-Am league agreed to a lease of $400,000 a year.

To manage the team, which, to the amusement of many cynics, was named the Champions, Wolff hired Hal Lanier, a one-time manager of the Houston Astros who had managed in the independent leagues for 16 years, 10 of them with the Winnipeg Gold-eyes. The veteran roster included two players with major league experience, pitchers Andrew Werner (who led the league with 12 wins) and Wilmer Font (who won 10 and lost four), two with Triple A and four with Double A experience, and several from the inde-pendent leagues, including Sebastian Boucher, who had spent the previous five seasons with Quebec City.

The Champions and Trois-Rivières spent the season in a neck-and-neck race for the fourth and final playoff spot in the six-team league. (The Shikoku Island All-Stars from Japan and the Garden State Grays also competed, playing road games that counted in the records of the other six teams.) Pete LaForest was back for the third consecutive sea-son as manager of the Aigles and, over the season, 16 returnees, including Steve Brown and David LeBlanc, each back for a third year, appeared on the roster. Trois-Rivières fin-ished strong, winning seven of their final eight games, closing the season in fourth place, 4.5 games ahead of the Champions. A playoff berth assured, the Aigles had part-owner and former major leaguer Eric Gagne, now 39 years old, start a game. (He allowed one earned run in 4.3 innings). The Aigles went on to defeat regular-season champion Rock-land three games to two in the semifinals and then New Jersey three games to two in the finals to win the Can-Am pennant. Neither Ottawa nor Trois-Rivières placed anyone on the all-star team. In its first year, Ottawa attracted 115,880 fans. Trois-Rivières final total of 96,997 (an increase of more than 24,000 over the previous season) would be the club's all-time highest attendance.

2016. In their second season the Ottawa Champions lived up to their name. Although they finished fourth in the regular season, only two games above .500, they defeated first place New Jersey three games to one in the semi-finals and second place Rockland three games to one bringing the pennant to Canada for the second consecutive year. The team was not strong at the plate, finishing sixth in the league with a .255 batting average, and tied for fifth in home runs with only 41. All-star second baseman Albert Cartwright was the team's top batter at .292. The pitching was stronger: the Champions' ERA of 3.97 was third best, while their strikeout total of 733 was second. All-star Austin Chrismon had a league-leading ERA of 2.39. Eric Gagne made a late season appearance for Ottawa, allowing one earned run and striking out six in five innings. The 2015 champion Trois-Rivières Aigles crashed, finishing a distant sixth, 26 games out of first place. With the team virtually eliminated by midseason, officials replaced manager Pete LaForest with 10-year independent league mound veteran T.J. Stanton. Third baseman Danny Mateo made the all-star team and led the Aigles at the plate with a .315 average. In Ottawa, attendance rose to 127,618, an all-time high. Trois-Rivières attendance dropped by 13,000.

2017. For the third consecutive season, a Canadian team won the Can-Am pennant. Les Capitales de Quebec finished first during the regular season and went on to win their seventh playoff championship. (See Chapter Eleven.) For the other two Canadian teams, the season was one best forgotten. Trois-Rivières finished again in sixth place, 26 games out of first and 6.5 out of the playoffs. One of the most interesting names on the roster was Trevor Gretzky, the son of the hockey great. Also an aspiring actor, the 24-year-old posted a .206 average in 95 games. The defending champions, Ottawa, dropped to fifth place, missing out on a playoff berth during the last week of the season. Thirty-five-year-old Sebastien Boucher led the team with a .296 average. More distressing than the two teams' on-field performances were their attendance figures. Trois-Rivières attracted 77,703 paying customers, certainly not enough to meet expenses. Ottawa's attendance dropped by 40,000 to 87,029, an alarmingly low total considering that the Champions' annual lease payments were over $400,000.

2018. In what would prove to be the penultimate season of the Can-Am League, the Trois-Rivières Aigles earned a playoff berth for the second time in their six-year history, while the Ottawa Champions found themselves out of the playoffs for the third time in four seasons. The Aigles' 53–49 record placed them in fourth place, 10.5 games behind Sussex County Miners, who would defeat them three games to two in the semifinals. Although the Aigles' .250 team batting average was sixth in the six-team league and the top batter, Sam Dexter, who was named the league's defensive player of the year, posted only a .287 average, the team was second in home runs with 101, and all-star third baseman and league player of the year Taylor Brennan had a league-high 32 round-trippers. Veteran outfielder Javier Herrera, now in his fourth season with Trois-Rivières, was also named to the all-star team. The Aigles' improved on-field performance led to an increase in attendance of over 13,000. The Champions were anything but; their final record of 41 wins and 60 losses put them in sixth place, 12 games out of the playoffs. Sebastian Boucher (.328), a native of nearby Gatineau, Quebec, was named to the all-star team as designated hitter. Jordan Kurokawa, who topped the league with 12 wins and had the lowest ERA (2.21), was named to the all-star team and was voted pitcher of the year and rookie pitcher of the year. Surprisingly, Ottawa attendance increased by 6,300.

2019. In the Canadian-American League's final season, Trois-Rivières enjoyed its best year to date, finishing in second place with a 58 wins, 37 losses record, 3.5 games behind the Sussex County Miners. T. J Stanton was named manager of the year. All-star outfielder Raphael Gladu led the team with a .302 batting average. All-star relief pitcher Garrett Mundell led the league with 20 saves. Catcher Anthony Hermelyn also made the all-star team. The Aigles lost the first round of the playoffs, winning two to New Jersey's three. In spite of the club's successes attendance dropped by 6,000.

During the offseason, long-time independent league player and player coach Sebastian Boucher had replaced Hal Lanier as manager of the Ottawa Champions, ending the latter's 57-year career as a player and manager. Boucher's team finished in fifth place, three games out of the playoffs. Two Champions made the all-star team: career independent leaguer outfielder Steve Brown (.302) and former major league pitcher Phillippe Aumont, a native of nearby Gatineau, Quebec, who set a league record with 145 strikeouts. For the third straight year, home attendance was below 100,000: 88,119.

During the season, there were several reports that cast doubt on the futures of both the Ottawa Champions and Trois-Rivières Aigles. On June 28, the City of Ottawa cancelled the Champions' ballpark lease. The team owed $418,942 in back lease and other payments to the city. An arrangement was made for the games to continue, with the Champions paying $128.25 an hour for use of the park and an additional forty-eight dollars an hour for the use of the lights. Miles Wolff offered to sell the team for the assumption of its debts and, a few weeks after the close of the season, found local buyers. In Trois-Rivières, attendance of less than 100,000 fans per season simply hadn't generated sufficient income to meet expenses. There was doubt that the club would be able to continue operating. However, in September meetings, club officials, civic leaders, and local businessmen came up with a solution: the team would sell naming rights to the Stade, local businesses would become sponsors, and a vigorous season's ticket sales campaign would be launched. The Aigles would fly for at least another year.

On October 16, 2019, the Canadian-American League ceased operations. In 2020, Quebec City, Trois-Rivières, New Jersey, Rockland, and Sussex County would become members of the Frontier League, the oldest continuously operating independent league. The Ottawa franchise, which did not have a lease, was not admitted. The 2020 season was cancelled because of the Covid pandemic. A new franchise for the 2021 season was granted to Ottawa. The team would be called the Titans.

LONDON RIPPERS: *Frontier League (2012)*

In the fall of 2011, the baseball fans of London, Ontario, learned that during the summer of 2012, the city would host its fourth professional team in two decades. The club had operated as the Oakland (Michigan) Crusaders in 2010 and, lacking a suitable home field, played most of its games on the road. The franchise, which was inactive during 2011, was owned by Othman Kari, a Michigan gynecologist and obstetrician, and David Martin, who had had some experience coaching at the junior college and amateur level. Neither had experience in professional baseball. The new team's relationship with the city of London got off to a bad start late in the fall, when club officials announced that the team would be called the Rippers and unveiled a logo that showed a sinister man wearing a black hat and pulling a dark cloak over his face. The citizenry, particularly groups fighting violence against families and women, denounced the name and the logo, noting the not very implicit echoes of the notorious nineteenth-century serial killer of women. Just before the season's opener, Martin defiantly announced that the logo and name would remain and proudly announced that his club would bring tourists to the city and generate a great number of jobs.

There were, as well, two problems that didn't seem to be apparent to the new owners when they signed a lease to play at Labatt Park. They would have to share the field with the London Majors, a very popular semi-professional team. Moreover, the Majors owned the liquor license for the stadium and provincial regulations stipulated that only one license could be granted for a specific address. In June, David Martin publicly lamented the fact that the Rippers could not sell beer at their home games, where, after a home opener crowd of 2,700, the per-game attendance average had slipped to under 750. Martin challenged the Majors to a winner-take-all baseball game, the victor assuming the liquor license and, in effect, control of Labatt Park. The Majors declined the challenge. A few weeks later, the Rippers were evicted from their offices and the team store for failure to pay rent, and, on June 24, the owners announced that the team was suspending operations. The league created a travelling team to fill out the remainder of the Rippers' schedule.

11

Thriving in the Twenty-First Century

*Vancouver Canadians, les Capitales
de Quebec, Winnipeg Goldeyes*

Between 1946 and 2019, only seven Canadian minor or independent league franchises operated for twenty or more consecutive seasons: the Northwest League Vancouver Canadians (20 seasons), les Capitales de Quebec (21 seasons), the Toronto Maple Leafs and Pacific Coast League Vancouver Canadians (22 seasons each), the Edmonton Trappers (24 seasons), and the Medicine Hat Blue Jays and the Northern League/American Association Winnipeg Goldeyes (26 seasons each). Only three of these, the Northwest League Vancouver Canadians, les Capitales de Quebec, and the Winnipeg Goldeyes, were still active at the end of the 2019 season.

Quebec City and Vancouver play in ballparks that are well over half a century old, while Winnipeg plays in a two decades old, state-of-the art park. The Vancouver Canadians, the only one of the three that is a member of an affiliated minor league, the Northwest League, offers a first stage in young rookies' quest to make it to the major leagues. Les Capitales and the Goldeyes, members of independent leagues, offer a chance to those who were never drafted and second and often last chances for those released by major league organizations. Nearly all players for the Canadians would spend a year or less with the team. Years later, fans would look back at those who became major league stars and murmur, "I remember when...." By contrast, many players for Winnipeg and Quebec City would spend three, four, or more seasons with their teams, becoming adopted "home-town players."

The Canadians, les Capitales, and the Goldeyes have not only survived, they have also thrived. The clubs are located in metropolitan areas ranging in population from Vancouver's 2.4 million to Quebec City's just over and Winnipeg's just under 800,000, areas large enough to draw the number of fans necessary to support the increasingly expensive business of running a professional baseball team. The clubs have local owners and are run by people who are very knowledgeable and well-trained in the business of operating professional baseball teams, who know how to make coming to the ballpark a complete entertainment experience, one in which the performance of the home team is only part. And, finally, because the seasons begin in mid–May, in the case of Quebec City and Winnipeg, and mid–June in the case of Vancouver, the clubs avoid having to deal with the possibility of mid- or late spring cold, rain, or sometimes even snow and with competition from the televised games of the first, and often later rounds of hockey's Stanley Cup playoffs.

Vancouver's New and Young Canadians: Northwest League (2000–2019)

In late October 1999, just weeks after the PCL Canadians had played their final game at Nat Bailey Stadium, the Southern Oregon Timberjacks' principal owner Fred Hermann, a one-time minor league pitcher and a former school administrator, had been granted permission to move his Northwest League franchise from Medford, Oregon, to Vancouver. After several years in which Canadian franchises had been transferred to American cities that had built new stadiums, an American team was moving to a city with a stadium that was nearly half-a-century old. When Vancouver opened its 2000 home season on June 25, the team was still called the Canadians, the Oakland Athletics supplied all the players, and the game was played at Nat Bailey Stadium. That is where the similarities with the 1999 team ended. The previous year's Canadians had played in the Pacific Coast League, one step below the major leagues, and nearly all of the players were "a phone call away" from joining the big-league team. The Northwest League, a short season Class A league, featured recently drafted players and a few with two to four years' experience. League regulations stipulated that each team could have no more than four players 23 years of age or older and no more than three players with four or more seasons' experience. Most likely, 17 of the rookies on the 2000 Canadians had remained close to their phones in early June to see if they had been drafted by a major league organization—they had. Only four members of the 41 to appear on the Canadians' roster would

Built in 1951 in hopes of attracting a Pacific Coast League team to Vancouver, Nat Bailey Stadium (originally called Capilano Stadium) is now the home of the very popular Vancouver Canadians of the Northwest League (courtesy Vancouver Canadians Professional Baseball Club—Mark Steffens).

ever get that call they had dreamed of for years, the call telling them to report to the parent team. The four would appear in a combined 262 major league games over a combined nine seasons.

2000. Playing under the direction of Dave Joppie, a first-year manager who had never played professional baseball, the Canadians started slowly, losing seven of their first nine games, including their home opener, 7 to 3 to Spokane in front of 5,462 fans. The team hovered around the .500 mark, in contention for first place in the Southern Division (which is where the Medford team had played the previous year). With five days to go in the regular season, the Canadians were in first place, two games ahead of Eugene; however, three straight losses precipitated them into second, with a final record of 39 wins and 37 losses. The Canadians had no .300 hitters among their regulars; the team batting average of .238 was the lowest in the eight-team league. Their 21 home runs were also lowest in the league. However, the team earned run average of 3.24 was tops in the league. Second round draft choice Fred Bynum was named all-star shortstop.

The Canadians' home attendance of 109,576, second lowest in the league, was over 40,000 more than that of Medford (who'd had the league's lowest attendance for four straight years) in 1999. This would be the lowest attendance the Canadians would experience; for all but four of the next 16 seasons, attendance would increase. The season had been a learning experience for both fans and owners. Many people in the Vancouver area had thought of the club as a semi-pro team and only gradually realized the difference in focus and purpose and in the caliber of play between a short season Class A team and a Triple A team. Fred Herrmann and his small front office crew discovered the difference between running a team playing in a 2,000-seat ballpark in a community of just over 66,000 and one playing in a nearly 6,000-seat stadium in a city with a metropolitan population of just over two million, a city which had dozens of other ways for people to spend their entertainment dollars.

2001. Attendance at Nat Bailey Stadium rose by a modest 231 a game. On the field, the team, led by another rookie manager, Webster Garrison, won two fewer and lost two more than in 2001, but finished in second place in the Southern Division, 14 games behind Salem-Kaiser. Three Canadians, none of whom would progress to the major leagues, were voted to the league all-star team: catcher Casey Myers, outfielder Matt Allegra, and pitcher Brett Price, who tied for the league lead in strikeouts with 100. Six players would eventually make the majors, including pitcher Rich Harden, a native of Victoria, British Columbia, who, over nine seasons, would appear in 170 games for Oakland, the Chicago Cubs, and Texas Rangers.

2002. The Canadians entered the season filled with optimism. Rookie manager Orv Franchuk, a former schoolteacher from Edmonton, Alberta, had a roster that included Oakland's top six draft picks—all of them first-rounders. Three of them, Nick Swisher, Jeremy Brown, and Mark Teahen, were promoted to the High Class A California League, early in the season, while the other three, pitchers Joe Blanton, Ben Fritz, and Steve Obenchain, got "the call to the Cal" in mid-season. In late July, the Canadians had been only two games out of first place in the Southern Division, but the core of their pitching staff having been stripped away, they won nine and lost 16, as the season wound down. They finished with the same record as they had in 2001, 37 wins and 39 losses—but this time they ended up in fourth place in the division. No Canadian was named to the all-star team. Nick Swisher would go on to play 1,527 games over 12 major league seasons. Attendance increased by over 10,000 to 127,099, second only to Spokane.

2003: The Canadians once again had a new manager, a roster that included most of Oakland's top choices from the current draft, and a losing season, but increased attendance. The new manager was Dennis Rogers, who had played only one season of minor league baseball but had gone on to a long and successful career coaching college teams in the spring and managing short-season minor league teams in the summer. Although the top draft choices of the Athletics played at Nat Bailey Stadium, only two of them would make it to the majors: first choice Omar Quintanilla and Andre Ethier. Both were called up to the next level during the season, Ethier after 10 games as a Canadian, Quintanilla after 32. Although Quintanilla did not have enough at bats to qualify for the batting title, his .341 average was sufficiently impressive to earn him a place as third baseman on the all-star team. Playing in the newly-formed and relatively weak Western Division, the team played at or just below the .500 level but were in contention for division title until mid–August, when a losing streak dropped them into third place, with a record of 35 wins and 41 losses, their poorest since moving to Vancouver. Nonetheless attendance again rose, this time by nearly 10,000, to 137,026, second only to Spokane.

2004. The Vancouver Canadians reversed three trends: they didn't hire a new manager—Dennis Rogers was back for a second season; they finally qualified for the post-season playoffs; and attendance didn't rise by around 10,000. Even though the Oakland Athletics sent most of their top draft choices to Vancouver, the Canadians started the season slowly, winning only 16 of their first 35 games. That was in part because two first-round choices, Landon Powell and Richie Robnett, and their second-round pick, Kurt Suzuki, were not assigned to the club until late July. The club won 19 of its last 27 games to clinch the West Division championship on the last day of the season. In the league final, the Canadians were swept three games to none by the Boise Hawks. The star of the team was Javier Herrera, a 19-year-old Venezuelan outfielder who played the entire season for the Canadians and who led the team with a .331 batting average and in home runs with 12 and stolen bases with 23. He was voted to the all-star team and named Northwest League most valuable player. Ten Canadians would eventually make it to the major leagues, with Suzuki (a catcher) playing in 1,504 games over 13 seasons and Gregorio Orgando, a pitcher, appearing in 284 over eight. In spite of the Canadians' first-place divisional finish, which capped an exciting pennant race, attendance rose by only 3,000.

2005. The Canadians won the West Division championship, but this time with a new manager: Juan Navarette, who had managed for 10 years in the Mexican League before spending seven managing the Oakland Athletics' lower-level affiliates. The A's again sent most of their top draft picks to Vancouver, although Travis Buck, the number one selection, didn't join the team until late July and appeared in nine games before being promoted to the Kane County Cougars of the full-season Class A Midwest League. After losing their first game, the Canadians won 17 of their next 22 games and never dropped out of first place, although a slump in August made for an exciting race in the last two weeks. With two days remaining in the season, Vancouver clinched the division championship and finished with a one-game lead over the Salem-Keiser Volcanoes. In the league final against the Spokane Indians, the Canadians established a 2–1 lead, but lost the next two, and the pennant. Two pitchers made the all-star team: twenty-first round selection Mike Madsen won six games while losing one and had a league-leading 1.69 ERA, while Brad Kilby was credited with 14 saves. Attendance dropped to 124,708, a decline of 15,329. Herrmann was operating the club with a small staff and on limited budget and this decrease would certainly have been troubling, especially in view of the fact that the aging Nat Bailey Stadium was in need of expensive renovations.

2006. Rumors circulating over the summer of 2005 about the sale of the Canadians became a reality early in the 2006 season. Jake Kerr, a major player in the Canadian forest products industry and a frequent negotiator for Canada in international trade agreements, and Jeff Mooney, CEO of the Canadian division of the fast-food chain A & W, reached an agreement in principle to purchase the team.

For the 2006 season, the Canadians would again have a new manager, Rick Magnante, who'd only played 35 games of professional baseball, but had begun his managerial career in 1987. He'd also coached South Africa's national team and, since 1996, had been an area scout for the Oakland Athletics. Oakland did not supply him with a strong team: the highest pick to come to Vancouver, third rounder Matt Sulentic, played only 38 games before being called up to Kane County. In all, the Canadians lost 10 players through call-ups. During the first half of the season, the club won 23 and lost 15; however, in the second, their record was 15 and 22. They finished in third place, 16 games behind division champion Salem-Keiser. Two Canadians were named to the all-star team: Sulentic (.354) in the outfield, and Alex Valdez (.273) at third base. Attendance dropped by 830.

2007. In January the sale of the Canadians was finalized, for $7 million (U.S.). The Canadians were now owned by Canadians! The Partnership signed a 25-year lease with the Vancouver Parks Board for the use of the park. Rent would be free for the first five years as the new owners had pledged $500,000 (with the city pledging an equal amount) for the first phases of much-needed renovations and improvements to the aging stadium. As the Oakland Athletics had wished, outfield fences would be moved in 10 to 15 feet in order to make it easier to hit home runs, the infield sod would be replaced, and dugouts and locker rooms would be modernized. For the fans, washrooms would be modernized and concession outlets upgraded. The entire stadium would be repainted and the outside walls decorated with portraits of such legendary baseball stars as Jackie Robinson and Ted Williams.

Recognizing their lack of experience in the baseball business, the two partners hired Aileen McManamon, an experienced sports marketer, as president and CEO. Then they brought on as a consultant Mike Veeck, who had made the St. Paul Saints of the independent Northern League one of the most popular summer sports attractions in Minnesota. He, in turn, recommended the hiring of Andy Dunn as consultant. Dunn had worked on both the business and baseball sides and at the major and minor league levels for the Montreal Expos, Washington Nationals, and Florida Marlins. He had a depth of experience and a wealth of contacts that would prove to be instrumental in the Canadians becoming one of the most successful minor league franchises. McManamon resigned just after his arrival and, after the 2007 season, Dunn was named president and part-owner of the team.

While the off-field fortunes of the Canadians had been turned around, the on-field product had not. The baseball team, again led by Rick Magnante, did finish in second place in the Western Division and had the second-best overall record in the Northwest League. However, they played below .500 ball and ended the season 19.5 games behind the powerhouse Salem-Keiser Volcanoes. Moving the fences increased the home run total by 10. Half of the 44 round trippers were belted by two players: all-star first baseman Danny Hamblin and first-round draft choice Corey Brown; each hit 11. Attendance increased 2,623 to 126,491.

2008. The Canadians continued their slide on the field but were watched by more fans than in the previous year. The parent Oakland Athletics returned 12 members of the 2007 squad to Vancouver, not good news for these players, as yearly advancement at the lower levels of professional baseball is considered essential to the continuation of baseball careers. Only one of these players, pitcher Pedro Figueroa, would ever reach the majors. In addition, the parent club sent fewer of its top draft picks, only the fifth, eighth and ninth round selections of the top 10. None of these would become major leaguers. During the season, 10 Canadians who did show promise were promoted to Oakland affiliates in higher classifications. The Canadians dropped and stayed below the .500 mark after the second game of the season and finished in third place with a record of 34 wins and 42 losses, six games out of first place in the West Division. The club couldn't hit: the .234 batting average was seventh in the league. And they had no power: in spite of the pulled-in fences, home run production dropped to 28. Pitching was stronger: Jose Guzman had a league-leading 15 saves and made the all-star team; Ronny Morla and Pedro Figueroa tied for the league lead in strikeouts with 77.

Off the field, attendance increased by 2,582, as Andy Dunn and his crew arranged a number of special days, as well as celebrity guest appearances. "Nooner at the Nat," the name of midweek day games that had been popular during the Canadians' PCL games, was revived. "A&W Sunday Family Day" included special kids' events and one dollar root beer floats. Ladies Day, a special Saturday morning clinic, invited female fans on to the field for instruction by the team's coaches. Bob the Brown Bear, whose name echoed that of the founder of professional baseball in Vancouver and was an oblique reference to the A&W Root Bear character, became a popular mascot. Ferguson Jenkins, the Famous Chicken, and wrestler Bret Hart made guest appearances.

2009. In what would turn out to be the penultimate season of the Vancouver-Oakland affiliation and Rick Magnante's tenure as the team's manager, the Canadians improved only marginally on the field, but played before the largest number of spectators in the first 10 years of their time in Vancouver. On the third day of the season, the team had a 2–1 record; for the rest of the season they would spend all but four days below the .500 mark. Their final record of 36 wins and 40 losses left them in third place in the West Division 12 games behind Salem-Keiser. Two high-ranked draft choices, fourth rounder Max Strassi (who signed for $1.5 million U.S.), and sixth rounder Ian Krol ($925,000 U.S.), did not show up until last late August. Five members of the team were promoted to Kane County during the season. None of the regulars hit .300. Dan Straily, a twenty-fourth round choice who would enjoy an extended major league career, led the moundsmen with five wins against three losses. One of the season's outstanding performances was by relief pitcher Paul Smyth, who appeared in 20 games and allowed only 12 hits and no earned runs over 29 innings. He struck out 37. The Canadians often played before 5,000 plus crowds over the season. Their attendance rose by over 20,000 to 149,297. Although there were no all-stars, the Canadians did win one award: their concessions menu was voted one of the top 10 vegetarian-friendly menus in the minor leagues.

2010. Shortly before the season began and then two weeks after it ended, the Vancouver Canadians issued important press releases. The first announced that Scotiabank had signed a naming-rights agreement with the city and the ball club. The park would be named Scotiabank Field at Nat Bailey Stadium. No financial details were released; however, the fees would certainly help ongoing renovations and enhancements to the nearly 60-year-old park, renovations like the one for the current season—a giant, high-definition video screen/scoreboard. The second announcement concerned the club's signing a new affiliation agreement: after 10 years with the Oakland Athletics, it would become the short season farm team of the Toronto Blue Jays in 2011.

On the field, the Canadians got off to a slow start, winning 17 and losing 21, to finish the first half of the split-season (which the Northwest League had reintroduced) in third place in the West Division, 10 games behind first place Everett. During the second half, they came alive, winning 20 and losing eight in August, and clinching first place in the division three days before the close of the regular season. Part of their resurgence was due to the arrival during the first week of August of Michael Choice, the Athletics' first-round pick in the June draft. His .284 average, along with all-star designated hitter A.J. Kirby-Jones's 14 home runs, and pitchers Mike Long's eight wins and two losses record, and all-star A.J. Griffin's 15 saves, was an important factor in the championship run. The Canadians, in their first playoff appearance in five seasons and the first of five consecutive seasons in the post-season, lost the division finals to Everett two games to none. Attendance rose to 154,490, with an average of just over 4,000 per game.

2011. The Canadians opened their first season as an affiliate of the Toronto Blue Jays with six Canadians, none of whom would make the major leagues, on the roster. Over the season it would be a more experienced team than Oakland had generally supplied: only 18 of the 39 men to appear on the roster were rookies. Unlike the Athletics in previous seasons, the Blue Jays did not send Vancouver any of the players they had selected in the first 10 rounds of the current year's draft. The C's led the West Division until the last day of the first half, when a loss to Boise dropped them into a tie with Eugene, which was awarded first place because it had won the majority of the meetings between the two teams. The second half was worse for the club; their record of 15 wins and 23 losses left them in fourth place in the West Division. John Schneider, a career manager in the lower minors, took family leave in early August and was replaced by Rick Miller, a roving instructor in Blue Jay's system. Vancouver's overall record of 39 wins and 37 losses was the second-best in the division and good enough for them to make the post-season. Although they'd backed into the playoffs, the Canadians made good once they arrived, defeating Eugene two games to one in the first round and Tri-City two games to one in the final. All-star third baseman John Berti led the team with a .291 average and stole 23 bases, third-best in the league. Pitcher Justin Nicolino, although he was promoted during the season to the full-season Class A Lansing Lugnuts, also made the all-star team with a 5–1 record, along with a 1.03 ERA and 64 strikeouts. Beginning with Aaron Sanchez, who debuted with Toronto in 2014, four Canadians would go on to play for Toronto. Despite a dismal showing on the field in the second half, there were eight consecutive sell-outs in August, and, for the fifth consecutive season, attendance increased—this time to 162,162.

2012. The Canadians, under the guidance of Clayton McCullough, who had been managing and coaching in the Blue Jays' system since 2007, included 10 members of last year's championship squad and, among 19 rookies, six of Toronto's top draft choices. The team won eight of its first 10 games and ended the first half with a very strong 22–15 record which was only good for third place, 5.5 games behind first-place Everett. They won the second half, with a 24–15 record, but it took them until the bottom of the eleventh inning of the final game to clinch first place in the West Division and their third straight trip to the post-season playoffs. They defeated Everett two games to none and faced Boise for the championship, which they won two games to one. Venezuelan Javier Avendano, who posted an 8–1 record and struck out a league-leading 91, was named to the all-star team, as was Mexican shortstop Jorge Flores (.265). McCullough was voted manager of the year. Attendance increased modestly to 164,461; one third of the games were sell-outs.

2013. "Threepeat"—the term was on the minds of large number of Vancouver fans as the 2013 Northwest League season approached. Would the Canadians win their third consecutive playoff title, something that hadn't been done in the Northwest League since Boise achieved the feat in the mid–'90s? Much would depend on what players were assigned by Toronto and which of these the parent club might promote during the season. None of Toronto's top 10 draft picks made it to Vancouver. L.B. Dantzler, who was taken in the 14th round, led the team with a .302 batting average and the league in home runs with nine and was named league MVP. Jordan Leyland, one of 12 players returning to the club, was promoted to the Lansing Lugnuts after posting a .341 batting average in the first half, as was Thunder Bay native Eric Brown, a third-year Canadian who had won five and lost one during the first half. In all, 10 Vancouver players were promoted to the Lugnuts. The Canadians, with a record of 22 wins and 16 losses, finished in second place in the North Division during the first half, a game behind Everett. They had a chance at the second half division championship but stumbled in the closing weeks. Nonetheless, their season's total of 39 wins and 37 losses was second-best in the division, enabling them to enter the playoffs. The Canadians defeated Everett, North Division winners of both halves of the season, two games to none, and Boise, two games to one, to achieve their "threepeat." Richmond, British Columbia, native Tom Robson, who had been promoted to the Canadians in early August and won three games and lost none, was the playoff hero, pitching six strong innings in the championship-winning game. Attendance soared to 184,371. Over half of the home games were sell-outs.

2014. The Canadians once again reached the Northwest League finals; but there would be no "fourpeat." Under the guidance of John Schneider, who had managed the team during the 2011 season, they finished the first half with 23 wins and 13 losses, tied with the Spokane Indians, who were awarded first place by virtue of having won more games than the Canadians in head-to-head meetings. During the second half, they played under .500 ball until mid–August, after which they won 12 while losing only five, ending in first place, two ahead of Tri-City. They won the North Division championship in two games over Spokane but lost the finals to Hillsboro in two straight games. Three of Toronto's first 10 draft picks played with the Canadians, but only one of these, first rounder Max Pentecost, who hit .313 in 19 games, put up impressive numbers. The star of the team was second-year shortstop Franklin Barreto, an 18-year-old Venezuelan who posted a .311 batting average and stole 29 bases, earning him the league's MVP award and *Baseball America*'s Short Season A player of the year award. He was one of 11 Canadians who would later appear in the major leagues. The season of 2014 was the first season that former Canadians made the roster of the parent Toronto Blue Jays: Aaron Sanchez from 2011; and Max Stroman, Daniel Pompey, and Daniel Norris from 2012. No doubt because of two rainouts, home attendance dropped by 3,000, to 180,187, although the per-game average rose by 27.

2015. After five very successful seasons on the field, the 2015 and 2016 Canadians endured two losing seasons, not finishing above .500 for four consecutive half-seasons. While their standings diminished, the attendance figures for the two years rose dramatically. In 2015, the team finished fourth in the North Division, six games behind Tri-City in the first half, and third (only two behind Everett and Tri-City) in the second half. Although Toronto sent six of its top 10 draft choices to Vancouver, they provided minimal help to the team. First-rounder John Harris posted a 6.75 ERA for 36 innings of work, while eighth-rounder Danny Young, was slightly better with a 6.33 ERA in 27 innings. Fourth-rounder Carl Wise had a .231 batting average in 47 games, sixth-rounder J.C. Cardinas a .179 average in 41 games, and ninth rounder Connor Panas a .252 average in 45 games. Before the season opened, the owners added 900 new seats, including 250 in "Hey, Y'All" Porch, located beyond the left field wall. Tickets to the Porch sold for $50 and included an all-you-can-eat buffet—alcoholic beverages were extra. There was also a craft beer garden along third base. Attendance rose an amazing 34,000 to 215,535. There were 22 sell-outs.

2016. The team performed even more poorly on the field, winning only 29 of 74 games, finishing the first half in third place, only three games behind Spokane, but ending the second half in fourth place, 13 games out of first. John Schneider had been replaced as manager by John Tamargo, who, after seven years of playing in the minors, had gone on to manage and coach Toronto's lower-classification teams. The Blue Jays sent seven of their top 10 draft choices to the Canadians, two of whom would go on to the major leagues: first-rounder T.J. Zeuch, who posted a 3.52 ERA in 23 innings pitched; and fifth-rounder Cavan Biggio, son of Hall of Famer Craig Biggio, who led the Canadians at the plate with a .282 average. Patrick Murphy, who led the league with a 2.84 ERA, was named to the all-star team. Even though the on-field performance of Vancouver often left home fans little to cheer about, attendance at Nat Bailey Stadium increased to 222,363.

2017. After two dismal seasons, the Vancouver Canadians returned to championship form. Rich Miller, a veteran minor league manager and coach who, as a late-season replacement for John Schneider, had led the 2011 Canadians to the Northwest League championship, returned to lead the team. The Canadians won a very tight first-half race division race against Tri-City; their 21 wins and 17 losses placed them a game ahead of the Dust Devils. They started the second half slowly, losing their first six games, but ended with a slightly better record, 22 wins and 16 losses, than they had in the first half. However, they placed second, by one game, to the Spokane Indians. The Canadians defeated

Spokane in two straight games to win the North Division title, and then dominated Eugene, winning three and losing one, to win their fourth Northwest League championship. First-round choice Logan Warmoth batted .306 in 39 games, while third-round choice Riley Adams posted a .305 average in 52 games and earned a berth on the all-star team as designated hitter. Rick Miller was named manager of the year. The club was a champion off the field: a record-breaking attendance of 239,527 was not only tops in the league, but the highest total of all short season Class A teams and a higher total than 38 of the 60 full-season Class A teams.

2018. It seemed, as both the first and second halves drew to a close, that the Vancouver Canadians would once again be competing in the playoffs. When the regular season ended, they had the best overall record—40 wins and 36 losses—in the North Division; but they were on the outside, looking in. Under the direction of rookie manager Dallas McPherson, the team did not reach the .500 mark until three weeks into the season, when they began to chase the Everett Aquasox for North Division lead. They were eliminated in their quest for the first half-season title with a game to go and finished with a 19 and 19 record. For most of the second half, they maintained a very small lead over Spokane, but lost out on the second-to-last game. Their second half record was 21 and 17. Outfielder Otto Lopez, who posted a team-high .297 batting average. was named to the all-star team, as was pitcher Josh Winckowski, who struck out 71 batters, and posted a 2.78 ERA. Tanner Kirwer of Sherwood Park, Alberta, led the league with 28 stolen bases, and Will McAffer of North Vancouver had a league-leading seven wins. Attendance dropped by 11 people a game. However, Vancouver was still the top drawing team in the lower minors: the final figure of 239,086 was better than all other short season teams and 44 of the 60 full season class A teams.

2019. This was to be a celebration of the 20 seasons the Canadians had been a member of the Northwest League. There were fireworks nights, appearances by former major league stars, and great ballpark food, including three-foot-long hotdogs, vegetarian friendly items, and sushi. But except for the races of three characters dressed up as pieces of sushi who raced around the base paths, there wasn't much happening on the field to cheer about. Under the guidance of a new manager, Casey Candaele, the fifth in as many seasons, the team got off to the worst start in its two decade-long history: after 16 games, the Canadians had won only four of 16 and were well entrenched in the basement of the North Division. They finished the first half with 15 wins and 23 losses, eight games out of first place. With just over two weeks to go in the second half, they were only four games behind leader Spokane; but they won only four of their last 13 games, to finish in fourth place, again with a record of 15 wins and 23 losses. Sophomore pitcher Adam Kloffenstein was named to the all-star team: his 2.24 ERA and 64 strikeouts were second best in the league. In spite of the Canadians' dismal record, attendance dropped by only 3,100 and was still the best of all short season A teams, and better than 55 full-season teams. The per-game average of 6,210, represented 96 percent of Nat Bailey Stadium's capacity.

The 2020 Northwest League season was cancelled, as were the seasons of all the other minor leagues, because of the Covid pandemic. In 2021, as part of the restructuring of minor league baseball, the Northwest League became a full-season High Level Class A league, with six teams including Vancouver.

Les Capitales de Quebec—A New Team for the Old Ballpark: Northwest/Northern/Canadian-American League (1999–2019)

In the middle of the 1990s, le Stade, Quebec City's municipal baseball stadium, which had been built in 1938 and had last hosted professional baseball in 1977, was in danger of being demolished. However, a group of local citizens led by Jean-Francis Cote formed the Comite de Relance, the goal of which was not only to save the stadium from the wrecker's ball but also to bring professional baseball back to town. Seeking advice about how to acquire a professional baseball team, the Comite cold-called Miles Wolff, publisher of *Baseball America* and founder and commissioner of the Northern League. Wolff knew that the aging ballpark, no matter how extensively it might be renovated, would never be able to fulfill the rigid ballpark specifications set out by the National Association. However, properly restored, it would be a perfect fit for an independent league team.

Wolff had a league in mind: the Northeast League, which had begun operations in 1995 in smaller cities in eastern New York and, during its first four seasons, had gone through 14 different franchises with only two of original clubs surviving into 1999. Wolff had purchased one of the "inactive" franchises, the Bangor Blue Ox, after the 1997 season and he saw Quebec City, which had a metropolitan population of over half a million, as a very good place to relocate the franchise. The new team would be called les Capitales and would start play in 1999, after renovations were complete. That year, the Northeast League morphed into the Northern League East, becoming part of the circuit that had operated in the upper Midwest for six seasons.

Home of les Capitales de Quebec, of the Canadian-American (now Frontier) League, le Stade has hosted professional baseball since 1939 (photograph by Sebastien Dion, courtesy Les Capitales de Quebec).

At a press conference in February 1999, Wolff stated that he hoped the club would be playing in Quebec 20 years in the future and that it would become an integral part of the community. His vision for the team would be more than fulfilled. At the end of the 2019 season, les Capitales were the second-longest continuously operating minor or independent league team in Canada.

Wolff made sure that both front office and on-field personnel would include many locals. During the first season the key people running the business of the team were from Quebec, and six members of the team were from the province. Two of the players, Michel Laplante and Stephane Dionne, would also spend time in the front office. Laplante would later become field manager and after that team president. Between 1999 and 2018, 77 Quebecois would play for the team. In addition to Laplante, another Quebec player, Patrick Scalabrini, would manage the team.

1999. To lead the team on the field, Miles Wolff hired Jay Ward, a long-time minor league manager, who had also coached in the major leagues, and more recently had managed Thunder Bay of the Northern League. The roster itself was typical of the independent league teams of the time. One player, Mitch Lyden, had spent time (briefly) in the major leagues and another 23 had played for major league farm teams. Eight were veterans of the independent leagues and six were rookies. In later seasons, seven would sign contracts with major league organizations. Thirteen would continue their playing careers in the independent leagues. What is interesting is that of these thirteen, four would go on to play three or more seasons with les Capitales. Unlike the farm clubs of major league teams, where, below the Triple A level, it was two years (at most) and then up or out, in the independent leagues players would often spend several seasons with one team and, along the way, become part of the fabric of the community. Over the years, 25 players would spend four or more seasons in Quebec City. One member of the 1999 squad, Eddie Lantigua, would play for les Capitales for nine seasons, marry a local girl and settle down in Quebec.

For what was basically an expansion team cobbled together by Miles Wolff and Jay Ward from a variety of sources, les Capitales de Quebec enjoyed a respectable first season. They started off on the road with a 3–3 record, before coming home to an opening day near-capacity crowd of 4,743 at le Stade and winning over the Albany-Colonie Diamond Dogs 8–2, with Michel Laplante striking out nine. They hovered around the .500 mark for the rest of the first half, finishing with a 21–22 record in a three-way tie for second place, a game behind first place Adirondack. In the second half, les Capitales won 22 and lost 21, this time finishing in second place two games behind Albany-Colonie. The team did not make the playoffs. Laplante was the outstanding member of the team, winning the pitching triple crown with 11 wins against two losses, a 2.06 earned run average, and 143 strikeouts, a performance which earned him a contract with a major league organization. He was named to the all-star team and voted pitcher of the year. A total of 110,559 paid to watch the Capitales' home games, third best in the Northern League East, and over 50,000 more than had come to see the Quebec Metros in 1977, their last season in the Eastern League.

2000. Les Capitales improved significantly in their sophomore season. With manager Jay Ward and 12 players, several of them Canadians, returning, the club enjoyed a five-game win streak at the end of the first half to give them a record of 22 wins and 20 losses, unfortunately only good enough for third place in the North Division. However, the momentum carried into the second half, as they had one seven-game and two five-game win streaks and finished in a first-place tie with Waterbury, with a record of 27 wins and 17 losses. Their overall record of 48 wins and 37 losses earned them a playoff berth. They lost in the first round, three games to one to Adirondack, who would end up as overall Northern League champions. Newcomer Dave Kennedy, who led the NL East with 19 home runs and posted a .298 batting average, was named NL East all-star first baseman. Sophomore pitcher Luis Ramos led the team with 11 victories and a 2.89 ERA. His performance resulted in his signing a minor league contract with the Milwaukee Brewers. Michel Laplante, who had been signed by the Montreal Expos after his superb 1999 season and assigned to Ottawa but released early in the season, returned briefly to Quebec City. He was about to start a game when informed by Miles Wolff that he'd been picked up by the Atlanta Braves. He asked to pitch in the game, won it, and reported to Richmond of the International League. After unsuccessful arm surgery during the off season, he returned to les Capitales, coaching, managing, serving in the front office, and pitching occasionally. Attendance increased to 127,303, best in the NL East. It would be the first of five consecutive seasons that home attendance would increase for les Capitales.

2001. Before les Capitales' inaugural season, Miles Wolff had said that it would take three seasons before the team had firmly established itself in Quebec City. In the stands, it was a success: the team again led the East in attendance. The first half was a qualified success on the field: Quebec City and Albany-Colonie finished in first place with identical 26 and 20 records, but the New York team won a single playoff game 1–0. There was, however, considerable unrest in the clubhouse. Manager Jay Ward publicly criticized the performance of Quebecois catcher Olivier Lepine, a fan favorite, and traded him to Elmira. The unrest continued in the second half, with Ward again publicly criticizing both fans and players, and then trading another very popular player, Ryan Kane, to New Jersey. The team lost nine straight in July and finished the second half in third place with an 18 and 27 record. Les Capitales' B.J. Garrison (.310) was named the NL East's rookie of the year. For another rookie, pitcher Patrick Scalabrini, from Coaticook, Quebec, the season marked the beginning of a long career with les Capitales—first as a pitcher, then a coach, and then 10 years as a manager. In spite of the poor season, the fans stood by the team: attendance increased by 21,000. No one was disappointed when, two weeks after the end of the season, it was announced that Jay Ward had resigned.

2002. After Jay Ward's not unwelcome resignation, les Capitales had three managers in as many years. The first of these, Andy McCauley, who had not played professional ball but had managed four years in the independent Frontier League, led Quebec City to its second post-season appearance. During the first half, thanks in part to a six and then seven-game win streak, the team finished in first place in the North Division, with a 29–16 record. The team cooled down in the second half, winning 23, losing 22, and finishing in third place. In the first of five consecutive seasons appearing in the playoffs, les Capitales lost to Adirondack three games to two, in the first round. Three members of the club were named to the all-star team: pitcher Mark Cisar, who garnered 19 saves; catcher Rafael Pujols, who posted a .319 average, and second baseman Patrick Scalabrini, who led the team with a .325 average, and (because he still qualified as a rookie in his second season) was named NL East rookie of the year. Back with the team after two years with Duluth-Superior of the Northern League West, was Eddie Lantigua. He hit .314. Attendance increased by 3,701 to 152,121, tops in the NL East.

2003. After the 2002 season, the Western and Eastern Divisions of the Northern League ended their four-year relationship and the eastern teams resumed the name Northeast League. Quebec City's new manager was Joe Ferguson, who had been a 14-year major league star before managing for seven years in the Baltimore Orioles' system. During the first half of the season, les Capitals won 21 while losing 24 and finished in third place in the North Division. They started the second half hot, winning nine of their first 12 games and took the second half crown with a 28 and 16 record. However, the playoffs ended quickly for Quebec City, which lost the first round in three straight to North Shore Spirit (of Lynn, Massachusetts). Three members of les Capitales made the all-star team: Eddie Lantigua (.313) at third base; outfielder Carlos Rodrigues (one of the first of over a dozen Cubans to play for les Capitales over the years), who banged a league-leading 21 home runs; and pitcher Jordy Alexander, who, in spite of a 4–7 record, posted a 2.86 earned run average and struck out 124. Perhaps because three home games were rained out, attendance rose by only 32 people. It was still the best in the league.

2004. Darren Bush, the third new manager in as many years, led les Capitales to their third consecutive playoff appearance. After a disappointing fourth-place finish during the first half, the team put together three seven-game winning streaks to win the second half with an amazing 34–12 record. For the second year in a row, they faced the North Shore Spirit in the opening round of the playoffs and lost, this time three games to two. Again, Eddie Lantigua made the all-star team, this time as a designated hitter. His average dropped to .290, but he belted 18 home runs. Other all-stars were outfielder Benoit Emond (.327) and pitcher Keith Dunn (10 wins-two losses). Pitcher Paul Jacinto, playing in what would turn out to be his only professional season, won seven and lost none and was named rookie of the year. Although attendance increased by nearly 5,000 to 156,899, les Capitales lost the attendance crown to Brockton (Massachusetts) Rox, which drew 203,000.

After the 2004 season, the Northeast League changed its name to the Canadian-American Association, a name which honored an earlier league of the same name and indicated Miles Wolff's desire to expand the number of Canadian teams in the league.

2005. After manager Darren Bush announced his intention to move on, Quebec City owner Miles Wolff looked inside les Capitales' organization for a replacement and chose a person who'd been there since before the first pitch had been thrown in 1999. In fact, he chose the person who'd thrown that first pitch: Michel Laplante. After arm surgery had ended his playing career (except for an occasional game), the native of the northern Quebec city of Val D'Or had served as the team's pitching coach, while at the same time running a tennis school and investing in a factory that made bats out of birch wood. Laplante would serve five years as manager, during which the team made the playoffs four times and won the championship twice. He added the role of general manager in 2006, and in 2008 became vice-president. He became les Capitales president in 2012, a position he still held at the end of the 2019 season.

The team, which included eight holdovers from 2004, won its first eight games and cruised to the first half North Division title with a 32 and 15 record. Les Capitales played lackluster .500 ball during much of the second half—until the last 11 games of the season, when they won 10 and lost one, and were in contention for the second half crown until the last two days of the season. In the playoffs, they handled the Brockton Rox easily sweeping the semifinals in three games, reaching the finals for the first time, but then lost to Worcester three games to none. Three players received all-star team awards: relief pitcher Christian Mendoza, with a league high 21 saves; outfielder Geof Tomlinson (.322), playing the second of his nine seasons for Quebec City; and third baseman Eddie Lantigua, who led the league with 31 home runs. He was also named Can-Am player of the year and *Baseball America*'s independent leagues player of the year. Attendance dropped by 233. Given that seven games had been rained out (and that a triple header had been scheduled to make some of these games up), les Capitales actually showed an increase on a per-game basis.

2006. In the off-season, Miles Wolff attempted to sell les Capitales to local interests, something he had felt would strengthen the club's ties with the city. When his plan didn't succeed, he turned over his general manger duties to Michel Laplante. Also during the off-season, the league made the decision to abandon the division alignment, but to continue the split-season format. The winners of each half would meet the two of the other six teams that had the best overall records.

Before the season began, there was considerable optimism that les Capitales would be one of the dominant teams. Fifteen members from the previous season's roster would play during 2006, including all-stars Eddie Lantigua, Geof Tomlinson, and Christian Mendoza. This optimism was dampened during the first half, as the team won only 16 games while losing 27. However, during the second half, led by all-stars third baseman Eddie Lantigua, who had the league's best average—.343, and pitcher Gabe Ribas, who won 10, while losing three, and struck out 106, the team basically inverted its first half record, winning 28 and losing 17. Their combined record placed them in fourth place in the overall standings. In a tough semifinal series, they defeated the New Haven Cutters three games to two and went on to win their first championship defeating Brockton, three games to two. The one disappointment was in the attendance figures. Over 18,000 fewer Quebec fans had attended home games.

2007. After the euphoria over the outcome of the 2006 season, disappointment was the dominant note the next year. Playing in what was now a 10-team league, les Capitales performed adequately during the first half, winning 27 and losing 16, finishing in third place. But they dropped to sixth in the second half, winning 22 and losing 25. Eddie Lantigua once again made the all-star team—this time at first base—leading the league in RBIs with 82 and home runs with 21. Newcomer Boomer Berry, who posted a .325 average, was named all-star second baseman. It would turn out to be the first of five consecutive post-season championships. Quebec City was about to become an independent leagues dynasty. Attendance rose to its usual high level: the total of 161,789 was second-best in the league.

2008. During the offseason, Laplante assigned some of his managerial duties to Pat Scalabrini. Les Capitales improved greatly during their tenth anniversary season, winning the first half handily, their 31 wins and 16 losses record placing them five games in front of Worcester. In the second half they slowed down; their 27–20 record was again good for first place, but this time they had to share top spot with Worcester and Sussex. Pitcher Michel Simard earned an all-star spot with an all-time team high of 13 wins and a league leading earned run average of 2.32. Third baseman Pat Deschenes, who posted a .301 average, along with 10 home runs, also made the all-star team. After defeating Atlantic City three games to one in the semi-finals, Quebec City was favored to take the finals from Sussex but was defeated in three straight. Attendance plunged by nearly 21,000, mainly as a result of five rainouts during the first half.

2009. Fans, players, and officials were optimistic about les Capitales' 2009 season. Fourteen members of the previous year's club were returning and, just before the season's opener, Pete Laforest, a native of Hull, Quebec, and a veteran of three major league seasons, signed with les Capitales. As the team began play, it was announced that Eric Gagne, a Montreal native and star of 10 major league seasons, would begin pitching for Quebec City in mid–June. The optimism began to fade during June, as the team played below .500. It finished the first half in fourth place in the six-team league, six games behind New Jersey. During the second half, performance improved and, thanks to a hot streak in which les Capitales won 11 of their final 14 regular season games, they finished in first place, with a 31 wins 16 losses record, one game ahead of Brockton. Dan Sausville led the pitchers with nine wins; Gagne was six and six. Pete Laforest, who led the league in RBIs with 82, and home runs with 24, was named all-star catcher and league most valuable player. The team moved easily through the playoffs, first defeating Brockton and then Worcester, both three games to one. This was not only les Capitales' second league championship, but it would turn out to be the first of five consecutive pennants. Quebec City was about to become an independent leagues dynasty. Regular season attendance rose to 160,992.

2010. In the off season, Laplante turned over all managerial duties to veteran player-coach Pat Scalabrini. Sixteen members of the championship team would return in 2010. In his first season as manager, Patrick Scalabrini led les Capitales to their third championship. The team finished the first half first in the now six-team league with a 30–17 record and, for the first two-thirds of the second half, seemed bound for another first-place finish. But a five wins 10 losses record in the last 15 games of the season dropped them into third place, 1.5 games behind Pittsfield and Brockton. Quebec City regained its momentum in the playoffs, dumping New Jersey three games to none in the first round and Pittsfield three games to one in the finals. Two members of the team earned all-star team berths: outfielder Sebastien Boucher, whose team high .336 average was second-best in the league, and rookie relief pitcher Andrew Albers, a native of North Battleford, Saskatchewan, whose 17 saves earned him a contract in a major league organization. In 2013 he made his major league debut with the Minnesota Twins. The star of 2009, Pete Laforest, was traded to Somerset of the independent Atlantic League before the season, did not report, and was resigned by les Capitales during the second half. Although the home attendance of 147,978 led the Can-Am Association, it was a drop of 13,014 from the previous season.

At the end of the season, Miles Wolff sold the team to Quebec City businessman Jean Tremblay, who promoted Michel Laplante to the position of team president. In 2016, Pierre Tremblay, owner of area automobile dealerships, and Bob Bissonnette, a popular entertainer and former hockey player, purchased minority interests in the team.

2011. Another year, another championship, a "three-peat," and, as an added bonus, two first-place finishes during the regular season. During the first half, Quebec City won

35 games, a Can-Am League record, and lost 11, ending up 8.5 games ahead of New Jersey. In the second half, thanks to a season-ending eight game win streak, they again finished ahead of New Jersey, but only by .005 points. Had their final game not been rained out, they might have finished in second place. Newcomers Bryan Rembisz, who made the all-star team, and John Mariotti, who posted nine and one and 11 and one records respectively, led the mound corps. Sebastien Boucher was the team's only regular to hit above .300 (his final average was .326). As was the case in the previous year, the post season was relatively easy: Brockton fell three games to nothing in the semi-final, while New Jersey lost three games to one. Home attendance was again the best in the league: 149,330, an increase of 1,352.

2012. After the 2011 season, Pittsfield and Brockton withdrew from the league and the road team that had been formed to create an even number of teams was disbanded, leaving the Can-Am with only five teams. In order to avoid having one team idle every day, an arrangement was made with the American Association for each Can-Am team to play 20 games against select American Association teams. In addition, the split-season format would be abandoned and the top two finishers during the regular season would meet in a best-of-seven championship series. Les Capitales easily won first place during the regular season, compiling a 66–34 record and finishing seven games ahead of the New Jersey Jackals. New Jersey won the first game of the championship final, before les Capitals took over winning the next four and outscoring the opposition 19–6. Five Quebec City players were named to the all-star team: shortstop Jeff Helps (.294), outfielder Sebastien Boucher (.325), designated hitter Rene Leveret (whose .361 average was best in the league), catcher Josue Peley (whose 22 homers led the league), and pitcher Jeff Duda (who led the league with 15 wins and a 2.10 ERA). The final attendance of 152,663, second highest in the league, marked an increase of 3,333.

2013. The Trois-Rivières Aigles joined the league, and, once again, the province of Quebec would see a professional baseball rivalry that extended back to 1923. There would be no split season; teams would again play against American Association squads; and the two top finishers would meet in a best-of-seven final. Although les Capitales' regular-season record dropped to 56 and 42, they clinched first place with a week to go, then lost five of their final six, resulting in the surging New Jersey Jackals finishing only 1.5 games behind them. The final series was far more challenging than the previous year's one, with the Jackals pushing les Capitales to a seventh game, where at one point they established a four run lead, before Quebec City rallied to take its fifth consecutive championship. Two members of the 2012 all-star team repeated: catcher Josue Peley (.303) and designated hitter Rene Leveret (.292). Jonathan Malo, who had joined the team in 2012, posted a .305 average with 11 home runs and 27 stolen bases, which earned him the third base spot on the all-star team and the player of the year award. Pat Scalabrini was named manager of the year. Attendance dropped by over 11,000 to 141,396, second-best in the league.

2014. The dynasty ended abruptly. In 2014, les Capitales finished with their poorest season since joining what was then the Northern League East. Playing in what had become a four-team league, the team won 46 while losing 50 (which included a 10–9 record against American Association teams) to finish third, nine games out of a playoff spot.

Attendance dropped by 28,000 to 121,305, the lowest since Quebec's inaugural season. Nonetheless, four players won post-season awards. Sebastian Boucher won the league batting championship with a .356 average and was named an all-star outfielder. Jonathan Malo (.285) earned his second straight all-star berth, this time at shortstop. And Balbino Fuenmayor (.347 and 23 home runs) who had spent six seasons in the Seattle Mariner's organization, was named all-star third baseman, league most valuable player, and *Baseball America*'s independent leagues player of the year. Although he didn't make the all-star team, pitcher Karl Gelinas led the league with 123 strikeouts. Matt Helms (.313) was selected rookie of the year.

The most significant event for les Capitales, the Canadian-American Association, and, indeed, international baseball generally occurred on July 10, when Michel Laplante announced that the team had signed an agreement with the Cuban Baseball Federation and the National Institute of Sports, Physical Education, and Recreation, permitting Yuniesky Gurriel, a 32-year-old Cuban outfielder, to play for les Capitales. This was the first time since Fidel Castro had taken over as ruler of Cuba that a baseball player had been permitted to play for a Canadian or American team. Laplante had been in negotiations with Cuban baseball officials for two years, establishing a relationship of trust between the Quebec City team and Cuban officials. Gurriel would not defect and he would return to his country at the close of the season. He appeared in his first game on July 23, going two for four, and over the next several weeks played in 30 games, posting a .321 average. Over the next five seasons, eight more Cubans would play for les Capitales. Like Gurriel, each was older and considered less likely to be attractive to major league organizations and thus not a great risk of defecting.

2015. Two expansion teams, the Ottawa Champions and the Sussex County Miners, joined the league. In addition, members of the now six-team league would flesh out their schedules by playing games against select clubs in the American Association; the "Grays," a travelling team financed by the league; and the Shikoku Island All-Stars, manned by players from a Japanese independent league. Les Capitales returned to their winning ways, with a 54–42 record, good enough for a second-place finish. In the first round Quebec City faced New Jersey, who had finished half a game behind them in the regular season, and lost to the Jackals three games to two. Quebec City was led during the regular season by veteran pitcher Karl Gelinas, who won 10 while losing three and whose earned run average of 2.11 was the best in the league. Yuniesky Gurriel, back for his second season, won the batting championship, with a .374 average, while his fellow Cuban Alexei Bell was the only other Quebec City regular to have a .300 plus average—.317. Les Capitales' roster included two other Cubans, pitcher Ismel Jimenez (three wins and three losses) and Yordan Manduley (.259). It would be Gurriel's final season with Quebec City and the only one for Jimenez and Bell. Manduley would play for four more, becoming a mainstay of the team. Gelinas, outfielder Kalian Sams (.279, 16 home runs), and relief pitcher Deryk Hooker (24 saves, tied for first in the league), made the all-star team. Jonathan Malo, who played second, third, and shortstop, was named the league's defensive player of the year. Attendance increased by just over 9,000 to 130,510.

2016. Playing against the other five teams in the league, as well as against the Cuban National Team and the Shikoku Island All-Stars, les Capitales won 56 games and lost 44 to finish in third place, six games out of first. Quebec City took three out of four games against Cuba, and two out of three against Shikoku. After building a two-game lead over Rockland in the semi-finals, les Capitales lost three straight. Only one member of the team made the all-star team: relief pitcher Jon Fitzsimmons, a London, Ontario, native who had earned 13 saves before his contract was purchased by the Cleveland Indians' organization. The two Cuban regulars on the team posted .300 averages: Yurisbel Gracial (.320) and Roel Santos (.301). Jasvir Rakfar of North York, Ontario, was tied for tops in the league with 10 wins. Trevor Gretzky, son of the hockey great, played 23 games for Quebec City and had a .228 average before being sidelined with a shoulder separation. Attendance rose by 16,000 to 146,946.

2017. For the first time since 2013, les Capitales finished on top of the league during the regular season and, as had been the case then, went on to win the playoff championship. It was an unusual regular season: Quebec City played its first 14 games on the road as it awaited the installation of artificial turf on its home field. The club returned to what was now called Stade Canac with a 6–7 record. From the beginning of June to the middle of August, les Capitales compiled an impressive record, winning 51 and losing 23, and seemed about to ready to cruise to the regular season title. But then they seemed about to blow it, winning only seven of their last fourteen games. Only a sweep of a season-ending doubleheader allowed them to finish first, half a game in front of Rockland. They regained their winning ways for the playoffs, sweeping both Sussex County and then Rockland, each in three games, to win their seventh league championship, the most championships won by an independent league team since revival began in 1993. Quebec City dominated the league all-star team: first baseman Jordan Lennerton (.328 and 14 home runs), outfielder Kalian Sams (.291 and 23 home runs), catcher Maxx Tissenbaum (.344 and 13 home runs), relief pitcher Nolan Becker (a league leading 24 saves), and the team's three Cubans. Third baseman Yurisbel Gracial posted a .333 average with 13 home runs, shortstop Yordan Manduley batted .309, and Lazaro Blanco, had a league leading 2.98 ERA to go along with 11 wins and 118 strikeouts. Manager Patrick Scalabrini, with five championships in eight seasons, was named manager of the year. The only disappointment was a 5,000 drop in attendance to 141,923, second-best in the league.

2018. Les Capitales celebrated their twentieth anniversary season with their sixteenth trip to the playoffs and their tenth appearance in the finals. The team played above .500 all season, but didn't really take off until August, winning 20 of its last 30 games to finish in second place with a 58 and 44 record, 5.5 games behind Sussex County. Les Capitales defeated Rockland three games to one in the semi finals but lost the finals to Sussex County three games to one. Only one Quebec City player was named to the all-star team: Cuban Yordan Manduley, who won the league batting title with an average of .337, only .002 percent ahead of second place finisher, Mikey Reynolds of Sussex County. It was Manduley's second consecutive all-star appearance. Two members of the team passed milestones: Patrick Scalabrini achieved his five hundredth victory as a manager and pitcher Karl Gelinas, his hundredth victory in professional baseball. Attendance was down in Quebec City as it was throughout the league. The final total of 126,483, second best in the Can-Am, represented a drop of over 15,000.

2019. What would turn out to be the final season of operation for the Can-Am was, to put it mildly, a disappointment for Quebec City players and fans. The team won only four of its first 14 games, and, although there were occasional bright spots such as a three-game sweep of the Cuban national team in June and a five-game win streak in July, les Capitales showed little improvement over the course of the season, finishing in last place with a 36–59 record, 25.5 games behind the leader. Five-year Quebec City veteran Yordon Manduley again led the team at the plate with a .350 average; fellow Cuban Stay-ler Hernandez was second with .319. Former major leaguer Scott Richmond was 5 and 5 on the mound and had a 4.24 ERA. The attendance of 119,060 was the team's lowest since the inaugural season of 1999.

In mid–October, the Can-Am League ceased operations and five of its clubs were accepted as members of the Frontier League, which had been operating in the Midwest since 1993 and was the longest continuously-operating independent league. Quebec City and Trois-Rivières would now be members of a 14-team league that stretched from the Mississippi River to the St. Lawrence River and the shores of the Atlantic.

The "New" Winnipeg Goldeyes ... Third Time's the Charm: Northern League/American Association (1993–2020)

When the Winnipeg Goldeyes joined the Class C Northern League in 1954, many members of the press thought that it was the first step leading to the city's acquisition of a franchise in the Triple A American Association. It was not to be. When the second Gold-eyes team joined the Northern League (now a short season Class A league), the hopes were rekindled. Again it was not to be. In 2011, the third incarnation of the Goldeyes,

The Winnipeg Goldeyes of the independent Northern and later American Association leagues began play in 1994 with home games held in Winnipeg Stadium, home of the Canadian Football League Blue Bombers. In 1999, they moved to CanWest Global (now Shaw) Park at the edge of downtown Winnipeg (courtesy Winnipeg Goldeyes).

which had been a highly successful member of the independent Northern League, since 1994, switched to another independent league, one which had been formed in 2006 and called itself the American Association, the Triple A league of that name having ceased operations after the 1997 season.

When Miles Wolff was considering cities to be included in the Northern League, the new independent circuit scheduled to open in 1993, he called on Sam Katz, a Winnipeg entertainment promoter who had arranged visits to the Manitoba city by such luminaries as Kenny Rodgers, Tina Turner, and the Rolling Stones. Winnipeg, with a metropolitan population of nearly 700,000, and St. Paul, Minnesota, would be major cities to act as anchors for a league that would include such smaller cities as Duluth, Minnesota; Sioux City, Iowa; Sioux Falls, South Dakota; and Thunder Bay, Ontario. However, at the time, Katz was more interested in purchasing a Triple A team and moving it to Manitoba and had tried unsuccessfully to acquire the Oklahoma City 86ers of the American Association and the Edmonton Trappers of the Pacific Coast League. At the time of Wolff's inquiries, he was hoping to purchase the Denver Zephyrs, the American Association franchise that would have to relocate when the Colorado Rockies, the expansion National League team, began play in 1993.

However, Katz's bid for the Zephyrs failed and, after the Northern League's inaugural season, the Rochester (Minnesota) Aces, who had drawn just over 50,000 people, were candidates for relocation. Katz and Wolff reconnected and the Manitoba entrepreneur and the Winnipeg Enterprises Corporation purchased the franchise, with Katz owning 60 percent of the team. Ace's manager Doug Simunic and 11 members of the team that had made it to the Northern League finals in 1993 formed the nucleus of what, in 1994, would become the Winnipeg Goldeyes, the first professional baseball team to call Manitoba home since the Whips of the International League had departed after the 1971 season. The team would play on a makeshift diamond erected in the northwest corner of Winnipeg Stadium, the home field of the Blue Bombers of the Canadian Football League. It was a dream park for right-handed pull hitters and a nightmare for pitchers: the sign next to the left field foul pole said it was 300 feet from home plate, a generous measurement according to many veteran observers. But it could hold as many fans as wanted to come to a game. There were lots of tickets priced at $2.50.

1994. On June 4, 14,764 of the seats at Winnipeg Stadium were filled by paying customers, who were rewarded when the new home team clobbered the Duluth-Superior Dukes. The Goldeyes won the second and third games of the series, before a combined total of 7,685 fans. The remainder of the first half was not so bright. Winnipeg finished in fifth place in the six-team league, its 16 wins and 24 losses putting it 11 games behind first-place Sioux City. The second half was a reverse of the first, with the Goldeyes winning 27 and losing 13 and finishing in first place, two games ahead of Sioux City. Jeff Bittiger, one of five former major leaguers on the team, won nine and lost four, while striking out 100. Steve Dailey led batsmen with a .340 average and 14 home runs. Mike Hankins (.320) was named all-star shortstop. The Goldeyes handled the Sioux City Explorers easily in the championship series, winning three games to one. The final attendance of 212,571, the second highest in the league, included six crowds of over 8,000.

1995. Although only six members of the championship team returned for the second season, the Winnipeg Goldeyes again made the championship series. They finished second during the first half, their 25 and 17 record placing them one game behind St. Paul, but slipped in the second half to third, experiencing a nine-game losing streak early in the half, and losing eight of 10 as the season drew to a close. They won 22 while losing 21. However, because St. Paul had won both halves and Winnipeg had the second-best overall record, the Goldeyes made it into the post-season, losing three games to one to the Saints. Newcomer Terry Lee, who had appeared in 15 major league games, was the team's dominant player. He led the league with a .373 average, had the most RBIs with 73, and finished second in the league with 22 home runs. Although, inexplicably, he was not named to the all-star team, he was named the league's player of the year. Returnee Kevin Dattola, who had a .339 average and a league-leading 41 stolen bases, was named an all-star outfielder. Catcher Hank Manning (.284, 19 home runs) was also named to the all-star team. For one of the Goldeyes, playing in Winnipeg earned him a second chance with a major league organization. Released early in the season from the Texas Rangers' minor league system, Mike Cather posted four wins and two losses, with eight saves and a 1.48 ERA. After the season, he signed with the Atlanta organization and, in 1997, made his big-league debut, becoming the first Goldeye to graduate to the major leagues. Attendance dropped by over 16,000 to 196,460, second-best in the league. The drop might have been greater had a crowd of 20,749, a minor league record, not attended the final home game.

1996. During the off-season, the Northern League awarded expansion franchises to Madison, Wisconsin, and Fargo-Moorhead, Minnesota/Wisconsin, and reformed the league into two divisions. Winnipeg joined Fargo-Moorhead, Sioux City, and Sioux Falls in the Western Division. The Goldeyes did not offer manager Doug Simunic a new contract, noting that although he was a good on-field leader, he was a public relations detriment, having made denigrating statements about the team and the city's fans. Hal Lanier, a veteran major league player who had been managing since 1976, including three years with the Houston Astros, took over field duties, beginning a 10-year career with Winnipeg. The team posted identical records in both halves: 25 wins and 17 losses, finishing twice in second place, one and then two games behind Fargo-Moorhead RedHawks, managed by Doug Simunic, who, along with Jeff Bittiger, had signed on with the expansion team. The Goldeyes had been in first place late in August but dropped into second after suffering an eight-game loss streak. The Goldeyes and RedHawks met in the division finals, with Fargo-Moorhead winning two games to one. It was the beginning of what, over the decades, would become one of the fiercest rivalries of the Northern League. First baseman Terry Lee, who finished second in the league in batting average (.353) and RBIs (88), was named to the all-star team, as were pitchers Jaime Ybarra and Matt Jarvis, each of whom won 11 games. Chirs Kokinda (.316) was named rookie of the year. There was again a serious attendance drop—25,000 to 171,351, still the second-best in the league.

1997. In November 1996, Sam Katz bought out Winnipeg Enterprises Corporation to become the sole owner of the Goldeyes. WEC, however, would only sign a two-year lease for the team's use of Winnipeg Stadium. In addition, the corporation controlled the running of the stadium, including parking and concessions. That parking and concessions prices were high and that customer service was not highly ranked were given as some of the causes of the steep decline in attendance since the very successful inaugural season. If the Goldeyes were to continue operations, Katz realized that he would have to build a baseball-only stadium, one in which the Goldeyes controlled the revenue streams, and it would have to be ready for the 1999 season. Over 29 months, he worked diligently to find a suitable location, negotiate (with difficulty) with the City Council over legal matters, secure funding, and build the park.

The 1997 Goldeyes won nine of their first 11 games and went on to win the first half, winning 29 and losing 12, finishing 1.5 games in front of the Sioux City Explorers. During the second half, they were tied for first place going into the last week of the season, but managed to win only two of their last five games and, on the last day, were edged out of first by their arch rivals, the Fargo-Moorhead RedHawks. They lost the first two games of the semifinals to the RedHawks but came back to take the final three and reach the finals for the third time in their four-year history. They lost the championship series three games to two to the Duluth-Superior Dukes. The final attendance figure of 171,240 was only 111 fewer than the year before, but it included a crowd of 22,081 that attended a game on August 27.

Five Goldeyes earned post-season awards. Terry Lee, who won his second batting championship with a .358 average, was named all-star first baseman, while Brian Duva, who had a .332 average and a league-leading 55 stolen bases, was all-star second baseman and John Dorman (.310), all-star shortstop.

The other two award winners were pitchers whose names loom large in Goldeyes history: right-handed pitcher Rick Forney and rookie of the year Jeff Zimmerman. For Forney, who tied for league lead with 11 wins (he lost four), 1997 would be the start of a long career in Winnipeg. After five years in the Baltimore Orioles' minor league chain, he spent a year with Lubbock in the Texas-Louisiana League before coming to Winnipeg. After four years as a player, he became the Goldeyes pitching coach, a position he held until 2006, when he succeeded Hal Lanier as manager. Going into the 2020 season, he still held that post. Jeff Zimmerman, a resident of Calgary, had been undrafted after finishing his college career at Texas Christian University. Encouraged by his mother, he drove to Winnipeg to attend the Goldeyes' tryout camp and made the team. After six weeks, his record was no wins and two losses; but then he won nine straight games. After the season he was signed by the Texas Rangers and, in 1999, he made his major league debut.

1998. The Goldeyes started their final season at Winnipeg Stadium slowly, not rising above .500 until the twenty-first game of the season and finished the first half in second place with a 25–18 record, 6.5 games behind Fargo-Moorhead. The team improved greatly in the second half, thanks to two five and two six-game winning streaks. On the final day of the season, before a home crowd of 9,672, the best of the year, they defeated the RedHawks 13 to 0, to earn a tie for first place and their fifth consecutive trip to the playoffs. Brian Duva, who, with the retirement of Terry Lee, had become the team leader, won the batting title with a .367 average and had 26 stolen bases, third-best in the league, and was named all-star second baseman. Outfielder Tony Chance, who won the RBI crown with 81 and had a .325 average, was also named to the all-star team. Designated hitter Sean Hearn, who led the league with 29 homers and finished second with 80 RBI, was named all-star designated hitter and Northern League player of the year. Rick Forney led the mound corps with 11 wins and six losses and had a league-high 112 strikeouts. Jeff Sparks earned 17 saves, second highest in the league, and in the off-season signed with the Tampa Bay organization and made his major league debut the next year. The playoffs ended quickly for the Goldeyes, with Fargo-Moorhead winning three games to one. Attendance dropped by nearly 12,000 to 159,512, third highest in the eight-team league.

1999. During the winter, CanWest Global Park began to rise from the "old hydro site" located between downtown and the Red River. Naming rights had been purchased by the Canadian media company for $1.5 million, $500,000 of which was applied to construction costs. Other funding came from the federal government ($1.5 million), the provincial government ($1.5 million) and the city government ($1 million). During the inaugural season, the new park seated 6,140. In 2000, another 250 seats were added, and the skyboxes were completed. In 2002, with the help of $1.5 million each from the federal and provincial governments, a restaurant, picnic area, nursing station, and outfield berm were created. Later additions would bring the capacity up to 7,481.

On June 4, a few hours after the construction finishing touches had been completed and the park swept clean, 6,708 people jammed into CanWest Global Park to see the Goldeyes play their first game in the new stadium. They lost 14–5 to Sioux Falls and would win only two games in their opening seven-game home stand. A 15 wins and three losses streak in June moved them into first place in the West Division, where they finished the first half, one game ahead of Fargo-Moorhead. The team slumped in the second half, winning 20 and losing 23 to finish in third place eight behind Sioux City. The Goldeyes came alive in the post-season, sweeping both Sioux City and Fargo-Moorhead three games to none to win the Northern League Central championship. But there was one more round to go. The year of 1999 was the first year that the former Northeast League became the Northern League East. The Goldeyes faced the East champions, the Albany-Colonie Diamond Dogs, and lost the championship round three games to one.

The Goldeyes placed three players on the NL Central all-star team: first baseman Darin Everson (.306, 69 RBIs, 12 home runs), shortstop Chad Thornhill (.293), and right-handed pitcher Rick Forney. During the off-season, Forney had been signed by the Atlanta Braves organization and, although he had struck out 71 in 70 innings playing with the Greenville Braves of the Double A Southern League, he was 27 years old and deemed too long in the tooth to fit into the Braves' plans. He returned to Winnipeg, won nine while losing three, and posted the Northern League Central's top earned run average: 2.13. Pitcher Shawn Onley led the NL Central with 103 strikeouts. The opening day crowd was the first of 24 sellouts at CanWest Global Park. The final attendance of 248,488, second-best in both divisions of the league, represented an increase of nearly 90,000 over 1998.

2000. The Goldeyes finished both half-seasons with identical records: 24 wins and 19 losses. During the first half, that record placed them four games behind Fargo-Moorhead in the West Division. During the second half, they were tied with the RedHawks for first with two games to go but finished one game behind. However, their overall record, second best in the West Division, earned them their seventh consecutive berth in the playoffs. Fargo-Moorhead made short work of Winnipeg, defeating the Goldeyes in three straight games. Former major leaguer, 34-year-old Wes Chamberlain had a .327 average for the Goldeyes along with 14 homers and was named to the all-star team as an outfielder. Shortstop Jack Jones (.276) also made the all-star team. Jeff Kepper tied for the most wins in the Central Division with 11. Rick Forney, who appeared in only seven games before being sidelined with an injury, began his six-year stint as Winnipeg's pitching coach. There were 34 sellouts at CanWest Global Park and the final attendance of 271,513 was tops in all the Northern League. This was the first of 14 consecutive season that the Goldeyes would lead attendance figures, first in the Northern League and then, from 2011 on, the American Association.

2001. The Goldeyes won the North Division's first and second half championships, won the NL Central championship and advanced to the Northern League championship against NL East champions New Jersey. During the first half, Winnipeg posted a 29 and 16 record and finished eight games ahead of Duluth-Superior. However, in the second half, partly because of a stretch in which they won only three of 12 games, they ended up only one game above .500. Still, that was three ahead of second place St. Paul. In the Central Division semifinals, the team lost the first two games to Fargo-Moorhead, before winning the next three; the NL Central final against Lincoln was easier, as the Goldeyes won three games to one. The powerhouse New Jersey Jackals then overwhelmed Winnipeg three games to one for the Northern League pennant.

In spite of the disappointing end to Goldeyes season, there were many highlights. Catcher Ryan Robertson (.310), shortstop Brent Sachs (.305), and outfielder Carmine Cappuccio, whose .359 average was second-best in the NL Central and 80 RBIs the best, were named to the all-star team. Rafael Gross had the most wins in the Central, 14, and the top winning percentage, .875. In mid-season, Brian Myrow, who was hitting .386 at the time, had his contract purchased by the New York Yankees. In 2005 he would make his major league debut with the Los Angeles Dodgers. During the season, 292,095 fans turned out, an increase of 20,000 fans and, at that time, the highest season's total for any Northern League team.

2002. The Goldeyes did it again, winning both halves in the North Division and the NL Central finals before being defeated in the Northern League championship by the New Jersey Devils. The team played mediocre baseball until mid–June when a stretch of 16 wins and only two losses lifted them from fifth to first in the North Division standings. Their record of 28 wins and 16 losses placed them three games ahead of Fargo-Moorhead. The Goldeyes hung on to a very slender lead throughout most of the second half and finished one game ahead Fargo-Moorhead. Winnipeg went on to defeat the Lincoln Salt Dogs three games to two and the Sioux City Explorers three games to one before facing the New Jersey Jackals in what would be the final year that the East would be part of the Northern League. Again New Jersey dominated the championship series, three games to one. Attendance at CanWest Global Park rose by 12,000 to 303,786.

Three Winnipeg players were named to the all-star team. Brent Sachs was named all-star third baseman. His .346 average was second highest in the league. Harry Berrios turned in the first of four consecutive .300-plus seasons with a .323 average and was selected in the outfield. Bobby Madritsch, who after suffering a rotor cuff injury and missing a season had been released from the Cincinnati organization, won 11 and lost four, posted a 2.30 earned run average, and struck out a league leading 153 batters. He was not only named to the all-star team but selected as *Baseball America*'s independent leagues player of the year. A year later he was a member of the Seattle Mariners' organization and in 2004 made his major league debut.

Two other Goldeyes had Cincinnati Reds connections. Pitcher George Sherrill had also been released from the organization and would later make his major league debut with Seattle. For 32-year-old Pete Rose, Jr., son of the Cincinnati Reds' tarnished star, the summer in Winnipeg was one of 27 stops in a long and peripatetic career that included 11 games for Cincinnati. He posted a .344 average for the Goldeyes.

2003. The Winnipeg Goldeyes celebrated their tenth anniversary season with their ninth half-season first place finish, tenth consecutive trip to the playoffs, and seventh appearance in the championship series—which unfortunately they lost (for the sixth time). During the first half they settled into the North Division's second place in early June and, during the next 16 games, were never closer than three games to first-place St Paul. They started the second half with eight wins in the first 10 games and moved into first place to stay in mid–July. Their first-half record was 26 wins and 18 losses, three and a half games behind St. Paul, while their second half record of 29 wins and 16 losses placed them six in front of second place Schaumberg. They edged the St. Paul Saints three games to two in the semi-finals, but lost in the finals, three games to one, to their arch rivals, the Fargo-Moorhead RedHawks. Three Goldeyes made the post-season awards list. Outfielder Harry Berrios, who posted a .312 average and belted 15 home runs, second-best in the league, and pitcher Rafael Gross, who won the most games, 13, and had the best won-lost percentage (.867) and the lowest ERA in the league, 2.28, in the league were selected for the all-star team. Kris Cox, who hit .314, was named rookie of the year. One home game was rained out, which explains why attendance fell by 3,026 to 300,760. The per-game average was an amazing 7,161.

2004. The Goldeyes' eleventh season would be one when the streak ended: they didn't make the playoffs for the first time in their history During the first half, they spent two days tied for first, but the last two weeks in third place. Their record, 26 wins and 21 losses, put them 5.5 games behind Fargo-Moorhead. Things started well in the second half and, at one point the Goldeyes won 14 of 15 games. They were tied for top spot five times, but, on the last weekend of the season, they were eliminated from playoff contention. They finished second, one game behind St. Paul, their record 30 wins and 18 losses. Third baseman Pat Scalabrini (.322, 20 home runs) was named to the all-star team. Attendance rose to an all-time Winnipeg high: 323,241.

2005. The league expanded during the off-season, adding teams in Calgary and Edmonton. All three Canadian teams would play in the North Division in a league that extended 1,665 miles from Gary, Indiana, to Edmonton, Alberta. If '04 had been disappointing for the Goldeyes, '05 was even more so. Winnipeg won only one of its first nine games and, although it lost only two of its last 10, it finished the first half in fourth place with a 22–26 record, 5.5 games behind Fargo-Moorhead. The situation worsened in the second half. Although the team's record improved to 25 and 23, they dropped during the last month from six games to 15.5 games behind Fargo-Moorhead and again finished fourth. Harry Berrios was selected all-star designated hitter. His .349 average was fourth highest in the league. Attendance dropped very slightly, by 483. The final figure of 322,758 was still tops in the league.

After the season, two momentous changes took place, one for the Goldeyes, the other for the league in general. Owner Sam Katz, who by then was also mayor of Winnipeg, was not happy with the club's performance and delayed so long in offering Hal Lanier a new contract that the team's manager of 10 years asked for and received permission to negotiate with another club. He decided to sign with the Joliet Jackhammers, also of the Northern League. In late September, in an announcement that shocked many people, the St. Paul, Sioux Falls, Sioux City, and Lincoln (Nebraska) teams announced that they would be jumping from the Northern League to become the nucleus of a new independent league, the American Association. The Northern League would still stretch from Gary to Edmonton, but in 2006 it would contain only eight teams.

2006. The managers' exchange of lineups on May 19, opening day at CanWest Global Park, was a study in contrasts. Sixty-four-year-old Hal Lanier, former major league manager and player and, until the late fall of 2005, manager of the Winnipeg Goldeyes, presented the umpires with the lineups for the Joliet Jackhammers. Thirty-four-year-old Rick Forney, who had only reached the Triple A level, where he played three games, but who had been Lanier's pitching coach and understudy for five years, turned in the Goldeyes' lineup. Winnipeg swept the three game home series and, thanks to a June stretch that saw the team win 10 and lose only two, finished the first half in second place in what was now the West Division, five behind Fargo-Moorhead. Late in the second half, they moved from fourth place to second, clinching a wild-card berth with two games to go. Their final second half record was 25 and 23, second again to Fargo-Moorhead, this time by six games. The Goldeyes faced their arch-rivals for the eighth time (the RedHawks won four of the previous seven series), won the first two games of the semi-finals and then were eliminated as Fargo-Moorhead took three straight. Outfielder Fehlandt Lentini (.325) was named to the all-star team, as was designated hitter Jimmy Hurst, a former major leaguer who posted a .307 average and batted in a league-leading 78 runs. Attendance dropped by over 10,000, but the final figure of 312,213 was still best in both the Northern League and the newly formed American Association.

2007. The Goldeyes made the second of what would be a streak of four consecutive post-season appearances, but they made it into the playoffs by the back door. During the first half, they lost four of their first five games, but, later, won eight of their last ten, to finish second with 27 wins and 20 losses, 1.5 games behind Calgary in what was again the North Division. Their record slipped to 25 wins and 23 losses in the second half and, although they were in second place for most of the last five weeks of the season, they never seriously challenged first place Fargo-Moorhead, finishing six games out. The Goldeyes became a wildcard playoff team by virtue of having the best overall record of non-first place finishing teams. The Goldeyes took the semi-final series to the limit, losing to Gary three games to two. Catcher Luis Alen (.333) and outfielder Fehlandt Lentini (.321) were named to the all-star team. Attendance dropped by 11,000 to 300,938. It was the sixth consecutive and last season the Goldeyes would draw over 300,000 fans during the regular season.

2008. With the departure of the troubled Edmonton and Calgary franchises, which bolted to the Golden Baseball League after the 2007 season, the Northern League was reduced to six teams. The split-season format was abandoned and all the teams played in one division. The Goldeyes started slowly, winning only five of their first 15 games. In mid–July, they had reached first place, but a streak in which they won only three of 16 games plunged them into fourth place. Their final record of 51 wins and 45 losses placed them in third, 11 behind regular season winner Fargo-Moorhead, and gained them a spot in the four-team playoffs, where they faced second-place Gary and lost three games to one. Three Goldeyes made the all-star team: Fehlandt Lentini, who posted a .298 average and stole a league-leading 37 bases, was named an all-star outfielder for the third consecutive season; Kevin West (.317, 18 homers) was selected as first baseman, and pitcher Brian Beuning, with a league-leading 1.75 ERA, was chosen as right-handed pitcher. The home attendance total of 284,398 was still the best in the league, but was nearly 16,000 fewer than in the previous year.

2009. From the beginning of the season on May 16 until August 18, there had been only two days when the Goldeyes were not either alone in first place or tied for first. On August 17, they clinched a playoff spot (four of the six Northern League teams would qualify). Then they lost six over a seven-game stretch and ended up finishing second. Their 55 wins and 41 losses record left them two games behind Gary. For the ninth time, Winnipeg met Fargo-Moorhead in the playoffs, and for the ninth time they lost: this time three games to two. Three Goldeyes were named to the all-star team: second baseman Josh Asanovich (.285), designated hitter Juan Diaz (.317 and a league-leading 29 home runs), and right-handed pitcher Ace Walker, whose 12 wins and six losses record also earned him the pitcher of the year award. Rookie pitcher Ian Thomas would play three years for the Goldeyes before being signed by the Atlanta Braves, with whom he'd make his major league debut in 2014. Attendance, although still tops in the league, dropped by 5,299 to 278,099. Three games were rained out and a great many cool and moist nights dampened fans' enthusiasm.

2010. In what would prove to be its final season, the Northern League added two teams: the Rockford River Hawks (who had been a member of the Frontier League) and the Lake County Fielders. All eight teams would play in one division and there would be no split-season format. The Goldeyes were never really in contention for the regular season pennant and, after completing 53 games, dropped below .500 for the rest of the season. They finished in fifth place with 46 wins and 53 losses, their worst record since joining the league. Outfielder Kevin West, now in his third and final season in Winnipeg, won the Northern League batting championship with a .337 average and was named to the all-star team. Attendance dropped again—to 271,399, still tops in the league.

A month after the season, rumors circulated that the Northern League would soon cease operations. The loss of St. Paul, Sioux City, Sioux Falls, and Lincoln had weakened the league. The Edmonton and Calgary franchises had departed two seasons later, and now both Schaumberg and first year Lake County were on shaky financial ground. During the season, Winnipeg owner Sam Katz, worried about the future of the league, had met with Miles Wolff about the possibility of the league's strongest franchises joining the American Association. On October 14, the American Association announced that Winnipeg, Gary, Fargo-Moorhead, and Kansas City would become members.

2011. The 14 teams of the American Association were divided into three groups: the South Division (Grand Prairie, Amarillo, Fort Worth, and El Paso, Texas, along with Shreveport-Bossier, Louisiana), the Central Division (Wichita and Kansas City, Kansas; Lincoln, Nebraska; Sioux City, Iowa; and Gary, Indiana), and the North Division (Winnipeg; Fargo-Moorhead, Minnesota/North Dakota; St. Paul, Minnesota; and Sioux Falls, South Dakota). During the 2011 season, the Goldeyes would only play against teams from the North and Central Divisions. After the first month of play, they had won 15 and lost 14 and found themselves in third place in their division. But a spectacular streak from mid–June to later July, in which they won 21 and lost nine, moved them into first place, where they would remain for the rest of the season. They set a record for most wins by the team, 60, lost 40 and finished four games ahead of St. Paul. Hopes for their first pennant since 1994 were dashed when St. Paul, the wild-card team, defeated them three games to two in the semi-finals. Price Kendall (.324) won the rookie of the year award, while Rick Forney was named manager of the year. Kody Kaiser led the league with 37 stolen bases. The Goldeyes did win one championship: their attendance of 275,521, an increase of 4,122 over 2010, was the best in the American Association.

2012. The Goldeyes opened their season deep in the heart of Texas, first in Amarillo and then, along the Rio Grande in Laredo and El Paso, winning six and losing three, and coming home in first place in the North Division. They maintained that position until mid–July, when they had a 32 and 21 record. There followed a steady descent, as the team dropped steadily behind the new North Division leaders, Fargo-Moorhead. The question became, not would the team repeat as division leaders, but would they earn a spot in the playoffs as the wildcard team. The Goldeyes finished the season 10 games behind the RedHawks, but three ahead of St. Paul. Not the favorites they had been in 2011, the Goldeyes surprised everyone, sweeping first Fargo-Moorhead and then Wichita to bring Winnipeg its first championship since 1994. Outfielder Chris Roberson (.317), who'd played 85 games in the major leagues, earned a berth on the all-star team. Pitcher Matt Rusch, the team's best pitcher with a 10 and four record, led the league in strikeouts with 113 and earned run average at 2.40. Once again, the Goldeyes topped the league in attendance: the final figure of 285,263 represented a rise of nearly 10,000 over the previous year.

2013. During the first three weeks of their twentieth anniversary season, the Goldeyes looked as if they would celebrate by winning a second consecutive championship. They won 12 of their first 20 games and occupied first place. However, over the next month, their fortunes were reversed and 12 wins in a 30-game stretch dropped them into third place at the season's mid-point. By the end of July they had moved into second place, and although they won 19 and lost 11 during the last month of the season, they were unable to catch up with front-running Fargo-Moorhead. Their final record of 56 wins and 44 losses put them six games behind the RedHawks. Nor were they able to win the wild-card spot in the playoffs, finishing 1.5 games behind Gary.

No member of the team earned a berth on the all-star team. The Goldeyes were one of the most travelled teams in the independent leagues. They opened the season deep in the heart of Texas, playing in Grand Prairie and Amarillo, and in mid–July, in an interlocking schedule with the Canadian-American League, played games near the shores of the St. Lawrence River (Quebec City and Trois-Rivières) and the Hudson River (Rockland, New York). Attendance dropped by 9,000 to 276,359, still tops in the American Association.

2014. The Goldeyes opened their season once again in Texas, winning four and losing three, and were in and out of first place for the next month. After their thirty-fifth game, they had a record of 22 wins and 13 losses, were in the top spot in the North Division and didn't leave it for the rest of the season. When the regular season ended, they were 15 games ahead of St. Paul, with a record of 63 wins, the most in team history, and 37 losses. But they didn't make it past the first round of the playoffs, which they lost to Central Division leader Lincoln, three games to two. First baseman Casey Haerther and shortstop

Tyler Kuhn, who posted identical .360 batting averages, second highest in the league, were named to the all-star team, as was pitcher Nick Hernandez, whose 12 wins tied for the league lead. Attendance plunged by 18,000—three games were rained out. But the figure of 258,429 was again highest in the American Association.

2015. If Winnipeg's faithful fans and the team's 10 returning players hoped that the Goldeyes' 2015 performance would help people forget the disappointing end to the 2014 season, they were all disappointed. When, on May 28, Winnipeg lost 3–4 to Wichita, the team dropped below the .500 mark and would remain below it the rest of the season. When the season ended, they were in second place, but were 26.5 games behind the St. Paul Saints. Their final record, 47 wins and 52 losses, was not their worst finish, but finishing 9.5 games out of a playoff spot was. Designated hitter Casey Haerther, who had a .312 batting average along with 79 RBIs, was named to the all-star team for the second year in a row. Third baseman Josh Mazzola, whose 20 home runs led the league, and outfielder Adam Heisler, who led the team in hitting with a .328 average, also made the all-star team. Attendance rose by 493 to 258,992, far below the 404,528 that the St. Paul Saints drew to their luxurious new stadium.

2016. The Goldeyes again finished in second place but had improved greatly since 2015. The team hovered around .500 until mid–July when they moved into second place, 9.5 games behind St. Paul. They were in contention for first place in the division until the final week of the season. They clinched a wildcard playoff berth on the last day of the season, edging out Laredo by half a game. In both the semi-finals and finals, they trailed two games to one but came back to the last two games against St. Paul and Wichita, respectively, to earn their third pennant. Pitcher Edwin Carl won three games during the playoffs, and Reggie Abercrombie belted three homers and 11 RBIs. Two Goldeyes made the all-star team, first baseman Dave Rohm, who had a team-high batting average of .339, and outfielder Willie Cabrera (.324). The final attendance of 231,206 represented a drop of nearly 29,000.

2017. With four position players, who among them had 84 stolen bases and 50 home runs, along with two .300 averages and one just below .300, and four pitchers with a combined 29 wins against 14 losses and 245 strikeouts, returning, the Goldeyes were preseason favorites to win a second consecutive championship. They started with seven wins and three losses and bounced around between first and fourth in the Northern division before moving into second place for all of June and the first two weeks of July. They took over first place on July 15, won 31 of their last 46 games, and clinched first place with four games left in the season. Their final record of 62 wins and 38 losses was the best in the League. They defeated Lincoln, Central Division winner, three games to one in the semi-finals and Wichita, the Southern Division champion, in the finals three games to two to win their fourth championship. Four Goldeyes, each of them a .300 hitter, were selected for the all-star team: Shortstop Andrew Sohn (.302), third baseman Wes Darvill (.309), designated hitter David Bergin (.323), and outfielder Josh Romanski (.324), who was also named league player of the year. Ironically, Shaun Pleffner, who won the league batting title with a .340 average, did not make the all-star team; nor did pitcher Kevin McGovern, whose 13 wins tied for the most in the league. The attendance dropped significantly for the third consecutive year: the figure of 219,556 was nearly 12,000 fewer than in 2017.

2018. As the opening of the Goldeyes' twenty-fifth anniversary season approached, newspaper headlines reported the team's "high expectations" and its hoping for a "three-peat," something that had not happened to any team during the 26-year combined operation of the Northern League and American Association. In late June, the expectations and hopes seemed a distinct possibility: Winnipeg had not been more than three games out of first in the six-team Northern Division and were now tied for first place. But the Goldeyes then lost 20 of their next 26 games and dropped to fourth place and in the final two and a half weeks of the season won only four of 18 games. Their final record of 41 wins and 59 losses represented the worst regular season record in the club's 25-year history. They finished in fifth place, 18 games behind co-division leaders St. Paul and Gary. What had happened? Two of last year's .300 hitters, David Bergin and Andrew Sohn, had only .250 averages, while former all-star Kevin McGovern won only five while losing 12. Thirty-seven-year-old Reggie Abercrombe, now in his fifth season with the Goldeyes, led the club with a .317 average. In spite of the dismal season, attendance dropped by only 226; the final total of 219,370 was still second best in the league.

2019. Players and coaches hoped that the 2019 season would be one of redemption. It was—partially at least. When spring training began, there were only eight holdovers on the roster, the most notable of whom were slugger/stolen base artist Reggie Abercrombie, and starters Kevin McGovern and Mitch Lambson. Wes Darvill, the Langley, BC, native whose all-star 2017 season had earned him a season in the Los Angeles Dodgers organization, was back in Winnipeg. The Goldeyes spent all but four of the first 21 games either tied for or in sole position of first place. However, they then played .500 ball until the midpoint of the season and dropped into third, then fourth place. For the rest of the way, they occupied fourth place, although they were in playoff contention until nine days to go. Nonetheless, the club improved greatly, its 57 wins and 43 losses record 16 percent higher than the year before. Mitch Lambson and Kevin McGovern, whose combined 2018 record was 13 wins and 18 losses, won 13 and 12 games respectively. Lampson's total, tops in the league, along with his 133 strikeouts (second-highest), earned him an all-star berth. Darvill led the team with a .317 average; his 26 stolen bases were second-best in the league. Three rainouts during the first half of the season contributed to a 23,000 drop in attendance, to 195,787, the first time the Goldeyes had dropped below the 200,000 mark since 1998, their last season in Winnipeg Stadium.

2020. The Goldeyes were the only Canadian minor or independent league team to play in 2020, as the American Association was the only league to operate, the Covid-19 pandemic having caused the cancellation of all minor league seasons as well as those of the other independent leagues. Six of the Association's 12 teams played during the 2020 season. Because of the strict quarantine regulations imposed on all people entering Canada, the Goldeyes played all their home games in the short, 60-game season in Fargo-Moorhead. On August 21, Winnipeg was in first place, but then lost 11 in a row and 14 of their final 18 games, finishing in fourth place, five games out of first and three out of the two-team playoffs. First baseman Kyle Martin (.301/16 home runs) was named all-star first baseman and Rick Forney manager of the year. With no actual home games to generate revenue, expenses were estimated to be in the high six figures.

Conclusion

There are many similarities between the history of minor and independent league baseball in Canada and the United States. The two countries saw a rapid expansion of minor league baseball right after World War II, followed by a steady decline in the 1950s and 1960s, as attendance dropped, teams folded or were relocated, and leagues were dissolved. In the 1970s, financially struggling teams relocated and, mainly at the Class A and Rookie levels, leagues frequently struggled to field enough teams to create a viable schedule. Although the number of league and teams did not increase measurably during the 1980s, attendance rose steadily and the value of franchises increased dramatically. Beginning in the 1990s, minor league teams frequently relocated as wealthy owners or ownership groups purchased and moved teams to cities that had built bigger and better stadiums. During the 1990s, independent leagues appeared and disappeared, with only four leagues surviving: the Northern League, which morphed into the American Association; the Atlantic League; the Frontier League; and the Northeast League (which was renamed the Canadian-American League and which merged with the Frontier League after the 2019 season). After the 2019 season, two of Canada's three independent league teams, the Winnipeg Goldeyes of the American Association and les Capitales de Quebec of the Frontier League, along with the Vancouver Canadians of the Northwest League, were among only seven Canadian minor and independent league teams that, since 1946, had operated for 20 or more consecutive seasons.

In the later 1950s and early 1960s, minor leagues and teams counted on the subsidies provided by the major leagues to remain financially solvent. In addition, the large majority and, after the early 1990s, all teams that were members of National Association leagues relied exclusively on major league teams for their players, coaches and training staff and much if not all of their salaries. Between 1946 and 1951, when the Montreal Royals of the International League were owned by and were the top farm team of the Brooklyn Dodgers, they won three regular-season and four playoff championships and were twice winners of the Junior World Series, played against the champions of the American Association. Over the six seasons, attendance at Montreal's Delorimier Downs averaged over 400,000. By contrast, the Toronto Maple Leafs finished out of the playoffs each of these seasons. They had working agreements with the Philadelphia Athletics and the Philadelphia Phillies, who had weak farm systems, and the Boston Red Sox, who sent their best Triple A players to their American Association team in Louisville. Attendance at Maple Leaf stadium only began to match or exceed Montreal's in 1952, when Jack Kent Cooke, who had bought the team in 1951, started regular promotions, celebrity entertainer appearances, and giveaways. The Royals' attendance dropped steadily during the 1950s, particularly after the Dodgers had moved to Los Angeles and began to send their top prospects to the Spokane Indians of the Pacific Coast League. When Los Angeles unsuccessfully attempted to sell the team after the 1960 season, the Royals' franchise was terminated.

Other Canadian minor league teams folded when they were unable to retain or acquire affiliation agreements with major league clubs. When the Philadelphia Athletics relocated to Kansas City, Missouri, after the 1954 season and decided to locate their Triple A farm team in Columbus, Ohio, the Ottawa Athletics departed from the International League. In the mid–1950s, the St. Louis Cardinals, who in 1954 had a minor league system of 22 teams, decided to cut back the number of affiliates and after 1955 divested themselves of ownership in the Hamilton Cardinals. The next year, the locally owned Hamilton Red Wings, with no major league support, folded three weeks into the season. The entire Provincial League didn't even make it to the beginning of the 1956 season. In early April, only three teams had secured an affiliation with a major league team and league officials, realizing that the financial risk involved in proceeding with three unaffiliated teams was too great, suspended operations. After the 1969 season, when the Montreal Expos and Seattle Pilots (two major league expansion teams) decided that they would no longer supply players to Vancouver's Triple A team in the Pacific Coast League, the Mounties were sold and the franchise relocated to Salt Lake City. Since 1956, when the Hamilton Red Wings disbanded, only two Canadian minor league teams have operated without major league support—the 1974 New Westminster Frasers and the 1978 to 1980 Victoria Mussels/Blues of the Northwest League. Their stays in the league were short, their on-field performances mediocre at best, and their fan support extremely low.

Although the history of Canada's minor and independent leagues and teams has followed patterns of minor and independent baseball in general, there have been significant differences. One of these is very positive, another has been an ongoing problem, and one, since the late 1960s, a uniquely Canadian phenomenon.

Canadian teams were among the leaders in the integration of black players into what had been an exclusively white profession. The Montreal Royals, under the direction of Branch Rickey of the Brooklyn Dodgers, led the way, beginning with the signing of Jackie Robinson in October 1945, and following with such future stars as Roy Campanella, Don Newcombe, and Johnny Roseboro. In addition to the Montreal Royals, who fielded 24 black players, Canada's other Triple A teams included black players on their rosters: Toronto (17), Ottawa (eight), and Vancouver (11).

Other Canadian teams and leagues played significant roles. Most notable was the Provincial League of Quebec, where, according to *Black Baseball Players in Canada: A Biographical Dictionary, 1881–1960*, 86 black players performed. Many of these were veterans of the Negro Leagues, which were facing severe financial crises. Others were young players like Vic Power (Drummondville) and Dave Pope (Farnham), who would go on to the major leagues. One, Sam Bankhead, became the first African American manager in the minor leagues, when he piloted the 1951 Farnham Pirates. Players in Quebec did not face the racism that they would have encountered playing for many American minor league teams.

When the St. Louis Cardinals, who in 1953 had only two of their 13 lower-level farm teams in non-southern states, decided to sign and develop black players, they needed a location suitable for sending their young prospects. Winnipeg, Manitoba, was their choice for a Class C club (they had a Class D team in Hamilton, Ontario). Since 1950, the city had been hosting teams in the ManDak (as in Manitoba, Dakotas) League, a high-level semi-professional circuit whose clubs frequently signed black players. Between the 1954 and 1960 seasons, the Goldeyes, as the team was named, included fifteen black players on their roster. Three of these, Johnny Lewis, Ed Olivares, and Julio Gotay, would later play in the major leagues.

Canada's minor league teams may have provided welcoming environments for black players in the late 1940s and through the 1950s. However, throughout the history of baseball in Canada, the natural environment in the early weeks of the season has often been anything but welcoming. Late bursts of winter into mid–May resulted in cancellations, games played on nearly frozen fields, and small crowds stamping their feet not to encourage the home team but to keep warm. On the Canadian prairies early home stands were snowed or even frozen out. Breaking even at the box office was often the best outcome front office officials could hope for. Needless to say, major league farm directors were often leery of sending their players to the "great white north" and worried about injuries, especially to pitching arms. Members of the Edmonton Trappers front office team remembered a cold, blustery day in 1991, when Whitey Herzog of the California Angels paid an early season visit to aging John Ducey Park. As he watched snowflakes drift down, he grumbled about the playing conditions and the condition of the park. At the end of the season, the Angels did not renew their affiliation with the Trappers.

The same thing happened a decade later, when Minnesota Twins General Manager Terry Ryan, along with Minor League Director Jim Rantz, visited Edmonton. The Trappers had a new stadium, but the same old early-season weather. They'd lost three of four games in their opening home stand and had to play the second one in Iowa because the home field was deep in snow. The Minnesota brass had arrived on Sunday to check on the players that had come to Edmonton, but the game had been postponed because of snow. The makeup doubleheader the next day was played in weather not many degrees above freezing, and the following day's contest was cancelled because of snow. The Twins officials took a late afternoon flight back to Minneapolis. At the end of the season, they terminated their affiliation agreement with the Edmonton Trappers.

Owners of Canadian minor league franchises faced another challenge related to winter—the Stanley Cup playoffs of the National Hockey League. Until the late 1960s, the National Hockey League's regular season ended in late March and the playoffs by mid- to late April. However, in 1967, when the League began the first of many expansions, the regular season grew longer and the playoffs extended first into May and later into June. As long as there was a Canadian team in the playoffs, most Canadians stayed indoors watching the games on television, especially if the hometown team were playing. Going to the ballpark, even if it was a warm and sunny day, wasn't an option. From the 1978 playoffs, during which time the Vancouver Canadians were enjoying their first season back into the Pacific Coast League, to the 2007 season, during which the Ottawa Lynx began their final season in the International League, 10 Canadian teams won the Stanley Cup, while eight others were in the finals. Twelve times, the Stanley Cup finals were played in cities that had Triple A baseball teams. Some fans came to the ballpark with transistor radios when the home hockey team was playing—but not in great numbers.

During the 1950s, the Canadian Triple A franchises were relocated to American cities. Those in the lower minors, and often the leagues they played in, simply disappeared. They were part of the great contraction that swept through the minor leagues in the 1950s. Many minor league cities lost their teams in the 1990s and into the twenty-first century. However, they were not part of a great contraction. In fact, the number of full-season minor leagues expanded by 10. These cities were victims of relocation. From the end of the 1990 season to the end of the 2007 season, 72 minor league teams, nearly half of those operating in 1990, moved to new cities, where they found homes in new, state of the art ball parks. The percentage was far higher in Canada. All of the 10 teams, from Triple A to rookie level, that operated in Canada in the 1990s relocated to the United States.

The 2008 season started with only one affiliated minor league team: the short season Class A Northwest League Vancouver Canadians, who had replaced the Triple A Canadians after the 1999 season. There has been no other Canadian minor league team since. Given the fact that in the fall of 2019, Major League Baseball announced that it would be cutting down the number of minor league franchises that big league teams would be supplying with players, the likelihood of another Canadian city acquiring a minor league team seems very slight. The Canadian cities that once hosted full-season minor league teams before are either too far from most major league cities or do not have the stadia that would meet increasingly strict standards; moreover, they suffer from those two Canadian early-spring problems: the weather and the Stanley Cup playoffs. Two of the short-season leagues, the New York–Pennsylvania League and the Pioneer League, which are fairly close to southern Canadian cities, have been disbanded as professional leagues. A third, the Northwest League, which includes Vancouver which has become the most successful short season minor league team of the twenty-first century, has been elevated to full-season status. However, Vancouver is the only western Canadian city with the population and the weather that would meet the Northwest League's footprint.

There is a small chance that one or a few of the Canadian cities who briefly hosted unsuccessful teams in independent leagues might acquire an independent league franchise. There was talk, when the Canadian-American League, of which the Trois-Rivières Aigles and the highly successful Capitales de Quebec were members, merged with the Frontier League after the 2019 season, that Ottawa and London might be granted franchises; Ottawa was to operate in 2021. The American Association, of which the Winnipeg Goldeyes franchise is the crown jewel, has shown no interest in expanding its geographical footprint into other western Canadian cities. Former independent league cities like Victoria, Kelowna, Edmonton, Medicine Hat, Regina, and Thunder Bay now host teams in the amateur collegiate summer leagues. In southern Ontario and Quebec, high level senior amateur/semi-pro teams are solidly entrenched.

An era of minor and independent league baseball in Canada that began on October 24, 1945, when Jackie Robinson signed a contract to play with the Montreal Royals and which survived the lean years of the 1960s and 1970s before rebounding in the last two decades of the twentieth century, has, with three exceptions—in Winnipeg, Quebec City, and Vancouver, languished and virtually ended. Winter weather and Stanley Cup playoffs, changing entertainment tastes, American owners with eyes on greener American pastures, and the general reluctance of American teams to travel north of the border have all contributed to the demise.

Appendix

*Directory of Canadian Minor League
and Independent League Teams
by Year: 1946-2020*

From **1946 to 1962** minor leagues, those operating under the aegis of the National Association of Professional Baseball League (Minor League Baseball since 1999), were classified alphabetically from Class AAA (the highest classification) to Class D (the lowest). There was one exception: from 1952 to 1955 to 1957, the Pacific Coast League was designated Open Classification which signified that the league was higher than AAA, but lower than the major leagues. Beginning with the **1963** season, Class B, C, and D leagues were reclassified as Class A leagues. The Rookie classification was added. Four leagues became short season leagues, operating between mid–June and early September: the Appalachian League (1963) and the Pioneer League (1964) at the Rookie level, and the Northern League (1965), the Northwest League (1966), and the New York–Pennsylvania League (1967) at the Class A level. Since the 1960s, nearly all teams in the National Association leagues have had affiliations with major league teams.

Independent leagues are those that have not operated under the aegis of the National Association. Neither the leagues nor the teams in them have affiliations with major league teams.

An asterisk (*) indicates that a team or a league discontinued operations during the season.

1946 (10 minor league teams)

International League (AAA): Montreal Royals, Toronto Maple Leafs
Western International League (B): Vancouver Capilanos, Victoria Athletics
Border League (C): Granby Red Sox, Kingston Ponies, Sherbrooke Canadians
Canadian-American League (C): Quebec City Alouettes, Trois-Rivières Royals
PONY League (D): Hamilton Cardinals

1947 (9 minor league teams; 8 independent league teams)

International League (AAA): Montreal Royals, Toronto Maple Leafs
Western International League (B): Vancouver Capilanos, Victoria Athletics
Border League (C): Kingston Ponies, Ottawa Nationals
Canadian-American League (C): Quebec City Alouettes, Trois-Rivières Royals
PONY League (D): Hamilton Cardinals
Provincial League (independent): Acton Vale*, Drummondville Cubs, Farnham

Pirates, Granby Grand Bs, Lachine Red Sox*, Sherbrooke Black Sox, Saint-Hyacinthe Saints, St. Jean Braves

1948 (9 minor league teams: 6 independent league teams)

International League (AAA): Montreal Royals, Toronto Maple Leafs
Western International League (B): Vancouver Capilanos, Victoria Athletics
Border League (C): Kingston Ponies, Ottawa Senators
Canadian-American League (C): Quebec City Alouettes, Trois-Rivières Royals
PONY League (D): Hamilton Cardinals
Provincial League (independent): Drummondville Cubs, Farnham Black Sox, Granby Red Sox, Sherbrooke Athletics, Saint-Hyacinthe Saints, St. Jean Braves

1949 (9 minor league teams: 6 independent league teams)

International League (AAA): Montreal Royals, Toronto Maple Leafs
Western International League (B): Vancouver Capilanos, Victoria Athletics
Border League (C): Kingston Ponies, Ottawa Senators
Canadian-American League (C): Quebec City Braves, Trois-Rivières Royals
PONY League (D): Hamilton Cardinals
Provincial League (independent): Drummondville Cubs, Farnham Pirates, Granby Red Sox, Sherbrooke Athletics, Saint-Hyacinthe Saints, St. Jean Braves

1950 (15 minor league teams)

International League (AAA): Montreal Royals, Toronto Maple Leafs
Western International League (B): Vancouver Capilanos, Victoria Athletics
Border League (C): Kingston Ponies, Ottawa Senators
Canadian-American League (C): Quebec City Braves, Trois-Rivières Royals
Provincial League (C): Drummondville Cubs, Farnham Pirates, Granby Red Sox, Sherbrooke Athletics, Saint-Hyacinthe Saints, St. Jean Braves
PONY League (D): Hamilton Cardinals

1951 (16 minor league teams)

International League (AAA): Montreal Royals, Ottawa Giants, Toronto Maple Leafs
Western International League (B): Vancouver Capilanos, Victoria Athletics
Border League (C)*: Cornwall Canadians*, Kingston Ponies*
Provincial League (C): Drummondville Cubs, Farnham Pirates, Granby Red Sox, Quebec City Braves, Sherbrooke Athletics, Saint-Hyacinthe Saints, St. Jean Braves, Trois-Rivières Royals
PONY LEAGUE (B): Hamilton Cardinals

1952 (12 minor league teams)

International League (AAA): Montreal Royals, Ottawa Athletics, Toronto Maple Leafs
Western International League (A): Vancouver Capilanos, Victoria Tyees
Provincial League (C): Drummondville Cubs, Granby Phillies, Quebec City Braves, Saint-Hyacinthe A's, St. Jean Canadians, Trois-Rivières Yankees
PONY League (D): Hamilton Cardinals

1953 (16 minor league teams)

International League (AAA): Montreal Royals, Ottawa Athletics, Toronto Maple Leafs

Western International League (A): Calgary Stampeders, Edmonton Eskimos, Vancouver Capilanos, Victoria Tyees

Provincial League (C): Drummondville Royals, Granby Phillies, Quebec City Braves, Sherbrooke Indians, Saint-Hyacinthe A's, St. Jean Canadians, Thetford Mines Mineurs, Trois-Rivières Yankees

PONY League (D): Hamilton Cardinals

1954 (15 minor league teams)

International League (AAA): Montreal Royals, Ottawa Athletics, Toronto Maple Leafs

Western International League (A): Calgary Stampeders*, Edmonton Eskimos, Vancouver Capilanos, Victoria Tyees*

Northern League (C): Winnipeg Goldeyes

Provincial League (C): Drummondville A's, Quebec City Braves, Sherbrooke Indians, St. Jean Canadians, Thetford Mines Mineurs, Trois-Rivières Yankees

PONY League (D): Hamilton Cardinals

1955 (9 minor league teams)

International League (AAA): Montreal Royals, Toronto Maple Leafs

Northern League (C): Winnipeg Goldeyes

Provincial League (C): Quebec City Braves, Sherbrooke Indians, St. Jean Canadians, Thetford Mines Mineurs, Trois-Rivières Phillies

PONY League (D): Hamilton Cardinals

1956 (5 minor league teams)

Pacific Coast League (Open Classification): Vancouver Mounties

International League (AAA): Toronto Maple Leafs, Montreal Royals

Northern League (C): Winnipeg Goldeyes

PONY League (D): Hamilton Red Wings*

1957 (4 minor league teams)

Pacific Coast League (Open classification): Vancouver Mounties

International League (AAA): Montreal Royals, Toronto Maple Leafs

Northern League (C): Winnipeg Goldeyes

1958 (4 minor league teams)

International League (AAA): Montreal Royals, Toronto Maple Leafs

Pacific Coast League (AAA): Vancouver Mounties

Northern League (C): Winnipeg Goldeyes

1959 (4 minor league teams)

International League (AAA): Montreal Royals, Toronto Maple Leafs

Pacific Coast League (AAA): Vancouver Mounties

Northern League (C): Winnipeg Goldeyes

1960 (4 minor league teams)

International League (AAA): Montreal Royals, Toronto Maple Leafs

Pacific Coast League (AAA): Vancouver Mounties

Northern League (C): Winnipeg Goldeyes

1961 (4 minor league teams)

International League (AAA): Toronto Maple Leafs
Pacific Coast League (AAA): Vancouver Mounties
Northern League (C): Winnipeg Goldeyes

1962 (3 minor league teams)

International League (AAA): Toronto Maple Leafs
Pacific Coast League (AAA): Vancouver Mounties
Northern League (C): Winnipeg Goldeyes

1963 (2 minor league teams)

International League (AAA): Toronto Maple Leafs
Northern League (A): Winnipeg Goldeyes

1964 (2 minor league teams)

International League (AAA): Toronto Maple Leafs
Northern League (A): Winnipeg Goldeyes

1965 (2 minor league teams)

International League (AAA): Toronto Maple Leafs
Pacific Coast League (AAA): Vancouver Mounties

1966 (2 minor league teams)

International League (AAA): Toronto Maple Leafs
Pacific Coast League (AAA): Vancouver Mounties

1967 (2 minor league teams)

International League (AAA): Toronto Maple Leafs
Pacific Coast League (AAA): Vancouver Mounties

1968 (1 minor league team)

Pacific Coast League (AAA): Vancouver Mounties

1969 (2 minor league teams)

Pacific Coast League (AAA): Vancouver Mounties
Northern League (Short Season A): Winnipeg Goldeyes

1970 (1 minor league team)

International League (AAA): Winnipeg Whips (midseason transfer from Buffalo, New York)

1971 (3 minor league teams)

International League (AAA): Winnipeg Whips
Eastern League (AA): Quebec City Carnavals, Trois-Rivières Aigles

1972 (3 minor league teams)

Eastern League (AA): Quebec City Carnavals, Sherbrooke Pirates, Trois-Rivières Aigles

1973 (3 minor league teams)

Eastern League (AA): Quebec City Carnavals, Sherbrooke Pirates, Trois-Rivières Aigles

1974 (4 minor league teams)

Eastern League (AA): Quebec City Carnavals, Thetford Mines Pirates, Trois-Rivières Aigles

Northwest League (Short Season A): New Westminster Frasers

1975 (4 minor league teams)

Eastern League: Quebec City Carnavals, Thetford Mines Pirates, Trois-Rivières Aigles
Pioneer League (Rookie): Lethbridge Expos

1976 (3 minor league teams)

Eastern League (AA): Quebec City Metros, Trois-Rivières Aigles,
Pioneer League (Rookie): Lethbridge Expos

1977 (5 minor league teams)

Eastern League (AA): Quebec City Metros, Trois-Rivières Aigles
Pioneer league (Rookie): Calgary Cardinals, Lethbridge Dodgers, Medicine Hat A's

1978 (5 minor league teams)

Pacific Coast League (AAA): Vancouver Canadians
Northwest League (Short Season A): Victoria Mussels
Pioneer League (Rookie): Calgary Cardinals, Lethbridge Dodgers, Medicine Hat Blue Jays

1979 (5 minor league teams)

Pacific Coast League (AAA): Vancouver Canadians
Northwest League (Short Season A): Victoria Mussels
Pioneer League (Rookie): Calgary Expos, Lethbridge Dodgers, Medicine Hat Blue Jays

1980 (5 minor league teams)

Pacific Coast League (AAA): Vancouver Canadians
Northwest League (Short Season A): Victoria Blues
Pioneer League (Rookie): Calgary Expos, Lethbridge Dodgers, Medicine Hat Blue Jays

1981 (minor league teams)

Pacific Coast League (AAA): Edmonton Trappers, Vancouver Canadians
Pioneer League (Rookie): Calgary Expos, Lethbridge Dodgers, Medicine Hat BlueJays

1982 (5 minor league teams)

Pacific Coast League (AAA): Edmonton Trappers, Vancouver Canadians
Pioneer League (Rookie): Calgary Expos, Lethbridge Dodgers, Medicine Hat Blue Jays

1983 (5 minor league teams)

Pacific Coast League (AAA): Edmonton Trappers, Vancouver Canadians
Pioneer League (Rookie): Calgary Expos, Lethbridge Dodgers, Medicine Hat Blue Jays

1984 (4 minor league teams)

Pacific Coast League (AAA): Edmonton Trappers, Vancouver Canadians
Pioneer League (Rookie): Calgary Expos, Medicine Hat Blue Jays

1985 (4 minor league teams)

Pacific Coast League (AAA): Calgary Cannons, Edmonton Trappers, Vancouver Canadians
Pioneer League (Rookie): Medicine Hat Blue Jays

1986 (5 minor league teams)

Pacific Coast League (AAA): Calgary Cannons, Edmonton Trappers, Vancouver Canadians
New York–Pennsylvania League (Short Season A): St. Catharines Blue Jays
Pioneer League (Rookie): Medicine Hat Blue Jays

1987 (5 minor league teams)

Pacific Coast League (AAA): Calgary Cannons, Edmonton Trappers, Vancouver Canadians
New York–Pennsylvania League (Short Season A): St. Catharines Blue Jays
Pioneer League (Rookie): Medicine Hat Blue Jays

1988 (6 minor league teams)

Pacific Coast League (AAA): Calgary Cannons, Edmonton Trappers, Vancouver Canadians
New York–Pennsylvania League (Short Season A): Hamilton Redbirds, St. Catharines Blue Jays
Pioneer League (Rookie): Medicine Hat Blue Jays

1989 (8 minor league teams)

Pacific Coast League (AAA): Calgary Cannons, Edmonton Trappers, Vancouver Canadians
Eastern League (AA): London Tigers
New York–Pennsylvania League (Short Season A): Hamilton Redbirds, St. Catharines Blue Jays, Welland Pirates
Pioneer League (Rookie): Medicine Hat Blue Jays

1990 (8 minor league teams)

Pacific Coast League (AAA): Calgary Cannons, Edmonton Trappers, Vancouver Canadians
Eastern League (AA): London Tigers
New York–Pennsylvania League (Short Season A): Hamilton Redbirds, St. Catharines Blue Jays, Welland Pirates
Pioneer League (Rookie): Medicine Hat Blue Jays

1991 (8 minor league teams)

Pacific Coast League (AAA): Calgary Cannons, Edmonton Trappers, Vancouver Canadians
Eastern League (AA): London Tigers
New York–Pennsylvania League (Short Season A): Hamilton Redbirds, St. Catharines Blue Jays, Welland Pirates
Pioneer League: Medicine Hat Blue Jays

1992 (9 minor league teams)

Pacific Coast League (AAA): Calgary Cannons, Edmonton Trappers, Vancouver Canadians

Eastern League (AA): London Tigers

New York–Pennsylvania League (Short Season A): Hamilton Redbirds, St. Catharines Blue Jays, Welland Pirates

Pioneer League (Rookie): Lethbridge Mounties, Medicine Hat Blue Jays

1993 (8 minor league teams; 1 independent league team)

International League (AAA): Ottawa Lynx

Pacific Coast League (AAA): Calgary Cannons, Edmonton Trappers, Vancouver Canadians

Eastern League (AA): London Tigers

New York–Pennsylvania League (Short Season A): St. Catharines Blue Jays, Welland Pirates

Pioneer League (Rookie): Lethbridge Mounties, Medicine Hat Blue Jays

Northern League (Independent): Thunder Bay Whiskey Jacks

1994 (8 minor league teams; 4 independent league teams)

International League (AAA): Ottawa Lynx

Pacific Coast League (AAA): Calgary Cannons, Edmonton Trappers, Vancouver Canadians

New York–Pennsylvania League (Short Season A): St. Catharines Blue Jays, Welland Pirates

Pioneer League (Rookie): Lethbridge Mounties, Medicine Hat Blue Jays

North Central League (Independent): Regina Cyclones, Saskatoon Riot

Northern League (independent): Thunder Bay Whiskey Jacks, Winnipeg Goldeyes

1995 (7 minor league teams; 8 independent league teams)

International League (AAA): Ottawa Lynx

Pacific Coast League (AAA): Calgary Cannons, Edmonton Trappers, Vancouver Canadians

New York–Pennsylvania League (Short Season A): St. Catharines Blue Jays

Pioneer League (rookie): Lethbridge Mounties, Medicine Hat Blue Jays

North Atlantic League (independent): Welland Aquaducks

Northern League (independent): Thunder Bay Whiskey Jacks, Winnipeg Goldeyes

Prairie League (independent): Brandon Grey Owls, Moose Jaw Diamond Dogs, Regina Cyclone, Saskatoon Riot

Western Baseball League (independent): Surrey Glaciers

1996 (Canadian minor league teams: 7; independent league teams 7)

International League (AAA): Ottawa Lynx

Pacific Coast League (AAA): Calgary Cannons, Edmonton Trappers, Vancouver Canadians

New York–Pennsylvania League (Short Season A): St. Catharines Stompers

Pioneer League (Rookie): Lethbridge Black Diamonds, Medicine Hat Blue Jays

North Atlantic League (independent): Welland Aquaducks

Northern League (independent): Thunder Bay Whiskey Jacks, Winnipeg Goldeyes

Prairie League: Brandon Grey Owls, Moose Jaw Diamond Dogs, Regina Cyclone, Saskatoon Smokin' Guns

1997 (7 minor league teams; 6 independent league teams)

International League (AAA): Ottawa Lynx
Pacific Coast League (AAA): Calgary Cannons, Edmonton Trappers, Vancouver Canadians
New York–Pennsylvania League (Short Season A): St. Catharines Stompers
Pioneer League (Rookie): Lethbridge Black Diamonds, Medicine Hat Blue Jays
Northern League (independent): Thunder Bay Whiskey Jacks, Winnipeg Goldeyes
Prairie League (independent): Brandon West Man Wranglers, Moose Jaw Diamond Dogs*, Regina Cyclones, Saskatoon Stallions

1998 (7 minor league teams; 2 independent league teams)

International League (AAA): Ottawa Lynx
Pacific Coast League (AAA): Calgary Cannons, Edmonton Trappers, Vancouver Canadians
New York–Pennsylvania League (Short Season A): St. Catharines Stompers
Pioneer League (Rookie): Lethbridge Black Diamonds, Medicine Hat Blue Jays
Northern League (independent): Thunder Bay Whiskey Jacks, Winnipeg Goldeyes

1999 (6 minor league teams; 3 independent league teams)

International League (AAA): Ottawa Lynx
Pacific Coast League (AAA): Calgary Cannons, Edmonton Trappers, Vancouver Canadians
New York–Pennsylvania League (Short Season A): St. Catharines Stompers
Pioneer League (Rookie): Medicine Hat Blue Jays
Frontier League (independent): London Werewolves
Northern League–Central (independent): Winnipeg Goldeyes
Northern League–East (independent): les Capitals de Quebec

2000 (5 minor league teams; 3 independent league teams)

International league (AAA): Ottawa Lynx
Pacific Coast League (AAA): Calgary Cannons, Edmonton Trappers
Northwest League (Short Season A): Vancouver Canadians
Pioneer League (Rookie): Medicine Hat Blue Jays
Northern League–Central (independent): Winnipeg Goldeyes
Northern League–East (independent): les Capitales de Quebec
Frontier League (independent): London Werewolves

2001 (minor league teams 5; independent league teams 3)

International League (AAA): Ottawa Lynx
Pacific Coast League (AAA): Calgary Cannons, Edmonton Trappers
Northwest League (Short Season A): Vancouver Canadians
Pioneer League (Rookie): Medicine Hat Blue Jays
Northern League–Central (independent): Winnipeg Goldeyes
Northern League–East (independent): les Capitales de Quebec
Frontier League (independent): London Werewolves

2002 (5 minor league teams; 2 independent league teams)

International League (AAA): Ottawa Lynx
Pacific Coast League (AAA): Calgary Cannons, Edmonton Trappers
Northwest League (Short Season A): Vancouver Canadians
Pioneer League (Rookie): Medicine Hat Blue Jays
Northern League–Central (independent): Winnipeg Goldeyes
Northern League–East (independent): les Capitales de Quebec

2003 (3 minor league teams; 10 independent league teams)

International League (AAA): Ottawa Lynx
Pacific Coast League (AAA): Edmonton Trappers
Northwest League (Short Season A): Vancouver Canadians
Canadian Baseball League (independent)*: Calgary Outlaws*, Kelowna Heat*,
   London Monarchs*, Montreal Royales (road team)*, Niagara Stars (Welland)*,
   Saskatoon Legends*, Trois-Rivières Saints*, Victoria Capitals*
Northeast League (independent): les Capitales de Quebec
Northern League (independent): Winnipeg Goldeyes

2004 (3 minor league teams; 2 independent league teams)

International League (AAA): Ottawa Lynx
Pacific Coast League (AAA): Edmonton Trappers
Northwest League (Short Season A): Vancouver Canadians
Northeast League (independent): les Capitales de Quebec
Northern League (independent): Winnipeg Goldeyes

2005 (2 minor league teams; 4 independent league teams)

International League (AAA): Ottawa Lynx
Northwest League (Short Season A): Vancouver Canadians
Canadian-American League (independent): les Capitales de Quebec
Northern League (independent): Calgary Vipers, Edmonton Cracker-Cats,
   Winnipeg Goldeyes

2006 (2 minor league teams; 4 independent league teams)

International League (AAA): Ottawa Lynx
Northwest League (Short Season A): Vancouver Canadians
Canadian-American League (independent): les Capitales de Quebec
Northern League (independent): Calgary Vipers, Edmonton Cracker-Cats,
   Winnipeg Goldeyes

2007 (2 minor league teams; 4 independent league teams)

International League (AAA): Ottawa Lynx
Northwest League (Short Season A): Vancouver Canadians
Canadian-American League (independent): les Capitales de Quebec
Northern League (independent): Calgary Vipers, Edmonton Cracker-Cats,
   Winnipeg Goldeyes

2008 (1 minor league team; 5 independent league teams)

Northwest League (Short Season A): Vancouver Canadians

Canadian-American League (independent): Ottawa Rapids/Rapides/Rapidz, les Capitales de Quebec
Northern League (independent): Winnipeg Goldeyes
Golden Baseball League: Calgary Vipers, Edmonton Cracker-Cats

2009 (1 minor league team; 5 independent league teams)

Northwest League (Short Season A): Vancouver Canadians
Canadian-American League (independent): les Capitales de Quebec
Golden Baseball League: Calgary Vipers, Edmonton Capitals, Victoria Seals
Northern League (independent): Winnipeg Goldeyes

2010 (1 minor league team; 5 independent league teams)

Northwest League (Short Season A): Vancouver Canadians
Canadian-American League (independent): les Capitales de Quebec
Golden Baseball League (independent): Calgary Vipers, Edmonton Capitals, Victoria Seals
Northern League (independent): Winnipeg Goldeyes

2011 (1 minor league team; 4 independent league teams)

Northwest League (Short Season A): Vancouver Canadians
American Association (independent): Winnipeg Goldeyes
Canadian-American League (independent): les Capitales de Quebec
North American League (independent): Calgary Vipers, Edmonton Capitals

2012 (1 minor league team; 3 independent league teams)

Northwest League (Short Season A); Vancouver Canadians
American Association (independent): Winnipeg Goldeyes
Canadian-American League (independent): les Capitales de Quebec
Frontier League (independent): London Rippers* (team disbanded, replaced in mid-season by a league-sponsored travelling team)

2013 (1 minor league team; 3 independent league teams)

Northwest League (Short Season A): Vancouver Canadians
American Association (independent): Winnipeg Goldeyes
Canadian-American League (independent): les Capitales de Quebec, Trois-Rivières Aigles

2014 (1 minor league team; 3 independent league teams)

Northwest League (Short Season A): Vancouver Canadians
American Association (independent): Winnipeg Goldeyes
Canadian-American League (independent): les Capitales de Quebec, Trois-Rivières Aigles

2015 (1 minor league team; 4 independent league teams)

Northwest League (Short Season A): Vancouver Canadians
American Association (independent): Winnipeg Goldeyes
Canadian-American League (independent): Ottawa Champions, les Capitales de Quebec, Trois-Rivières Aigles

2016 (1 minor league team; 4 independent league teams)

Northwest League (Short Season A): Vancouver Canadians
American Association (independent): Winnipeg Goldeyes
Canadian-American League (independent): Ottawa Champions, les Capitales de Quebec, Trois-Rivières Aigles

2017 (1 minor league team; 4 independent league teams)

Northwest League (Short Season A): Vancouver Canadians
American Association (independent): Winnipeg Goldeyes
Canadian-American League (independent): Ottawa Champions, les Capitales de Quebec, Trois-Rivières Aigles

2018 (1 minor league team; 4 independent league teams)

Northwest League (short season): Vancouver Canadians
American Association: Winnipeg Goldeyes
Canadian-American League (independent): Ottawa Champions, les Capitales de Quebec, Trois-Rivières Aigles

2019 (1 minor league team; 3 independent league teams)

Northwest League (short season): Vancouver Canadians
American Association (independent): Winnipeg Goldeyes
Canadian-American League (independent): Ottawa Champions, les Capitales de Quebec, Trois-Rivières Aigles

2020 (1 independent league team)

Because of the Covid-19 pandemic, all minor and independent leagues but one suspended their 2020 seasons. Six American Association teams, including the Winnipeg Goldeyes, played an abbreviated 60-game schedule. Because of travel restrictions to and from Canada, the Goldeyes played all their home games in Fargo-Moorhead, North Dakota/Minnesota.

Bibliographical Essay

In researching *Minor League Baseball in Canada: A History Since War World II*, I have consulted thousands of sources—books, magazines, team programs, media guides, newspapers, and online materials. For gathering the yearly standings, statistics, individual category leaders, award winners for Canadian minor league teams, I have relied mainly on four sources. The third edition of *The Encyclopedia of Minor League Baseball* (Durham, NC: Baseball America, 2007), edited by Lloyd Johnson and Miles Wolff, contains yearly standings and, where available, season's attendance, names of managers, all-star teams, and category leaders for every minor or independent league operating between 1876 and 2006. For each of the seasons from 1990 to 2019, I have drawn on information published in the annual *Baseball America Almanac* (Durham, NC: Baseball America). The online site *baseball-reference.com* includes yearly league, team, and individual statistics, along with team rosters (with links to the career statistics of individual players) for all minor leagues. I have also accessed the weekly issues of *The Sporting News* from 1946 to 2003, available from *www.paperofrecord.com*.

Two books, along with introductory chapters of the first two editions of *The Encyclopedia of Minor League Baseball* (1993 and 1997), have provided overviews of the changes and trends in minor league baseball: Robert Obojski, *Bush League: A History of Minor League Baseball* (New York: Macmillan, 1975) and Neil J. Sullivan, *The Minors: The Struggles and the Triumph of Baseball's Poor Relations from 1876 to the Present* (New York: St. Martin's Press, 1990). More specific histories I've consulted include William Humber, *Diamonds of the North: A Concise History of Baseball in Canada* (Toronto: Oxford University Press, 1995); Bill O'Neal, *The International League: A Baseball History 1884–1991* (Austin, TX: Eakin Press, 1992); Bill O'Neal, *The Pacific Coast League 1903–1988* (Austin, TX: Eakin Press, 1990); and Barry Swanton and Jay-Dell Mah, *Black Baseball Players in Canada: A Biographical Dictionary, 1881–1960* (Jefferson, NC: McFarland, 2009). Michael Benson's *Ballparks of North America: A Comprehensive Historical Reference to Baseball Grounds, Yards and Stadiums, 1845 to the Present* (Jefferson, NC: McFarland, 1989) has been a very useful reference.

For the narratives of individual seasons, I have consulted the four general sources noted above, along with books on individual teams or leagues, league and team media guides when those have been available, and particularly local newspapers' season-long coverage of specific teams. The relevant sources for the information are listed in the chapter notes below.

Part I

1946–1951: The Minors Expand
and Contract in Canada

For a general overview of the years 1946 to 1951 I have drawn on William Marshall's *Baseball's Pivotal Era: 1945–1951* (Lexington: University of Kentucky Press, 1999) and Jules Tygiel's *Baseball's Great Experiment: Jackie Robinson and His Legacy* (New York: Oxford University Press, 1983).

1. From Jackie Robinson to Jack Kent Cooke

Detailed information about both in-season and off-season events have been collected from the files of *The Montreal Gazette*, *The Globe and Mail*, *The Toronto Star*, and *The Ottawa Citizen*. William Browning's *Baseball's Fabulous Montreal Royals: The Team that Made Baseball History* (Montreal: Robert Davies Publishing, 1996) is a readable account of the team from 1928 to 1960. Accounts Jackie Robinson's 1946 season with the Montreal Royals, particularly his early season games and those of the Junior World Series, draw from game stories in *The Montreal Gazette*, Arnold Rampersad's *Jackie Robinson: A Biography* (New York: Alfred A. Knopf, 1997) and Jackie Robinson's *I Never Had It Made* (New York: G.P. Putnam's Sons, 1972). Neil Lanctot's *Campy: The Two Lives of Roy Campanella* (New York: Simon & Schuster, 2011) includes an account of the catcher's season in Montreal.

2. Canada's Border Leagues Teams

The sports pages of the *Hamilton Spectator*, *Sherbrooke Daily Record*, *The Quebec Chronicle-Telegraph*, *St. Maurice Valley Chronicle*, *Kingston Whig-Standard*, *Ottawa Evening Citizen*, *Victoria Daily Times*, *Daily Colonist*, *Vancouver Daily Province*, and *Vancouver Sun* have provided information about on-field events and important off-field stories of individual teams' seasons. The website *www.wilbaseball.blogspot.com* includes newspaper stories relating to nearly all Western International League cities between 1945 and 1954. The unfortunately inactive *www.quebec.sabr.org* contained many articles about Quebec's minor league teams during this era. David Pietrusza's *Baseball's Canadian-American League: A History of Its Inception, Franchise, Participants, Locales, Statistics, Demise and Legacy, 1936–1951* (Jefferson, NC: McFarland, 1990) is a valuable compendium of facts and figures. David McDonald's "Baseball in Ottawa" (*Ottawa Citizen*, April 15, 2005, p. B1) and Don Russell's "An Evening with a Big City Sports Promoter" (*Standard-Freeholder*, June 9, 2001, p. 24) contain useful information about the Ottawa Nationals/Senators and the short-lived Cornwall Canadians, respectively, in the Border League.

3. Mexican Jumping Beans, Hockey Players, and Negro Leaguers

Game stories in the *Sherbrooke Daily Record*, *Quebec Chronicle-Telegraph*, and *St. Maurice Valley Chronicle* provided much of the information for the yearly season's summaries. Quebec.sabr.org, the website of the Quebec chapter of SABR, the Society for American Baseball Research, which is no longer online, was a treasure trove of photographs, rosters and statistics (especially for the 1947 and 1948 seasons), reprints of contemporary articles, and historical essays on the Provincial League. Bill Young's

"Ray Brown in Canada: His Forgotten Years" and "Les belles annees de la Provinciale"; Christian Trudeau's "La Provinciale: une ligue de haut caliber"; Daniel Papillon's "The Drummondville Cubs of 1949" first published or reprinted in the website contain much valuable information. William Humber's *Diamonds of the North* (pages 117–122) has a succinct summary of the league's history. Chapters 4 and 13 of William Marshall's *Baseball's Pivotal Era* discusses the Mexican Jumping Beans and their careers in the Provincial Leagues, including, on page 243, the amazing salaries they received. Bill Young's retrospective essay about the 1951 fire that destroyed the Sherwood ballpark, "The Day Sherbrooke Baseball Died," appeared in the *Sherbrooke Record*, September 19, 2006, p. 7.

Part II

1952–1977: The Lean Years

The decline of the minor leagues and their struggle for survival are detailed in Neil J. Sullivan's *The Minors* (pages 235–255), Robert Obojski's *Bush League* (pages 26–31) and Miles Wolff and Lloyd Johnson, *Encyclopedia of Minor League Baseball*, 1st ed. (263). The major league's "rescue programs" of 1956, 1959 and 1962 are discussed in *The Sporting News*, August 15, 1956 (pages 3, 4, 12); *The Sporting News*, December 15, 1959 (pages 1, 2); and *The Sporting News*, June 2, 1962 (page 13).

4. International League Departures

In compiling the yearly narratives I have drawn on accounts in *The Globe and Mail, The Toronto Star, The Montreal Gazette* and *The Ottawa Citizen*. Bill O'Neal's *The International League* chronicles the fortunes of the league, including the vicissitudes of the three Canadian franchises. William Browning's *The Fabulous Montreal Royals* traces in detail the decline and demise of the once mighty franchise. Stew Thornie, in "Was Roberto Clemente Hidden in Montreal," *http//quebec.sabr,org/1950*, offers interesting speculations about the Hall of Fame great's season as a Montreal Royal. The announcement of the Continental League's formation is discussed in *The Sporting News*, Wednesday, August 5, 1959 (pages 7, 8, 12).

5. The Pacific Coast League Mounties Come and Go ... and Come and Go

Bill O'Neal's *The Pacific Coast League* provides a good overview of the PCL during the years that the Vancouver Mounties were members of the league. Narratives of specific Mounties seasons are based on information in *The Sporting News* and *The Vancouver Sun*. In his "kiss and tell" memoir, *Ball Four: My Life and Hard Times Throwing the Knuckleball in the Big Leagues* (Cleveland: World, 1970), Jim Bouton begins his brief account of his trip from the expansion Seattle Pilots to the Mounties, by lamenting: "I died tonight. I got sent to Vancouver" (p. 111).

6. Canada's Border League Teams Go South

The sources for the Western International League seasonal narratives are *www.wilbaseball.blogspot.com*, the *Victoria Daily Times, Vancouver Sun, Edmonton Journal,* and *Calgary Herald*. Brent E. Ducey's *The Rajah of Renfrew* (Edmonton: University of Alberta Press, 1998), Chapter 16, contains accounts of John Ducey's efforts to obtain and then preserve a Western International Franchise for Edmonton. Reports in *Quebec Chronicle-Telegraph Sherbrooke Record,* and *St. Maurice Valley Chronicle,* as well as information in the now-defunct *quebec.sabr.org,* provided facts for the description of the on and off field events of the Provincial League. The *Hamilton Spectator* was the source for information on the PONY League's Hamilton Cardinals and Red Wings. The *Winnipeg Free Press* along with pages 9 to 35 in Scott Taylor and Dr. Kris Row's *Home Run: The History of the Winnipeg Goldeyes and CanWest Global Park* (Winnipeg, Manitoba: Studio Publications, 2005) were the main sources consulted for information about the Winnipeg Goldeyes.

7. *Struggling to Survive in the '70s*

The *Winnipeg Free Press, Quebec-Chronicle-Telegraph, Lethbridge Herald, Calgary Herald,* and *Medicine Hat News* have provided the information for the seasons' narratives. Scott Taylor's *Home Run* provides background on the Winnipeg Whips, as does Bill O'Neal's *The International League.* Daniel Papillon's *En lieu sur ... un stade pour la capital* (Quebec: Commission de la capital nationale du Quebec, n.d.) is a richly illustrated history of Quebec City's le Stade and the teams that have played in it since 1939. Ken McIntosh and Rod Drown have chronicled the short history of the New Westminster Frasers in *The New Westminster Frasers Baseball Club* (New Westminster, BC: Raised Seams Fanatic Publishing, 2010).

Part III

1978–2020: Boom and Bust II— Independence and Survival

Attendance statistics have been provided in an email from Steve Densa of Minor League Baseball.

8. *Another Minor League Boom in Canada*

Neil J. Sullivan's *The Minors,* Chapter 13, "The Rebound" and *Encyclopedia of Minor League Baseball,* 1st edition, "The Revival," p. 355 present overviews of the period 1978–1990. For narratives of individual seasons, I have consulted the *Vancouver Sun, Edmonton Journal, Edmonton Sun, Calgary Herald, Victoria Daily Times, Daily Colonist, Lethbridge Herald, Medicine Hat News,* and *Hamilton Spectator. Baseball America's Almanac* (Durham, NC: Baseball America, published annually since 1988) contains statistics and summaries for each minor league beginning with the 1987 season. Bill O'Neal's *The Pacific Coast League* provides an overview of the league up to the end of the 1988 season. David Lamb's *A Stolen Season: A Journey Through America and Baseball's Minor Leagues* (New York: Random House, 1991) does not discuss Canadian teams, but is an excellent first-hand account of the minor leagues at the end of the 1980s. Allen Abel's "Living it up in baseball's bushes; These Jays have busses, big dreams, and burgers," *The Globe and Mail* (August 22, 1978), p. S1; Marty York's "Albertan builds baseball empire," *The Globe and Mail* (February 2, 1985) p. S5; and Steven Wolf's "The Babes of Summer," *Sports Illustrated* (July 23, 1990), accessed in *https://vault.si.com/vault/1990/07/23,* are feature articles about the Medicine Hat Blue Jays.

9. *Canada's Minor League Teams Go South Again*

The following newspapers were consulted in preparing the season-by-season summaries of the various league and their Canadian teams: *Calgary Herald, Edmonton Journal, Edmonton Sun, Hamilton Spectator, Lethbridge Herald, London Free Press, Medicine Hat News, Ottawa Citizen, St. Catharines Standard, Vancouver Sun. Baseball America's Almanac* from 1991 to 2008 provided annual summaries and statics for each minor league. Hank Davis's *Small-Town Heroes: Images of Minor League Baseball* (Iowa City: University of Iowa Press, 1997) includes chapters on the London Tigers, Hamilton Redbirds, Welland Pirates, and St. Catharines Blue Jays. *The Circus is in Town: A Baseball Odyssey*, by Robert A. Hilliard (Denver: Outskirts Press, 2016) contains a detailed account of how the Hamilton Redbirds were purchased and then relocated to New Jersey. Kelly Whiteside, in "Every Day Is Ladies Day" (*Sports Illustrated*, November 2, 1992—accessed in *https://vault.si.com/vault/1992/11/02*), profiles the St. Catharine's Blue Jays' all-female front office staff. "Birth of a Triple-A Baseball team," *Ottawa Citizen* (September 19, 1991, p. C12), provides a timeline of Ottawa's quest for an International League franchise.

10. *On Their Own: Canadian Teams in the Independent Leagues*

The annual *Baseball America's Almanac* has seasonal summaries and statistics of every independent league that has operated since 1993. Jon C. Stott's *Leagues of Their Own: Independent Professional Baseball, 1993–2000* (Jefferson, NC: McFarland, 2001) and David Kemp and Miles Wolff's *The History of Independent Baseball Leagues 1993–2002* (Bismarck, ND: Mariah Press, 2003) chronicle the earlier years of the independent leagues. The archives of *www.oursportscentral.com* provide links to newspaper stories appearing since 2000 about minor and independent leagues and teams. Since 2002, off-field business of teams and leagues is reported in *www.ballparkdigest.com*. The following newspapers have been consulted for information about individual teams: *Victoria Times-Colonist, Vancouver Sun, The Province, Edmonton Sun, Edmonton Journal, Calgary Herald, Saskatoon Star-Phoenix, St. Catharines Standard, Quebec Chronicle-Telegraph, London Free Press, Ottawa Citizen*. Steve Perlstein's *Rebel Baseball: the Summer the Game was Returned to the Fans* (New York: Henry Holt and Company, 1994) and Stefan Fatsis, *Wild and Outside: How a Renegade Minor League Revived the Spirit of Baseball in America's Heartland* (New York: Walker and Company, 1995) recount the 1993 and 1994 seasons of the Northern League and include detailed discussions of the Thunder Bay Whiskey Jacks. The website of the Trois-Rivières Aigles, *www.lesaiglestr.com*, includes detailed accounts of each season. *Can-Am League Media Guide* (Dayton, OH: Canadian-American Association, 2019) has summaries and statistics for each season from 2005 to 2019, along with all-time records.

11. *Thriving in the Twenty-first Century*

In addition to the annual editions of *Baseball America Almanac* from 2000 to 2020 and *The Encyclopedia of Minor League Baseball*, 3rd edition (Durham: NC: Baseball America, 2007), and *www.baseball-reference.com*, I have drawn on articles in the archives of *www.ballparkdigest.com* and the links in *www.oursportscentral.com*.

Specific information about individual seasons of les Capitales de Quebec comes from the *Quebec Chronicle-Telegraph; Les Capitales de Quebec Guide de Press 2019*

(Quebec City: Les Capitales de Quebec, 2019), and *www.capitalesdequebec.com*. Daniel Papillon's *En lieu sur … un stade pour la capital* (Quebec City: Commission de la Capitale Nationale, n.d.) is a fully illustrated history about the team's ballpark. The role of Miles Wolff in the founding of Les Capitales is examined in Chris Jones' "Wolff Storms the Plains," *National Post* (February 11, 1999, p. B15), and Don Retson, "Wolff Steps Up to the Plate to Recapture Quebec City Market," *Ottawa Citizen* (May 12, 1999), p. 3C. The signing of Cuban baseball players is recounted in Robert Grant, "Diamond Diplomacy," *The Globe and Mail* (December 16, 2015, p. S1) and "Cuban Baseball Player Sings to Play in Quebec," *https://amateursport.wordpress.com/2014/08/01.*

The *Vancouver Sun* and *The Province* are the principal sources for accounts of individual seasons. *Vancouver Canadians 2014 Official Media Guide* (Vancouver, BC: Vancouver Canadians, 2014) provides detailed information about game scores and statistics for the 2000 through 2013 seasons.

Articles in the *Winnipeg Free Press*, along with detailed information in Nigel Barchelor's *Winnipeg Goldeyes' 2020 Media Guide* (Winnipeg, MB: Winnipeg Goldeyes, 2020), are the main sources for information on the Goldeyes' individual seasons. Hoffman Wolff, *American Association 2020 Media Guide* (Moorhead, MN: American Association, 2020) includes information about the Goldeyes since they joined the league in 2011. Scott Taylor and Dr. Kris Row's *Home Run: The History of the Winnipeg Goldeyes and CanWest Global Park* (Winnipeg, MB: Studio Publications, 2005) is a lavishly illustrated account of the team's first 12 seasons.

Index

Note: Dates in parentheses following league abbreviations refer to the years of operation after World War II.

Abbott, Kyle 141
Abercrombie, Reggie 205–206
Abrams, Carl 60
Acre, Mark 146
Acton Vale (Prov) 43, 44, 211
Adair, Bill 65
Aker, Jack 75
Albers, Andrew 191
Allensworth, Jermaine 146
Alston, Walter 17–18, 55, 56
Altobelli, Joe 63
American Association (AA; 2006–) 1, 3, 108, 153, 166, 170, 171, 176, 195, 202, 203–206, 207, 210, 220–221
Amoros, Sandy 55, 56, 57, 61, 62
Anderson, George "Sparky" 58, 59, 60, 61, 62, 63, 64, 66
Anderson, Rick 171
Andrews, Mike 67
Applegate, Gideon 29
Armour, Al 47
Ashford, Emmett 79
Atlantic League 207
Ault, Doug 154

Babe, Loren 57
Bailey, Nat 36, 70, 74
Bamberger, George 69, 70, 71, 73, 74
Bando, Sal 75, 76
Bankhead, Dan 16, 17
Bankhead, Sam 49, 208
Barajas, Rod 139
Barbee, Quincy 48
Barreto, Franklin 184
Beamon, Charlie 70
Becker, Joe 19, 54
Bell, Alexei 193
Bell, Derek 125
Benson, Vern 91, 92
Bergin, David 205, 206
Berrios, Harry 200, 201
Berroa, Geronimo 124
Betzel, Bruno 58, 59
Bevington, Terry 117, 165, 166
Bigbie, Larry 169
Biggio, Cavan 184
Bird, Doug 97
Bissonnette, Del 16
Bittiger, Jeff 196, 197
Blake, Casey 150
Blanco, Lazaro 194
Blowers, Mike 143
Bomback, Mark 111

Boone, Bret 143, 169
Border League (BL; 1946–51) 2, 9, 20, 25–31, 211–212
Borders, Pat 122
Boston, Daryl 158
Boston, D.J. 137
Boucher, Sebastien 173, 174, 191, 192, 193
Bouton, Jim 76
Bowers, Brent 168, 169
Bowman, Eleanor 127
Boyer, Cloyd 124, 125
Boyer, Ken 24–25, 124
Brace, Murray 158, 159
Brandon Grey Owls (Prairie) 217
Brandon West Man Wranglers (Prairie) 158, 218
Breard, Stan 145
Breeding, Marv 71, 72
Brenner, Bill 33, 34, 35, 36, 83
Bridges, Rocky 17, 18
Brinkley, Darryl 167, 168
Brown, Adrian 133
Brown, Bob 31, 33, 36
Brown, Eric 183
Brown, Ray 48
Burgess, Tom 23
Burkhart, Morgan 168, 169
Busch, Mike 165, 167
Bush, Darren 189
Butler, Rob 127
Bynum, Fred 178

Cabrera, Willie 205
Calgary Cannons (PCL) 109, 114–119, 136, 137, 141–151, 165, 216–219
Calgary Cardinals/Expos (Pioneer) 104–105, 114, 120–123, 215
Calgary Outlaws (CBL) 163–164, 219
Calgary Stampeders (WIL) 51, 79–84, 213
Calgary Vipers (GBL) 167–169, 202, 220
Calgary Vipers (NAmL) 169–170, 220
Calgary Vipers (NL2) 164–167, 201, 219–220
Calvert, Paul 45
Campanella, Roy 14, 208
Campbell, Mike 117
Campbell, Peter 11, 13, 14
Canadian-American League 1 (CA1; 1946–51) 9, 13, 22, 31, 37–42, 99, 211–212
Canadian-American League 2 (CA2; 2003–19) 1, 108, 171–174, 186–195, 207, 210, 219–221
Canadian Baseball League (CBL; 2003) 163–164, 219
Candiotti, Tom 120
Les Capitales de Quebec (NLE, NEL, CA2) 1, 3, 102, 109, 171, 172, 174, 176, 186–195, 207, 210, 218–221

Carlton, Steve 94–96
Carrasquel, Alex 47
Carter, Gary 100
Casanova, Bruno 24
Castro, Nelson 167, 168
Castro, Ramon 149
Cather, Mike 197
Cerutti, John 122
Chamberlain, Wes 199
Chambliss, Chris 126, 149
Chapman, Jim 119
Charles, Ed 73, 85
Chavez, Endy 135
Chorlton, K. 35, 83
Church, Ryan 152
Cisco, Galen 667
Clapp, Stubby 165, 166
Clark, Jim 23, 36, 79, 80, 83
Clarkson, Buzz 45
Clarkson, Reg 33, 35, 36
Clemente, Roberto 56–57
Coleman, Rip 64
Connors, Chuck 14, 16, 17
Constable, Jim 65
Contini, Hal 89
Cooke, Jack Kent 11, 19–20, 53–54, 55, 57, 58, 60, 61, 62, 63, 64, 66, 207
Cornelius, Brian 157, 158, 159
Cornwall Canadians (BL) 25, 30–32, 212
Coste, Chris 157
Cote, Jean-Francis 186
Craig, Roger 58
Crandall, Del 28
Creeden, Connie 45
Crimian, Jack 57, 58, 62
Cromarte, Warren 100
Cruz, Enrique 170
Cruz, Fausto 145

Darvill, Wes 205, 206
Darwin, Howard 132, 133, 134, 135
Davis, Tommy 61
Dawson, Andre 101–102, 104
Day, Leon 20, 81, 82
Dean, Paul "Daffy" 27
Delgado, Carlos 125
Demeter, Don 59
Demeter, Steve 64
Deschenes, Pat 190
Didier, Bob 111
Dionne, Stephane 187
Dore, Carlos 93
Downs, Scott 152
Dragicevich, Scott 141
Dressen, Charlie 64, 65
Driessen, Dan 99
Drummondville Cubs/Royals, A's (Prov) 43, 44, 45, 46, 47, 48, 49, 85–88, 211–213
Drysdale, Don 58
Duany, Claro 45, 48
Ducey, John 80–81, 83, 84
Dunn, Andy 180–181
Duren, Rhyne 70
Dussault, Norm 25, 28, 48
Duva, Brian 198

Eastern League (EL; 1946–2019) 51, 88, 96, 98–102, 125–126, 130–131, 187, 214–17

Edmonton Capitals (NAmL) 169–170, 220
Edmonton CrackerCats/Capitals (GBL) 167–169, 202, 220
Edmonton CrackerCats (NL2) 164–167, 219
Edmonton Eskimos (WIL) 51, 79–84, 213
Edmonton Trappers (PCL) 5, 6, 109, 112–119, 136, 141–152, 164, 165, 176, 209, 215–219
Eichorn, Mark 121
Ellis, Matt 138
Ellis, Mike 138, 140
Encarnacion, Angelo 146
Erskine, Carl 18
Estalella, Bobby 45
Ethier, Andre 179

Farnham Black Sox/Pirates (Prov) 43, 44, 45, 47, 48, 49, 50, 85, 211–212
Feldman, Henry 47
Felice, Jason 155, 156, 157
Felske, John 111
Ferguson, Chris 155–156
Ferguson, Dave 155–156, 158, 159
Ferguson, Joe 189
Fernandez, Sid 122
Finn, Marilyn 127
Fitzsimmons, Jon 194
Foote, Barry 99
Forney, Rick 198, 199, 202, 204, 206
Foy, Joe 67
Franchuk, Orv 170, 178
Frazier, Joe 70
Fricano, Marion 53
Friend, Owen 93
Frietas, Bob 72
Frontier League (Frontier; 1993–) 108, 153, 161–163, 168, 174–175, 188, 195, 203, 207, 218, 220
Fryman, Travis 126
Fuenmayor, Balbino 193

Gagne, Eric 171, 172, 191
Galarraga, Andres 121
Garcia, Sylvio 48
Gardella, Danny 45, 47
Garriott, Cec 78–79
Garrison, Webster 178
Gee, George 25
Geiger, Gary 90
Gelinas, Karl 193, 194
Giambi, Jason 145
Gibbons, Jay 140
Gidney, Jeff 165, 166
Giles, Brian 159
Gilliam, Jim "Junior" 19, 54, 55
Gionfriddo, Al 15, 16, 17, 86
Gladstone, Granny 5, 79
Gladu, Roland 45, 48
Golden Baseball League (GBL; 2005–10) 167–169, 202, 220
Goliat, Mike 59, 60, 61, 62
Gomez, Ruben 49
Goosen, Greg 76
Gorman, Tom 20–21, 26, 30, 31
Gotay, Julio 92, 209
Gott, Jim 105
Gracial, Yurisbel 194
Granby Grand B's/Red Sox, Phillies (Prov) 29, 43–45, 47–49, 85–87, 212–213
Granby Red Sox (BL) 9, 25, 26, 211

Gray, Brett 161, 162
Gray, Lorenzo 112
Green, Lenny 71
Greene, Todd 146
Gretzky, Trevor 173, 194
Grieve, Ben 146
Griffey, Ken, Sr. 99
Griffith, Tommy 156
Grimes, Burleigh 54, 55
Gurriel, Yuniesky 193

Haerther, Casey 204, 205
Hamilton Cardinals/Red Wings (PONY) 9, 22–25, 41, 78, 89–90, 208, 211–213
Hamilton Redbirds (NYP) 108, 125, 127–128, 216–217
Hansen, Ron 71
Harden, Rich 178
Harrigan-Charles, Ellen 127
Harshman, Jack 33, 34
Harvey, Doug 1, 27, 28, 29
Hayworth, Red 47
Heard, Jehosie 5, 79
Hendricks, Elrod 93
Henley, Gail 121, 122
Hentgen, Pat 125
Hermann, Fred 177, 178, 180
Hernandez, Stayler 195
Hill, Rob 171
Hitchcock, Billy 73
Hoak, Don 54, 55
Hodge, Jean 90
Holle, Gary 112
Hopper, Clay 16, 17
Horton, Tony 67
Hough, Stan 135
Howard, Elston 57
Howell, Jack 115
Hriniak, Walt 104
Huppert, Dave 151
Hurst, Jimmy 202

International League (IL; 1946–2019) 2, 9, 10–21, 51–52, 53–68, 96, 97–98, 131–137, 147, 171, 196, 207, 208, 209, 211–214, 217–219
Izturis, Cesar 130

Jarrell, Arnie 26, 29
Jaster, Larry 93
Jenkins, Ferguson 163, 164, 181
Jethroe, Sam 15, 16, 17, 57 , 61
Johnson, Don 55, 58, 60, 61, 62
Johnson, Mike 166, 168
Johnson, Syl 33
Jones, Gary 146
Jones, Willie "Puddin' Head" 15, 16
Jorgensen, Spider 69, 70, 97
Jose, Felix 168

Kane, Ryan 188
Karpuk, Peter 26, 27, 29
Kasko, Eddie 68
Katz, Sam 118, 196, 197, 201, 203
Kehoe, Stu 160
Kelly, Pat 134
Kelowna Heat (CBL) 163–164, 219
Kerr, Jake 180
Key, Jimmy 122
Kingston Ponies (BL) 22, 25–31, 211–212

Kirwer, Tanner 185
Kittle, Ron 105, 112–113, 150
Klein, Lou 47
Knoop, Bobby 63–64
Knorr, Randy 124
Konstanty, Jim 13, 14, 15, 16
Kowalchuk, Mel 112, 118, 142, 146, 149, 150, 151, 165, 166
Krausse, Lew 75
Kuhn, John, Jr. 161
Kuld, Pete 154
Kurkowski, Whitey 93
Kurokawa, Jordan 173
Kutyna, Marty 93

Laboy, Coco 94
Lacey, Bud 80, 82
Lachine Red Sox (Prov) 43, 44, 212
LaForest, Pete 171, 172, 173, 191
Lamabe, Jack 67
Lamb, David 150
Lanier, Hal 172–174, 197, 198, 201, 202
Lanier, Max 47
Lantigua, Eddie 187, 188, 189
Laplante, Michel 187, 188, 189, 190, 193
Larker, Norm 59
Lasorda, Tom 17–18, 19, 54, 55, 56, 58, 59, 61, 62
Lawing, Garland 40, 41
Laws, Brick 69, 70
Lee, Derrick 122
Lee, Terry 197, 198
Lehman, Ken 57–58
Leiper, Tim 135, 136
Lemaster, Denny 73
Lentini, Fehlandt 168, 202, 203
Lepine, Olivier 188
Lethbridge Expos/Dodgers/Mounties/Black Diamonds (Pioneer) 102, 103–105, 120–123, 137–140, 215, 217–218
Leveret, Rene 192
Lewis, Johnny 93, 209
Lillard, Gene 80, 82
Lind, Jose 117
Lintz, Larry 99
Lipon, Johnny 64
Liu, Charlton 163
London Monarchs (CBL) 131, 163–164, 219
London Rippers (Frontier) 131, 174, 220
London Tigers (EL) 108, 125–126, 130–131, 216–217
London Werewolves (Frontier) 161–163, 218
Lopez, Hector 49
Lorraine, Andrew 145
Lovenguth, Lynn 58
Loviglio, Jay 112
Lucchesi, Frank 33
Lumley, Mike 130
Lyden, Mitch 187
Lyle, Sparky 68

Macha, Ken 101
Mackanin, Pete 133
Madritsch, Bobby 200
Maglie, Sal 45, 47, 48
Magnante, Rick 180, 181
Majtyka, Roy 101
Maldonado, Candy 121
Mallett, Jeff 163–164
Mallette, Mal 54
Malo, Jonathan 192, 193

Manduley, Yordan 193, 194
Marini, Jean 90
Marshall, Jim 111
Marshall, John 35
Marshall, Mike 121
Martin, Fred 47
Martinez, Edgar 116–117
Martinez, Manny 147
Martinez, Tino 118, 141
Matthews, Walt 92
Mauro, Carmen 54, 55
Maxvill, Dal 93
May, Rickey 154, 155
McCauley, Andy 161–162, 188
McCormack, Frank 40, 41
McCullough, Clayton 183
McDonald, Bob 125
McDougald, Gil 34, 35
McDuffie, Terris 45
McGaha, Mel 62, 63
McGovern, Kevin 205, 206
McIntosh, Ken 103
McQuinn, George 41, 87
Mead, Charlie 33, 34, 80
Medicine Hat A's/Blue Jays (Pioneer) 103–104, 108,
    120–124, 137–141, 165, 176, 215–219
Mendoza, Christian 190
Metkovich, George 69, 70
Metro, Charlie 71, 73
Metzig, Bill 27, 28, 29, 30
Miller, Rick 182, 184, 185
Mohorcic, Dale 119
Molini, Albert 48, 49
Montreal Royales (CBL) 163–164, 219
Montreal Royals (IL) 1, 2, 5, 9, 10–21, 51, 53–63, 207,
    208, 211–213
Mooney, Jeff 180
Moose Jaw Diamond Dogs (Prairie) 156–158, 217–218
Morrison, Greg 139, 165
Morton, Lew 55–61
Moseby, Lloyd 121
Myers, Rodney 138
Myrow, Brian 200

Nelson, Rocky 56, 57, 58, 60, 61, 65
New Westminster Frasers (NWL) 102–103, 208
New York-Pennsylvania League (NYP; 1957–2019) 90,
    102, 110, 124–125, 127–130, 135, 159, 210, 216–218
Newcombe, Don 15, 16, 208
Nichols, Chet 73
Nicklous, Mike 118
Norris, Daniel 184
North American League (NAmL; 2011–12) 169–170, 220
North Atlantic League (NAL; 1995–96) 159–160, 217
North Central League (NCL; 1994–95) 15–16, 217
Northeast League (NEL; 1995–98; 2003–04) 108, 171,
    186, 189, 207, 219
Northern League (NL1; 1946–71) 9, 51, 64, 78, 90–95,
    97–97, 195, 213–214
Northern League (NL2; 1993–2010) 1, 6, 153–155, 156,
    164–167, 170, 187, 195–203, 207, 217–220
Northern League Central (NLC; 1999–2002) 155–156,
    218–219
Northern League East (NLE; 1999–2002) 102, 171,
    186–188, 218–219
Northwest League (NWL; 1955–2019) 2, 84, 96,
    102–103, 119–120, 160, 207 208, 210, 215, 218–221
Nunez, Vladimir 139

O'Doul, Lefty 69, 71
Olivares, Ed 209
Olivares, Max 143
Orgando, Gregorio 179
Orlich, Dan 165, 166, 167, 168
Ornest, Harry 110–111, 112
Ottawa Champions (CA2) 172–174, 193, 220–221
Ottawa Giants/Athletics (IL) 18, 20–21, 53–56, 208,
    212–213
Ottawa Lynx (IL) 2, 6, 51, 52–56, 109, 131–137, 171, 209,
    217–219
Ottawa Nationals/Senators (BL) 20, 22, 25, 31, 87,
    211–212
Ottawa Rapids/Rapides/Rapidz (CA2) 171, 220

Pacific Coast League (PCL; 1946–2019) 5, 10, 36, 52,
    59, 60, 64, 65, 66, 69–77, 84, 85, 110–119, 123, 160,
    164, 208, 209, 213–214, 215–219
Pagliaroni, Jim 71
Parker, Darren 168
Parker, Russ 104, 114, 123, 143, 144, 146, 148, 149, 165, 168
Parris, Clyde 59
Parrish, Larry 100
Partlow, Roy 13, 38
Pascual, Lauro 45
Patterson, Reg 31, 80
Pattison, Jim 112, 113, 114
Pecor, Roy 135
Peley, Josue 192
Pendleton, Jim 54, 56
Pennsylvania Ontario New York League see PONY
    League
Perranowski, Ron 63
Pettis, Gary 113
Phillips, Dick 113, 160
Piche, Ron 73
Pinkston, Al 85, 86
Pioneer League (Pioneer; 1946–) 2, 103–105, 114,
    120–124, 137–141, 165, 210, 215–219
Pocklington, Peter 112, 142, 143, 144, 147, 148, 150
Podres, Johnny 54, 55
Pompey, Daniel 184
PONY League (PONY; 1946–56) 9, 22–25, 51, 73,
    89–90, 211–213
Pope, Davie 45, 48, 208
Pote, Lou 167, 168, 168
Potter, Rick 164
Power, Vic 46, 48, 208
Prairie League (Prairie; 1995–97) 156–159, 217–218
Pries, Don 36, 79, 82
Prior, Bill 79
Provincial League (Prov; 1947–55) 2, 22, 29, 42, 43–50,
    84–88, 99, 208, 211–213

Quade, Mike 132, 147
Quebec City Alouettes/Braves (CA1) 9, 22, 37–42,
    211–212
Quebec City Braves (Prov) 43, 49, 50, 85–88, 212–213
Quebec City Capitals see Les Capitales de Quebec
Quebec City Carnavals/Metros (EL) 99–102, 104, 125,
    187, 214–215
Quintanilla, Omar 179

Rackley, Marv 12
Radmanovich, Ryan 166
Rakfar, Jasvir 194
Randall, Scott 151
Randolph, Willie 101

Regina Cyclones (NCL) 155–156, 217
Regina Cyclones (Prairie) 155–156, 217–218
Reichert, Dan 165
Restovich, Michael 151
Richard, Maurice 43
Richmond, Scott 165, 166, 167, 195
Rickey, Branch 10–11, 17, 19, 57, 208
Ridzik, Steve 18, 62, 63, 64
Rios, Alex 140
Ritchie, John 36, 37, 79
Riviera, Tony 163, 164
Robertson, Sandy 35, 36
Robinson, Bill 88
Robinson, Brooks 71–72
Robinson, Jackie 5, 11–14, 180, 208, 210
Robson, Tom 183
Rodas, Rick 121
Rodriguez, Alex 145
Rodriguez, Carlos 180
Rodriguez, Hector 19, 58, 61, 62
Rodriguez, Larry 138
Rodriguez, Roberto 76
Roebuck, Ed 54, 55
Roenicke, Gary 101
Rogelstad, Don 119, 120
Rogers, Dennis 179
Rogers, Steve 98, 100
Romanski, Josh 205
Rose, Pete, Jr. 201
Roseboro, Johnny 58, 208
Roy, J.P. 45
Rusch, Matt 172, 204

Sadecki, Ray 92
Sadowski, Rob 92
St. Catharines Blue Jays/Stompers (NYP) 108, 110,
    124–125, 127–131, 216–218
Saint Hyacinthe Saints/A's (Prov) 43–44, 45, 47–49,
    84–86, 212–213
St. Jean Braves, Canadians, les Canadiens (Prov)
    43–45, 47–49, 84–88, 212–213
Ste Marie, Ulysses 39, 40, 41
Sakata, Len 101, 111
Salmon, Tim 143
Sanchez, Aaron 184
Santos, Roel 194
Saskatoon Legends (CBL) 163–164, 219
Saskatoon Riot (NCL) 155–156, 217
Saskatoon Riot/Stallions/Smoking Guns (Prairie)
    156–158, 217–218
Savage, Art 143
Sawatski, Carl 59
Sawkiw, Warren 154
Sawyer, Eddie 15
Sax, Dave 121
Sax, Steve 121
Scalabrini, Pat 188, 190, 191, 192, 194
Scantlebury, Pat 61, 62
Schley, Van 119, 120
Schneider, John 182, 183, 184
Schofield, Dick 113
Seamon, Leonard "Lefty" 28, 29
Sherbrooke Athletics/ Black Sox/Indians (Prov)
    43–45, 47–50, 84–88, 211–213
Sherbrooke Canadians (BL) 9, 25, 26, 211
Sherbrooke Pirates (EL) 99–100, 214
Sherrill, George 200
Shetrone, Barry 71, 72

Shuba, George "Shot Gun" 12, 18
Shwam, Dan 154
Sick, Emil 31
Simard, Michel 190
Simunic, Doug 196, 197
Sinclair, Steve 164
Skalbania, Nelson 111, 113
Sledge, Terrmel 151
Smith, Reggie 67
Snider, Duke 15
Sohn, Andrew 205, 206
Soriano, Dewey 73, 80, 82
Sparks, Jeff 198
Speier, Chris 139
Stanton, T.J. 173, 174
Stevens, Ed 14, 54, 59
Straily, Dan 81
Strong, Joe 160
Sturgeon, Bob 37, 81, 83
Sullivan, Haywood 74, 75
Surhoff, B.J. 115
Surrey Glaciers (WBL) 160–161, 217
Suzuki, Kurt 179
Sweet, Rick 134
Swisher, Nick 178, 179

Tallis, Cedric 69, 70
Tamargo, John 184
Tanner, Chuck 28
Tartabull, Danny 115
Taylor, Dean 103
Taylor, Joe 72
Teahen, Mark 178
Tekulve, Kent 100
Templeton, Gary 149
Terlecky, Bill 155
Thetford Mines Mineurs (Prov) 86–88, 213
Thetford Mines Pirates (EL) 100–101, 215
Thomas, Ian 203
Thompson, Tim 54, 55, 56, 61, 62, 64
Thunder Bay Whiskey Jacks (NL2) 153–155, 187,
    217–218
Tiefenauer, Bob 59, 61
Tilmon, Pat 154, 155
Timlin, Mike 124
Tomlinson, Geof 190
Toronto Maple Leafs (IL) 1, 2, 9, 10–21, 51, 53–68, 176,
    207, 211–214
Tracy, Jim 132
Trice, Bob 55, 85, 86
Trois Rivieres Aigles (CA2) 171–173, 195, 210, 220–221
Trois Rivieres Aigles (EL) 99–102, 125, 214–215
Trois Rivieres Royals (CA1) 9, 13, 37–42, 211–212
Trois Rivieres Royals/Yankees/Phillies (Prov) 43, 49,
    85–88, 212–213
Trois Rivieres Saints (CBL) 163–164, 219
Trouppe, Quincy 46

Unser, Al 92

Valentin, Javier 150
Valenzuela, Fernando 141, 142
Vancouver Canadians (NWL) 2, 3, 6, 9, 176, 177–185,
    207, 210, 218–221
Vancouver Canadians (PCL) 108, 135, 110–119, 141–148,
    160, 176, 177, 209, 215–218 (dates)
Vancouver Capilanos (WIL) 22, 31–37, 51, 78–84,
    211–213

Vancouver Mounties (PCL) 36, 64, 69–77, 84, 85, 208, 213–214
Van Gallen, Aric 165
Van Iderstine, Ben 162, 164
Vernon, Mickey 75
Victoria Athletics/Tyees (WIL) 5, 9, 31–37, 51, 78–83, 211–213
Victoria Capitals (CBL) 163–164, 219
Victoria Mussels/Blues (NWL) 84, 119–120, 208, 215
Victoria Seals (GBL) 168–169, 220
Villafuerte, Brandon 169

Wakefield, Tim 125
Walker, Dixie 59, 61
Ward, Jay 155, 187, 188
Waslewski, Gary 67
Weathers, David 125, 144
Webster, Mitch 105
Welland Aquaducks (NAL) 159–160, 217
Welland Niagara Stars (CBL) 163–164, 219
Welland Pirates (NYP) 108, 125, 127–128, 216–217
Wells, David 122
Wells, Vernon 130
West, Kevin 203
Western Baseball League (WBL; 1995–2002) 160–161, 217
Western International League (WIL; 1946–54) 5, 9, 22, 31–37, 51, 78–84, 102, 211–213
White, Charlie 20, 71, 73
Whiten, Mike 124
Whitt, Ernie 128

Wilkie, Leftie 35
Williams, Dick 66, 67
Williams, George 145
Williams, Marv 83
Williams, Stan 59
Williams, Wally 29
Williams, Woody 125
Wilson, Archie 34, 57, 58, 59, 60, 61, 62
Wilson, Nigel 144
Winnipeg Goldeyes (AA) 1, 3, 109, 176, 203–206, 207, 210, 220–221
Winnipeg Goldeyes (NL1) 51, 64, 90–95, 96–97, 208, 213–214
Winnipeg Goldeyes (NL2) 1, 78, 109, 153, 172, 176, 195–203, 217–220
Winnipeg Whips (IL) 97–98, 196, 214
Wolff, Miles 107, 153, 171, 172, 174, 186, 187, 188, 189, 190, 191, 196, 203
Wood, Jason 151
Wooten, Sean 157
Wright, John 13, 38

Young, Ken 149
Young, Michael 130
Young, Peter 165
Yuill, Bill 104, 140

Zabala, Adrian 45, 47
Zeuch, T.J. 184
Zimmerman, Jeff 198
Zimmerman, Roy 45, 47